THE DESKTOP DESIGN WORKBOOK

Don Busché
Saddleback College

Bernice T. Glenn
Glenn and Associates

Regents/Prentice Hall
Englewood Cliffs, New Jersey 07632

Library of Congress Cataloging-in-Publication Data

Busché, Don.
The desktop design workbook/Don Busché, Bernice T. Glenn.
p. cm.
Includes bibliographical references and index.
ISBN 0-13-202425-X
1. Desktop publishing. 2. Printing, Practical—Layout—Data processing. I. Glenn, Bernice. II. Title.
Z286.D47B889 1991 91-28579
686.2'2544—dc20 CIP

Simon & Schuster / A Viacom Company
Upper Saddle River, New Jersey 07458

Printed in the United States of America

10 9 8 7 6 5 4 3 2

ISBN 0-13-202425-X

Prentice-Hall International (UK) Limited, *London*
Prentice-Hall of Australia Pty. Limited, *Sydney*
Prentice-Hall Canada Inc., *Toronto*
Prentice-Hall Hispanoamericana, S.A., *Mexico*
Prentice-Hall of India Private Limited, *New Delhi*
Prentice-Hall of Japan, Inc., *Tokyo*
Simon & Schuster Asia Pte. Ltd., *Singapore*
Editora Prentice-Hall do Brasil, Ltda., *Rio de Janeiro*

ACKNOWLEDGEMENTS

This book would not have been possible without the guidance, help, and advice of many other people. Our thanks go to the following individuals who reviewed the manuscript and provided valuable criticism and suggested improvements: Patricia R. Allen, Otis Art Institute of Parsons School; Janet Buzzard, Emporia State University; Sonsie Carbonara Conroy, Catalyst Communications; Mary E. Gribble, Lee College; Hans Krommenhoek, Milwaukee Area Technical College; Luetta K. Linder, Lee College; Tony Longson, California State University, Los Angeles; Scott Persky, McHenry County College; James L. Pomeroy, Clark County Community College; Marjorie Webster, Bergen Community College.

To the Prentice Hall staff for their support and understanding, especially to Liz Kendall, Senior Editor, Office Technology for seeing the need for this text, agreeing to this project, and never loosing interest in our work.

Sonsie Conrad, Catalyst Communications, performed an exceptional job of copyediting our prose.

To the individuals involved in producing the final book for Glenn and Associates, for their interest, cooperation, and work beyond the pale under the stress of a tight deadline: Jack Lanning, Jeanne Wong, Anne Cook, Eve Meng, Sue Linville , June Rubin, Emmanuel Robért. Our thanks also to Toni Hollander, The Design Works; René Sheret, Sheret Design; Einer Vigne, Vigne Design Inc. for providing examples of graphic design done on computer.

To all these people and companies who aided us, we are forever indebted for their efforts on our behalf. However, we take full responsibility for the contents and accuracy of this text.

COLOPHON

The Desktop Design Workbook manuscript was produced on a DOS machine by one author, and on a Macintosh by the other. Editing was done on both DOS and Macintosh platforms. Communication hardware and software was used to translate from one platform to another. Final pages were produced on a Macintosh FX and an SE. Graphics were produced mainly on Macintosh, secondarily on a DOS machine; a variety of software was used.

Type faces used include: chapter openers, Lithos bold and black; main text, New Century Schoolbook; headlines, Lithos bold and light; callouts and captions, Gill Sans.

CREDITS

Design, art direction and project management: Bernice Glenn

Page makeup and coordinator: Jack Lanning

Computer graphics and forms design: Jeanne Wong

Computer illustration: Anne Cook

Page makeup, Workshop/Forms Appendix: Eve Meng

Illustrations: Sue Linville and June Rubin

Flat art photography: Emmanuel Robért

Other photography unless otherwise indicated: Bernice Glenn

CONTENTS

PART THREE: DESIGN WORKBOOK APPLICATIONS /149

PART FOUR: PLANNING, PRODUCTION, AND PRINTING /203

PART ONE

INTRODUCTION TO DESIGN FOR DESKTOP PUBLISHING

INTRODUCTION : Why Knowledge of Design is Important in the Desktop Publishing Field

1. The Publishing Process: People, Tasks, and Equipment

2. Communications: Visual and Verbal

INTRODUCTION:

WHY KNOWLEDGE OF DESIGN IS IMPORTANT TO DESKTOP PUBLISHING

GOOD DESIGN IS GOOD COMmunication. We all communicate with each other through speech, the written word, the printed page. All too often, though, our messages do not get across exactly as we want them to. You might want to complement a friend by saying, "You look nice today." Your friend, though, may interpret this remark to mean that she doesn't look "nice" on other days.

Just as good choice of language reduces the possibility of problems in oral communication, a good publication design reduces the possibility of visual communication problems. Whether your publication is an annual report or a party invitation, a term paper or a sales proposal, a company newsletter or restaurant menu, good design carries with it an implied message of excellence.

This book is not intended to be a panacea for achieving the most beautiful graphic design or the most eloquently written document, but it will help you get your message across to the recipient clearly and as *you* want it to be understood. This book will also guide you through some basic principles of design aesthetics so that your messages are pleasing to look at and communicate a feeling of well-being to the reader.

Our focus in this book will be primarily on business usage, since that is where most people do their publishing. The standards for good design and communication, however, are the same for any setting where desktop publishing is done.

The book is divided into four parts. Part One, *Introduction to Design for Desktop Publishing* is an overview to the desktop publishing process, and the basics of communication for desktop publishing. Part Two, *Design as Communication,* covers the basics of document structure, typography, and illustration. Part Three, *Design Workbook Applications,* consists of practice activities for business publications, newsletters, brochures, manuals, and magazines. Part Four, *Planning, Production, and Printing,* describes how to work with service bureaus and print shops; how to prepare camera-ready art, and how to plan, schedule, and budget a publication.

Each chapter contains exercises to help you "learn by doing." Workbook exercises contain pages for you to work on at the back of the book. In addition, *Desktop Design Workbook* provides you with ready-to-use desktop publishing forms and checklists that can be photocopied for every day use.

The appendices include a bibliography and a glossary of commonly used terms, and the disks provided with this book contain materials you will need to complete the exercises, plus additional information you will find helpful.

THE DATA DISK

A data disk has been prepared for use with the exercises in the Workbook. If you are using this book as a classroom text, your instructor will supply copies from the original included in the Teacher's Guide package. If you are using this book on your own and would like to purchase a data disk, use the order form on the last page of this book. Most of the exercises can be performed without the convenience of the data disk.

OBJECTIVES:

Upon completion of this text, you should be able to:

- ✔ Use visual language to communicate effectively
- ✔ Use basic design principles in your desktop published documents
- ✔ Design and use a publication grid
- ✔ Design simple page layouts and use thumbnails
- ✔ Use type fonts that are appropriate for your publication and its audience
- ✔ Effectively use photographs and illustrations in your desktop publications
- ✔ Design and create a variety of simple publications for business use:
  - — Newsletters
  - — Manuals, proposals, and reports
  - — Directories
  - — Catalogs and price lists
  - — Brochures and flyers
  - — Magazine layouts
- ✔ Plan, schedule and prepare budgets for simple publications
- ✔ Work with a service bureau or print shop
- ✔ Work with authors, editors, professional designers, photographers, and illustrators on complex publications

CHAPTER OVERVIEW

PART ONE: INTRODUCTION TO DESIGN FOR DESKTOP PUBLISHING

Chapter 1 describes the publishing process, including both the people and the involved. Advice is included on choosing appropriate hardware and software.

Chapter 2 spotlights the content of the message: How the content affects the publication's form or visual arrangement, and how the publication is received by its audience of one or many.

PART TWO: DESIGN AND COMMUNICATION

Chapter 3 focuses on how publications are organized. Document structure is analyzed, the parts of a document are described, and the use of style guides is covered.

Chapter 4 discusses form and content and how design is tied together with the text for better communication.

Chapter 5 discusses the basics for working with type. Type families and sizes, the structure and history of type faces, and measuring type are all described.

Chapter 8 discusses illustrations—where to get them and how to place them on the page so as to enhance your message once you have the images you need. Electronic and traditional sources for photography, pictorial illustration, and charts and graphs are reviewed.

PART THREE: DESIGN WORKBOOK APPLICATIONS

Chapters 9 through 13 show you how to prepare some basic publication types such as business reports, overhead presentations, newsletters, brochures, advertisements, and long documents (including magazines and manuals).

PART FOUR: PLANNING, PRODUCTION, AND PRINTING

Chapter 14 covers details on how to work with service bureaus and print shops. You will learn how and when to consult with these outside resources, how to determine the quality levels of the output, deciding on the printing process you will need, how to get bids, and to select paper stock. You are given basic information on working with color and black and white halftones.

Chapter 15 describes the process for preparing camera-ready art.

Chapter 16 provides you with forms you can fill out that will show you how to plan and prepare production schedules and how to put together a publications budget.

This book is designed to be a self-teaching tool as well as a textbook for classroom use. If you do desktop design as part of your job assignment, for a club or organization, or simply for your own personal use, you will find *Desktop Design Workbook* to be an invaluable reference.

1. THE PUBLISHING PROCESS: PEOPLE, TASKS, AND EQUIPMENT

When you finish this chapter you should be able to:

- *Describe the publishing cycle.*
- *Contrast traditional publishing with the computer-based desktop publishing process.*
- *Explain how each part of the publishing process interacts with the others.*
- *Discuss the hardware and software needed to implement the kind of publishing you intend to do.*

JUST ABOUT EVERYONE AGREES THAT desktop publishing has revolutionized publishing. Only a few years ago, producing a typical publication required the separate services of artists and graphic designers, writers, editors, layout people, typographers, and printers.

Publishers today can work from their desktop, taking over many of the functions performed by these craftspeople in the traditional publishing arena. Although there are many definitions for the term "desktop publishing," it is most simply described as the kind of publishing people can do using personal computers at their office, school, or home. Desktop publishing involves the use of specialized software and near-typeset quality printers to design and print high-quality documents.

In essence, desktop publishing sounds simple.

If you expect to produce material that communicates the information that you want it to — to the audience you are aiming at — and looks good too — there's a lot to be learned.

This book covers the important concepts, chapter by chapter, and gives you the chance to practice on your own using workbook assignments.

As a start, a basic knowledge of the history and development of the publishing process will help you to understand the significance of the technological advances that have made desktop publishing possible.

HISTORY: HIGHLIGHTS OF THE PUBLISHING PROCESS

Johann Gutenberg is credited with inventing both the printing press and movable type during the fifteenth century. He is rarely given full credit for the influence he had on the development of what we know as the traditional publishing process.

Before 1450, information was disseminated mainly by word of mouth. The general population was illiterate. Only about one person in a hundred could read simple text, and few had a complete grasp of the written word. Books were scarce because they were created by hand, letter by letter, by monks in monasteries. The use of written documents was restricted to the church, royalty, and the wealthy, and even they could afford to own only a relatively small number of books. The Vatican Library, one of the largest in Europe at that time, held about 750 books.

The ability to read represented power and ordinary people of the fifteenth century recognized this fact. Learning to read and having access to books would lead to the Gutenberg "Revolution."

Gutenberg's methods and inventions were revolutionary because they changed not only the way in which publishing was done but also the pathways through which knowledge spread. The Gutenberg "Revolution" had a profound affect on the structure of publishing as it was known at the time. Published documents were no longer made by hand. Gutenberg took a craft process, one that needed many people to produce a single hand-lettered book, and introduced a method that allowed one person to produce many duplicates of a single document. The Gutenberg process permitted printers to become publishers as well.

By the end of the fifteenth century, Gutenberg and his associates had produced more than 10 million printed pages, forever changing the way in which published documents

Figure 1.1: A typical fifteenth century print shop; in the foreground, the printer at the right is inking type at a printing press. The back of the shop is devoted to storing cases of type.

were used in business, politics, education, and leisure pursuits. The "Gutenberg Revolution" not only changed the way printing and publishing were done; it also changed the social structure of Western Europe through increased literacy and broader access to information for the general population (see Figures 1.1 and 1.2.)

Many improvements were made to the printing process between the fifteenth and eighteenth century, but in the nineteenth century the Industrial Revolution introduced another wave of technological innovation. The invention of the typewriter, the Linotype machine, the camera, and halftone plates had a dramatic impact on the way books and newspapers were reproduced. Like Gutenberg's fifteenth century revolution, the inventions of the nineteenth century revised the writing and editorial process as well as the visual appearance of printed matter.

The publishing industry continued with little change until the invention of the desktop computer and the laser printer. Over the past ten years, rapidly changing technology has created new methods of solving design and communication problems and interpreting a design's aesthetic values.

TRADITIONAL METHODS AND CONTEMPORARY PROCESSES

The foundation for desktop publishing is based on the traditional publishing process. While some desktop publishers try to perform the entire publishing process on a computer, often the traditional process can offer better, easier, and quicker solutions. This means that you need to know something about the traditional publishing process, and also something about computers and the electronic tools available for effective desktop publishing.

EARLY HISTORY OF PRINTING

1418	First European example of xylography (block printing from wood engraving.)
1445	Chinese developed copper type.
1446	First dated block print.
1450	Johann Gutenberg invented printing press and movable type matrices. His type face resembles the hand-lettered black-letter script used for manuscripts.
1455	Gutenberg's 42-line Bible, the first book printed from moveable type.
1457	Printer's marks used for the first time.
1460	Albert Pfister, a printer, produces the first book that includes woodcut illustrations with text.
1465	Music printed for the first time.
1469	John de Spire produces first book in Venice.
1470	First French printing press set up at the Sorbonne in Paris.
	The first roman type face produced in Venice.
1477	First book printed in English by William Caxton.
1486	First use of colored inks for illustrations.
1494	First English paper mill established.
1501	Aldus Manutius developed an italic typeface
1508	First use of paper printing in Scotland
1525	Newsletter developed as an early type of newspaper and widely used to keep trading houses informed.
1535	First use of printing in the New World (in Mexico.)

Figure 1.2

Figure 1.2: Timeline showing the spread of printing in the fifteenth century.

STEPS IN THE PUBLISHING PROCESS

1. **The authoring process**

   – A formal expression of the writer's mental intention.

2. **Planning, scheduling, budgeting**

3. **Editing and correcting the publication**

   – Maintains integrity with the author's intentions and client requirements.

4. **Designing the publication**

   – A visible portral of the intentions that the author wishes to communicate. The text is designed to reflect the organization of the written text.

   – Projects visible standards of excellence for the organization.

5. **Production**

   – Typesetting, art, photography, and page makeup, with editorial and proofing correction cycles

6. **Producing multiple copies**

   – A variety of methods are used: copying machines, 1-color, 2-color, or full color printing presses

7. **Distribution and inventory**

THE PUBLISHING PROCESS

In publishing, the goal is to produce a printed document. The publishing process consists of seven basic steps that are required to meet that goal. These seven steps are illustrated in Figure 1.3 and are described in this section.

CREATING THE BUILDING BLOCKS FOR A PUBLICATION

In this book we have used the word "publication" to refer to flyers, brochures, newsletters, reports, manuals, and any other material created by the desktop publishing process. Before you can lay out the pages of any publication, you need to develop its building blocks. These are constructed from *text* — the written (or typewritten) word, and *artwork* — the graphics, figures, and illustrations used to enhance the text. In both the traditional and the desktop publishing processes, authors and artists use many kinds of tools to furnish text and artwork for a publication.

PREPARING COPY

Written text for a publication is called *hard copy*, or just *copy*; in longer documents such

THE PUBLISHING PROCESS

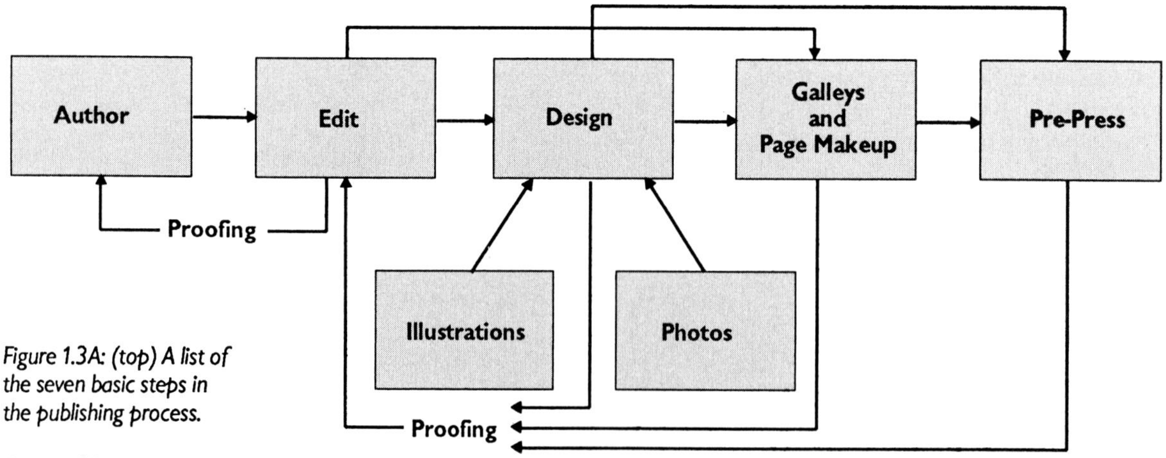

Figure 1.3A: (top) A list of the seven basic steps in the publishing process.

Figure 1.3B: A flow chart illustrating the publishing process.

as books, text is called the *manuscript*. Before computers became popular writing tools, writing and copy development was done on typewriters. Editing was done by hand on the typewritten copy or on printer's proofs. Because this procedure was not automated, it was a very time-consuming part of the publishing process. Today, however, the words, numbers, and symbols used to make up the copy are entered into a computer by typing them on a computer keyboard in a process called *keyboarding*. The keystrokes are saved and are used in subsequent phases of the publishing process.

In traditional publishing today, copy submitted by the author is typeset by a *compositor*. A compositor is a person who operates a computer-driven typesetting machine. The compositor either keys in the text from typewritten copy, or uses the disk containing text provided by the author. As the copy is typeset, codes are entered into the text so that the typesetting machine will produce the desired output. The typeset copy produced by the compositor is called a *galley*. Galleys are long columns of material typeset to the designer's specifications and output as paper proofs. These are used for editing purposes. After the galleys are edited, they are corrected and output on photographic paper. The photographic typeset output is known as *repro*. Repros are used to produce camera-ready copy.

In contrast with traditional methods, the nucleus for desktop publishing involves keyboarding text on a disk using a word processing software program. The keystrokes are saved, and as you will see, are used in the layout and assembly process.

EDITING

Copy carries the basic message of the publication and is usually edited before it is used in a layout. Copy editing involves checking the copy for its writing style, correct information, proper use of grammar and language, and correct spelling, capitalization, and punctuation.

The person who performs these functions is called an *editor* or *copy editor*. As you can imagine, the editor has a considerable amount of influence over the copy to be used in a publication. Using today's computer software, an editor frequently performs the editing process on-screen, using the same keystrokes that the author has entered.

PREPARING THE ARTWORK

The person who prepares artwork for a publication is called a *graphic artist*. Graphic artists who work in a traditional manner use tools like pen and ink, rulers, type, cameras, and so on to produce appropriate art. Today's graphic artists employ a diversity of electronic tools to produce tables, charts, graphs, and illustrations. Computers are used together with paint and draw programs, digitizers, and scanners. Even though these new tools make creating artwork much easier, when working electronically, you are still free to use some traditional methods if it is more efficient to do so. For instance, drawings done by hand can be pasted into final electronic hard copy output, and photographs can be placed into the layout.

DESIGN PROCEDURES

Once the copy and any appropriate sketches of the artwork are created, they are given to a *graphic designer*. A graphic designer is the person who analyzes the copy, the artwork, and the message the author wishes to convey and makes decisions as to how to design the publication. As illustrated in Figure 1.4 on the next page, a number of steps are involved in the design of a typical publication.

In both the traditional and desktop publishing process, the graphic designer selects pages of the text that contain all the representative elements to be used in the publication: its title, any headings, the main text and associated tables, charts, photographs, captions, and so on.

At the first stage of the design process, the designer makes small rough sketches to represent the various elements used in the publication. These sketches, called *thumbnails*, are miniature indications of the design layout. Thumbnails may be done with paper and pencil or on a computer screen. The best thumbnails are selected from which to create full-sized, more detailed sketches of the design. At this point these full-sized sketches are called *roughs*.

Once the graphic designer is satisfied with the rough representation, text, artwork, and other graphic elements are indicated in fairly finished form. At this point, the sketch is called a *comprehensive layout* or simply a *comp*. The comp is used as a guide showing the placement of text, the size and placement of artwork, the type, and other graphic treatments to be used in the publication. A *type specification sheet* or *type specs*, with descriptions of the type and placement of all the page elements generally accompanies the comprehensive design. Type specs are very similar to the style guides included with many page layout and word processing programs. Chapters 2 through 8 cover these design procedures.

PAGE LAYOUT

Using the comp as a guide, the graphic designer assembles the copy and artwork into a layout of the publication. In traditional publishing, this process is called making a *layout dummy*. This process consists of pasting photocopies of all text galleys and artwork into position as they are to appear on the final pages.

When the dummy is proofread, corrected, and approved, type reproduced on photographic quality paper is ordered for the final mechanical or pasteup. The term "pasteup" came from traditional publishing and describes the process in which copy and artwork are pasted on to stiff boards. A triangle, T-square, and a variety of other tools are used to align the elements; rubber cement or wax are used to paste the elements on the boards. Chapter 15, *Preparation of Camera Ready Art*, explains and illustrates how this is done.

In desktop publishing, the "pasteup" is created directly on a computer, often the same one used to create the copy and artwork. One of the advantages of desktop publishing is that copy and artwork files as well as the comp created during the design phase can be used to lay out the pages. The finished layout is also saved as a computer file, and in most cases, it is printed out and pasted as one piece on a board.

PROOFREADING

The layout or pasted-up mechanical is then proofread for accuracy and neatness, regard-

THE PUBLISHING PROCESS

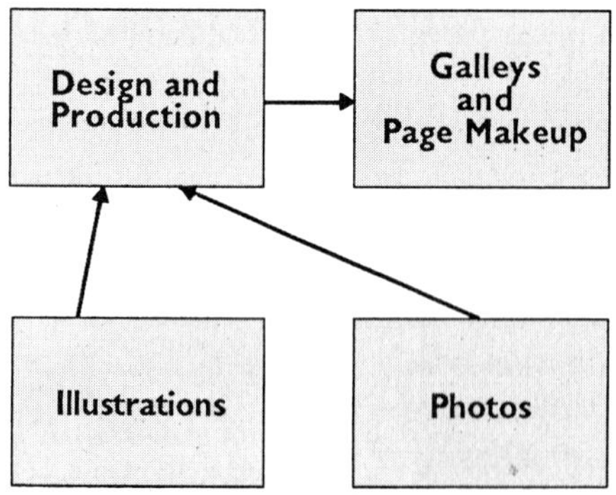

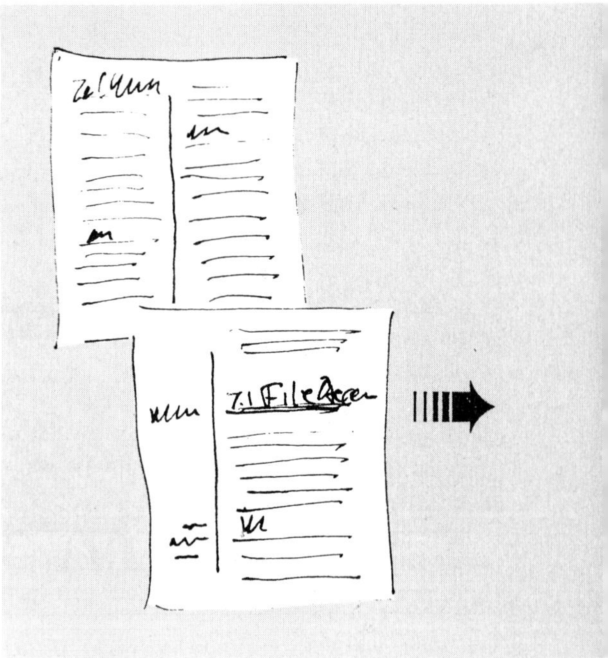

Figure 1.4: (above) A flow chart of the design process in publishing. (right) The design process illustrating steps a designer follows from thumbnails to roughs to comps.

less of whether a traditional or desktop publishing process is used. Proofreading includes checking for completeness—making sure all the copy and artwork are included. The copy is also checked for accuracy, such as making sure charts and other graphics are on the same pages as their text references and caption text is correct both for the image and its page reference. Any corrections are indicated on photocopies of the original work, or on tissues laid over the pasteup. Corrections are made either through traditional cut-and-paste methods or through the computer. The corrected pasteup is proofread once again, and corrections and proofs are made until the pasteup is determined to be accurate and ready for printing. At this point, the pasteup is referred to as a *camera-ready art* or *final mechanical,* or simply, the *pasteup.*

PRINTING

When the last correction is made, the mechanical is ready for the print shop or office copier. If only a few copies of a publication are needed, such as for a proposal or a report, the publication is usually duplicated on a copier. If larger quantities are needed, or if special treatment is required for color or print sizes other than 8 1/2 x 11, the publication is printed on a printing press.

In desktop publishing, a laser printer is used mainly to produce publications that are to be distributed in an office environment or for documents that do not require a high-quality look. Later in this chapter you will be introduced to color laser printers and others than can handle output for different paper stocks and sizes. When high-quality printing is required, the laser printer is used only to make paper proofs. For better quality, a high-resolution device is used to produce the final output. If you do not have access to a high-quality output device such as a typesetter, companies known as *service bureaus* can provide output for you at reasonable prices per page.

FINISHING

The printed pages of a multi-page publication must be collated, folded, trimmed, and bound. This process is called finishing. Once the finishing process is complete, the document is distributed to its intended audience.

For more information on high-resolution printing, color output, and binding, see Chapter 14, *Working with Service Bureaus and Print Shops.*

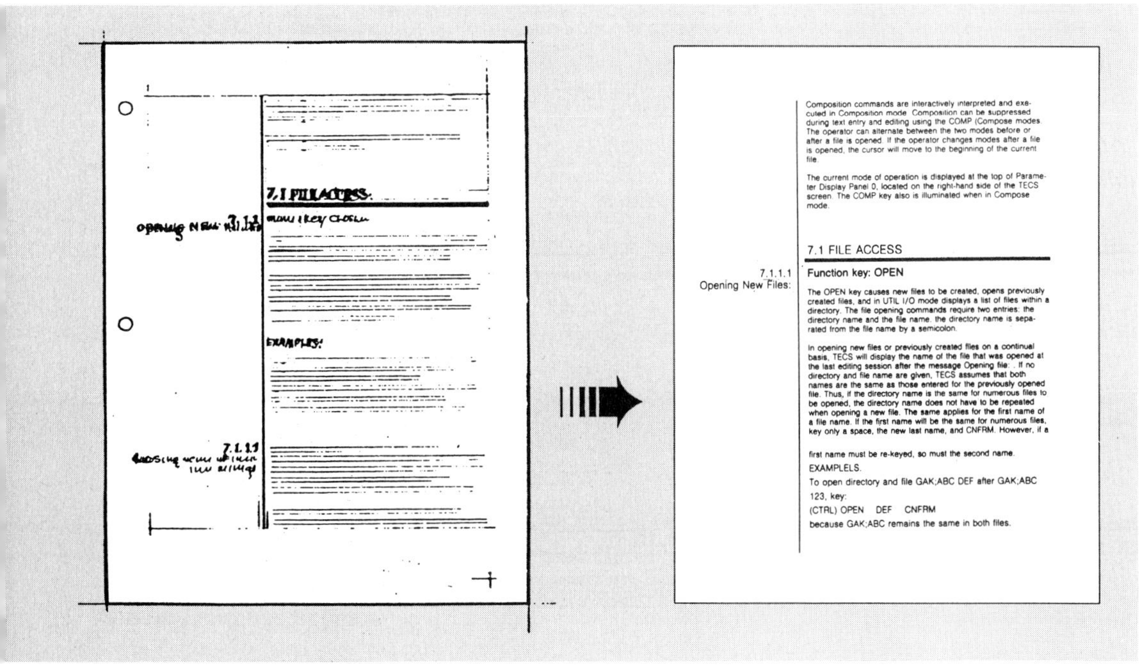

CHECKLIST OVERVIEW FOR PUBLICATIONS DESIGN

✔ What kind of publication is it?

☐ Report ☐ Newsletter ☐ Long document ☐ Other

Size ______ Number of Pages ______

✔ Who is it for (target audience)?

☐ ______

✔ What are the messages to be conveyed?

☐ ______

☐ ______

✔ Will it have competition? Yes (Indicate) ______

______ ☐ No ______

✔ How many copies will you need?

☐ ______

✔ What illustrations will be used?

☐ Charts ☐ Line Drawings ☐ Half-tones

☐ Other ☐ None

✔ How will the publication be distributed?

☐ Mail ☐ By hand ☐ Sold ☐ Other

Figure 1.5: A full-sized version of the Checklist Overview for Publication Design will be found in the Workshop/Forms Appendix.

DEVELOPING A PUBLICATION PLAN

Desktop publishers also need to be decision makers. You will want to be sure that your publication is produced within your budget and that it is finished on time. To accomplish these goals, you will have to make decisions prior to publication as to where you will be spending your time and your money in order to get things done. To answer these questions, you will need a *publishing plan.* To develop the plan, you will need to answer some questions, as illustrated in Figure 1.5.

DETERMINING THE SCOPE OF THE JOB

Before developing your publishing plan, the first thing you need to know is the scope of your job. This is done simply enough by listing all the tasks that need to be done in order to finish the job. List all the processes and their components required to produce the finished publication, starting with text creation or delivery of copy. (Refer to Figure 1.3.) Review your list, rearranging and adding steps until you are confident that all processes are listed. Once you have determined what must be done, you can develop a timeline for performing each task.

DEVELOPING A PRODUCTION SCHEDULE

The first thing you need to know when developing a production schedule is the absolute delivery date of the finished document. In order to get this date, you'll need to know how the publication will be used or delivered. Knowing this, you can determine the delivery date. For example, if you are producing a report that will be handed out at a meeting, the delivery date will be a day or two before the meeting. If you are producing a monthly newsletter to be mailed to members of a homeowners' association, you will need to allow enough time for mail delivery in your schedule.

After you have established the final delivery date, you will need to work backwards to figure out how much time each task on your list will take to finish. Allow a little extra time for revisions, corrections, or problems. Convert the times you have allotted to calendar dates in your time line. Continue assigning time and date for each task in your process from finish to start. Remember, you are working back from the delivery date. If, when you are finished, your schedule has "extra" days before the delivery date, you can add time between the steps. If your completed schedule exceeds the deadline, you may have to rethink how some of the tasks in your process need to be done in order to meet the deadline. This may require changing or eliminating art that takes too long to do, or working overtime on some days in order to pick up a day or two on the schedule.

BUDGETING

A major reason that a company uses desktop publishing is to save money, so budgeting and controlling costs are important even for in-house operations. A detailed description of planning, budgeting, and scheduling publications, along with sample forms you can use, are covered in Chapter 14.

THE DESKTOP PUBLISHING WORKSTATION

Desktop publishing got its start when low-cost page layout software and laser printers were created. Desktop publishing is the fastest growing personal computer application.

Almost any personal computer can be turned into a desktop publishing workstation. A professional desktop publishing computer system, however, requires more and better hardware than the typical personal computer system does (see Figure 1.6.) Apart from hardware and software, your working environment should also be considered, especially if you will be working for many hours at a stretch. Check out your space for glare, and eliminate it by moving your monitor, adjusting the window shades, or switching light sources. Make sure that your chair and desk heights are comfortable, and that your keyboard and mouse are placed for extended use without causing strain.

DESKTOP PUBLISHING WORKSTATION HARDWARE

The typical desktop publishing workstation consists of a personal computer with a hard disk, graphics monitor, a mouse, and a laser printer (see Figure 1.6.) Many professional

Figure 1.6: Illustration of the hardware for a typical workstation; (below left) a scanner; (center) a computer, monitor, keyboard and mouse; (below right) a printer.

desktop publishing computer systems also include a scanner for converting photographs, line art, and drawings to a format that can be manipulated by the computer.

WHAT KIND OF COMPUTER IS BEST?

In desktop publishing, the more power the computer has, the faster and better it performs the task. The Macintosh computer is based on the Motorola 6800 microprocessor chip. This chip was designed for use in graphics applications and the Mac, therefore, was the first microcomputer to be used for desktop publishing. In recent years, DOS-based computers (IBM or IBM clone) have been enhanced with extended graphic-handling capabilities. For desktop publishing on DOS-based machines, an 80286, 80386, or higher microprocessor chip is essential. The newer Unix-based machines (ATT and NEXT) have been designed for sophisticated applications like desktop publishing.

Along with a high-speed processor, the computer must have a lot of internal memory, both to run your programs and to store electronic information. Page layout programs are very complex and so are the documents you create with them. For fast operation, it's important to hold as much of both the program and the document in memory as possible. A few page layout programs operate with as little as 640K (640,000) bytes, but 1.2Mb (1,200,000 bytes) is desirable on DOS equipment. Macintosh programs usually need at least 2 to 4 megabytes to operate with efficiently.

A large-capacity hard drive is also necessity for two reasons: it provides more storage and is faster than a floppy disk drive. The speed of your hard drive is also important. Because the computer is constantly reading information from your drive, the faster it can find the information and store it back again, the faster you can get your job done.

MONITORS

A desktop publishing workstation needs a high-resolution monitor and a graphics card to allow graphic images to appear on the monitor. Most DOS-based machines come with a twelve- to fourteen-inch monitor that displays 23 to 25 lines. Although low-end Macintoshes come with a nine-inch screen, this provides excellent resolution and definition for desktop publishing. Twelve- to fourteen-inch monitors are standard for other Macintoshes.

A full or dual page monitor is more expensive, but is definitely easier and more efficient to work on. Although desktop publishing can be done using screens of any size, with smaller screens, you'll be spending a fair amount of time scrolling back and forth to see all parts of the page.

A color monitor is not as important as one with high resolution unless you work with color a good deal. If you work with photographs and illustrations, a gray-scale monitor is useful. They show levels of gray from very light to black on the screen. Gray-scale monitors are a little more expensive than monochrome monitors, but considerably less costly than color. A high-resolution screen for any monitor, usually about 100 dots per inch (about double that of a standard screen), makes working at the computer much more pleasant.

MOUSE

A mouse is used to send instructions to your page layout program. It is a small pointing device designed to fit under the operator's hand. When the mouse is moved, its progress is duplicated on the screen; selections are made by clicking on a mouse button. The mouse is used to make selections from menu options, to identify page elements, and to issue computer commands.

PRINTERS

As mentioned earlier, the invention of the laser printer was a major contributor to the development and popularity of desktop publishing. A graphics dot matrix printer can produce a rough version of your finished publication, but its output is not acceptable for publication.

A printer's output quality, or resolution, as it is more appropriately called, is measured in *dots per inch (dpi)*. The minimum printing resolution that is acceptable for desktop publishing is 300 dpi (see Figure 1.7.) At this resolution, documents are considered *near-typeset quality*. This resolution is adequate for practically all business documents, and many types of newsletters, workbooks, and manuals.

Higher resolution typesetters (1200 dpi and above) are used when quality output is important, are expensive machines, and need experienced people to run them. As mentioned earlier, if you don't have a typesetter, you can take or send your disk to a service bureau and have your document run out on their equipment.

Color laser printers are quite expensive, but prices keep coming down. If you do a lot of covers and interior pages and illustrations in color, these printers are useful for color comps. Color output in these printers is not true to the screen original but it is close enough to give you or your client a good idea of what the finished color work will look like once the document is printed on a two- or four-color press.

PMS COLORS

PMS colors are sets of printer ink color samples used as a standard by the printing industry for many years. PMS colors are matched in two ways. For spot color output, inks are mixed to match a numbered PMS sample. If you are working with four-color process for full color, percentages of cyan (blue), yellow, magenta, and black are used to get the desired color.

A number of page layout programs now specify color output, but beware: It is almost impossible to match the screen colors to the PMS color samples.

Color printer manufacturers are aware of the color matching problem and are trying to provide solutions. For more detailed coverage on colors and printing output see Chapter 14.

DESKTOP PUBLISHING SOFTWARE

The basic software requirements for desktop publishing are a good word processing program and a page layout program. An application program that will manipulate type, a paint program, a drawing program, and a charting and graphing program are also helpful when you have a heavy work load.

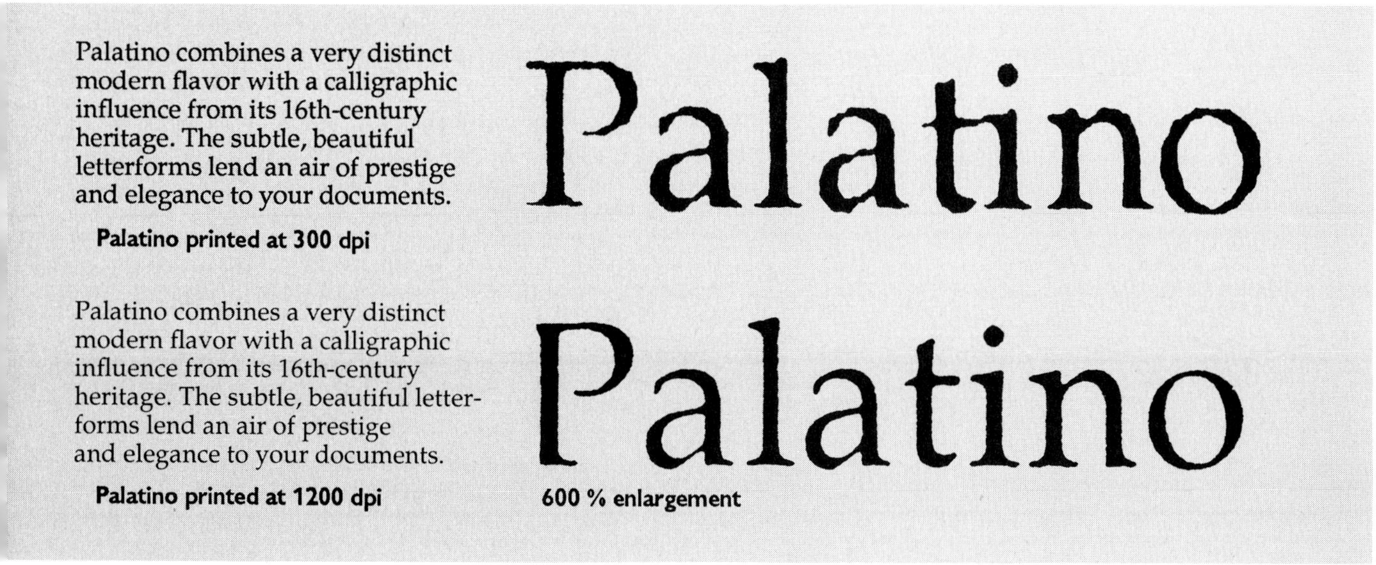

Figure 1.7

POPULAR PAGE LAYOUT PROGRAMS

Low End Programs ($90 – $395)	DOS-Based	Macintosh
Finess	✔	
Gem Desktop Publisher	✔	
MaxPage		✔
PFS: First Publisher	✔	
Publish It	✔	
Quark Style		✔
Springboard Publisher	✔	
Springboard Publisher II		✔

High End Programs ($400 – $900)	DOS-Based	Macintosh
Design Studio		✔
FrameMaker	✔	✔
Interleaf Publisher	✔	
Legend	✔	
The Office Publisher	✔	
PageMaker	✔	✔
Quark Express		✔
Ventura Publisher	✔	✔

Table 1.1

WORD PROCESSING PROGRAMS

Text composition, the most basic publishing requirement, is handled with a word processing program. In fact, lengthy text should be composed with word processing software and placed or imported into your page layout program. Word processing programs are especially designed for text applications because they contain features such as search and replace, hyphenation and justification, widow and orphan control, spell checkers and style sheets. There are word processing programs with additional components including mathematical symbols, table-making features, a thesaurus, and even a gauge for ascertaining a document's reading level.

Some word processing program will allow you to design, style, and prepare many types of documents directly, similar to the features of a simple page layout program.

You should select a word processing program that contains the features you will need. If you use foreign words frequently, you will need hardware and software that will support accent marks, umlauts, circumflexes and other foreign language markings. If your publications require mathematical symbols, you will need an application that can represent them in the text.

PAGE LAYOUT PROGRAMS

You will frequently hear the term "desktop publishing software" used when referring to the software used on a desktop publishing system. However, since the function of these programs is to merge text and artwork on screen and to produce near-typeset quality output, people in the field refer to them more accurately as *page layout programs.* These programs should not be confused with some of the full-featured word processing software packages on the market today. Page layout programs provide higher-quality hyphenation and justification than word processing, and they give you greater flexibility over the type of artwork than can be merged into a document and where it can be positioned.

Page layout programs are designed for a range of complexity levels, aimed at different types of publications and user needs. Page layout programs are often classified as either high- or low-end programs. The popular page layout programs for each category available at the time of this writing are shown in Table 1.1.

DOS-BASED PROGRAMS

Xerox Ventura Publisher is best for lengthy publications with fairly standardized text elements throughout. If your publication needs fine-tuning and variations, PageMaker is a better choice. If you work with simple publications, GEM Publisher and First Publisher may serve your needs.

MAC-BASED PROGRAMS

Xerox recently released a Macintosh version of their popular Ventura Publisher. Likewise, Aldus PageMaker is available for both Macintosh and DOS machines.

Unlike Ventura Publisher, Mac and DOS PageMaker publications files are completely compatible with each other when transferred back and forth on a network. Microsoft Word is also compatible with both versions of PageMaker. PageMaker has a color extension that allows you to specify color by PMS numbers or by process color percentages to be used for film separation.

Quark Express is another robust page layout program — one that professional typographers like to work with. It has excellent features for adjusting the spaces between characters and words. It also has good capabilities for color film separation. Another page makeup program, DesignStudio, provides color specification and allows extensive type manipulation, including rotations. For long documents, FrameMaker is an excellent program, with many additional features for text and graphics adapted from its applications in Unix environments.

For more information on working with color, see Chapter 14.

GRAPHICS PROGRAMS

While all page layout programs allow you to draw lines, boxes, and circles, none allow you to create more involved illustrations and charts. If you plan to use line drawings and illustrations in your documents, similar to the ones illustration in Figure 1.8, you will need one or more graphics programs.

Facts on software programs for illustration purposes are found in Chapter 8, *Working with Photos and Illustrations.* More

Figure 1.8: (right) Three images rendered in a draw program. (far right) A line drawing done in a paint program. Note the rough lines typical of paint programs (drawing courtesy of June Rubin.)

specific suggestions for particular kinds of publications are included in Chapters 10 through 14. Basic illustrations programs include those listed in Table 1.2.

IMAGE SCANNERS

Scanners or digitizers allow you to include art in desktop publishing documents that has been created in another medium such as pencil, chalk, oil, or photography. With the aid of a scanner, original artwork can be recorded electronically at various resolutions and stored, displayed, or printed according to a number of menu choices. You can manipulate scanned images in various ways, using software that comes with the scanner or bought for that purpose.

When a scanned image is placed into a desktop publishing document it can be scaled and cropped like any other piece of artwork. If you have to scan images frequently, especially large pieces of artwork, a desktop scanner is needed. A desktop scanner, as illustrated in Figure 1.6, is about the size of a computer. A smaller hand-held scanner sells for much less than the desktop model, but produces a lower resolution image. Hand-held scanners can be used to capture a low-resolution image for placement and alignment in a document. When the final document is sent to the print shop, the actual artwork is pasted into place rather than using the low-resolution copy.

More recently, color scanners have been introduced on the market. These scanners permit the desktop publisher to scan and place four-color artwork into a document.

NETWORKING BETWEEN DIFFERENT USERS AND DIFFERENT PLATFORMS

While good page layout software exists for both Macintosh and DOS-based machines, the kind of work each type of machine does best varies from one software application to another. For example, since the Macintosh has a strong graphic interface, graphic software for the Macintosh has many more capabilities than the software for DOS-based machines. Happily, networks such as Tops and Ethernet can tie DOS-based and Mac computers together, as well as mainframes and NEXT machines, to get the best of all worlds. Conversion software to convert programs from one format to another is supplied with the network. Additional software is available, depending on your requirements for converting text and graphics from one environment to another.

Table 1.2

POPULAR PAINT AND DRAW PROGRAMS

Programs	Dos-Based	Macintosh
Arts & Letters	✔	
Corel Draw	✔	
MacDraft		✔
MacDraw		✔
MacPaint		✔
Pixel Paint Professional		✔
PC Paintbrush	✔	
Superpaint		✔
Windows Paint	✔	

CHECKING YOUR UNDERSTANDING

1. Briefly describe the influence Johann Gutenberg had on the traditional publishing process.

2. List the seven steps in the publishing process.

3. Contrast the tools used by the traditional graphic artist with those used by a desktop publisher.

4. Discuss how the copy preparation process has changed with the advent of the computer.

5. Explain how an editor influences the copy to be used in a publication.

6. What is the use and purpose of a thumbnail, a rough, and a comp in the design process?

7. Explain how traditional methods of page layout differ from the desktop publishing methods.

8. List the questions that must be answered in order to develop a publication plan.

9. Explain why planning and budgeting are necessary before you begin your publication design.

10. Describe the hardware requirements for a typical desktop publishing workstation.

11. Why are both a page layout program and a word processing program considered necessary software for the desktop publisher?

BUILDING YOUR DESKTOP PUBLISHING DESIGN SKILLS

1. Secure a newsletter from work, school, or home that you consider to be well-designed. Assume you are a desktop publisher and have accepted the task of producing this newsletter.

    a) Indicate the steps you would follow to produce the newsletter and how you would accomplish each step. For example, indicate how you would obtain and edit the copy, the artwork, and any other elements that are part of the newsletter.

    b) Select a date two months from today and create a schedule and time line to produce the newsletter.

2. Assume you have obtained a desktop publishing position with a small business. The accounts are being done on a DOS-based machine, and all printed documents are currently produced on an electric typewriter. You know that the owner does not want to put too much money into equipment at this time; however, the company creates a lot of charts and graphics and also needs to present financial information on slides to small client groups.

    Survey the available hardware and software by reading personal computer magazines; visiting local computer and software stores; or talking with knowledgeable friends, teachers, or colleagues at work; then do the following:

    a) Describe the type of firm (a financial planner, a small manufacturing company, an investment broker, etc.) for which you are working.

    b) Prepare a one- to two-page recommendation for the purchase of hardware and software. Indicate the brand and model and indicate the reasons for your selections.

3. Study the hardware and software available to you in your school's computer lab or at your work location, then do the following:

a) Describe the desktop publishing workstation you are using. Include the brand and model of hardware item (computer, printer, scanner, and so on) and your personal evaluation of each item's strengths and weaknesses.

b) Develop a list of the application software packages available to you. Include a description of the purpose, strengths, and weaknesses of each. Consult personal computer magazines for additional information if necessary.

DESKTOP DESIGN WORKSHOP

The purpose of this section is to provide you with opportunities to develop and/or improve your desktop publishing design skills. The worksheet pages have been placed at the back of the book, and are designed so they can be removed and you can write, draw, or place your responses directly onto the pages.

WORKSHEETS 1.1 AND 1.2

Using the information presented in this chapter or other material you may have available, compose a 1000- to 1500-word theme on the history of publishing and do the following: (Keep track of the time you spend on each of these activities.)

a) Keyboard your theme using a word processing program and save the file on the data disk that accompanies this book. Use the file name "History." Answer questions 1 and 2 on Worksheet 1.1.

b) Proofread your theme by reading the screen, and make any necessary corrections. Replace your original file with your corrected copy, if appropriate.

c) Print your theme on at least two different types of printers (i.e., dot matrix and laser.) Compare the two outputs, then answer questions 3 and 4 on Worksheet 1.1.

d) Select and proofread one of the printed copies. Mark all corrections.

e) Using your marked copy, make any necessary corrections. Replace your file with the corrected copy, if necessary.

f) Reformat your document into a 3-inch-wide column.

g) Print a copy in this format to simulate a galley proof.

h) Using scissors and rubber cement or transparent tape, paste up the galley proof in the columns provided on Worksheet 1.2. You may have to edit the story to fit the available space.

i) Answer question 5 on Worksheet 1.1.

2. COMMUNICATION: VISUAL AND VERBAL

When you finish this chapter you should be able to:

- *Discuss how visual language can be used as a communication medium.*
- *Summarize the basic requirements for desktop publishing text.*
- *Describe how graphic design and aesthetics aid in the communication process.*
- *Define communication problems and discuss how visual communications can help solve these problems.*
- *Identify basic visual communication principles and explain how they aid in the design of aesthetically pleasing publications.*

DESKTOP PUBLISHING IS A form of communication, not only in the verbal content of its message, but also in the visual signals a message sends to the reader. Communication exists on many levels, and messages are sent in many forms. Animals communicate with howls, grunts, or birdsong. Humans read facial expressions and body language along with listening to words. People also communicate using messages in the form of pictures or images. Red and green lights, when used as traffic signals, are visual messages that tell a driver when to stop and go on the road. Red and green signs in December let us know that it's time to do Christmas shopping. Apart from color, messages can be sent through texture, size, or spatial arrangements (in a room, on a page, or in the outdoor environment). Visual messages are common in our everyday lives.

THE WAY THINGS LOOK IS A FORM OF COMMUNICATION

Speech is one of our most basic forms of communication. It is fluid and expressive. We punctuate our utterances by speaking soft or loudly and varying the pitch to make it higher or lower. Ending a sentence by going up in tone usually signifies a question. The message is made more emphatic when it is coupled

Figure 2.1: Examples of body language, facial expression, and gesture (courtesy Sue Linville.)

with a visual gesture such as raising the eyebrows. The sound and expression of spoken exchange coupled with bodily accents is part of what we respond to when we talk to each other, as illustrated in Figure 2.1.

Speech is ephemeral. The sounds of the spoken word disappear unless they are recorded. According to Marshall McLuhan[1], before printing became widespread, the communication of a message was based on word inflection, using audible sound cadences for meaning. As printed communication became more widespread, the order of words in a visually presented text message replaced sound as a communicant. Grammar and rules for the written word replaced the rhetoric used in a vocal expression. The written word can be thought of as a kind of frozen speech, a permanent record when compared to verbal dialogue.

Apart from the messages in text as written language, the printed word can use visual messages to express moods and feelings. This chapter will introduce you to ways in which sounds, gestures, and the body language of human communication can be represented in the printed pages you produce.

COMPARISONS BETWEEN SPEECH AND PUBLICATION ELEMENTS

Verbal Format Elements	Publication Format Elements
The conversation opener	Title
Individual topics and events, with opening announcements for each	Stories and individual sections of a publication
Small talk — actual contents of each event	Contents of a story or article
Audible emphasis punctuating speech	Subheadings used as visual punctuation
Gestures	Graphical images
Silences	White space such as margins and paragraph space markers

Table 2.1

COMPARING ELEMENTS IN SPEECH AND IN PRINT

Elements in a publication are similar to those used in verbal communication, as seen summarized in Table 2.1. When people start a new topic of conversation, they usually use some *opening phrase* to introduce it. In text, the *title* functions similarly. Conversation may consist of many different topics and events, with opening announcements for each. This equates to the individual stories and sections of a publication. After a topic is introduced, the conversation that follows consists of small talk, equivalent to the actual contents of a story or article. Vocal emphasis punctuating a conversation is like the use of headings, while the use of gestures corresponds to graphical images — their size, color, and texture. Silences in verbal communication are similar to the white spaces on a printed page.

COMPARISONS BETWEEN SPEECH AND PUBLICATION ELEMENTS

Imbedded in any publication are many different kinds of messages. The text containing the content of the written message is the most obvious. All publications also embody subliminal messages that are expressed visually. Non-textual messages in a publication are called its *visual language*.

Examples of visual language used in communication are illustrated in Figure 2.2. The typeface you use; the way you arrange the text on the page; the number, size, and kind of illustrations you use; and the quality, color, and size of paper all work together to form a setting. This setting acts as a visual frame for the messages in your publication, and becomes part of the total message to be received by your reader audience.

To learn more about how to translate speech elements into those used in publications, read Chapter 3, *Document Structure: Organizing Your Publication.* It discusses the parts of a publication and shows you how to work with them as a desktop designer.

Powerful

Professional

Jazzy

Stylish

Playful

Distinguished

Figure 2.2

BASIC REQUIREMENTS FOR DESKTOP PUBLISHING TEXT

This book is not intended to cover the writing aspect of desktop publishing. However, the checklist illustrated in Figure 2.3 summarizes some of the basic requirements for an author to follow when producing desktop publishing text. If you need more help when writing material for your publications, consult your local library.

When you are preparing to design a booklet, newsletter, or report, keep the following in mind:

> *Only part of the message carried by your publication is expressed through the printed words. Another part of the message is sent through the appearance of your publication.*

✔ **CHECKLIST FOR TEXT:**

The text:

- ☐ Is written clearly, simply, and as briefly as possible.
- ☐ Contains short, concise sentences.
- ☐ Uses concrete language and avoids abstractions.
- ☐ Sounds as if I am speaking.
- ☐ Is free of jargon.
- ☐ Is logically presented; each sentence and paragraph flow meaningfully to the next.
- ☐ Is consistent.
- ☐ Uses active verb forms.
- ☐ Avoids sex bias language.
- ☐ Has been proofread, edited, and rewritten so as to present the message I wish to convey.

Figure 2.3

Figure 2.4: The transportation network is an example of how we use our visual sense in daily life.

Communication through appearance is called *visual communication.*

VISUAL COMMUNICATION

Studies have shown that as much as 80 per cent of what we perceive in the world around us is through our visual sense. Unconsciously, our visual sense guides us to "read" more than the words on a page (see Figure 2.4.)

> *We read not just words and their meaning, but also how the words are arranged, where they are placed, and what they look like.*

Receivers of messages classify them based on what they see. Supposedly, you can't judge a book by its cover, but the person who pulls a book off a shelf and opens it is responding to a message that the publisher makes about the content of the book (see Figure 2.5.)

Visual language can send a reader messages that help organize and clarify the text. It acts as an aide to better understanding by reflecting the information structure of the text. Messages contained in the text of a pub-

Figure 2.5: The visual language that is inherent in the design of the cover of a book may or may not reflect the message within its interior.

lication can be changed based on the way the reader perceives those messages visually. Visual communications reflect the mood of the text message, whether it is serious or humorous, elegant or unpolished.

CHARACTERISTICS OF VISUAL MESSAGES

So far we have discussed visual language in comparison to speech. Visual messages have other characteristics that contribute to their impact. Figure 2.6 illustrates the composite nature of communication. It shows the publication as a composite message, sent by the publication designer and editor, to be received by the reader audience. The medium that carries the communication is print. The message itself is made up of its text messages and its visual elements set within the context of the publication.

REPRESENTATION OF VISUAL ELEMENTS

Visual elements can be very realistic, as in the letters of the alphabet or in photographs. They can also be very abstract, and presented in symbolic form. Look at the photograph shown in Figure 2.7. Realistically it shows a spider in its web. Imbedded in the image are other messages — for example, the concept of evil and intrigue. These messages are "coded"— they are set in a visual

Figure 2.7: A photograph with a realistic and a symbolic representation.

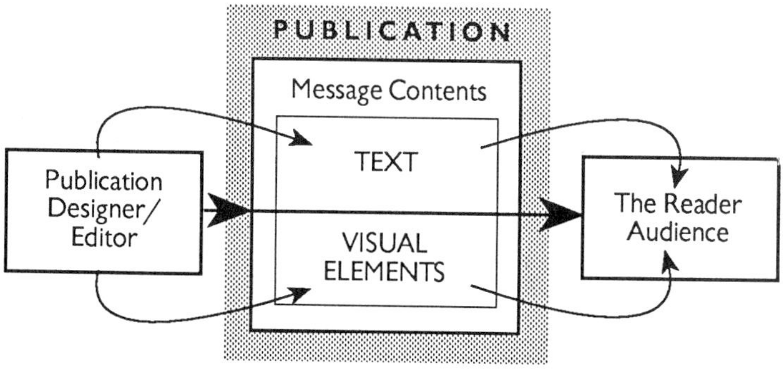

Figure 2.6: The visual presentation in a publication sends messages along with those sent by the words that compose its text.

Figure 2.8: Two versions of an advertisement for Purina HiPro — the ad at the top was used for a Los Angeles audience, while the one below was aimed at New Yorkers.

shorthand that the mind interprets. Some codes are very personal, but many are universal. These are the ones that graphic designers rely on, according to Paul Rand. "The symbol is . . . the common language between [designer] and spectator . . .The graphic designer's task is to find the essential meaning in the material and then to abstract and symbolize."[2]

RULES FOR VISUAL COMMUNICATION

Rules for visual communication exist by convention, by their context or environmental setting, and by how our minds organize information.

RULES BY CONVENTION

We define some visual arrangements by our cultural expectations, such as reading from left to right in European languages, and right to left in Semitic ones. Arabic numerals and mathematical symbols, too, are symbols that are agreed to conventionally. They usually do not convey information about their numerical value symbolically in their shape. In design, it is important to pay attention to the way people *expect* certain kinds of messages to be sent. Otherwise you will not be understood.

RULES DERIVED FROM CONTEXTS AND SETTINGS

The environmental setting and the medium that is used to carry the message affect how it will be received by its audience. A reader has different visual expectations when reading a report in the office than in reading a play program designed by school-age children for their parents. Advertising agencies take advantage of this fact when designing advertisements for people living in different parts of the country. (See Figure 2.8.)

RULES BY HOW OUR MINDS ORGANIZE INFORMATION

The mind organizes the information it receives into mental formats that are quickly processedand acted on. Cognitive psychologists have defined some of the formats that designers have used intuitively when organizing page layouts. See Chapter 4, *Designing Form With Content,* for a discussion on cognitive research and graphic design.

When you learn how to use visual communication in your publications, it will be easier for you to design a document that transmits your messages clearly and explicitly. Visual communication, appropriately used, will help you to communicate with your intended audience more specifically and with greater power.

DESIGN AS A SKILL

Publication design is an ability that can be learned. It is a sophisticated skill, but one which you can develop through practice, like playing the piano or learning how to become a better swimmer. Not everyone will be an Olympic champion in the area of graphic design, but you can learn to improve your designs through repeated effort and practice.

- ✔ Get as much information as you can about the project. Find out why it needs to be done in the first place. Get the budget and schedules, if possible. Ascertain the scope of the project — large or small. Read Chapter 16, *Publication Planning, Budgeting, and Scheduling,* for help in this area.
- ✔ Study the nature of the design problem, now that you have the basic information.
- ✔ Develop several possible solutions in rough form.
- ✔ Review and criticize your solution possibilities.
- ✔ Rework your solutions. Repeat steps 4 and 5 until you (and your clients) are satisfied.
- ✔ Create the final design.

HOW TO SOLVE PROBLEMS WITH DESIGN

The first step when designing a publication is to learn what the problems are and solve them. It will set the direction that guides your graphic design.

You will need to know *who* your audience is, *what* you want to say to them, and *how* you want to frame the message. For example, you may want to present statistics for a financial report so that it is received clearly and without bias. When designing a restaurant menu, you might want to indicate a feeling of elegance about the restaurant's atmosphere, along with information about the food and prices. A newsletter to company employees may need a light touch, as compared to a more serious newsletter sent to stockholders of the same company. A term paper and a business report both need to show the reader that the information is presented effectively and explicitly.

Unless you define the problems your design is meant to solve and use a design that fits those needs, the publication will not communicate your message or serve its purpose—no matter how attractive its design is.

- ✔ *Define your audience.*
- ✔ *Know the purpose of your publication.*
- ✔ *Know how you want your audience to react.*
- ✔ *Know the image you wish to project.*

Use the checklist in Figure 2.9 on the following page to help you define your communication problems so that you can use visual communications as a way of solving the problems. Consciously define the audience, and what your document requires to reach them. Define your content message as well, in relation to how you want it to be received.

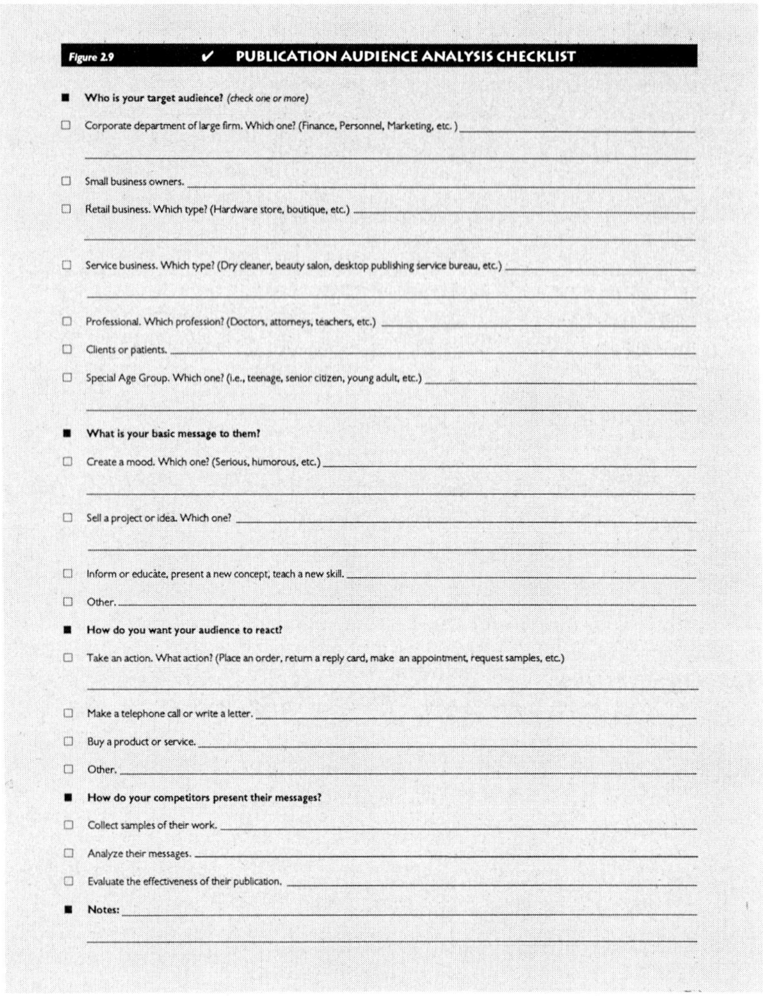

Figure 2.9 ✔ PUBLICATION AUDIENCE ANALYSIS CHECKLIST

- ■ **Who is your target audience?** *(check one or more)*
- ☐ Corporate department of large firm. Which one? (Finance, Personnel, Marketing, etc.) ____
- ☐ Small business owners. ____
- ☐ Retail business. Which type? (Hardware store, boutique, etc.) ____
- ☐ Service business. Which type? (Dry cleaner, beauty salon, desktop publishing service bureau, etc.) ____
- ☐ Professional. Which profession? (Doctors, attorneys, teachers, etc.) ____
- ☐ Clients or patients. ____
- ☐ Special Age Group. Which one? (i.e., teenage, senior citizen, young adult, etc.) ____
- ■ **What is your basic message to them?**
- ☐ Create a mood. Which one? (Serious, humorous, etc.) ____
- ☐ Sell a project or idea. Which one? ____
- ☐ Inform or educate, present a new concept, teach a new skill. ____
- ☐ Other. ____
- ■ **How do you want your audience to react?**
- ☐ Take an action. What action? (Place an order, return a reply card, make an appointment, request samples, etc.)
- ☐ Make a telephone call or write a letter. ____
- ☐ Buy a product or service. ____
- ☐ Other. ____
- ■ **How do your competitors present their messages?**
- ☐ Collect samples of their work. ____
- ☐ Analyze their messages. ____
- ☐ Evaluate the effectiveness of their publication. ____
- ■ **Notes:** ____

Figure 2.9: A full-sized version of the Publication Audience Analysis Checklist can be found in the Workshop/Forms Appendix.

DEFINE YOUR AUDIENCE AND ITS ENVIRONMENT

Publishing can be defined as the act of using written or printed words to make something public or known, that was previously unknown. This definition implies that the publishing process involves the transfer of knowledge from a sender to an audience. The audience for the printed message can vary in size from one person to a hundred or even several thousand. The audience may be a boss, a coworker, an employee, a prospective customer or client, a professor, a friend.

The way the audience will receive the information you are sending in your publication depends on the *form* in which the published message is presented—its *look*. But don't assume that your intended audience will actually *read* your printed message.

> *You do not have a reader until you have* ***involved*** *that person in your message. Defining or identifying your audience helps you choose the techniques that engage readers.*

A good speaker always considers the audience to whom the message is directed. Don't you speak differently to a child than to a grownup? Words said in anger have a different tone than those expressing love. A request for a raise sounds different than a discussion of where to go for dinner. Most of us have learned to change or vary our spoken communication depending on circumstances, on who we are talking to, and what the subject matter is. We have learned to "read the audience." If the listener does not appear to understand, we repeat the message, speak more slowly, or rephrase the information. Sometimes we use gestures to make the message even more clear. (See Table 2.2.)

The printed word can also be modulated and changed in its presentation to depend on who you are reaching, the mood you wish to convey, and how you would like the reader to

SPEECH AND PUBLICATION MESSAGE FORMATS

Speech Context *(ephemeral and fleeting)*	**Publication Context** *(Frozen and specific)*
Topic of conversation	Function or purpose of publication
Mood or key of the conversation	Mood or key of the pages
Participants in a conversation	Audience for desktop publishing
Message form: spoken	Message form: written
Conversation is two-way most of the time. Rules for interaction depend on the participants and the time allotted: client, boss, child.	Audience to whom message is directed is specific but is one-way only.

Table 2.2

react. It is important to understand that the extent and manner in which your audience becomes involved is directly connected to the form in which your message is sent.

KNOW THE PURPOSE OF YOUR PUBLICATION

Desktop publishing is used to produce a variety of different publications. These documents fall into one or more of the categories illustrated in Figure 2.10. Identifying the category to which your document belongs can help you develop the right approach for its purpose.

KNOW HOW YOU WANT YOUR AUDIENCE TO REACT

The printed word is a one-way communication. When your printed message is being read, you usually are not present to watch and listen to your reader, filling in with speech when the printed message has not expressed your intentions clearly. The printed message needs to communicate to your audience *directly* as to how you want them to react while they are looking at and reading the text.

One of the most important design objectives is knowing what action you want your reader to take. Among the more common reactions promoted by business publications are: to buy (or sell); to feel good about a company, product, or service; to define and convey information or data; to change an attitude; to agree (or disagree) with a philosophy; and to support a point of view.

KNOW THE IMAGE YOU WANT TO PROJECT

A third important design objective is knowing what image you would like your publication to project. The arrangement of elements on the page and the design elements you select must fit your purpose and audience.

CATEGORIES OF BUSINESS PUBLICATIONS

When you can identify the category to which your publication belongs, it will help you to make better design decisions. A publication may be classified in more than one category, depending on how it will be used.

A Publication Can...

...identify

- Business card
- Corporate standards manual
- Label
- Stationary

...provide data

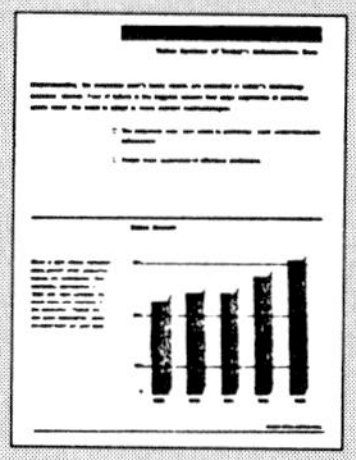

- Application
- Documentation sheet
- Order form
- Questionnaire
- Resume
- Specification sheet
- Survey

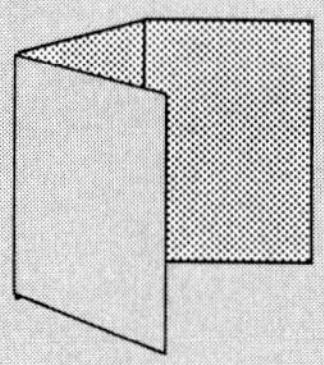

...inform

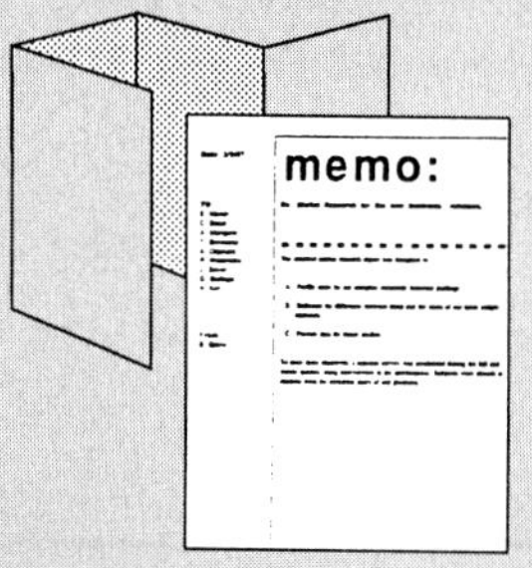

- Brochure
- Bulletin
- Business report
- Factsheet
- Magazine
- Marketing plan
- Newsletter
- Newspaper
- Product list
- Program
- Resume
- Specification sheet

...be a reference

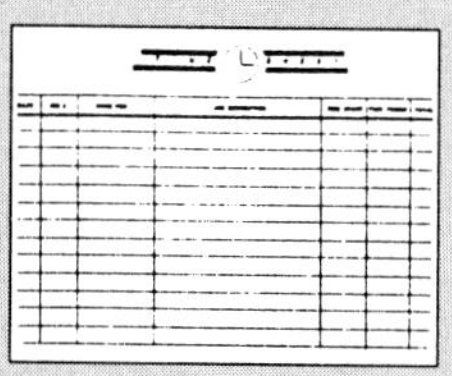

- Calendar
- Directory
- Glossary
- List
- Schedule
- Timetable

...sell

- Advertisement
- Catalog
- Invitation
- News release
- Poster
- Promotional flyer
- Prospectus
- Resume
- Sales brochure

...teach

- Curriculum guide
- Documentation manual
- Instruction manual
- Textbook
- Training guide

Figure 2.10: Categories of business documents.

If you are preparing the annual report for a Fortune 500 company, your text should be informative and authoritative and your design should project a feeling of prosperity. If, on the other hand, you are designing a business plan, the mood would be bold, energetic, and confident.

Before you begin to design your publication, list the impressions you want to make.

DESIGN AESTHETICS AND VISUAL COMMUNICATION

Visual communication seems to have mysterious qualities to those who have had little exposure to page layout and design. It can take several years to master the nuances of visual communications, but you can begin to design aesthetically pleasing publications that reinforce your message if you apply the basic principles reviewed in this book.

FORM AND CONTENT

The well-designed document or publication is easy to read, although the reader is not conscious of it. It just *looks* inviting. The messages it transmits are communicated to the reader clearly and unambiguously. Visual and verbal elements do not conflict with each other. If the text is a serious one, the publication looks serious. Each element within the text visually echoes the content of the written word. Important headings are large; less important elements look less important because they are smaller or lighter in tone. In design language this is known as *form* echoing *content.*

Form and content use two different channels for communication: visual and written

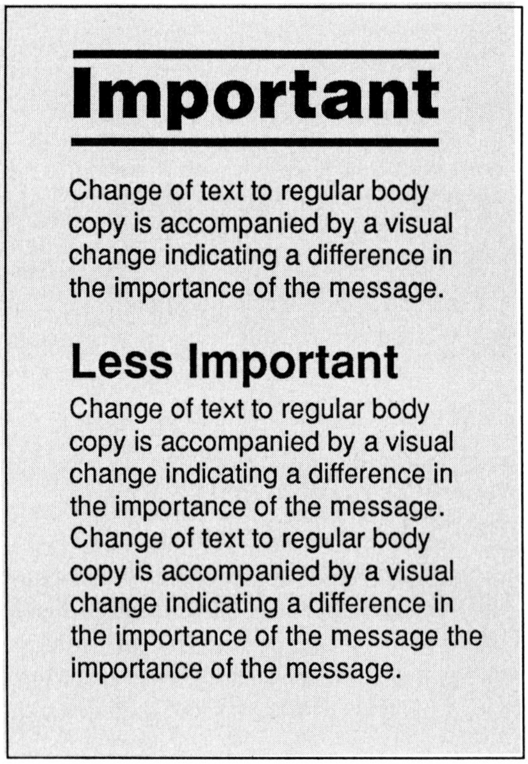

Figure 2.11: (right) The differences between an upscale restaurant and a fast food place are reflected not only in their pricing, but in the visual design of their menus.

Figure 2.12: (far right) Levels of importance in text are reflected by the size and boldness of the type that is used.

language. The visual appearance of the text — how it looks and how it is arranged on a page — is called form. The written word of a publication, the text, is called content. As described earlier, form contains visual messages that can enhance or conflict with the content. When a message is communicated so that form and content echo each other, the reader finds the message easier to understand and to remember. Figure 2.11 illustrates how changes in visual presentation reflects differences in messages portrayed in printed pieces. Chapter 4 discusses this concept in greater detail.

STRUCTURE AND SPACE

Other aspects of form and content deal with structural and spatial arrangements. Breaks in the text are reflected by visual breaks on the page. As shown in Figure 2.12, important elements are made visually more important, bigger or bolder than the accompanying text. A change of text category is accompanied by a visual change in structure. For example, notice that there is a distinct difference between the chapter headings, paragraph headings, and subheading used in this text. In this way, a reader is able to follow, with visual cues, the intent and arrangement of the text or written message.

A publication whose visual presentation is not coordinated with its text is the equivalent of wearing a sneaker on one foot and a dress shoe on the other.

Another support for good visual communication is through the use of a regular and repeated arrangement of text and illustrations that the reader unconsciously follows (see Figure 2.13.) The page layout follows an underlying skeleton, paragraph to paragraph and page

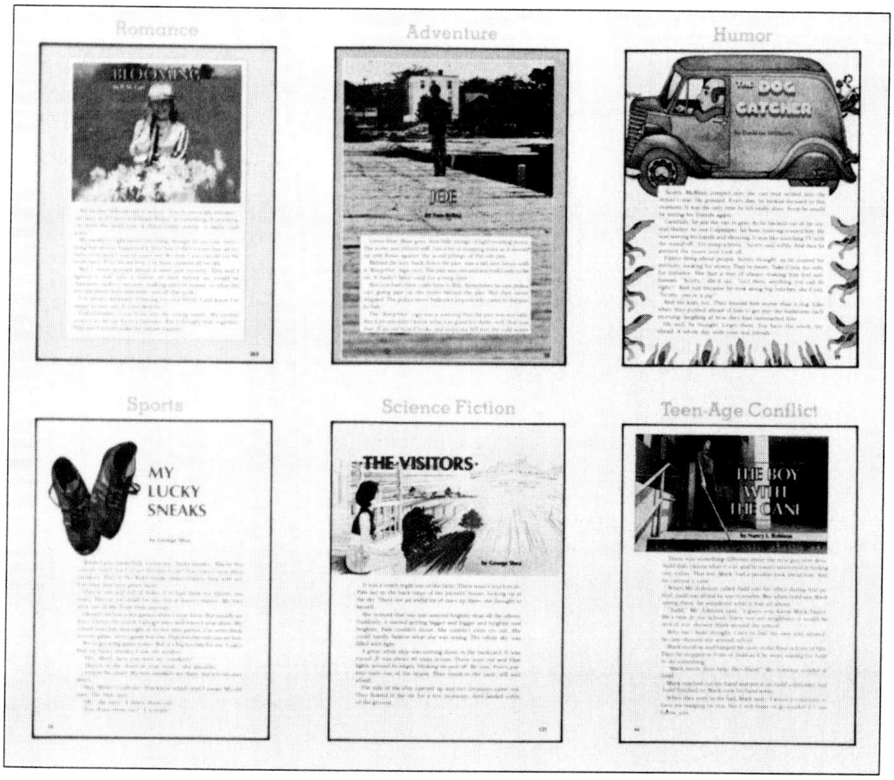

Figure 2.13: A regular arrangement of text and illustrations.

Figure 2.14: Comparison of publications for different audiences: (top) a book for teen-aged girls, (center, courtesy KCRW) a radio station newsletter, and (bottom) an annual report.

to page. Chapter 7, *Grids: Working With Structure and Space,* covers this aspect of design.

MOOD AND FEELING

In a well-designed document or publication, the mood and tone that the text communicates is replicated visually. When the message is a serious one, type and text arrangements also look serious. An annual report that looked like a new-wave graphic or an MTV music presentation would convey an ambiguous message — one of frivolity conflicting with a serious statement. A publication for teenagers, on the other hand, would be inappropriately designed if it looked like a corporate financial report (see Figure 2.14.)

TEXT AND VISUAL COMMUNICATION

When designing a publication for good communication you must also think about how well the material on the page can be read. Consideration must be given to four elements: legibility, readability, consistency, and relevance.

LEGIBILITY

Legibility is the extent to which the print is large enough and sufficiently well-formed to actually be read. Overinked, filled-in letters or smeared print are examples of text that is hard to read because it is not legible.

Print for beginning readers and the elderly, even when it is clean, is not actually legible unless it is larger than average.

READABILITY

Readability is a gauge of the amount of effort needed to read a document. Readability differs from legibility in that legibility is concerned with the clarity of the text; readability is concerned with the ease or difficulty in reading the type face design, size, and placement. Convention also affects what people think is readable. In the fourteenth century, the German black letter printing was easily read, but it is considered almost unreadable today (see Figure 2.15.)

CONSISTENCY

It is easier to read a publication when its page design is *consistent.* Consistency demands that any page elements used in the same way throughout a publication should always look the same and have the same locations and relationships to each other, page after page. For example, a main head should always be set using the same type face and size throughout a story. Likewise, the body text in that story should have the same width throughout, unless there is an illustration.

Inconsistent page design is confusing to the reader. A publication that is confusing to the reader is a poorly designed publication

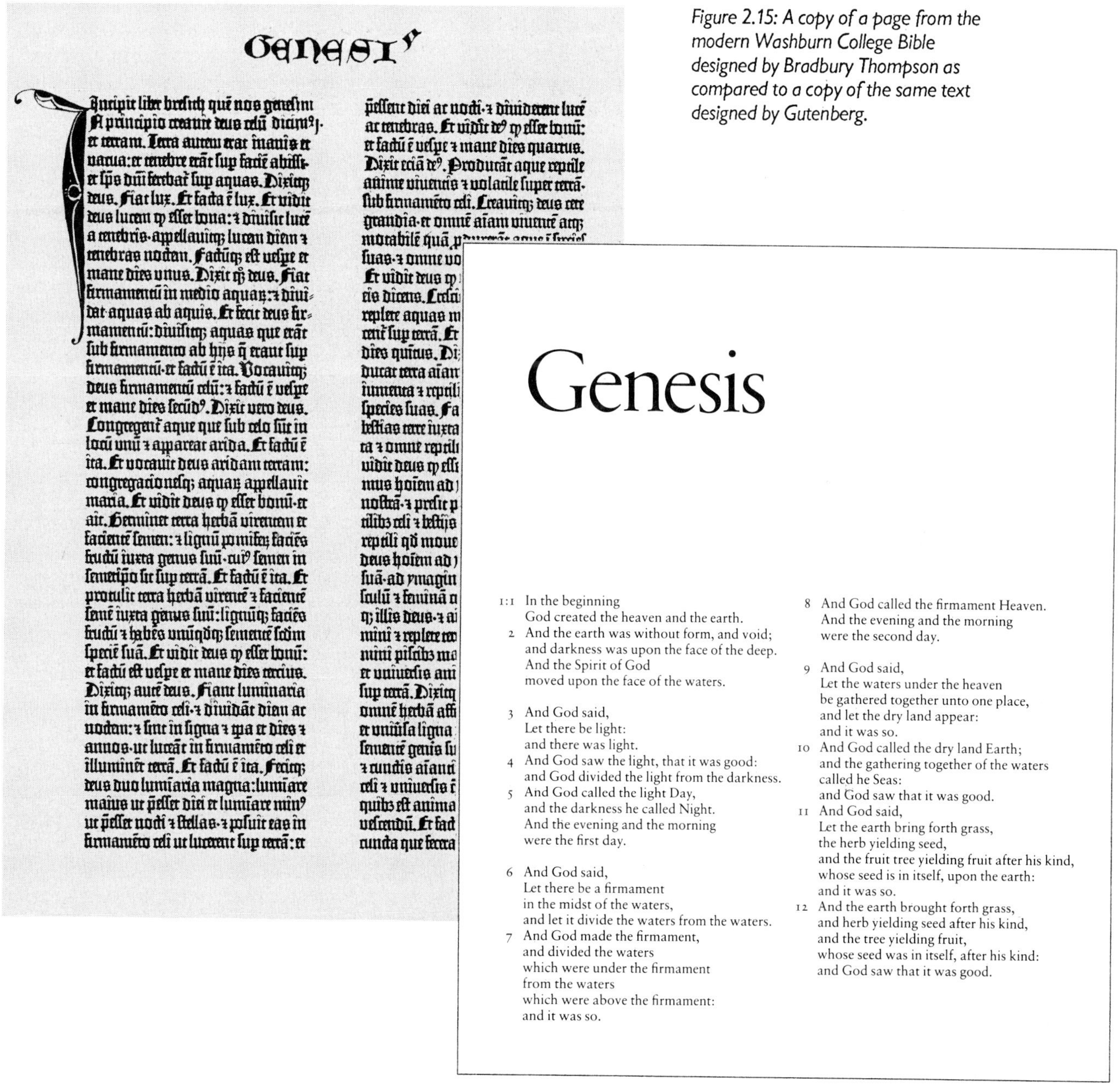
Genesis

1:1 In the beginning
God created the heaven and the earth.
2 And the earth was without form, and void;
and darkness was upon the face of the deep.
And the Spirit of God
moved upon the face of the waters.

3 And God said,
Let there be light:
and there was light.
4 And God saw the light, that it was good:
and God divided the light from the darkness.
5 And God called the light Day,
and the darkness he called Night.
And the evening and the morning
were the first day.

6 And God said,
Let there be a firmament
in the midst of the waters,
and let it divide the waters from the waters.
7 And God made the firmament,
and divided the waters
which were under the firmament
from the waters
which were above the firmament:
and it was so.
8 And God called the firmament Heaven.
And the evening and the morning
were the second day.

9 And God said,
Let the waters under the heaven
be gathered together unto one place,
and let the dry land appear:
and it was so.
10 And God called the dry land Earth;
and the gathering together of the waters
called he Seas:
and God saw that it was good.
11 And God said,
Let the earth bring forth grass,
the herb yielding seed,
and the fruit tree yielding fruit after his kind,
whose seed is in itself, upon the earth:
and it was so.
12 And the earth brought forth grass,
and herb yielding seed after his kind,
and the tree yielding fruit,
whose seed was in itself, after his kind:
and God saw that it was good.

Figure 2.15: A copy of a page from the modern Washburn College Bible designed by Bradbury Thompson as compared to a copy of the same text designed by Gutenberg.

RELEVANCE

Relevance, the fourth member of the text type quartet, is concerned with visual emphasis. The importance of a text or graphic element is indicated by the size, type style, and the space it takes up. Its level of importance should be equal to its visual and spatial emphasis on the printed page. Newspaper headlines, for example, are larger and blacker than the rest of the text on the page to call attention to important news events. Magazines use headings that are large enough to stand out from the advertisements on the page to show the beginning of a story (see Figure 2.16.) For a more detailed discussion of legibility, readability, consistency, and relevance, see Chapter 6, *Type Aesthetics*.

The major elements that make up text in a document are covered in the next chapter. Publication elements require design using visual and spatial emphasis that is appropriate to the text reference and to the audience that you are reaching. These elements are similar to those used in speech, as shown in Table 2.2.

---

[1] McLuhan, M (1960), "The Effect of the Printed Book on Language in the 16th Century," in *Explorations in Communication.* McLuhan, M. and Carpenter, E.. (eds), MA, Beacon Press, 1960.

[2] Rand, P. (1970) *Thoughts on Design.* London, Studio Vista, 1970.

10 Minutes Without Blood

RACING RESULTS-ENTRIES

Los Angeles Times

SATURDAY MORNING FINAL

VOL. XCI FOUR PARTS—PART ONE | SATURDAY MORNING, APRIL 29, 1972 | 78 PAGES | DAILY 10¢

PLANET X

Evidence of Huge Body Beyond Pluto

SOVIET SHORTAGE

Rezinoproekt in Big Trouble Over Pacifiers

40,000 Reds Start Siege of Quang Tri City

Squadrons of Tanks Cut Highway 1 Into Capital; Hue Also Under Threat

UC Scientists Cite Shifts of 3 Comets

Figure 2.16: Typographic emphasis is shown by sizes of type and its placement.

CHECKING YOUR UNDERSTANDING

1. Give three examples of how visual language is used in our daily lives.

2. Briefly explain how the content of a publication may be changed based on the way the reader visually perceives the message.

3. Give five of the basic requirements for writing desktop publishing text.

4. List the four problem areas that must be addressed before you can begin a publication design.

5. Contrast how a speaker and a desktop publishing designer considers the audience to which the message is addressed.

6. List ten different publications currently available at your local library or school and then classify each of the publications according to purposes shown in Figure 2.9.

7. Explain the difference between the form and the content of a publication.

8. Give two examples of how this text uses structural and spatial arrangement as a design element.

9. Explain how mood and feeling of a publication's text can be replicated visually.

10. Explain the differences between each element of the text/type communication quartet: readability, legibility, consistency, and relevance.

BUILDING YOUR DESKTOP PUBLISHING DESIGN SKILLS

1. Collect samples of five different publication designs (brochure, magazine advertisement, flyer, form, newsletter, and so on) that illustrate good use of the basic principles of design discussed in this chapter, and five different samples that illustrate poor use of basic design principles. Prepare a cover sheet for each of your publications using a copy of the Publication Cover Sheet, Figure 2.17 in the Workbook/Forms Appendix.

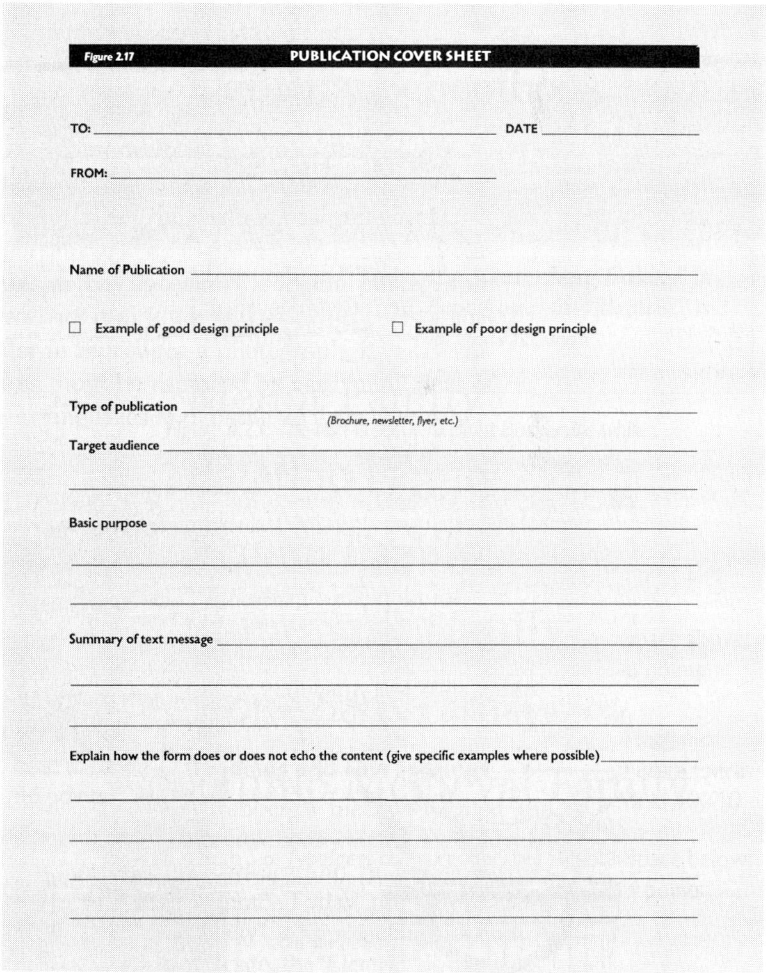

Figure 2.17 PUBLICATION COVER SHEET

TO: ______ DATE ______

FROM: ______

Name of Publication ______

☐ Example of good design principle ☐ Example of poor design principle

Type of publication ______ (Brochure, newsletter, flyer, etc.)

Target audience ______

Basic purpose ______

Summary of text message ______

Explain how the form does or does not echo the content (give specific examples where possible) ______

Figure 2.17: Reduced copy of Publication Cover Sheet

2. Collect a minimum of four different publications (i.e., brochures, stationery, business cards, newsletters, and so on) for an organization or firm with which you are familiar. The organization may be a school club, an academic department within your school or college, a professional organization to which you belong, or the company for which you, a friend, or relative works.

Prepare a one- or two-page report that answers the following questions about the organization or company. Include your samples with your written report.

a) What is/are the primary product(s) or service(s) provided by the organization or firm?

b) Explain how this organization or firm differs from others that provide the same products or services.

c) List three adjectives that can be used to describe the audience to which your samples are directed.

d) List three adjectives that best describe the image the organization or firm image conveys in your samples.

e) Describe any identifying logo, motto, or slogan, and explain the image that is conveyed.

3. Prepare the text for an unsolicited letter of application that you can use to obtain a position in a field of your choice.

a) Before starting to write, take the time to answer the following:

- Who is my audience?
- How do I want my target audience to react?
- What image do I want to project?

b) After writing your text, check it over using the following criteria:

- Evaluate your writing style using the check list for text on page 23 as a guide.
- Proofread your text carefully for spelling, grammar, punctuation, and sentence structure.

c) Edit your first draft if necessary, and prepare a final copy. Include an introductory paragraph to the text that describes the target audience, the image you wish to project, and any other information that will help the reader evaluate the effectiveness of your message.

DESKTOP DESIGN WORKSHOP

The purpose of this section is to provide you with opportunities to develop and/or improve your desktop publishing design skills. The worksheet pages have been placed at the back of the book, and are designed so they can be removed and you can write, draw, or place your responses directly onto the pages.

WORKSHEET 2.1

Study the two sample desktop publishing publications. Review their accompanying "makeovers" along with the description of the firm using each publication. Working with the design principles presented in this chapter, and the description accompanying each publication, indicate why the changes reflected in the "makeovers" were made. Give suggestions for further improvement, if appropriate.

PART TWO

DESIGN AS COMMUNICATION

3. DOCUMENT STRUCTURE: ORGANIZING YOUR PUBLICATION

When you finish this chapter you should be able to:

- *Describe text elements that can add character, animation, and shape to a page.*
- *Use design elements that add emphasis and variety to a page that is text-intensive.*
- *Recognize the grid structure of a simple publication design.*
- *Discuss the purpose and use of a style sheet.*

IN THIS CHAPTER YOU WILL BE INTRODUCED to the basic forms that publications take. These basic elements are part of the desktop designer's palette. Some parts of a publication are typographic elements; others deal with spatial structure — where to put what on the blank page. Learning what page design elements are and how they are used will introduce you to some of the basic technical and aesthetic concepts practiced in graphic design. This information will help you to design a publication that delivers your message the way you want it to be sent. More detailed information on typographic usage and page design is covered in the chapters that follow.

DESIGNING PUBLICATIONS USING DOCUMENT STRUCTURES

In Chapter 2, *Communication: Visual and Verbal,* you learned that designing and assembling pages on a computer is a communications task as well as an electronic one. Publications need to be tailored to fit their audiences. This chapter shows you how to look at a page and identify the elements that give it shape and character.

SIZE AND SHAPE ARE DESIGN ELEMENTS

Think about the magazines, manuals, and reports you read, the letters and memos you send, and the flyers and brochures you receive. Although they may be cut and folded into a variety of final sizes, many of them start out using a standard page size of 8-1/2 x 11 as shown in Figure 3.1A. While larger sizes of paper are frequently used for desktop publishing (see Figure 3.1B) this chapter will focus on designing for 8-1/2 x 11 inches since that is the output size of most laser printers.

Pages and their elements can be arranged either lengthwise or sideways on document pages. In desktop publishing lingo, a page that is taller than it is wide is said to be designed in the *portrait* mode. A page that is wider than it is tall is designed in the *landscape* mode.

PAGE ELEMENTS OF A TYPICAL PUBLICATION

There are a number of terms that the publishing community uses to describe page elements in a publication. This shared vocabulary has traditionally allowed writers, editors, graphic designers, layout artists, printers, and publishers to communicate quickly and easily. Desktop publishing can benefit from this tradition. The page elements of a typical publication are illustrated in Figure 3.2. Each term is explained in the chapter text that follows.

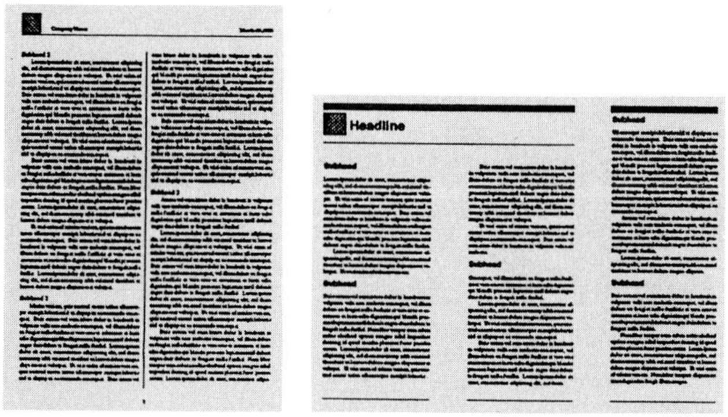

PORTRAIT LANDSCAPE

Figure 3.1A

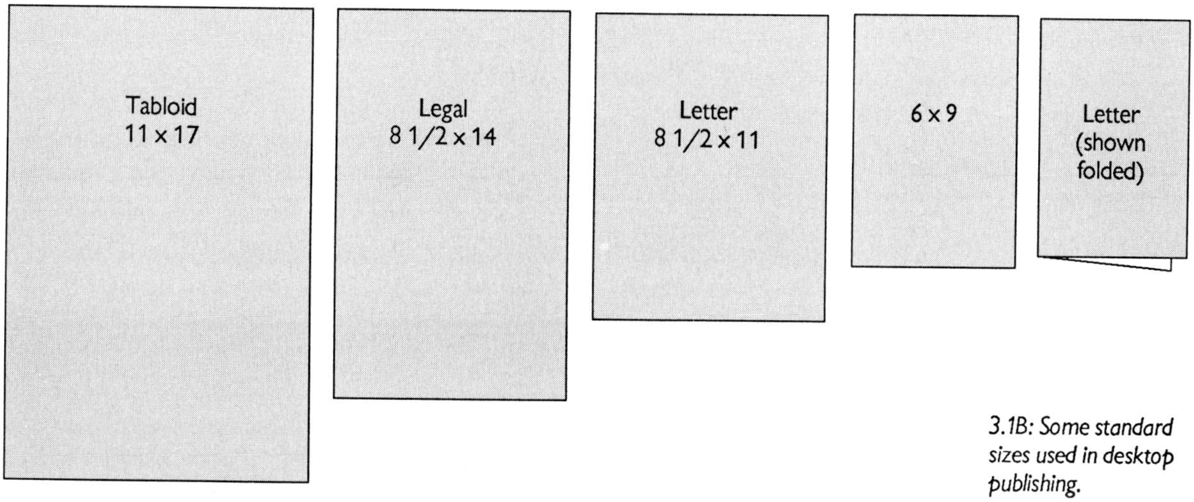

3.1B: Some standard sizes used in desktop publishing.

Figure 3.2
THE ANATOMY OF A PRINTED PAGE

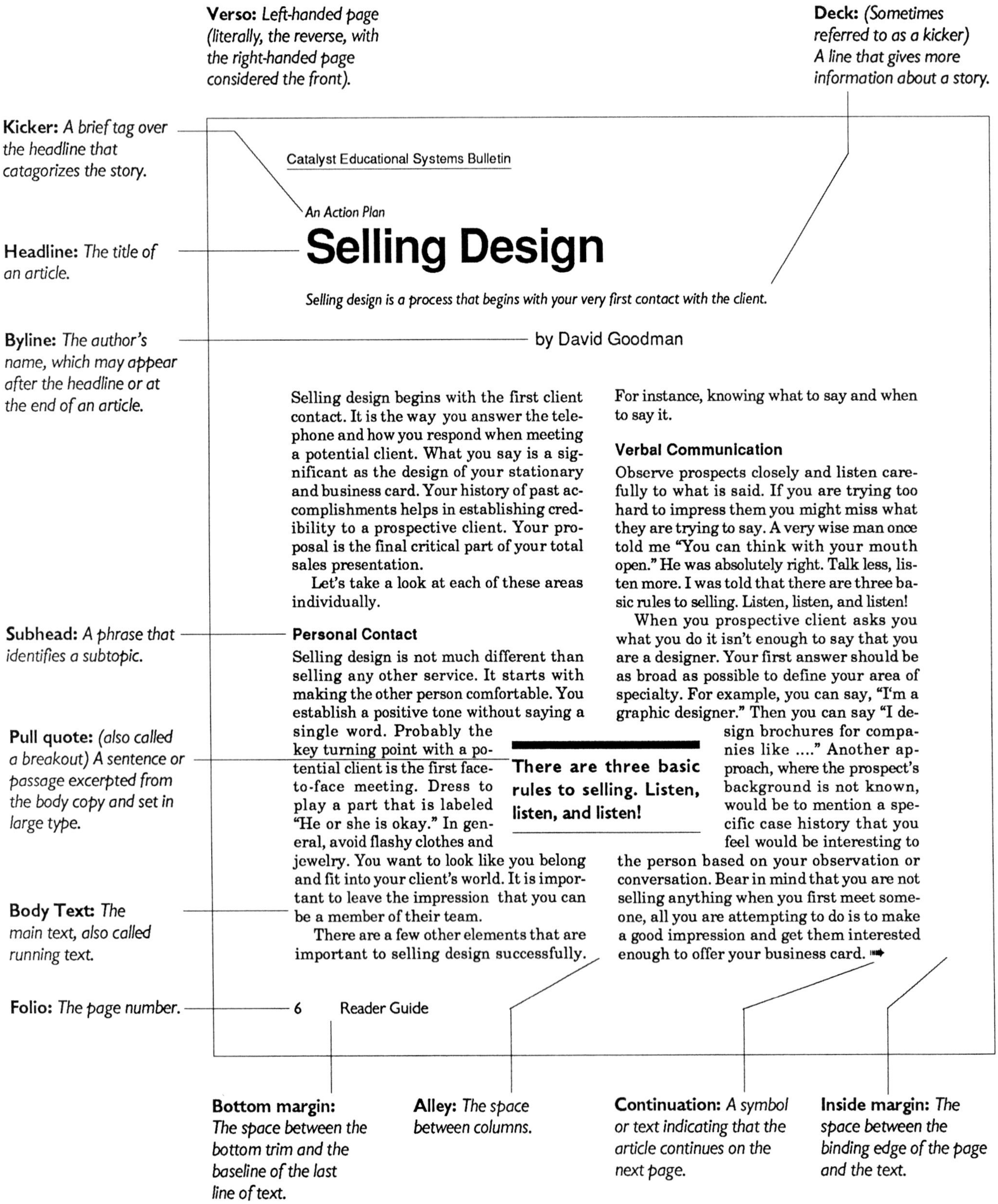

Catalyst Educational Systems Bulletin

An Action Plan

Selling Design

Selling design is a process that begins with your very first contact with the client.

by David Goodman

Selling design begins with the first client contact. It is the way you answer the telephone and how you respond when meeting a potential client. What you say is a significant as the design of your stationary and business card. Your history of past accomplishments helps in establishing credibility to a prospective client. Your proposal is the final critical part of your total sales presentation.

Let's take a look at each of these areas individually.

Personal Contact

Selling design is not much different than selling any other service. It starts with making the other person comfortable. You establish a positive tone without saying a single word. Probably the key turning point with a potential client is the first face-to-face meeting. Dress to play a part that is labeled "He or she is okay." In general, avoid flashy clothes and jewelry. You want to look like you belong and fit into your client's world. It is important to leave the impression that you can be a member of their team.

There are a few other elements that are important to selling design successfully. For instance, knowing what to say and when to say it.

Verbal Communication

Observe prospects closely and listen carefully to what is said. If you are trying too hard to impress them you might miss what they are trying to say. A very wise man once told me "You can think with your mouth open." He was absolutely right. Talk less, listen more. I was told that there are three basic rules to selling. Listen, listen, and listen!

When you prospective client asks you what you do it isn't enough to say that you are a designer. Your first answer should be as broad as possible to define your area of specialty. For example, you can say, "I'm a graphic designer." Then you can say "I design brochures for companies like ...." Another approach, where the prospect's background is not known, would be to mention a specific case history that you feel would be interesting to the person based on your observation or conversation. Bear in mind that you are not selling anything when you first meet someone, all you are attempting to do is to make a good impression and get them interested enough to offer your business card. ➠

There are three basic rules to selling. Listen, listen, and listen!

6 Reader Guide

Top margin: *The distance from the top trim to the top of the text area. Running heads, feet, and folios are often positioned in the top and bottom margin.*

Recto: *Right-handed page.*

Catalyst Educational Systems Bulletin

Visual Communication.

The exchange of business cards becomes a moment of truth. You card says much more about you than the words printed on it. The design itself says that you are contemporary or dated. The typography says whether you are nouveau or conservative/classic. The use of four-color, die-cutting, embossing, or foil stamping could make you look impractical or flamboyant. All of these associations, thoughts, or feelings take place in milliseconds.

The most important fact about your visual communication is that **you** are completely in control of your design.

Proposal

The proposal , when signed, becomes a contract. This fact alone makes it a little scary. You are making a legal commitment to execute a specific amount of work within a designated period of time for a specified sum of money. This is something they don't teach you at school.

Break down what you are offering to do into work packages. Call them phases or stages, and estimate how much time you plan to spend on each. Then multiply this by your hourly rate. Be certain to spell out what you will or will not do. Say, too, what is expected of the client. If they are to select a final design from your comps by a certain date, say that.

Take all your experience to date in dealing with clients and use it to construct a sound working relationship. Organize it, write it out, and use it as the procedural aspect of your agreements. Even if you are dealing with a small job that requires only a single page letter of agreement, follow the procedure you have mapped out for yourself. ●

THE CHALLENGE OF SELLING DESIGN

✧✦✧✦✧

Selling design is not easy for most designers. The reason is that the emphasis is on *selling*, not on *design*. Selling design actually has very little to do with design. It has to do with people. Selling is a person-to-person activity. Designing isn't.

It is a fact that the most successful designers are fantastic salespeople. The bottom line is simple. If you want to be successful in this business, learn how to sell. It can be hard work, but you are rewarded many times over with new skills and increased confidence that will bring about tangible results to you and your business.

Flow chart showing phases to include in your sales proposal.

Reader Guide 7

Running head: *A line of text across the top of the page that helps orient the reader within a document. It might include the document's title, author, chapter, subject of current page, or page number.*

Dingbat: *A decorative or symbolic device used to separate items on the page or denote items on a list.*

Sidebar: *A smaller story inside a larger one, boxed with its own headline to set it apart from the main text. It can be positioned anywhere on the page.*

Screen: *(also called tone) A tint, either a percentage of black or a second color, behind text or art.*

Art window: *Contains illustrations, photographs, charts, or diagrams.*

Caption/Cutline: *The text describing a photograph or illustration. A caption is known as a* ***cutline*** *when used in newspapers.*

Outside margin: *The space between the outside trim and the text.*

Gutter: *The space between two facing pages.*

End of article: *Symbol or text indicating end of article.*

Running Foot: *A line across the bottom of the page that helps orient the reader within a document.*

Page trim: *The edge of the page. In commercial printing, the size of the page after it is cut during the binding process.*

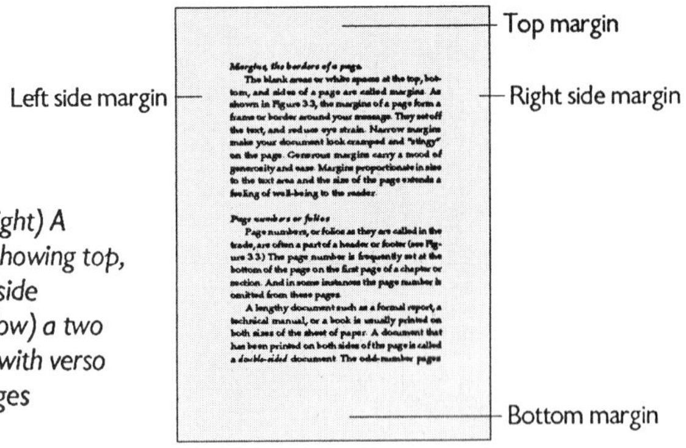

Figure 3.3: (right) A single page showing top, bottom, and side margins. (below) a two page spread with verso and recto pages indicated.

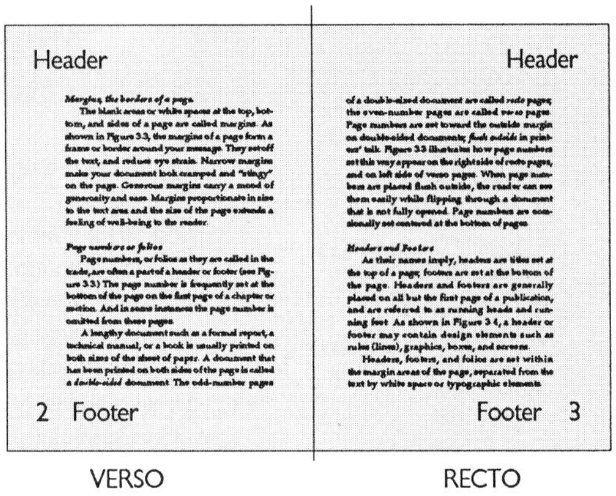

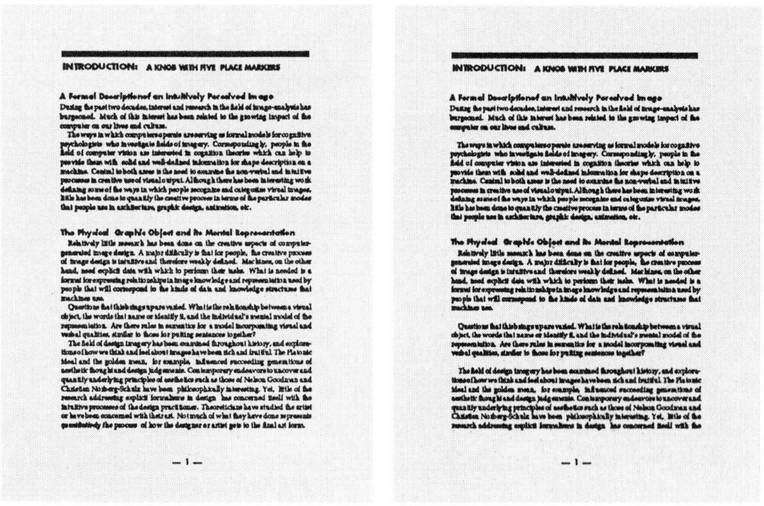

[A] [B]

Figure 3.4A: (left) A page of text with paragraphs set solid. Figure 3.4B (right) A page of text with extra space between paragraphs.

MARGINS: THE BORDERS OF A PAGE

The blank areas or white spaces at the top, bottom, and sides of a page are called margins. As shown in Figure 3.3, the margins of a page form a frame or border around your message. They set off the text, and reduce eye strain. Narrow margins make your document look cramped and "stingy" on the page. Generous margins carry a mood of generosity and ease. Margins proportionate in size to the text area and the size of the page extends a feeling of well-being to the reader.

PAGE NUMBERS OR FOLIOS

Page numbers, or folios as they are called in the trade, are often a part of a header or footer (see Figure 3.3.) The page number is frequently set at the bottom of the page on the first page of a chapter or section. And in some instances the page number is omitted from these pages.

A lengthy document such as a formal report, a technical manual, or a book is usually printed on both sizes of the sheet of paper. A document that has been printed on both sides of the page is called a *double-sided* document. The odd-number pages of a double-sided document are called *recto* pages; the even-number pages are called *verso* pages. Page numbers are set toward the outside margin on double-sided documents; *flush outside* in printers' talk. Figure 3.3 illustrates how page numbers set this way appear on the right side of recto pages, and on left side of verso pages. When page numbers are placed flush outside, the reader can see them easily while flipping through a document that is not fully opened. Page numbers are occasionally set centered at the bottom of pages.

HEADERS AND FOOTERS

As their names imply, headers are titles set at the top of a page; footers are set at the bottom of the page. Headers and footers are generally placed on all but the first page of a publication, and are referred to as running heads and running feet. As shown in Figure

3.4, a header or footer may contain design elements such as rules (lines), graphics, boxes, and screens (shading).

Headers, footers, and folios are set within the margin areas of the page, separated from the text by white space or typographic elements.

TEXT ELEMENTS

Many desktop publications are documents in which text is predominant. In these documents, the words used to present your information are referred to as *body text.* In addition to its content, the appearance of body text can be used well, or to your disadvantage. For example, a page of solid body text, depending on the type face you have chosen, conveys an image of overall grayness and can be dull and uninteresting (see Figure 3.4A.) The bland appearance of a solid page of text can be made more interesting by using one or more additional text elements.

> *Many common text elements used in graphic design add character, vitality, and shape to a publication.*

PARAGRAPH SPACING

A simple but effective way to reduce the "grayness" on a solid-text page is to provide extra space between paragraphs in the body text. As shown in Figure 3.4B, this extra space will appear as white space between the gray lines of text.

HEADINGS AND HEADLINES

Books and magazines, reports and newsletters contain major and minor headings. *Major headings* are headings such as *section* or *chapter titles* and the most important level of heading in articles. *Minor headings* are used within the text between paragraph headings of lesser importance. Minor headings are also referred to as secondary headings or subheads. Major and minor headings such as those used in this book are used to organize your message and add an element of design to your publication.

As shown in Figure 3.5, the largest headings used in newsletters are called *headlines.* In magazines these headings are usually *titles* of sections or articles. In addition to titles, headlines, major and/or secondary headings called *subheads* are used. These guide the reader's eye movement around the page to pick up the information you are stressing. In addition, headings help to break up the gray

"All the News That's Fit to Print"

The New York Times

National Edition

VOL.CXXXIX . . . . No. 48,140 — THURSDAY, FEBRUARY 8, 1990 — Printed in California 50 CENTS

SOVIET LEADERS AGREE TO SURRENDER COMMUNIST PARTY MONOPOLY ON POWER

Drug for Babies' Seizures Is Found Ineffective and Perhaps Harmful

By GINA KOLATA

Judge Nullifies Law Mandating Use of English

By FELICITY BARRINGER

Communism by Decree . . .

or by Choice

"Society itself will decide whether it wishes to adopt our politics."

ALEKSANDR N. YAKOVLEV

GORBACHEV BACKED

A Western-Style System of Government Urged as Meeting Ends

By FRANCIS X. CLINES

Caution: The Soviet Party Is Not Over

By BILL KELLER

Figure 3.5: A front page showing a variety of headlines and subheads. These differences convey levels of importance. (Copyright © 1990 by the New York Times Company. Reprinted by permission.)

masses of text. In Chapter 5, *Type Basics,* you will learn how to emphasize major and minor headings by varying their font size and style.

BANNERS

The title of most desktop publications is placed on the cover or first page. The publication title, date, volume, and number form an element know as a *banner.* As shown in Figure 3.5, a banner is often made more eye-catching with a graphic or logo. In newspapers, a large, bold headline that runs across the entire page is called a *banner headline.*

CONTINUATION ELEMENTS

Publications such as newspapers, magazines, and newsletters often begin a story on one page and continue the story on a subsequent page or pages. As illustrated in Figure 3.6, two elements —*jump lines* and *continuation lines* — are used to direct the reader through the publication.

Jump lines refer the reader to the page on which the story is continued. Continuation lines indicate that a story has been continued from a previous page. Continuation lines are not needed for stories that continue from one column to another on the same page.

TYPOGRAPHIC DESIGN FOR EMPHASIS AND VARIETY

There are a number of design elements you can use to add emphasis and variety to gray text-intensive pages. These design elements can also be used in newsletters and magazines to fill out the pages when the stories don't fill up the available space.

> *Design elements can also be used to focus the reader's attention on ideas in the text you want to be noticed or emphasized.*

The following material describes and illustrates some of the more common elements you can use to add diversity and interest to your pages.

KICKERS

A *kicker* is a brief phrase or "lead-in" to a story or chapter. Story kickers can be placed above or below the headline or title. In newsletters and magazines, publication kickers are often placed above the banner —as a preview of stories within the publication (see Figure 3.7.)

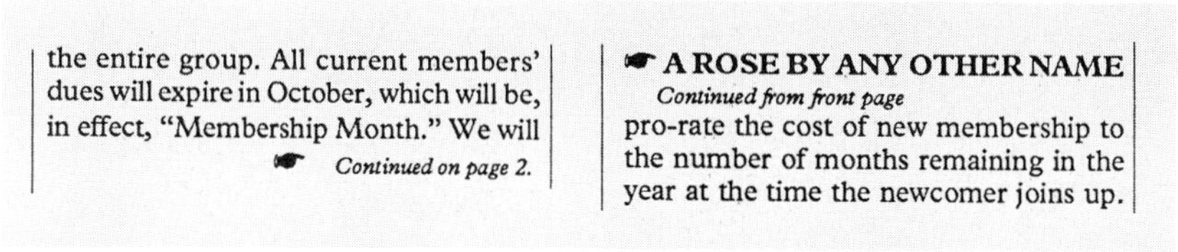

Figure 3.6: Sections from two pages; the section on the left illustrates a jump line, the one on the right shows the corresponding continuation line.

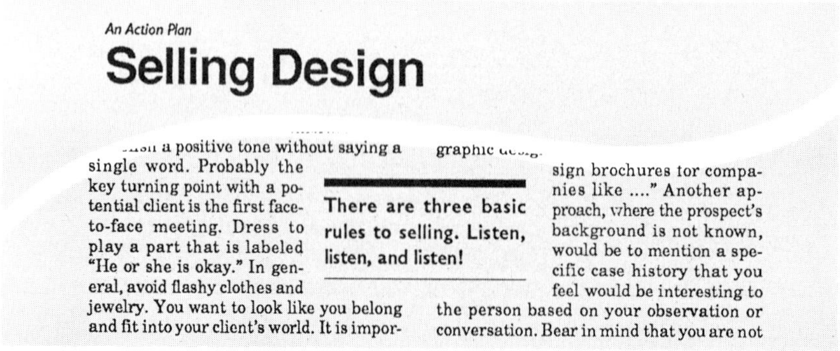

Figure 3.7: Page elements from Figure 3.2, illustrating use of a kicker and a pull quote. The kicker is the line of text above the title. A pull quote is text repeated from the body text, set larger to give it visual importance.

PULL QUOTES

A *pull quote* is a brief phrase taken from the body text, enlarged and set off from the text with rules, a box, and/or a gray tint. As illustrated in Figure 3.7, the pull quote is usually set right in the middle of a text block, not between paragraphs nor at the bottom or top of a column. The pull quote is often set in type that is larger than the body text, for emphasis or to fill space. Rules are also used to isolate the quote from the main text and to give it yet more punch. A pull quote should not be confused with a block quote or extract. A pull quote is brief (usually less than six lines), and repeats a phrase from the body text.

SIDEBARS

A *sidebar* is a related story or block of information that is set apart form the main body text. As illustrated in Figure 3.8, a sidebar is usually boxed and/or screened. Despite their name, sidebars can be placed anywhere on a page.

DINGBATS

A variety of elements are used in association with text type, either for emphasis, embellishment, or to identify elements in a list. Some of these elements are part of the standard type font, such as asterisks, bullets, and numbers. *Bullets* look like enlarged dots and are used for emphasis at the beginning of each entry in a list. Other decorative elements can be substituted, such as filled or open boxes, arrows, check marks or other *dingbats*. Dingbats are assortments of decorative elements that can be used in place of those that come as part of the standard type font (see Figure 3.9.) The name dingbat comes from traditional printing and typesetting days and means whatever you think a dingbat is.

ILLUSTRATIONS

It is possible to create a complete publication entirely with text. If illustrations are included, however, the appearance and communication value of most publications are enhanced. Illustrations are drawings, charts,

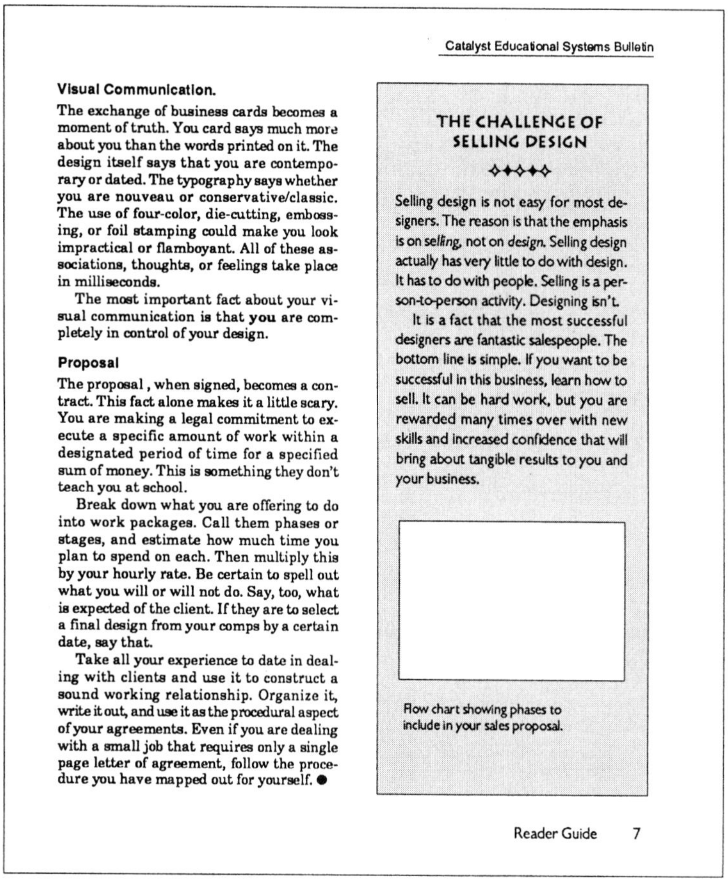
Catalyst Educational Systems Bulletin

Visual Communication.

The exchange of business cards becomes a moment of truth. You card says much more about you than the words printed on it. The design itself says that you are contemporary or dated. The typography says whether you are nouveau or conservative/classic. The use of four-color, die-cutting, embossing, or foil stamping could make you look impractical or flamboyant. All of these associations, thoughts, or feelings take place in milliseconds.

The most important fact about your visual communication is that you are completely in control of your design.

Proposal

The proposal, when signed, becomes a contract. This fact alone makes it a little scary. You are making a legal commitment to execute a specific amount of work within a designated period of time for a specified sum of money. This is something they don't teach you at school.

Break down what you are offering to do into work packages. Call them phases or stages, and estimate how much time you plan to spend on each. Then multiply this by your hourly rate. Be certain to spell out what you will or will not do. Say, too, what is expected of the client. If they are to select a final design from your comps by a certain date, say that.

Take all your experience to date in dealing with clients and use it to construct a sound working relationship. Organize it, write it out, and use it as the procedural aspect of your agreements. Even if you are dealing with a small job that requires only a single page letter of agreement, follow the procedure you have mapped out for yourself. ●

THE CHALLENGE OF SELLING DESIGN

Selling design is not easy for most designers. The reason is that the emphasis is on *selling*, not on *design*. Selling design actually has very little to do with design. It has to do with people. Selling is a person-to-person activity. Designing isn't.

It is a fact that the most successful designers are fantastic salespeople. The bottom line is simple. If you want to be successful in this business, learn how to sell. It can be hard work, but you are rewarded many times over with new skills and increased confidence that will bring about tangible results to you and your business.

Flow chart showing phases to include in your sales proposal.

Reader Guide 7

Figure 3.8: A sidebar, tinted gray, is part of a page.

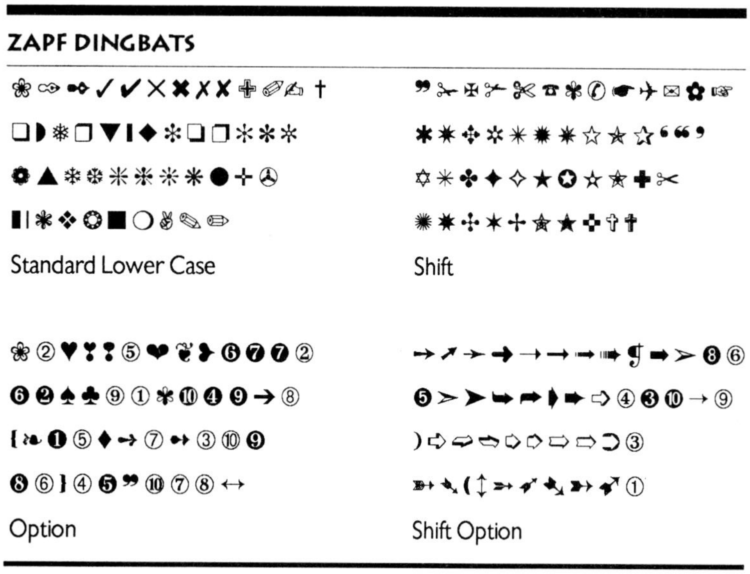

Figure 3.9: Zapf Dingbats is a typeface made up of an assortment of decorative elements.

or photographs used to strengthen a publication. They do this in two ways:

- ✔ *Illustrations can describe something or show comparisons.*
- ✔ *Illustrations add visual interest by breaking up the neutral appearance of a solid page of text.*

Illustrations are often accompanied by a text element that explains the illustrations or ties it to the context of the message. This element may be a caption, a cutline, or a callout.

CAPTIONS AND CUTLINES

As explained above, captions and cutlines are used to enhance an illustration. *Captions* are brief phrases; *cutlines* are full explanatory sentences that describe special points in illustrations (see Figure 3.10A.) In books and reports, the term "caption" refers to any explanatory text associated with photographs and illustrations.

CALLOUTS

Callouts are labels that refer to parts of an illustration, chart, or other graphic. As illustrated in Figure 3.10B, a callout often includes a line pointing to an area of the illustration.

TABLE OF CONTENTS AND INDEX

The *table of contents* is used within the first few pages of reports, newspapers books, magazines, and other documents to let you know what the major stories, sections, or chapters are and what pages they are on. *Indexes* are usually found at the end of the text material in longer documents. They contain a list of all important references in the document, arranged in alphabetical order. Some page layout programs allow you to produce a table of contents and an index automatically, similar to the ones illustrated in Figure 3.11. You need to code any section, phrase, or key word you want to appear as an entry. Once coded, these elements are referenced when the page layout program paginates the final copy of your report or manual. The contents and index list are updated each time a coded element is moved from one page to another.

COMMUNICATING INFORMATION THROUGH DESIGN AND DOCUMENT STRUCTURE

Although design is subjective, most designers agree that there are several principles by which designs can be judged. The following

The drawing at right shows the side and top view of a sculpin. Sculpins are a common inshore fish whose habitat in Pacific coastal waters ranges from Baja California to Alaska. The sculpin is characterized by its large head and long dorsal spines

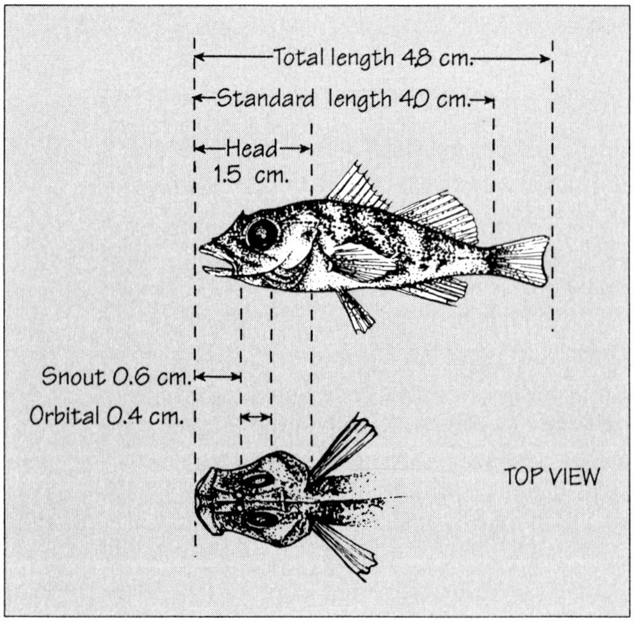

Figure 3.10A (top) An example of a caption. These are called cutlines when used in newspapers.

3.10B: (right) An illustration with callouts.

six design rules (discussed in depth in Chapter 4, *Designing Form With Content*) will help you get started in designing attractive page layouts.

- ✔ *Control the reader's eye movement.*
- ✔ *Balance the page elements.*
- ✔ *Keep the page elements in proportion to each other while observing information relevance.*
- ✔ *Use repetition for effect.*
- ✔ *Provide a dominant element.*
- ✔ *Keep the design simple.*

KEEP THE DESIGN SIMPLE

Simplicity is probably the most difficult design principle to apply in a consistent manner. That's because desktop publishing gives you the power to choose from many type faces and a variety of spatial arrangements. With so many options at your fingertips, it is easy to forget about simplicity. Remember that graphic design should be invisible to the reader. Keep in mind the KISS formula: Keep It Simple, Stupid!

THE GRID: THE UNDERLYING STRUCTURE OF YOUR PUBLICATION

All designs start with a blank page. The designer, however, sees a page with imaginary lines that define the number and size of the columns and the boundries for the top, bottom, and side margins. These imaginary lines make up what is called a *grid*. The grid is the underlying structure on which your publication is built. Figure 3.12 illustrates examples of a standard two-column and three-column grid frequently used by many types of publications.

Grids are the major approach to publication design because they are an effective way to organize page elements and allow you to

— Place text and graphics.

— Speed up layout time.

CONTENTS

xxiii

INDEX

Page numbers in italics indicate illustrations

Figure 3.11 (top) A contents page, and (bottom) an index page.

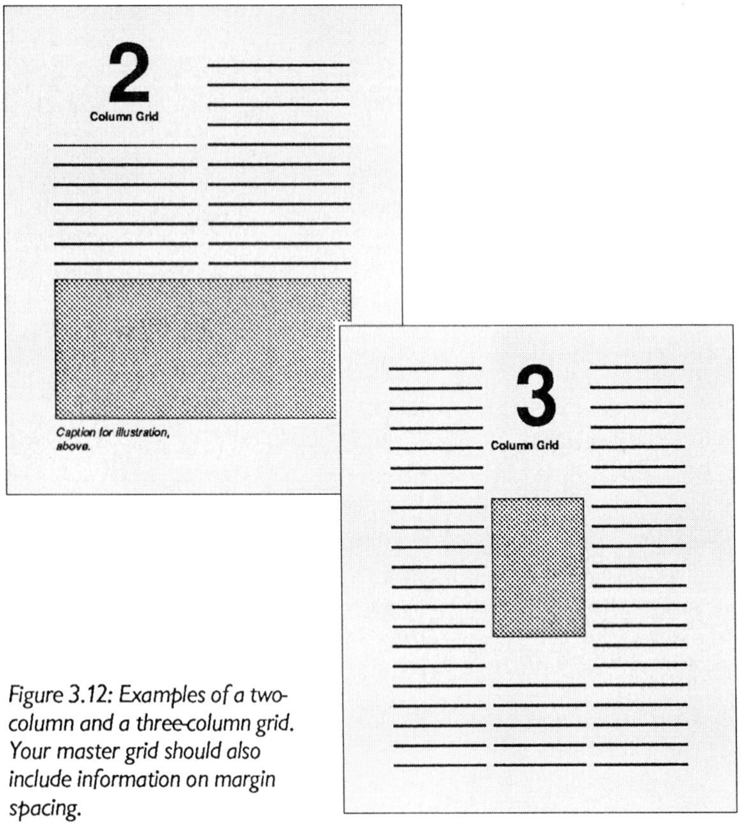

Figure 3.12: Examples of a two-column and a three-column grid. Your master grid should also include information on margin spacing.

ORIGINAL TEXT

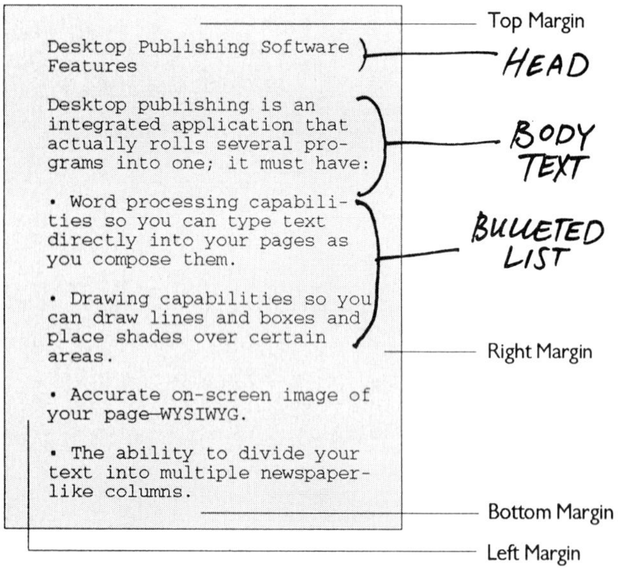

Figure 3.13: A simple document with its margins and structural elements indicated.

— Give a planned, cohesive look to your publication.

— Ensure consistency from one page to the next.

Whether you use a standard grid such as the ones shown in Figure 3.12 or design your own, it is a good idea to establish a master grid for each publication. Using a master grid will ensure that you have consistent margins and columns throughout your publication.

At a minimum, a master grid should include the following:

✔ *Page size (such as 8-1/2 by 11 inches).*

✔ *Margins.*

✔ *Number of columns and their width (two-column, three-column, four-column, etc.).*

In Chapter 5, *Type Basics,* you will learn that the type style and size are major factors in determining the appropriate column width and the space between columns. Chapter 7, *Grids: Working With Structure and Space,* will show you how to design custom grids for your own publications.

Not all graphic designers use the grid system in their work. Some designers use other techniques, such as perspective or an aesthetic, free-form approach to page layout and design. In general, however, desktop publishers find that a grid provides a consistent, planned look to their publications.

LINKING STRUCTURE TO STYLE

Learning to identify the structural elements in a document is not merely an academic pastime. Each element you use has a style description that includes its placement on the page and its type specification. Let's say, for example, you have the document illustrated in Figure 3.13.

This simple document contains body text, a single head, and a list with bullets. The page size is 8-1/2 x 11 inches. The structure you will be using will include:

— Top and bottom margins.

— Left and right margins.

— Type specifications for main or body text.

— Type specifications for the main heading.

— Type specifications for a bullet list.

As you can see, each of these structural elements will require that you make a design decision regarding the space it will occupy and the type in which it will be set.

When you make a visual design decision for an element, and select its position on the grid, you are linking the document structure to its style.

Most page layout programs allow you to record your design decision in the form of style guides.

USING STYLE GUIDES

A *style guide* is a collection of styles: formatting information for each element you have designed. Each style is called a *tag*, and each tag has two elements: a name (i.e. body text, headings, etc.,) and a format specification (i.e. font, alignment, spacing, and tabs). A style guide contains a tag for each text element in your document. For example, if your document contains a main head, a subhead, body text, and a bullet listing, your style guide for this document would contain four different tags. By associating formats with tags, you guarantee that your publication will have a consistent appearance throughout its length. Each time the tag appears, the proper font size and style, paragraph alignment, spacing, and so on are set in place automatically. Figure 3.14 shows you an example of an unformatted and formatted paragraph and the associated style sheet tag.

ORIGINAL TEXT

```
Desktop Publishing Software
Features

Desktop publishi
integrated appli
actually rolls s
grams into one;

• Word processin
ties so you can
directly into yo
you compose them

• Drawing capabi
can draw lines a
place shades ove
areas.

• Accurate on-sc
your page—WYSIWY

• The ability to
text into multip
like columns.
```

Desktop Publishing Software Features

Desktop publishing is an integrated application that actually rolls several programs into one; it must have:

- Word processing capabilities so you can type text directly into your pages as you compose them.
- Drawing capabilities so you can draw lines and boxes and place shades over certain areas.
- Accurate on-screen image of your page—WYSIWYG.
- The ability to divide your text into multiple newspaper-like columns.

FORMATTED TEXT

Tag Name	Font	Size	Style	Leading	Alignment
Heading	Helvetica	8	Bold	9	Flush Left
Body Text	New Century Schoolbook	8	Normal	9	Flush Left
Bulletted List	New Century Schoolbook	8	Normal	9	Hanging Indent

STYLE GUIDE

Figure 3.14: (far left) The original text, is the unformatted page illustrated in Figure 3.13; (center) the formatted version of the page; (right) a style guide that lists the tag names and attributes for each structural element.

Figure 3.15 **STYLE GUIDE SPECIFICATION WORKSHEET**

Publication: ______________________ Date: __________

Designer: ______________________

GRID DESIGN

Orientation: ☐ Portrait ☐ Landscape Page Size: __________

Margins: Top ______ Bottom ______ Right ______ Left ______

Columns: Number ______ Space Between ______

Folio/page number: Position: ______

Style: ______

Running head: Position: ______

Style: ______

Running foot: Position: ______

Style: ______

TAG FORMAT

Tag Name*	Font	Size	Style	Leading	Alignment

*For the Tag Name column, fill in with the names of the elements you are using in your page layout. (I.e. Banner Head, Body Text,or Pull Quotes. For a list of structural elements, see Figure 3.17 Publication Element Review Form in the Worksheets/Forms Appendix.)

Figure 3.15: The Style Guide Specification Sheet , shown reduced. A full sized version can be found in the Workshop/Forms Appendix.

STANDARD GENERIC MARKUP LANGUAGE (SGML)

Generic Identifier	Tag Name	Title	Macro
Title	Title	Title	SMT101
Introduction			

```
<p>
Text processing and word processing systems
typically require additional information to be
inset in the natural test of the document to be
processed. Thes added information, called
<q>markup</q>, serves two purposes:
<ol>
<li> Separating the logical elements of a
document, and<li> Specifying the processing
functions to be performed on those elements.
</ol>
```

Figure 3.16: Notation for generalized markup requires that each generic identifier is initiated by a less-than symbol (<) at the start of the generic identifier, and a greater than symbol (>) at its end. The generic symbols identify parts of the document structure, rather than its typographic styling.

As you can see in Figure 3.14, when you tag a paragraph, you are applying the style guide format. The appearance of the paragraph is then changed to reflect that format. Should you change your mind about a format, you can make the change throughout your document simply by changing the style format for the appropriate tag. For example, say you want to change the heading margin from flush left to centered. As shown in Figure 3.15, the reduced Style Guide Specifications Sheet, the change would be made to the heading tag . This change would then be made throughout your entire publication, wherever you have used the heading tag. The Style Guide Specifications Sheet can be found full size in the Workbook/Forms Appendix.

STANDARD GENERIC MARKUP LANGUAGE (SGML)

Standard Generic Markup Language or *SGML* as it is often called, is based on the style guide concept and takes advantage of electronic media. SGML has been developed as an international standard for interchange, manipulation, storage, and reuse of information (generally for longer documents). The U.S. Government supports the SGML concept for more than just design consistency because any document marked with SGML tags can be accessed and parts of it used in other documents. These tags allow the information to be manipulated electronically at a later date. Coding a document with SGML tags is very similar to using a style guide (see Figure 3.16.)

A company using SGML is using a standard that allows access to huge databases of information. SGML also allows data to be converted from any one electronic form to any other; for example, entries in a data base can be converted to a hard copy publication. While you may not be using SGML standards now, you will most likely be called upon to work with SGML in the future. The main thing to understand about Standard Generic Markup Language is that it is based on an understanding of document structure and each element is given a name or a tag for markup purposes. This descriptive tag can be accessed and used for many applications.

STANDARDIZATION AND DOCUMENT DESIGN

Style guides and SGML are aids to standardizing document formats. Whether you are preparing publications for personal use, for a large organization, or for a small business, you will find that using standardized document formats have many advantages. If you are working on a series publication such as a newsletter or company report, the use of a style guide will maintain design consistency from issue to issue. Style guides also save you time, since you only need to plan a design once. If you work with several people in a publications department, the use of predefined style guides will ensure consistency of company design standards.

Style guides not only maintain group design standards, they also help newcomers get up to speed more quickly when a document has been predefined with style for them. Moreover, documents standardization allows readers to recognize each publication style intuitively, preparing them for the content even before the text is read.

CHECKING YOUR UNDERSTANDING

1. Explain how page elements such as margins and page numbers can be used as design elements.

2. List five text elements that can be used as design elements and briefly explain their design purpose.

3. Explain the purpose of continuation elements and identify and distinguish between the two types.

4. Explain the purpose of a pull quote and explain how it differs from a block quote.

5. Explain the purpose of a sidebar and give an example of how it might be used as a design element.

6. Define the terms *caption, cutline,* and *callouts* and explain how they differ.

7. Discuss the purpose of the publication grid and indicate the minimum elements a grid should contain.

8. Explain how a style guide ensures a consistent appearance throughout your document.

BUILDING YOUR DESKTOP PUBLISHING DESIGN SKILLS

1. Use the Publication Elements Review Form (Figure 3.17 found in the Workshop Forms/Appendix) containing a list of all the publication elements covered in this chapter. At the top of the sheet, insert a line for the name of the publication and a second line for the number of pages it contains.

2. Locate three publications that contain most of the page and text elements discussed in this chapter. Examine the publications, select one, then identify the page elements and text elements discussed in this chapter. Circle the elements, number them, then list the numbers with their corresponding page element name on the publication review form you completed in the activity above.

3. Select a publication that contains most of the page and text elements discussed in this chapter. Study the publication, list the page elements on a copy of your publication review form, then indicate any modification to the element's format that would make the publication more attractive to you.

4. Using the text in this chapter as sample text, do the following:

   a) Write a kicker for the introduction on the first page of this chapter.

   b) Write a pull quote for the section titled "Communicating Information Through Design and Document Structure."

c) Develop a sidebar for the information in the section titled "Illustrations."

DESKTOP DESIGN WORKSHOP

The purpose of this section is to provide you with opportunities to develop and/or improve your desktop publishing design skills. The worksheet pages have been placed at the back of the book, and are designed so they can be removed and you can write, draw, or place your responses directly onto the pages.

WORKSHEETS 3.1 AND 3.2

1. Using the grid on Worksheet 3.1 at the back of the book, design an association newsletter using the contents elements on Worksheet 3.2, including the illustrations.

   a) Make a photocopy (you may want to make several) of the grid on the front side of Worksheet 3.1, then cut out the elements and position them on your grid.

   b) Create an appropriate footer with a page number for each page.

   c) Create a pull quote from the March Meeting Highlights story so that the text will fill the column.

   d) Key in the following callouts and place them in the illustration: Large Memory Capacity, High-Resolution Screen, Mouse, Software, Laser Printer.

   e) Place the caption, "The Professional Desktop Publishing Workstation," below the illustration.

   f) Assume that the shaded square is a photograph of David Webber, author of the article, "Silicon Valley at Your Fingertips," and place an appropriate caption below the picture.

2. Using your desktop publishing program and your layout, produce and print a copy of the April newsletter.

   a) Capture the text using your word processing program or use the GREEK.TXT (DOS) or GREEKED TEXT (Mac) text file provided on the Student Data Disk that accompanies this book. This text file consists of many lines of nonsense text. Since our major concern is with the layout and design of the newsletter, the same nonsense text can be used for all stories; its only purpose is to simulate the actual text. If you use the greek text file, add the appropriate headings, adjust the column lengths, and format the greeked text to fit your design.

   b) Scan the graphics or use shaded boxed to simulate the graphics.

   c) Include the footer, caption, callouts, and pull quote that you designed for problem 1.

4. DESIGNING FORM WITH CONTENT

When you finish this chapter you should be able to:

- *Analyze the text portion of a simple document, identify its structural elements, and classify the information from most important to least important.*
- *Work with an editor to analyze and identify structural elements of the text portion of complex documents.*
- *Use editor's mark-up codes to indicate a publication's structure.*
- *Mark up text for typesetting indicating appropriate word and letter spacing, tab settings, margins, and indents.*
- *Prepare thumbnails for the pages you design.*
- *Use size and weight to add importance to a publication's text elements.*
- *Use space visually to indicate relationships between different parts of a page.*
- *Use a minimum of six basic page design and layout rules in a publication design.*

PUBLICATION DESIGN AS A form of communication with an audience was discussed in Chapter 2, *Communication: Verbal and Visual.* Knowing your audience is a basic consideration for desktop designers. Chapter 3, *Document Structure: Organizing Your Publication,* described the major elements that make up a publication or document. In this chapter you will discover how to use this information to design a document that combines its visual form with its text content.

ANALYZING THE DOCUMENT

When publications are prepared for design, they are usually put through a process called design analysis. The analysis has less to do with the actual designing of the publication and more to do with identifying its design components and determining their relative importance in the text. As a desktop designer, you may not be familiar with the process of design analysis. In large companies with publication departments, an editor usually performs the design analysis task. An editor is a person who is specially trained to work with the content of a publication, checking its accuracy and defining its structure. Editors correct and revise manuscripts using standard *proofreader marks*. Frequently used marks are shown in Figure 4.1A; a complete Proofreaders Marks Chart is Figure 4.1B, in the Workbook/Forms Appendix. These marks are used by everyone in publishing to indicate changes and corrections in the text.

Many small businesses and desktop publishing firms don't have the services of an editor conveniently at hand. You, as the desktop designer, will need to know some of the basics involved in analyzing written text when designing a publication.

When you are given a flyer, a brochure, or a report to produce, you are ordinarily given its content — which can be unformatted text on disk, typewriter or printer hard copy output, or, hand-written scrawls on pieces of paper. Pictures may also be included. The content you are given is usually called document *copy* or *manuscript*.

PROOFREADER'S MARKS

Explanation	Margin Mark
Example	
A) Delete letter, letters or words indicated	
B) Replace with lowercase	lc
C) Replace with capital.	cap
D) Insert letter.	g
E) Insert word.	my
F) Transpose letters or word as indicated	TR

Copy Errors – Marked	Corrected Type
Example	
A) Seven joggged my elbow.	Seven jogged my elbow.
B) Seven Jogged my elbow.	Seven jogged my elbow.
C) seven jogged my elbow.	Seven jogged my elbow.
D) Seven joged my elbow.	Seven jogged my elbow.
E) Seven jogged elbow.	Seven jogged my elbow.
F) Seven my jogged elbow.	Seven jogged my elbow.

Figure 4.1A: Some frequently used proofreader marks. A complete Proofreaders Marks Chart (Figure 4.1B), can be found in the Workbook/Forms Appendix.

DISK PREPARATION GUIDELINES FOR EDITORS AND AUTHORS

When you receive manuscripts on disk from authors or editors, you will have an easier time analyzing the text if certain keyboarding guidelines are followed when the disk file is prepared. The five guidelines presented in Figure 4.2 are used by major publishers who accept text in disk file format.

Disk Preparation Guidelines for Editors and Authors

1. Use only single spaces after the period or other punctuation at the ends of sentences. While typists use two spaces, the single space is good typesetting form.
2. Do not use paragraph indents in your manuscripts. Instead, use a line space or hard carriage return between paragraphs, or use a "space after paragraph" setting if your word processing software permits it.
3. Use tabs to set any indents you may wish to use for lists and tables. Never use the space bar on your keyboard to line up text because the spacing will change as soon as the manuscript text is reformatted into final pages. Tabs can be moved to different indents, but they will always maintain the same alignment for the text.
4. Set your text ragged right. Do not use justified text for manuscript or other text copy.
5. If you can, design a basic style guide for authors and editors to use if their word processors permit it. You will find instructions on how to do so on pages 48 to 50.

Figure 4.2: Guidelines for Keyboarding and Formatting Disk Text Files

WHAT KIND OF PUBLICATION IS IT: A CHECKLIST ANALYSIS

The checklist analysis consist of reading through the text and identifying its structural elements according to a checklist of particulars. A simple checklist is provided for you in Figure 4.3. This analysis helps you to clarify and organize in your own mind exactly what will be involved in the production of the publication. The checklist will also serve as a written record that can be shared and verified with your client or boss. Once completed, the checklist can be used as a cover sheet for the manuscript you are given to design. Notice that the information recorded on the checklist covers topics covered in Chapters 1 and 2.

INSTRUCTION FOR COMPLETING A PUBLICATION DESIGN CHECKLIST

First, record the name and type of publication that is to be designed. Is it a report? A newsletter? A manuscript? Then, name the publication so you have a way of referencing the work. Third, identify the target audience so that the publication you design will be visually relevant to its prospective readership.

When you evaluate the manuscript prior to design, apply what you learned about document structure in Chapter 3. In most instances, you will notice that there is a main or body text and some headings. There may be an illustration or two, tables, charts, and graphs. Using the checklist as a guide, mark up every element that you can identify in the manuscript. As you identify an element, you should also indicate its level of importance as it is related to the document as a whole. The elements should be ranked in importance from most important to least important. Often, you will to work with the author to identify the major and minor text elements, rank their relative importance, and to determine their relevance to the intended audience. This information can be noted in the margin of the text manuscript or on overlay tissues for each page. Figure 4.4 shows a sample manuscript page that has been marked up for publication design.

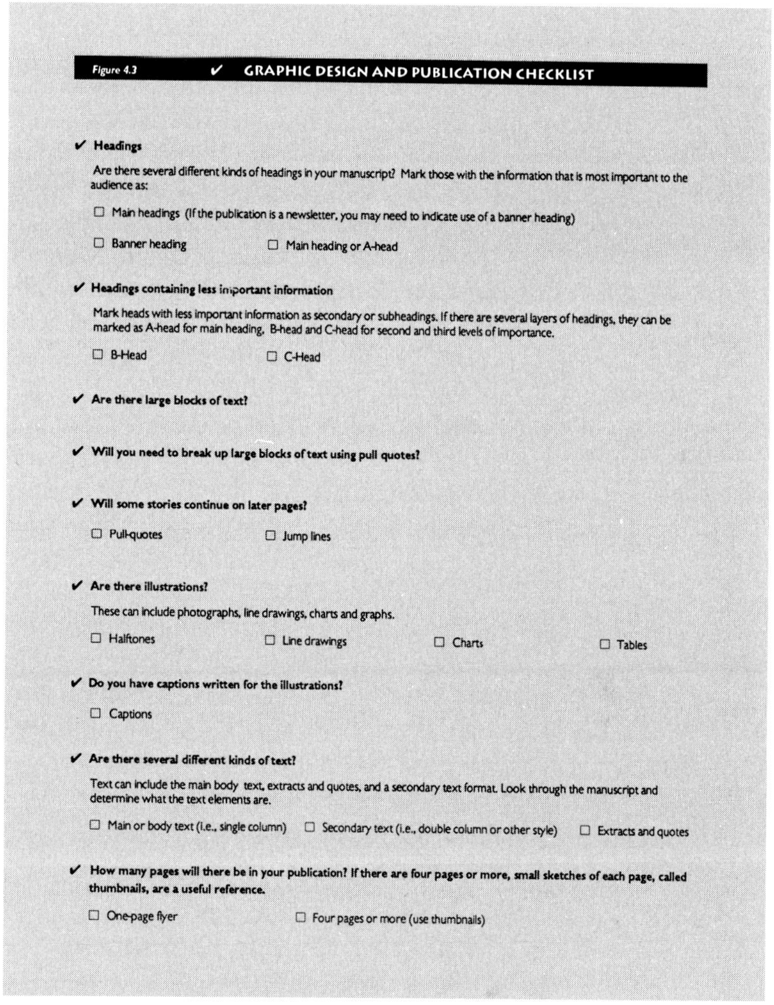
Figure 4.3 ✔ GRAPHIC DESIGN AND PUBLICATION CHECKLIST

✔ **Headings**

Are there several different kinds of headings in your manuscript? Mark those with the information that is most important to the audience as:

☐ Main headings (If the publication is a newsletter, you may need to indicate use of a banner heading)

☐ Banner heading ☐ Main heading or A-head

✔ **Headings containing less important information**

Mark heads with less important information as secondary or subheadings. If there are several layers of headings, they can be marked as A-head for main heading, B-head and C-head for second and third levels of importance.

☐ B-Head ☐ C-Head

✔ **Are there large blocks of text?**

✔ **Will you need to break up large blocks of text using pull quotes?**

✔ **Will some stories continue on later pages?**

☐ Pull-quotes ☐ Jump lines

✔ **Are there illustrations?**

These can include photographs, line drawings, charts and graphs.

☐ Halftones ☐ Line drawings ☐ Charts ☐ Tables

✔ **Do you have captions written for the illustrations?**

☐ Captions

✔ **Are there several different kinds of text?**

Text can include the main body text, extracts and quotes, and a secondary text format. Look through the manuscript and determine what the text elements are.

☐ Main or body text (i.e., single column) ☐ Secondary text (i.e., double column or other style) ☐ Extracts and quotes

✔ **How many pages will there be in your publication? If there are four pages or more, small sketches of each page, called thumbnails, are a useful reference.**

☐ One-page flyer ☐ Four pages or more (use thumbnails)

Figure 4.3: Graphic Design and Publication Checklist is shown here reduced. A full-sized version can be found in the Workbook/Forms Appendix.

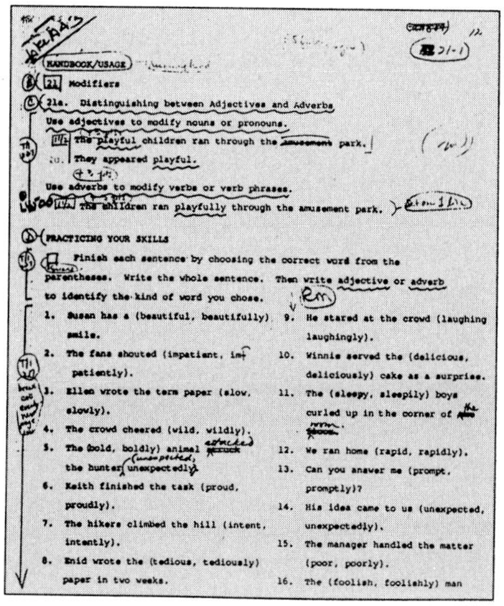
HANDBOOK/USAGE

21 Modifiers

21a. Distinguishing between Adjectives and Adverbs

Use adjectives to modify nouns or pronouns.

The playful children ran through the amusement park.

They appeared playful.

Use adverbs to modify verbs or verb phrases.

The children ran playfully through the amusement park.

PRACTICING YOUR SKILLS

Finish each sentence by choosing the correct word from the parentheses. Write the whole sentence. Then write adjective or adverb to identify the kind of word you chose.

1. Susan has a (beautiful, beautifully) smile.
2. The fans shouted (impatient, impatiently).
3. Ellen wrote the term paper (slow, slowly).
4. The crowd cheered (wild, wildly).
5. The (bold, boldly) animal struck the hunter (unexpected, unexpectedly).
6. Keith finished the task (proud, proudly).
7. The hikers climbed the hill (intent, intently).
8. Enid wrote the (tedious, tediously) paper in two weeks.
9. He stared at the crowd (laughing laughingly).
10. Winnie served the (delicious, deliciously) cake as a surprise.
11. The (sleepy, sleepily) boys curled up in the corner of the room.
12. We ran home (rapid, rapidly).
13. Can you answer me (prompt, promptly)?
14. His idea came to us (unexpected, unexpectedly).
15. The manager handled the matter (poor, poorly).
16. The (foolish, foolishly) man

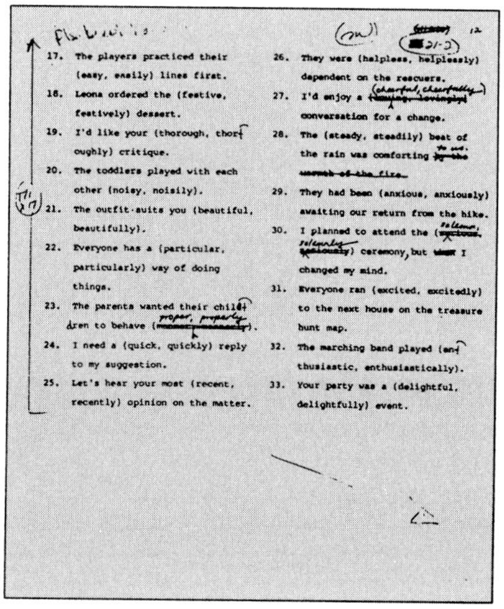
17. The players practiced their (easy, easily) lines first.
18. Leona ordered the (festive, festively) dessert.
19. I'd like your (thorough, thoroughly) critique.
20. The toddlers played with each other (noisy, noisily).
21. The outfit suits you (beautiful, beautifully).
22. Everyone has a (particular, particularly) way of doing things.
23. The parents wanted their children to behave (proper, properly).
24. I need a (quick, quickly) reply to my suggestion.
25. Let's hear your most (recent, recently) opinion on the matter.
26. They were (helpless, helplessly) dependent on the rescuers.
27. I'd enjoy a (cheerful, cheerfully) conversation for a change.
28. The (steady, steadily) beat of the rain was comforting to us.
29. They had been (anxious, anxiously) awaiting our return from the hike.
30. I planned to attend the (solemn, solemnly) ceremony, but I changed my mind.
31. Everyone ran (excited, excitedly) to the next house on the treasure hunt map.
32. The marching band played (enthusiastic, enthusiastically).
33. Your party was a (delightful, delightfully) event.

Figure 4.4: Manuscript pages marked up for a complex publication design.

USING THUMBNAILS

Thumbnails are publication pages in miniature, generally about one-fourth to one-eighth of the actual page size. They are rough drafts of a page showing the page elements and where they are located. As shown in Figure 4.5, headlines are usually legible and text is indicated by greeking. Greeking is nothing more than gray lines that indicate where actual text will appear in the finished document. Illustrations are usually indicated where they will appear by a gray box. The sketches may also feature a rough grid that includes the number of columns, the spaces allotted to margins, and the placement of text and artwork within the grid. Major headings are indicated and a visual rendition of heavy and light areas is prepared. The graphic designer may try out a number of arrangements in this smaller size. Thumbnails may also be included for successive pages in multiple paged publications to see how the page design flows from one page to the next.

Most graphic designers prepare their thumbnails at the start of the design phase in order to view the overall look of the publication and check for balance and consistency.

USING MARK-UP CODES FOR CONTENT STRUCTURE

Chapter 3 described the various elements present in a publication. Editors use a series of codes that represent the parts of the document when they mark up a manuscript for design and typesetting. These mark-up codes are shorthand words for text formats. For example, body text (or main text as it is sometimes called) may be coded with a BT for body text or with an MT for main text. Elements that have levels of importance, such as headings, may be coded with a level code such as A-head for the top or main level, B-head for the next level, C-head for the next level, and so on. (Refer to Figure 3.16.)

The names for the codes you use are generally up to you, but the code names should be part of a consistent vocabulary that is familiar to editors and publishers.

GROUPING IDEAS INTO RELEVANT SEGMENTS

Once you have marked up your copy to show its structure, you will need to select those elements that will best convey that structure visually. This is done by deciding what part of the text you need or want to emphasize.

The way that words and illustrations on the page can be grouped into meaningful "chunks" of information is up to you. Here are a few things you should consider. (See figure 4.6.)

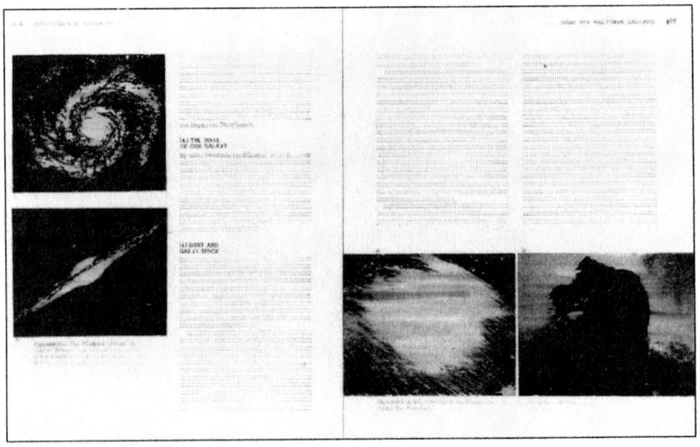

Figure 4.5: Thumbnails showing headlines with greeking for text.

You can examine the copy and ask yourself questions such as the following:

- ✔ *Will using headings in the body text help to break up the mass of gray text?*
- ✔ *Are some parts of the body text more important than others?*
- ✔ *Can subheads be used to break up long passages of text ?*
- ✔ *Do elements on the page go together? Does the information flow logically, one idea to the next? Is it coordinated with the visual information—does the visual structure convey the same information as the text, both logically and hierarchically?*
- ✔ *Text blocks composing the main text are customarily seen as gray blocks on a white page.*
- ✔ *Typefaces of varying sizes and weights can be used to organize the visual page structure. Heavier weights and larger sizes send messages of greater importance.*
- ✔ *Rules of different weight can be used to emphasize text or to separate different areas of the page.*
- ✔ *"White" space, used to separate objects on the page visually, also separate them in the mind of the view. Eliminating white space brings items closer together mentally as well as visually.*

Radius DirectColor™ Series

16 and 24-bit Color Interfaces for the Macintosh II

Product Description

The Radius DirectColor Series for the Macintosh II is the latest development in Radius high resolution color technology. Radius DirectColor/16™ and Radius DirectColor/24™ video interfaces display vivid, photographic quality images in a two-page format. Designed for the user interested in building a professional Macintosh II color workstation, DirectColor Interfaces combine superior hardware features with innovative software.

Professional Color Quality. Available in 16-bit or 24-bit format, the Radius DirectColor Series presents precise colors and sharp text on the Radius Color Display. A screen resolution of 1152 x 882 pixels offers [illegible] more workspace than the traditional 1024 x 768 resolution — ideal for two-page layouts and graphic design. A screen refresh rate of 72 Hz eliminates perceptible flicker for extended viewing comfort. DirectColor/16 displays 32,768 colors simultaneously. With DirectColor/24, the Macintosh II's full palette of 16.7 million colors is available for true color imaging. Both Radius DirectColor Interfaces are designed to work with the Radius Color Display.

Upgrade Path. DirectColor/16 is fully upgradable to 24-bit format via an upgrade kit that consists of high-speed video memory that plugs into sockets on the DirectColor/16 Interface.

Innovative Software. RadiusWare,™ a variety of powerful software features, is shipped with the DirectColor Series and includes Tear-off Menus, an Enlarged Menu Font, a 1, 8, 16 or 24-bit PICT Screen Capture capability, Screen Saver and Bit Depth Changer. The Bit Depth Changer lets you select between 1, 8, 16 or 24-bit pixel depth via the keyboard and mouse. All RadiusWare features are conveniently available through the standard Apple Control Panel.

Superior Performance. The digital design of the Radius DirectColor/16 and /24 provides maximum system performance. Radius supports the complete NuBus protocol, including Block Transfer, which allows up to 16 words of 32-bit data to be transmitted as a single transaction. This feature ensures a more productive environment for applications requiring extremely fast data transfer to the video interface card.

Complete Compatibility. Because of our dedication to the Macintosh, Radius products are designed with the highest standards of Macintosh hardware and software compatibility. The Radius DirectColor Series is completely compatible with Apple's full chunky 32-bit QuickDraw standard.

Figure 4.6: A publication page illustrating some of the elements to be considered during the design process. Note the use of subheads breaking up the text; rules to separate different areas of the page; white space between text blocks separating them visually. (Courtesy Toni Hollander, The Design Works.)

CONTROLLING LEVELS OF IMPORTANCE THROUGH VISUAL MEANS

Publication design is a creative process that lends itself more to rules of thumb than to hard-and-fast rules. There are, however, some essential concepts that are worth following.

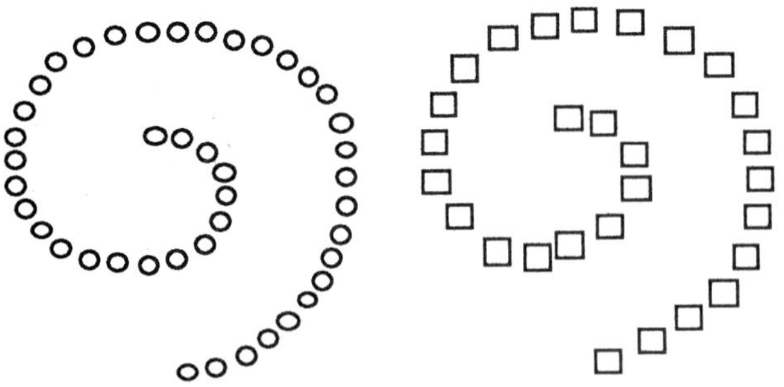

Figure 4.7A: Through the phenomenon of form quality, a viewer will perceive the overall shape of the objects shown above as the same, although the individual elements making them up are different.

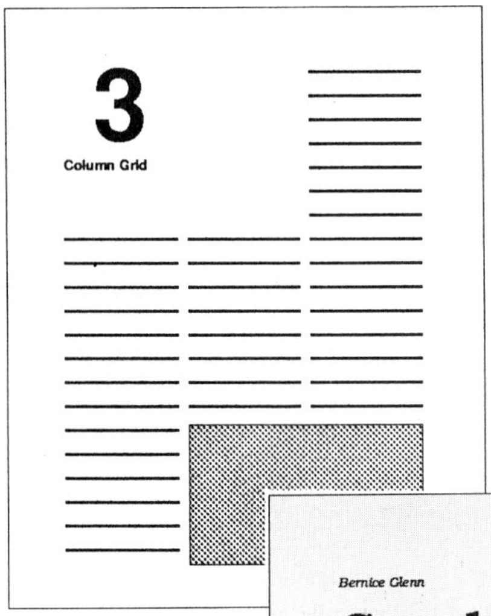

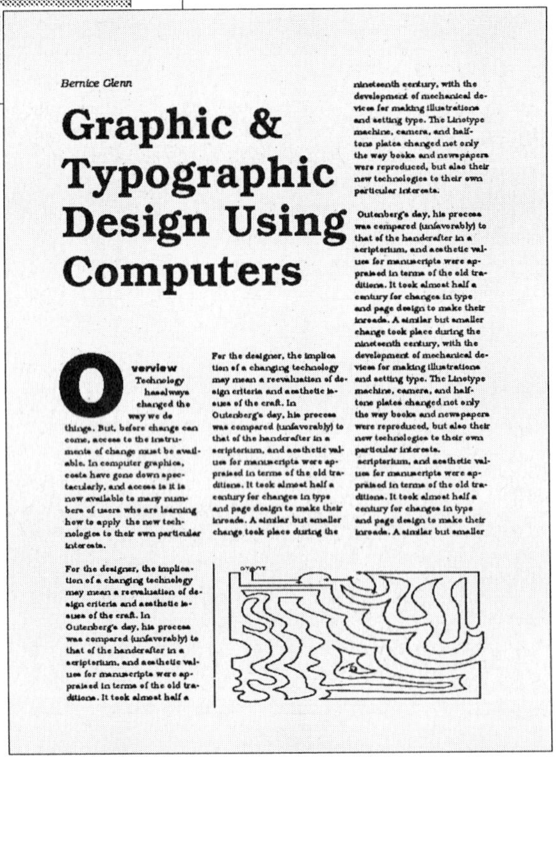

Figure 4.7B: Grids are an example of Form Quality in a publication.

Gestalt theory is an area of psychology that has been used as a guide for designers to follow since the 1930s, when the theory was developed. Since then, cognitive psychologists have enlarged on some of its concepts. This area of psychology investigates the way individuals process visual information in order to perceive meaning. Its central viewpoint is the notion that when the mind gathers data from the outside world, it interprets the data as an "organized whole." One example of an organized whole is in music; a tune or melody depends on hearing the notes as a whole in relation to each other, rather than on hearing each note as an individual sound. Visual objects in a graphic composition are likewise seen as related parts of the entire design.

USING SPATIAL RELATIONSHIPS TO INDICATE RELATIONSHIPS IN MEANING

When designers use cognitive theory, they refer to the notion that visual objects on a page they are designing are seen as parts of an entire design, whether they are text, graphic, or "white space." Understanding and applying these concepts to visual images can help the designer organize and control the visual page and its message. These concepts include form quality, proximity and togetherness, consistency and togetherness, repetition, dominance, balance, and organization.

FORM QUALITY AND CONSISTENCY

Through form quality, images can show an overall similarity of form although the individual elements that make up the image are different (see Figure 4.7A and B.) Form quality in publication design is concerned with the overall consistency of pages that results from the use of a grid.

CONSISTENCY AND TOGETHERNESS

According to visual cognition specialists, objects that look the same will appear to belong together, even when they are not placed close to each other. Using this concept as a guideline for design means that a reader will sense more organization in a publication when ideas of equal importance share the same design format. This might be done by using the same type for related ideas or by positioning related items in similar locations from page to page within the publication. You can confuse your reader when similar elements change visually from page to page within the same story or article (see Figure 4.8.)

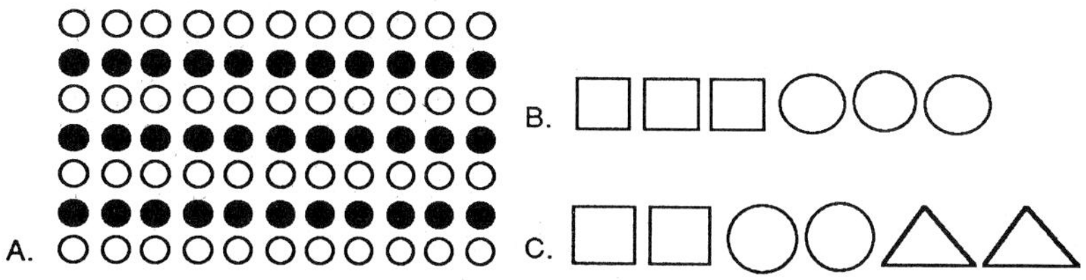

Figure 4.8: Objects that look alike are usually grouped together by the viewer. In illustration A, above, the open circles are seen as grouped together to form one set of rows, while the closed circles form a second set. B shows two groups of three similar objects; C is seen as three groups of two similar objects each. Designers make use of this when designing publications.

PROXIMITY AND TOGETHERNESS

The rule of proximity or closeness and togetherness implies that objects placed close together will appear to belong together. This rule of thumb can be applied to several concepts in page design.

One logical guideline states that captions should be placed close to the graphic they describe, and headings should be placed closer to the text they relate to. Allow more space between the heading and the paragraph above, and less space between the heading and the paragraph below to which it refers. As illustrated in Figure 4.9, when a heading is centered equally between two paragraphs, the reader finds its relationship to the text ambiguous.

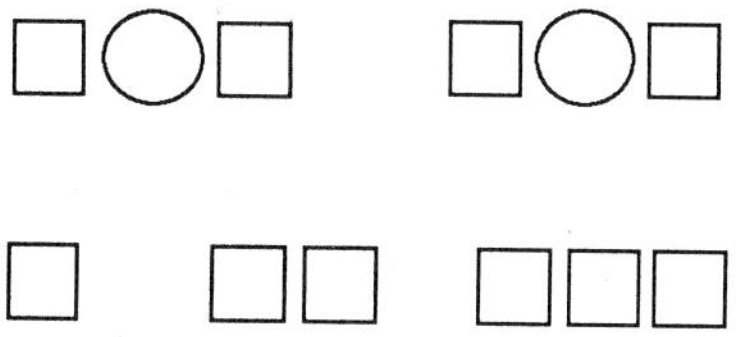

Figure 4.9: According to cognitive psychologists, elements that are close to each other will be viewed as belonging together, even when each elements looks different. In the top illustration, two distinct groups are seen, each made up of a circle and squares. In the illustration at the bottom, although made up of similar elements, three different groups are viewed because of their placement.

The illustration below demonstrates an application of proximity and togetherness as applied to the placement of headlines.

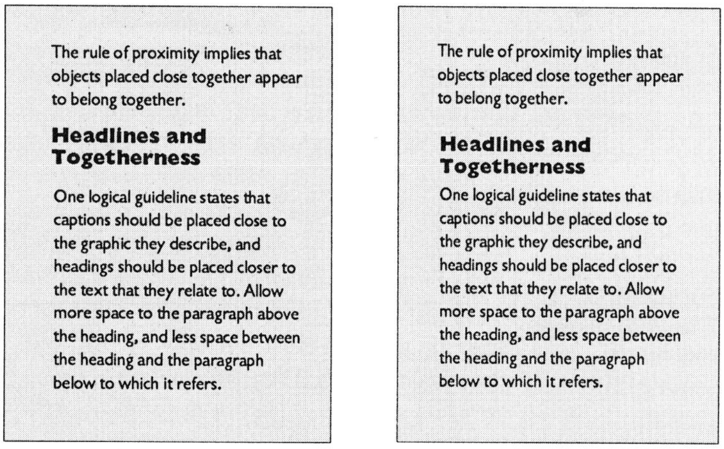

Ambiguous placement of the heading

Logical placement of the heading

USE OF REPETITION FOR EFFECT

Repetition of a shape or page element serves to unify the elements in a publication. Repetition can also be used to infer movement. If you look closely at this text, you will see that design elements are repeated from page to page and from chapter to chapter. The headers and footers are one such element. Also notice that each chapter has a similar opening page with a title, objectives, and an introductory paragraph. Repeating design elements in this manner unifies your publication by giving its pages a feeling of visual constancy and continuation.

PROVIDE A DOMINANT ELEMENT

Every layout needs a dominant element or shape. A single dominant element organizes the reader's eye movement and indicates relative importance. When one illustration

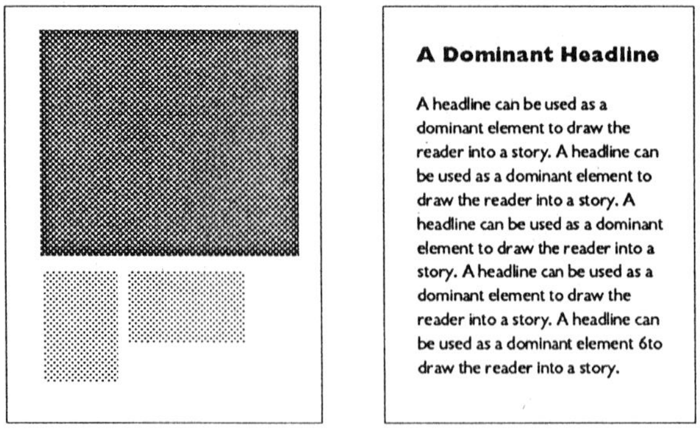

Figure 4.10: The page on the left is an example of a dominant image that will grab the reader's attention. The example on the right shows the use of a dominant headline.

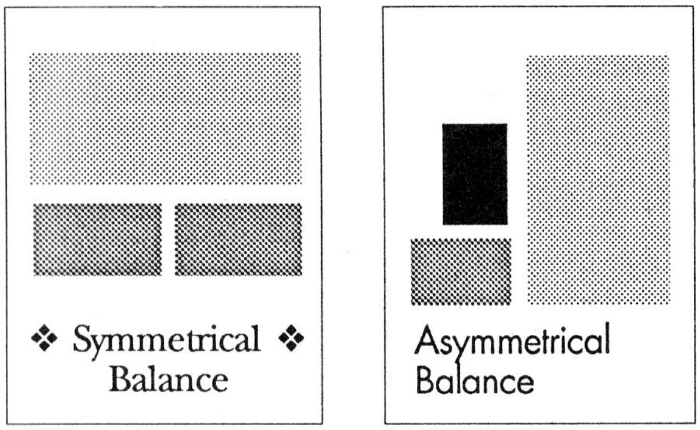

Figure 4.11: The page on the left demonstrates the principle of formal balance, while the page on the right is an example of informal balance.

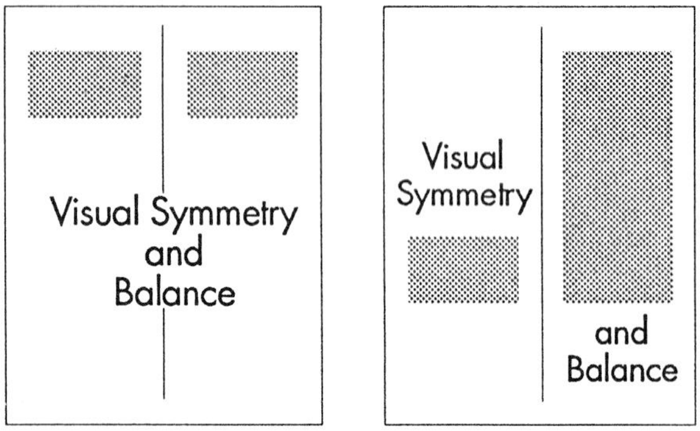

Figure 4.12: Two pages organized around a central axis. The illustration on the left is based on a symmetrical organization while the one on the right is based on asymmetric symmetry.

is larger than others, as shown in Figure 4.10, it sends a message to the reader to pay more attention to it rather than to the others. A headline can also be used as a dominant element to draw the reader into a story.

BALANCE THE PAGE ELEMENTS

In page layout, *balance* is accomplished by how you distribute the elements on a page. Think of balance as an old-fashioned scale where the elements on one side must weight the same as the other in order to be "in balance." Balance can be formal or informal. Formal, or *symmetrical balance*, as it is sometimes called, mirrors the elements out from a central axis, so that each half is a duplicate of the other (see Figure 4.11.) Informal, or *asymmetrical balance*, is created by the contrast of relative weights of elements on the page. The visual weight of elements are affected by their size, number, or density. All other factors being equal, a large element has more visual weight than a small element; a dark or dense element has more weight than a light element. As illustrated in Figure 4.11, a single large element may be balanced by a number of smaller elements.

STATIC AND DYNAMIC ORGANIZATION

When a page is organized around a central axis using symmetrical balance, the look that is conveyed is one of balance, tradition, and possibly even boredom.In an asymmetrical design, the organization of objects is different on each half of the page although the page is visually in balance. This type of organization is more dynamic (see Figure 4.12.)

VISUAL CORRESPONDENCE TO OTHER FORMS OF COMMUNICATION

Communication codes have what anthropologists call *correspondence*. That is, something expressed in one form can be translated in its essence to another form. For example, kinetic expression in a dance will reflect the music that is being played. Rhythm, cadence, and expression are replicated in each form. Visually, those forms can be repeated as well. For instance, when we say that a layout looks "jazzy," we are taking examples from jazz music and translating them into visual terms. Figure 4.13 demonstrates how rhythm, color, and primitive qualities found in a musical form can be replicated visually.

Our spoken language also has this facility for translation from textual to visual. Words such as light, massive, elegant, and plain, can be replicated visually through the elements you select and arrange on a page.

Figure 4.13: A jazzy layout for a party invitation. (Courtesy Toni Hollander, The Design Works.)

CHOOSING FEATURES FOR A VISUAL FORMAT

CONTROL THE READER'S EYE MOVEMENT

Studies show that when a person looks at a page, his or her eye will gravitate to the left-hand column about three-fifths up the page. Well-designed graphics can be used to control the reader's eye and keep it on the page. If you want the reader to concentrate on the important elements on the page for as long as possible, use a large or dominant illustration such as the one shown in Figure 4.14. A visually important element quickly draws the eye to it from its entry position on the page. Notice that the figure in the illustration is facing into the page and serves to guide the reader's eye movement.

Figure 4.14: An example of how a well placed illustration and heading will draw the reader's eye into the text of the printed page.

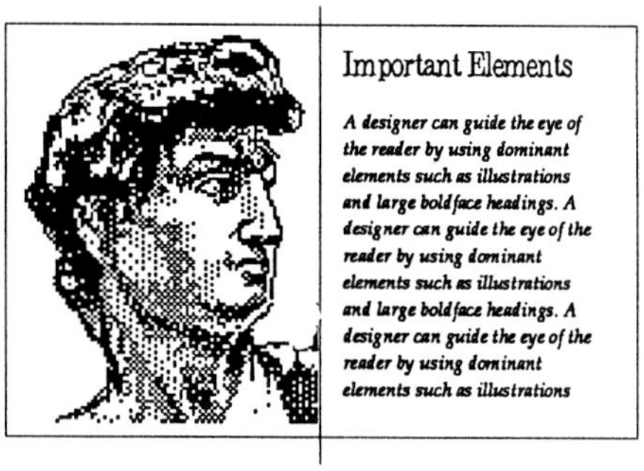

GROWTH AND DIRECTION

Space on a page can be used to convey growth and direction depending on the spatial relationships between text and its position on the page. Text that is placed very close to the bottom of page draws the eyes down. A heading placed low and flush right will move the eye down and to the right, in the direction that the text is read (see Figure 4.15.)

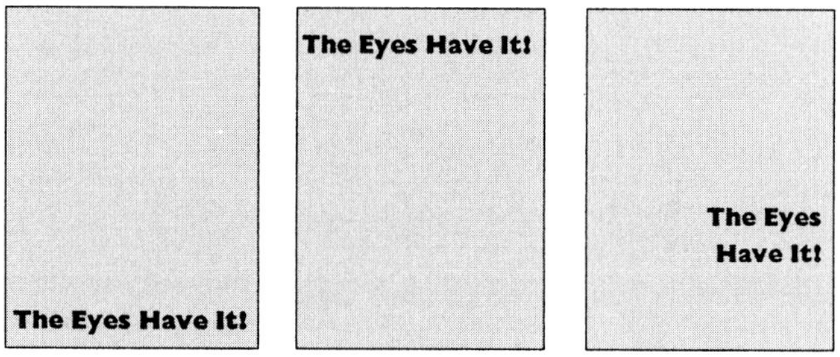

Figure 4.15: The designer has the ability to move the eye of the reader through the placement of dominant elements.

Pages can be organized bilaterally, in thirds, quarters, eighths, or whatever the design requires. If a publication has many similar pages, a grid or plan for consistent visual organization can be used (see Figure 4.16.)

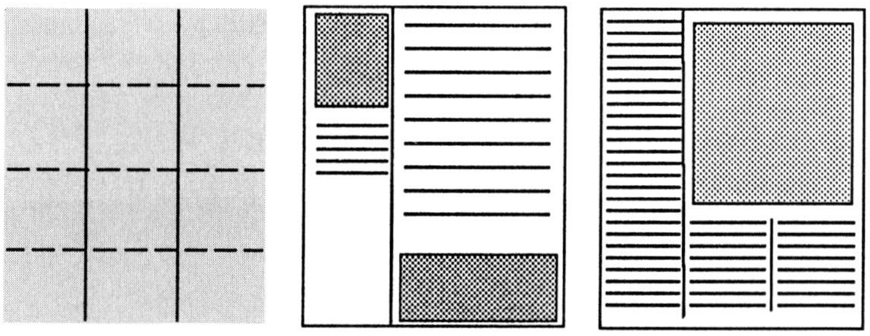

Figure 4.16: Pages can be organized bilaterally, in thirds, quarters, eighths, or whatever the design requires.

Figure 4.17: Note the variety of sizes the designer allocated to both text and photographs in this annual report executed on the desktop. (Courtesy Vinje Design, Inc.)

Figure #	Illustrated Design Principle	Additional Design Principle
4.8	Consistency and Togetherness	
4.9	Proximity and Togetherness	
4.10	Dominant Element	
4.11	Balance	
4.12	Static and Dynamic Organization	
4.14	Controlling Eye Movement	
4.16	Growth and Direction	

Figure 4.18: Prepare a sheet similar to the one shown above in order to answer question 1 in Building Your Desktop Publishing Skills on the opposite page.

COMMUNICATION USING SIZE, WEIGHTS, AND SPATIAL RELATIONSHIPS

KEEP THE PAGE ELEMENTS IN PROPORTION

A good design keeps its design element in proportion to its level of importance. Using elements of varying sizes, you can visually reflect the relative importance of the elements. Large bold type visually indicates topics of greater importance than small, light type does. Notice in this text that the headings are larger and bolder when compared to the lighter type used by the body text.

In interesting layouts, the areas allocated to text should be of different sizes than those occupied by the illustrations (see Figure 4.17.)

Because type comes in many sizes and densities, it is your primary vehicle for indicating levels of importance and insuring consistency between elements. You will learn more specific techniques for using type in Chapter 5, *Type Basics.*

CHECKING YOUR UNDERSTANDING

1. List the six design principles listed in this chapter.

2. Distinguish between formal and informal balance and give an example of each.

3. Describe the functions an editor performs in the design analysis task.

4. Give the major benefits in using a checklist analysis when analyzing design elements as discussed in this chapter.

5. Explain what a thumbnail is and tell why designers use them.

6. Explain the purpose of mark-up codes and give an example of a simple coding scheme.

7. What is the basic concept behind cognitive psychology as it is applied to design?

8. List each of the seven cognitive concepts for visual images and briefly explain each of the concepts.

9. Explain how well-designed graphics can control the reader's eye and keep it on the page.

10. Briefly discuss proportion as it applies to layout and design and give examples of how proportion may be achieved in a publication.

BUILDING YOUR DESKTOP PUBLISHING DESIGN SKILLS

1. The seven illustrations in Figure 4.18 demonstrate more than just the design principle indicated. Study each of these illustrations and then indicate the additional design principle or principles that you find in each figure.

Use the Publication Elements Review Form Figure 3.17 found in the Workbook/Forms Appendix and do the following:

2. Find a publication that consists mainly of text and is several pages long. Identify the type elements that had to be designed. Include all page headings, page numbers, each level of heading, body type, and any special treatment (bullets, etc.) within the body of the text.

3. Keyboard and save a disk copy of the three sections of text on pages 54 and 55 in this chapter, using your favorite word processing software. When keyboarding, follow the guidelines given in Figure 4.2. Then do the following:

   a) Print out a copy of your disk file.

   b) Use the proofreaders' marks, on page 327 in the Workbook/Forms Appendix. Mark up your copy, then go back and make the changes using your software. Print out a new copy incorporating your changes.

   c) Photocopy the Graphic Design and Publication Checklist, Figure 4.3, in the Workbook/Forms Appendix. Then complete the checklist for your text.

   d) Make up a set of easy-to-remember mark-up codes for each of the text elements indicated on your checklist.

   e) Mark up your text printout, noting the text elements in the margin using the mark-up codes you created.

DESKTOP DESIGN WORKSHOP

The purpose of this section is to provide you with opportunities to develop and/or improve your desktop publishing design skills. The worksheet pages have been placed at the back of the book, and are designed so they can be removed and you can write, draw, or place your responses directly onto the pages.

WORKSHEETS 4.1 AND 4.2

1. Use the boxes provided on Worksheet 4.1 to make thumbnails of layouts that you think might be suitable for a one-page flyer for the Good Dog Training Institute.

   a) Use the headline and text copy provided on the worksheet.

   b) Assume that an appropriate graphic will be used.

2. Select one of your thumbnails and create a "clean" version of your design on Worksheet 4.2.

   a) Make a copy of the Graphic Design and Publication Checklist, Figure 4.3 in the Workbook/Forms Appendix, and complete it, indicating all the text and graphic elements in your design.

   b) Create a set of easy-to-remember mark-up codes for each of the text elements you found.

3. Mark up your thumbnail on Worksheet 4.2, using your mark-up codes to note the text and graphic elements. Mark them in the margin.

5. TYPE BASICS

When you finish this chapter you should be able to:

- *Describe basic type characteristics such as type style, weight, slant, and proportion.*
- *Understand how to distinguish one typeface from another.*
- *Measure type and specify type for a publication.*
- *Use a type catalog.*
- *Make type specimen sheets.*

PUBLICATIONS HAVE BEEN DEscribed as consisting of a written message as well as a visual message. In this chapter, you will learn how to give form to the visual message by working with one of the fundamental building blocks of graphics design: type. Type is the stylized set of letters, numbers, and symbols used to tie together the written and visual messages. Readers seldom will notice the typefaces as they are reading, if your material has been well-designed. Misused type, on the other hand, can quickly discourage anyone from reading. If you want to exploit the use of type to its best advantage, it helps if you understand its history, nature, and structure.

Over the centuries, designers have developed hundreds of typographic arrangements intended to make type more attractive, readable, and eye-catching. As part of this historical design process, principles regarding the use of type emerged. If you use these principles as design guidelines, they can be of major value in producing attractive, well-designed documents.

For help on how to use type aesthetically, refer to Chapter 6, *Type Aesthetics*.

COMMUNICATING WITH TYPE

No doubt you have heard the saying, "a picture is worth a thousand words," but did you know that type talks just as pictures do? Type can be emphatic or dainty, light or heavy, small or big. What you select and how you place it will paint your manuscript page as color paints a canvas.

Type can be as small as that used in a telephone directory or big enough for a billboard. It can be light, medium weight, bold, and ultrabold. Typefaces can be chosen to attract attention, to provoke specific moods, to fit narrow spaces, to fit large spaces.

There are type designs made specifically for book and magazine text, newspapers, and wedding invitations. Figure 5.1 shows an assortment that exemplifies some of these characteristics. Learning about typographic attributes can help you create appropriate and interesting page designs.

THE LANGUAGE OF TYPOGRAPHY

With the arrival of desktop publishing, people could produce type in any size or slant, merely by selecting it on the computer. The terms traditionally used to describe type and its appearance on the printed page are often unknown to today's desktop publisher. In addition, the desktop publishing industry defines much more loosely, many of the terms used for centuries by typographers and printers. If you have a solid understanding of the terms discussed in this chapter, it will help you when working with printers, service bureaus, typographers, and professional designers.

SIZE

As shown in Figure 5.1, type can vary in size from small to large and can be classified according to its size. Type is usually specified in standard sizes, evolved from the ways in which it was used historically. The size of type is expressed in "points" rather than in inches. The point measurement system will be discussed in greater detail later in this chapter, but for now you only need to understand that the larger the number of points, the larger the type size.

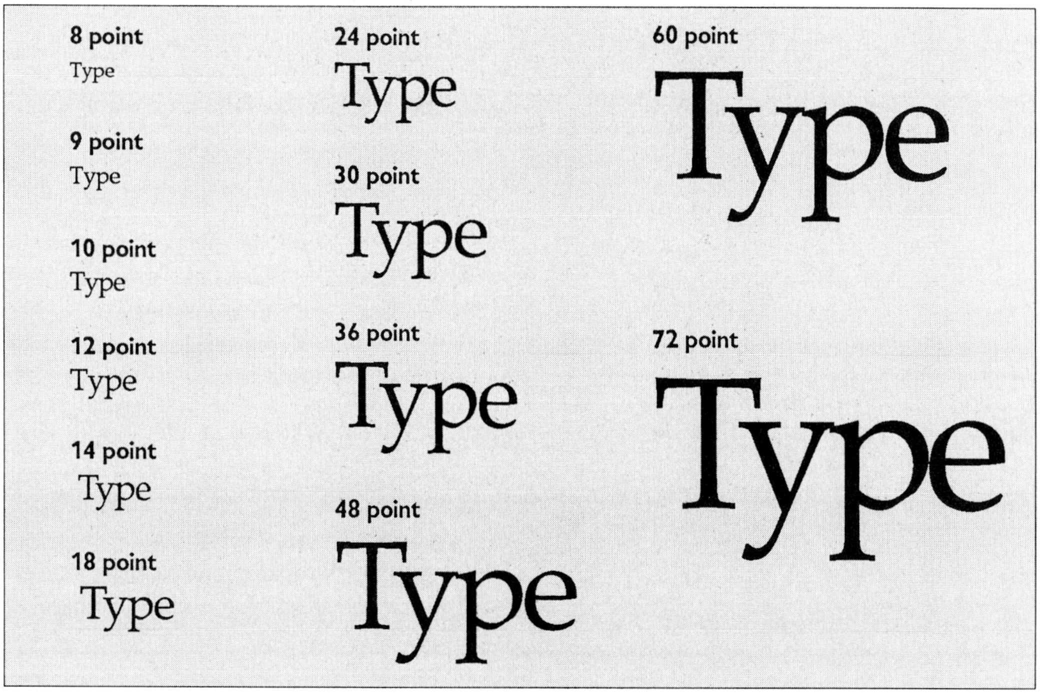

Figure 5.1: Typical sizes for use in desktop publishing, shown here in Palatino.

WEIGHT

As you can see in Figure 5.2, another typographic variation involves the thickness of the strokes that form the characters, and their proportion of height to width. The degree of stroke thickness coincides with the weight of the type. The thinner the stroke, the lighter the type character is. Loosely speaking, type may be described as light, medium, or bold in weight. The terms used to describe the variations of boldness are not standard, but some of the commonly used vocabulary refers to light, regular, book, medium, demibold, semibold, ultrabold, and heavy.

18 point Helvetica light

18 point Helvetica regular

18 point Helvetica bold

18 point Helvetica black

a a a a **a** ***a***

a a a a **a** ***a*** **a** ***a***

a a **a** ***a*** **a** ***a***

a ***a***

Figure 5.2: Samples showing various type weights available in Helvetica.

SLANT

Type may be completely vertical, like most of the text in this book, or slightly slanted (sometimes referred to as oblique). The terms *inclination* and *posture* are used to describe the slant of the lines that form the character. Type fonts of a standard or normal weight whose vertical members do not tilt to the right are traditionally called *roman* fonts. *Italic*, as shown in Figure 5.3, is a familiar slanted type style. Italic differs from oblique in that it usually is designed differently from the parent Roman face, not only to accommodate the slant, but to emulate some of the features in traditional handwriting. *Oblique* is a roman font that has been slanted without any basic design changes to the letter forms.

Bodoni roman letter form

Bodoni italic letter form

Bodoni oblique letter form

Figure 5.3: Illustration comparing the slants of Bodoni italic and oblique to its roman alphabet.

WIDTH

Type also varies in its proportion based on a classical or traditional standard. The width of a character of type is measured from where it begins at the left to where it ends at the right. Type can vary from its standard or classical width and be made narrower (condensed), or wider (expanded) as shown in Figure 5.4. When type is condensed, the vertical stokes composing the face are placed close together in proportion to the character width. When type is expanded the vertical strokes are placed further apart. The height remains the same.

Futura Book

Futura Condensed Light

Futura Book Expanded

Figure 5.4: A comparison of condensed and expanded fonts in Futura.

FONTS, FACES, AND FAMILIES

FONTS

Moveable type was originally developed using metal molds. Each separate character was cut as an individual piece separate from others in the alphabet and a mold was made from every character and symbol. A complete set of all individual characters (including punctuation, numerals, and symbols) of a given size and style was called a *type font,* or simply font. Each font was defined by its size and family name, such as 12-point Bodoni. The printer would use a set of molds to produce as many individual alphabet characters as were needed to set several pages at a time. This feature, called *moveable type,* allowed the printer to set the characters into various combinations to form words and sentences. Every single character for each different size of type was cut independently.

When more variation than just size was needed, heavier or lighter weights of type could also be cut. Each different type weight, such as light or bold, was a separate named font made up of individual characters. A bold version of the standard 12-point Bodoni font would be called 12-point Bodoni bold. Slanted or italic type was cut individually as well, and it, too had its own distinctive name (12-point Bodoni italic.) Figure 5.5 illustrates a family of type fonts.

TYPEFACES

A *typeface* design is a distinctive look or style, independent of size or weight. Bodoni, Helvetica, and Palatino are typefaces whose looks are distinctive, as shown in Figure 5.6. The design features for each typeface is preserved through all sizes, weights, and inclinations. The innate design stays the same; only its size, weight, or inclination changes.

18 point Bodoni Roman

18 point Bodoni Italic

18 point Bodoni Bold

18 point Bodoni Poster

Figure 5.5: A family of Bodoni type fonts.

Adobe Garamond Family

Bodoni Family

Century Schoolbook Family

Futura Family

Galliard Family

Helvetica Family

Melior Family

Palatino Family

Plantin Family

Stone Serif Family

Stone Sans Family

Trump Medieval Family

Figure 5.6: Typefaces compared for their distinctive looks.

Futura Bold

Futura Bold Oblique

Futura Condensed

Futura Condensed Bold

Futura Condensed Bold Oblique

Futura Condensed Light

Futura Condensed Light Oblique

Futura Condensed Oblique

Futura Condensed Extra Bold

Futura Condensed Extra Bold Oblique

Futura Book

Futura Light

Futura Book Oblique

Figure 5.7: The Futura family of fonts.

TYPE FAMILIES

A *type family* consists of all the sizes, weights, and inclinations of a particular typeface (Figure 5.7.) Within a type family, many variations are possible. Type families include so many variations of weight and size that you can design a graphically interesting publication using only one family. A rule for beginners to keep in mind: staying within a narrow range of type choices using a single type family will produce a cleaner, more consistent design.

In addition to the type characteristics described so far, typefaces may vary in other ways.

> *Typefaces frequently differ in the overall width of their characters and in the proportion of width to height. Other differences include unique shapes of individual characters in a given type face, such as the curl in the tail of the letter "Q" or the shape of the lower case "g."*

As you become more familiar with type structure, these characteristics will help you to identify particular type faces and also enable you to select faces that go well together. Figure 5.8 shows some of these variations.

Another major design difference between typefaces depends on how the weight of their strokes are interpreted. For example, typefaces that were developed at the start of the printing revolution were designed to look like the handwriting that preceded them, so the strokes that make up the typeface resemble the pen strokes that drew these traditional letterforms. These swells from thick to thin are still apparent in faces called *Old Style,* whose history goes back to the fifteenth century.

Garamond and Caslon are examples of faces we use today whose shadings from thick to thin come directly from a pen that drew letterforms with these characteristics —

that of a 20- to 30-degree slant from the perpendicular for the thinnest part of the letter (Figure 5.9). The angle at which the thick and thin weights are distributed is called the *weight stress.* In Old Style types faces, the thin strokes are relatively thick in proportion to the heavy strokes.

By the eighteenth century, typefaces were still designed using thicks and thins, but these forms were constructed with the thinnest part of the letter set at right angles to the perpendicular, using a vertical stress. The thin strokes became thinner when compare to those on Old Style. Typefaces whose thinnest parts are parallel to the base of the letter are the start of a new category of type face designs called *Transitional.*

Through time, these showed more and more contrast between the thicks and thins of the basic letter form. Older faces in the series are Transitional. Those showing the most exaggerated contrasts from hairline thins to thick bold strokes are called *Modern,* relating to the time that they were designed, not to the present day. Bodoni, a typeface illustrated in figure 5.10, is an example of a Modern face, designed by Giambattista Bodoni in 1788. In Modern typefaces, the weight stress is heaviest in its vertical strokes.

SERIF, SANS SERIF, AND MONO-WEIGHTED LETTERFORMS

Typefaces are also classified according to other characteristics of their letterform structure. Three common classifications are *serif, sans serif,* and *mono-weighted. Decorative* is another descriptive classification, referring to designs that are more elaborate or fanciful. Decorative fonts are usually members of the main structural groups: serif, sans serif, and mono-weight.

Throughout most of the long history of typographic design, letter forms had characteristic endings to their letter strokes called *serifs.* Serifs are most frequently used as endings to the vertical letter form strokes. Tails and curls are also used as stroke terminators, such as in the lower case "a" and "g." As you can see in Figure 5.11, the upper case

Old Style

Adobe Caslon

Garamond Old Style

Plantin

Transitional

Baskerville

Caslon 3

Figure 5.8: Examples of some old style and transitional faces.

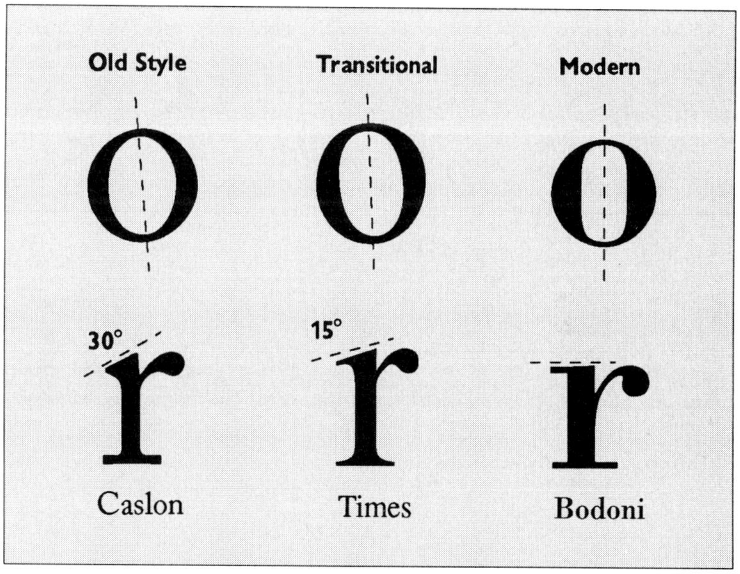

Figure 5.9: Illustration comparing the degrees of slope in several oldstyle and transitional letterforms.

Bodoni

Torino

Figure 5.10: Examples of the modern letterform. Note the hairline serif that marks their design.

Figure 5.11 A, B, and C: Illustration of serifs with serif comparison chart, Old Style through Modern
A. Old Style and Transitional serifs: Garamond, Times Roman, Baskerville, ,
B. Hair-line serif in the Moderns - Bodoni
C. Thick serif: Wild West

A. Old Style and Transitional

Adobe Caslon	a d r y R T
Adobe Garamond	a d r y R T
New Baskerville	a d r y R T
Palatino	a d r y R T

B. Modern

Bodoni	a d r y R T
Torino	a d r y R T

C. Wild West

Aachen Bold	**a d r y R T**

"A" has feet, while the lower case "a" has a slight curl on its tail. These feet and curls are serifs. Serifs help tie together the characters that make up words and text lines.

Serif styles also show stylistic transitions from Old Style to Modern and beyond. Caslon and Garamond use serifs that are bracketed — a curve is used to connect the serif to its main stroke. In Old Style lower case characters, some serifs, such as those at the top of the "r" and the "b," are drawn at the same angle as their weight stress — 20 degrees to 30 degrees to the left of the vertical. In Transitional faces, this angle gradually disappears as the weight stress becomes more vertical. In Modern faces, serifs are always horizontal and hairline-thin. Lower case "r" and "y" have ball terminals at the end of their tail strokes

In the nineteenth century, some typefaces were designed with exaggeratedly thick serifs. These faces are still used by American circus companies and movie studios to represent the Wild West (see Figure 5.11C.)

SANS SERIF TYPEFACES

Since the early twentieth century, machines have become a metaphor for design, and also have provided the mechanism for producing certain kinds of design "looks." Functional use and clean lines based on geometric forms were conspicuous in furniture design, houses, and typography. Sans (without) serif type was one of the results of this ongoing design revolution. As you can see in Figure 5.12, sans serif typefaces do not have the characteristic "feet" and "tails" of serif faces. They also follow the overall design trend of the time in their reliance on geometric forms.

The most popular sans serif typefaces, Univers, Futura, and Helvetica, came into general use in the 1950s and 60s. Helvetica was very widely used in the United States because it implied modernity and forward-thinking ideas at a time of cultural change after World War II. Annual reports, especially, used Helvetica to carry a message of fiscal responsibility and faith in the future to a company's stockholders.

MONO-WEIGHT TYPEFACES

Fonts with little or no variation in the widths of their strokes are referred to as mono-weight fonts. Their strokes appear equal to the eye, although there may actually be some variance in the letterforms. Mono-weight fonts can be found in both serif and sans serif styles. An early example is Gill Sans, now in a revival. Other mono-weight sans serif fonts include Futura and Helvetica. Many sans serif fonts, such as Univers, employ a subtle use of thicks and thins. Optima is usually classed as a sans serif face, although its strokes splay out at their endings — implying serif-like terminators to the letter forms.

Along with the sans serif typefaces, mono-weight serif faces were designed, such as

Avant Garde	**Gill Sans Extra Bold**
Eras Medium	**Helvetica Compressed**
Futura Book	Peignot Light
Futura Bold Condensed	**Peignot Bold**

Figure 5.12: Examples of sans serif type faces shown here in 18 point.

Glypha
Lubalin Graph
Memphis

Figure 5.13: Mono-weighted slab serif letter forms.

Memphis and Cairo. These faces, represented by characteristic "slab" serifs, can range from hairline thin fonts to ultra black (see Figure 5.13.)

DECORATIVE TYPEFACES

Unlike serif or sans serif type, decorative type is not designed for continuous reading. It is used primarily for headlines, layouts for flyers, special events, wedding invitations, and advertisements. Americana, Souvenir, Zapf Chancery, Cooper Black, University Roman, Brush, Stencil, Cottonwood, and Broadway are examples of decorative type. Script fonts whose characters are connected by a continuous line are often designed as decorative faces. Notice how much more difficult the decorative type samples illustrated in Figure 5.14 are to read than the serif or sans serif type faces illustrated above. But notice, too, how they grab the eye and make it focus on the page.

Americana
Duc De Berry
Korinna
Park Avenue
PEIGNOT
Tiffany
Torino

Figure 5.14: Decorative type samples.

TYPE STRUCTURE

Regardless of their design characteristics, all fonts have a similar structure. When you understand typographic structure you can better understand and recognize the differences in type.

Type font are measured by their height: from the highest part of the tallest letter down to the lowest part of the lowest letter. The font height description is broken down into several sections that make up the entire character. As shown in Figure 5.15, the main

Figure 5.15: Type structure showing x-heights.

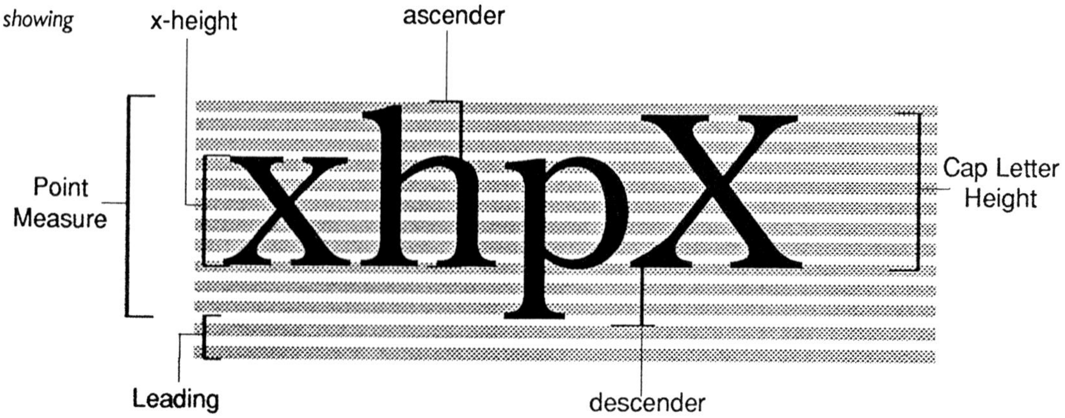

region or section is called the *x-height,* an area that corresponds to the lower case letter height. The x-height for any font is the distance measured from its baseline, the imaginary line for the bottom of most characters, to the top of a lower-case "x," whose top and bottom are clearly defined for measuring.

Some lower-case letters, such as "b," "d," "f," "h," "k," "l," and "t," extend above the x-height. The part of the font character that extends above the x-height is called the *ascender.* Capital letters also extend above the x-height. They are usually the same height as the ascenders, although in some faces they may be somewhat shorter.

The part of a character that goes below the baseline is called a *descender.* The lower-case letters "g," "j," "p," and "y" have descenders. Some capital letters have descenders, such as the tail of the Q or J, that can extend below the baseline (see Figure 5.16.)

You can identify type by its proportions, such as the size of the x-height as compared to the ascender or descender. These proportions have a great deal to do with the readability of the typeface. For example, type with a small x-height and elongated ascenders usually needs to be set larger than average in order for the text to be read easily. Letter forms with elongated ascenders and descenders can look elegant, old-fashioned, or conservative, depending on the choice of type. This style of letterform is often used for wedding announcements and jewelry advertisements.

A letter form with a large x-height as compared to its ascenders and descenders is more readable in small sizes. The large x-height letter was originally designed for use in newspapers because you could use a smaller type size (and therefore pack in more characters to the line) while still maintaining readability. Most contemporary faces are designed with a large x-height (see Figure 5.17.)

Other differences in fonts include the width of the letterform in proportion to its overall height, the style of its serifs if it has any, and certain characteristics of particular letterforms, such as the curl of the "Q" and the shape of the "g" (see Figure 5.18 on the following page.)

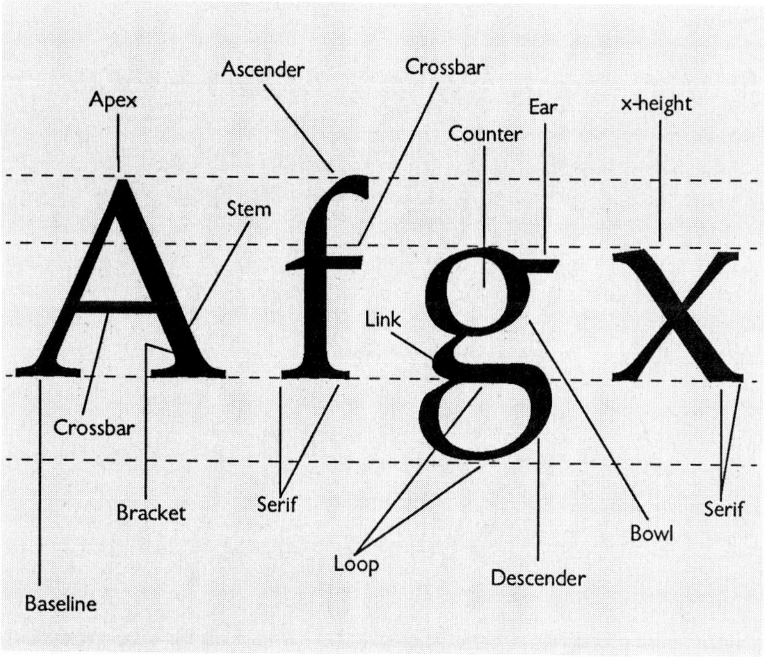

Figure: 5:16: Identification of the parts of letters in a type font.

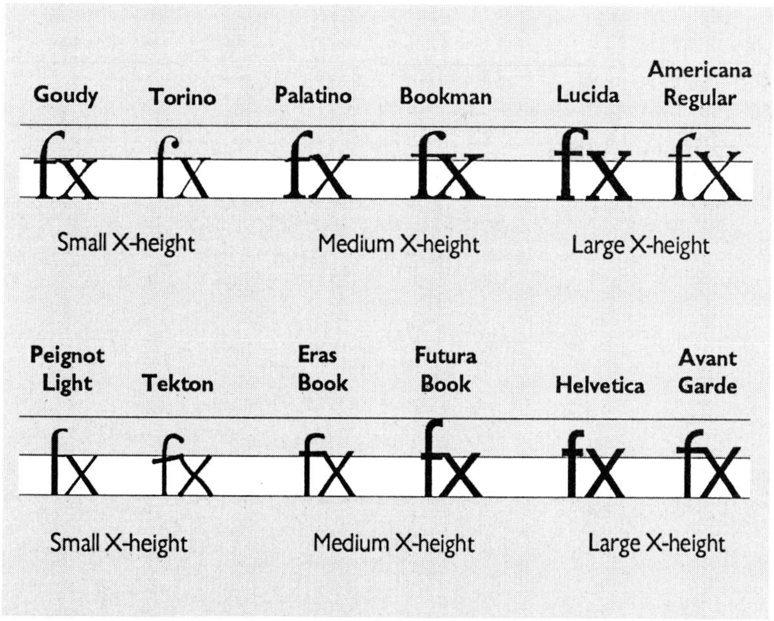

Figure 5:17: A comparison of X-heights for various type faces is shown at 36 point. The top row compares serif faces, while those on the bottom compare sans serif faces.

Figure 5.18: Chart comparing letterform characteristics.

Adobe Caslon	a	g	r	y	M	R	Q	Y
Adobe Garamond	a	g	r	y	M	R	Q	Y
Americana	a	g	r	y	M	R	Q	Y
Bodoni	a	g	r	y	M	R	Q	Y
Friz Quadrata	a	g	r	y	M	R	Q	Y
Futura	a	g	r	y	M	R	Q	Y
Gill Sans	a	g	r	y	M	R	Q	Y
Goudy	a	g	r	y	M	R	Q	Y
Lubalin Graph	a	g	r	y	M	R	Q	Y
New Baskerville	a	g	r	y	M	R	Q	Y
Palatino	a	g	r	y	M	R	Q	Y
Plantin	a	g	r	y	M	R	Q	Y

MEASURING TYPE HEIGHT AND WIDTH

As previously mentioned, type uses a different measuring system than our typical use of inches and feet. In the United States and England, type sizes and all typographical specifications are calibrated in *points*, a unit of measurement for type. Font size is determined by measuring the number of points in the overall font height, from its highest ascender to the lowest descender.

In the point system of measurement, there are approximately 72 points to the inch. A 12-point unit is called a *pica*. Figure 5.19 illustrates the relationship between the point/picas system and the inch/foot system. Notice that 12 points equal 1 pica, and 6 picas equal 1 inch. Since the measurement of 72 points to the inch is very close but not exact, when you measure type that is more than 3 or 4 inches long, you will notice a discrepancy showing up between points and inches.

Font size descriptions are expressed in points. While the menu choices in most desktop software lists only standard sizes, many programs allow you to select from 6 points up to 127 points or larger, merely by keying in your choice.

When measuring type from the top of its tallest letter to the bottom of its lowest letter a special ruler called a *type scale* is used. A typical type scale is shown, reduced, in Figure 5.20A, and full size on page 326 in the workbook section. Type scales are clear plastic with some of the frequently used type sizes and line spacing imprinted in black.

In Figure 5.20B, the type scale is used to determine the type size by measuring the letter "T" in the sample text. The letter "T" was selected because it is a capital letter and it is straight. A curved letter like the letter "s" rests slightly below the baseline and lower case letters like "j" or "d" have ascenders or descenders that extend above or below the baseline. A straight letter like the upper case "T" is easier to measure against.

In our example (Figure 5.20B), the "E" of the type gauge portion of the type scale is

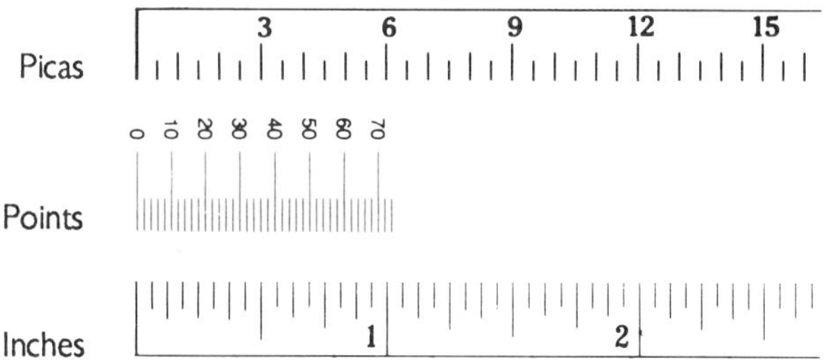

Figure 5.19 : Point/Pica— Inch comparison

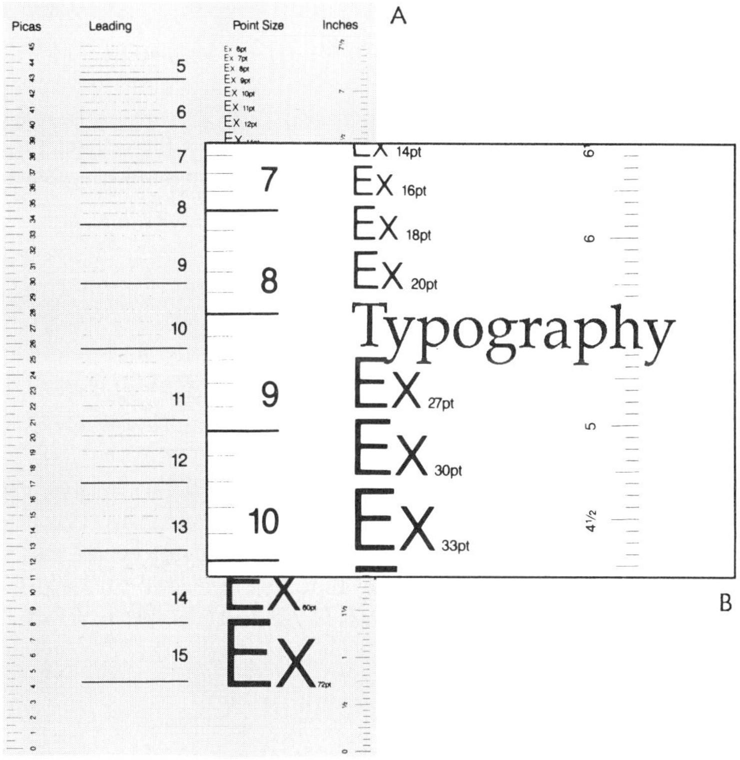

Figure 5.20A: Shown shaded and reduced is a typical type scale
B. The E-scale section of the type scale, shown actual size, is used here to measure the type size of the letter "T."

placed over the capital letter "T" and the gauge is moved up or down until the "E" that most closely matches the size of the text sample is found.

A type scale should be used only as a guide to the type size. Since each type font is unique, all sizes vary a little from one another depending upon the shape of the characters.

LEADING

The space between two lines of type is called interlinear spacing, or leading. *Interlinear spacing* is the term used by computer programmers. *Leading* (pronounced "ledding"), a term used by typesetters and publication designers, comes from the metal typesetting tradition, where strips of lead were placed between rows of type to provide more space between the lines. Leading by itself is no longer specified as a measurement, but is indicated as part of the measure from the baseline of one line of type to the baseline of the next.

As illustrated in Figure 5.20, the type scale contains line rules. The line rules are identified as 8-point, 9-point, and so on. As their name implies, line rules are used to measure line spacing. Leading is measured with the line rules by placing the sets of line rules over two line of type until you find a set of line rules that matches up at the baselines, as shown in Figure 5.21. For example, a 12-point computer font measures 12 points from its highest ascender to its lowest descender. If 2 points of leading are desired between the lines, it would be indicated as 12-point type on a 14-point measurement, from baseline to baseline, (or 12/14, b/b). In metal type fonts, a 12-point font actually measures 10 or 11 points since an additional point was included top and bottom, as part of the metal block belonging to the type character. In computer type, no such additional space is needed.

When you want to specify leading for page design, decide how much space you want between the lines in points, and add that amount to the type size. Your type specification would read as (type size)/(type size + leading) set baseline to baseline.

Fonts whose x-height is large in proportion to their ascenders and descenders require more leading space between the lines, to make reading easier.

Remember that the type scale is only a guide to measuring type size. In order to get the correct size, you need to find both the type gauge and line rules measurements. Between the two, you can usually determine the exact point size. You will realize how important it is to match the point size and line spacing when you are revising a document and need to match new type to that already used.

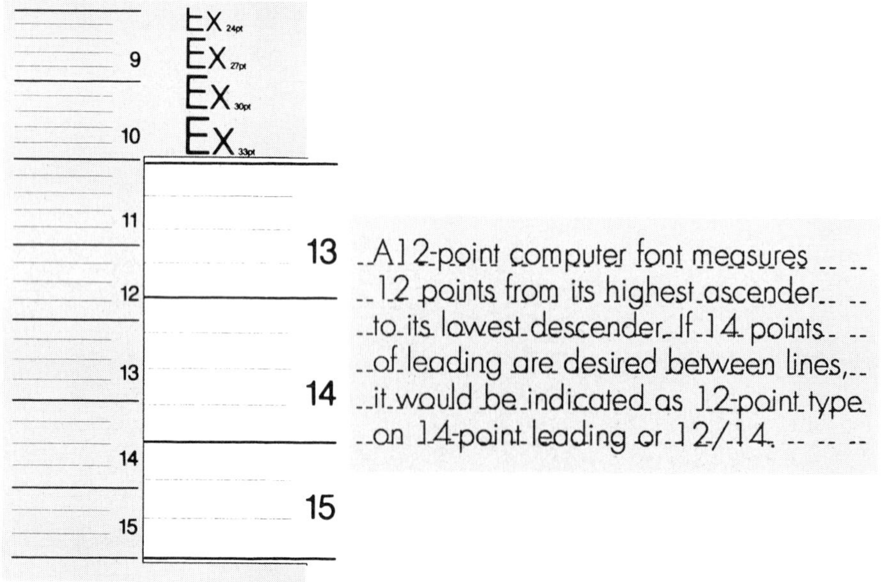

Figure 5.21: Using the type scale to determine leading.

LINE LENGTH

The length and width of a column of text are measured in picas, using the pica ruler section of the type scale. If you need to measure unjustified lines of text, first draw a line along the right edge of the longest line of the text block. Then, measure the line length from the left edge of the type to the pencil line, as shown in Figure 5.22.

ELECTRONIC FORMATS FOR TYPE

In the old days, fonts were made of metal. Today, the desktop publisher uses fonts that are electronic and are composed using information in the computer, in font software, and/or in the printer. For typographic and near-typographic quality, fonts need to be output on laser printers, using a smoothed line rendering. Two formats are in use today, and others are in development or ready for release. When you are buying fonts, make sure that they are compatible not only with the computer you are using, but also with your printer. Most desktop publishing programs will allow you to use both Type 1 and Type 3 fonts (see following paragraphs,) provided that you have installed all the software needed for the font to print.

POSTSCRIPT

The first format developed for laser output of fonts was Postscript, a language that calculates the font geometry electronically, as a graphic for any size that is requested in a program. Postscript Type 1 format fonts were first developed by Adobe, whose software incorporates "hints" for adjusting the type design to the size of its output. Type 1 contained hinting and other type structure information proprietary to Adobe. Until Type 1 was released to the public, other companies making Postscript fonts used a form known as Type 3, without Adobe's hinting structure. Adobe still uses undocumented information or "trade secrets" they apply to making their Type 1 fonts. Manufacturers today can make both Type 1 and Type 3 fonts, and are each developing their own methods for better type structures. Type 3 fonts tend to print darker in small sizes.

Adobe is developing a new font format, MultiMaster, a font master that will allow you to modify a type face to the weight and width that you specify for it.

TRUETYPE

Apple Computer's new System 7 supports a new font format known as TrueType. This format allows high-quality letterforms of any size to be displayed on both screens and printers of any resolution.

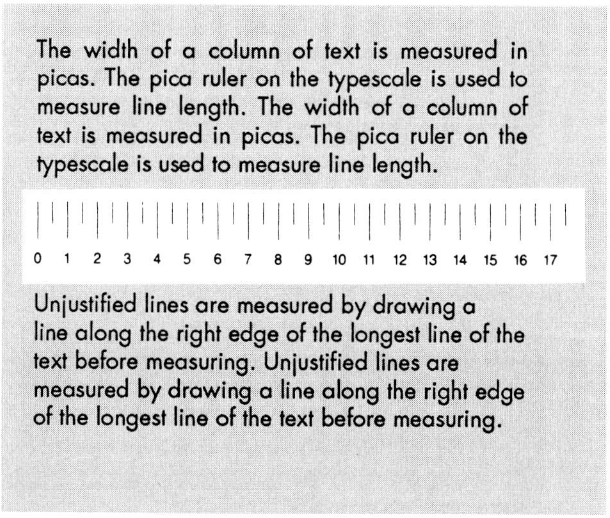

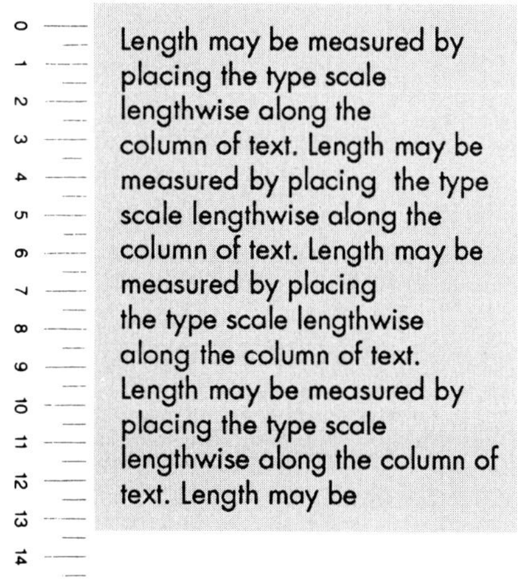

Figure 5.22: (far left, top) Measuring type. Lay the 0 point of the pica rule against the left end of the line of type. The length of the line is indicated on the pica scale at the right end point of the line of type. (far left, bottom) If the type block has a ragged right, draw a line lengthwise down the page, corresponding to the longest line of type in the type block you are measuring. The line you have drawn corresponds to the right end point of the type line. (left) Measuring the length of a column of type.

MONOTYPE BODONI * Volume 1008

Bodoni
Bodoni Italic
Bodoni Bold
Bodoni Bold Italic

MONOTYPE BODONI BOOK, Ultra Bold & Onyx** Volume 1009

Bodoni Book
Bodoni Book Italic
Bodoni Ultra Bold
Bodoni Ultra Bold Italic
Onyx

MONOTYPE BODONI BLACK & Bold Condensed Volume 1010

Bodoni Black
Bodoni Black Italic
Bodoni Bold Condensed
Bodoni Bold Condensed Italic

Bauer Bodoni** Roman	Hamburgefonstiv. Since 1886 Linot
Bauer Bodoni Italic	*Hamburgefonstiv. Since 1886 Linoty*
Bauer Bodoni Bold	**Hamburgefonstiv. Since 1886 Lin**
Bauer Bodoni Bold Italic	***Hamburgefonstiv. Since 1886 Lino***
Bauer Bodoni Black	**Hamburgefonstiv. Since 1886 L**
Bauer Bodoni Black Italic	***Hamburgefonstiv. Since 1886***
Bauer Bodoni Roman SC	HAMBURGEFONSTIV. SINCE 1886 LINOTY
Bauer Bodoni Italic OsF	*Hamburgefonstiv. Since 1886 Linoty*
Bauer Bodoni Bold OsF	**Hamburgefonstiv. Since 1886 Lin**
Bauer Bodoni Bold Italic OsF	***Hamburgefonstiv. Since 1886 Linot***
Bauer Bodoni Bold Condensed	**Hamburgefonstiv. Since 1886 Linotype**
Bauer Bodoni Black Condensed	**Hamburgefonstiv. Since 1886 Linotype**
Bodoni Book	Hamburgefonstiv. Since 1886 Linotype
Bodoni Book Italic	*Hamburgefonstiv. Since 1886 Linotype h*
• Bodoni	Hamburgefonstiv. Since 1886 Linoty
• Bodoni Italic	*Hamburgefonstiv. Since 1886 Linoty*
• Bodoni Bold	**Hamburgefonstiv. Since 1886 Lino**

Figure 5.23: Sample type catalogue pages from (top) Monotype Typography, Inc., and (bottom) Linotype-Hell Company. Linotype is a registered trademark of Linotype-Hell AG.

USING A TYPE CATALOG

The number of type font providers has multiplied, along with the variety of fonts that are available to the desktop publisher. Many of the fonts provided by one company have the same names as those provided by others. The design of similarly named fonts can vary, though, from one company to another. The only way to tell the difference is by looking at sample output in a *type catalog.*

Type catalogs illustrate the different kinds and styles of type that are available from a particular manufacturer or type supplier. Desktop publishers have access to a number of sources that show available typefaces. Some equipment manufacturers such as Hewlett-Packard, Qume, Varitype, and Apple have specimen sheets showing the faces that accompany their equipment. Type catalogs are also distributed by typographic software developers such as Bitstream, Monotype, Linotype-Hell and Adobe (see Figure 5.23.)

These specimen sheets and type catalogs generally show 12-point type only, in an alphabetic display. These are convenient for showing you what a face looks like, but a 12-point alphabet really does not help you very much to make good design decisions.

For design purposes, look at type in the actual sizes you are interested in using — including examples of bold and italic. When designing text, look at type specimen sheets that show one size of text with alternate leading choices.

MAKING YOUR OWN TYPE SPECIMEN SHEETS

If you want to see type as you plan to use it in headings or in text, you can use a software program that prints out specimen sheets for you, or you can make your own specimen sheet. You can easily prepare a specimen sheet on your computer that is similar to those provided by traditional typesetters.

Palatino

8 pt. ABCDEFGHIJKLMNOPQRSTUVWXYZabcdefghijklmnopqrstuvwxyz0123456789!?,"¢$&%{}*
9 pt. ABCDEFGHIJKLMNOPQRSTUVWXYZabcdefghijklmnopqrstuvwxyz0123456789!?,"¢$&%{}*
10 pt. ABCDEFGHIJKLMNOPQRSTUVWXYZabcdefghijklmnopqrstuvwxyz0123456789!?,"¢$&%{}*
12 pt. ABCDEFGHIJKLMNOPQRSTUVWXYZabcdefghijklmnopqrstuvwxyz0123456789!?,"¢
14 pt. ABCDEFGHIJKLMNOPQRSTUVWXYZabcdefghijklmnopqrstuvwxyz012
18 pt. ABCDEFGHIJKLMNOPQRSTUVWXYZabcdefghijklmno

48 pt. ABCDEFGHIJKLMN
OPQRSTUVWXYZ
abcdefghijklmnopqrs
tuvwxyz0123456789
!?,"¢$&%{}*

10/10

Our options for communication today range from the spoken word (on records and tapes) through handwriting and printing to the digital stored word or picture in a computer. Within the evolution of the spoken word, from the first letter-symbols in prehistoric caves to the electronically generated forms of the present, the developments and new techniques during the past centuries have been a continuous expansion of what preceded.

—Hermann Zapf

10/12

Our options for communication today range from the spoken word (on records and tapes) through handwriting and printing to the digital stored word or picture in a computer. Within the evolution of the spoken word, from the first letter-symbols in prehistoric caves to the electronically generated forms of the present, the developments and new techniques during the past centuries have been a continuous expansion of what pre.

10/14

Our options for communication today range from the spoken word (on records and tapes) through handwriting and printing to the digital stored word or picture in a computer. Within the evolution of the spoken word, from the first letter-symbols in prehistoric caves to the electronically generated forms of the present, the developments and new techniques during the past centuries have been a

Point size:	6	7	8	9	10	11	12	13	18	20	24	36
Chars/Pica:	4.49	3.85	3.37	3	2.7	2.45	2.25	2.07	1.5	1.35	1.12	0.75

Figure 5.24: A sample type speciman sheet for Palatino.

Caution! Typeface providers frequently use the same traditional name for their typefaces – such as Garamond or Futura. However, each firm will interpret the font design with some nuance of difference. Make sure, when printing out a document, that the type faces you or your service bureau use for printing are exactly the same as the ones used in the original document format.

As shown in Figure 5.24 on the previous page, a specimen sheet should show an entire type family in different sizes and weights. The sheet not only includes the alphabet, but one or more text elements in different sizes and leadings. It is customary to include information on the number of characters per pica for a given font size. This data allows the page designer to know in advance how much room a given type font will take, especially when compared to another font of the same size.

CHECKING YOUR UNDERSTANDING

1. Briefly explain how type can be classified according to size, weight, and slant.

2. Explain what is meant by type width and given an example.

3. Explain why the terms type font and typeface should not be used interchangeably.

4. Name at least three type families and give five variations for each.

5. Contrast between serif, sans serif, and mono-weight typefaces and give an example of each.

6. Hand print the word "Afghan" on your paper and label the parts of type that make up the letterforms.

7. Identify the units of measurement used in typography and explain their relationship to an inch.

8. Explain how the term "leading" is used differently by desktop publishers than in the traditional printing industry.

9. Distinguish between Postscript and other typographic formats

10. Explain the purpose and importance of using a type specimen sheet.

BUILDING YOUR DESKTOP PUBLISHING DESIGN SKILLS

1. Using your desktop publishing program and the text file you created for Design Skills, question 3, (on page 63, Chapter 3) do the following:

   a) Select typefaces for the formatting of your document. Assume your text will be used in a report that has a single-column (30-pica) format.

   b) Select main text and headline typefaces from those available on the system you are using.

   c) Print a copy of your document.

   d) Prepare a cover sheet that explains your choice of typefaces.

2. Collect four different publications (i.e., brochure, newsletter, advertisement or flyer, business report, and so on).

   a) Analyze the type used in each of the publications.

   b) Prepare a one- or two-page report that describes the classification of type used and provide an explanation as to why each typeface was used in each publication.

3. Using your desktop publishing system, make a sample type catalog for the available fonts. Use 12-point type and the format shown in Figure 5.23 as a guide.

4. Prepare a type specimen sheet for the type you used in exercise 1.

   a) Indicate all the faces and sizes used in the document.

   b) Format your specimen sheet similar to the specimen sheet shown in Figure 5.24.

DESKTOP DESIGN WORKSHOP

The purpose of this section is to provide you with opportunities to develop and/or improve your desktop publishing design skills. The worksheet pages have been placed at the back of the book, and are designed so they can be removed and you can write, draw, or place your responses directly onto the pages.

WORKSHEETS 5.1 AND 5.2

Knowing how to recognize type styles, type sizes, and line spacing will make planning your publications easier. This exercise will assist you in developing your skill identifying and matching type specifications.

1. Study the five sample fonts shown in column 1 of Worksheet 5.1. Indicate which of the following each font represents:

   a) Category
      — Serif
      — Sans serif
      — Decorative

2. Use the sample type scale on page 326 in the book or a commercial type scale and indicate the leading for the text samples in column 2 of Worksheet 5.1.

3. Use the sample type scale on page 326 in this book or a commercial type scale and indicate the size of each type used in sample text shown in column 3 of Worksheet 5.1.

4. Using the marked-up copy of the flyer shown in Worksheet 5.2, do the following:

   a) Using the fonts available on your desktop publishing system, select one or more fonts and prepared a type specimen sheet for the flyer. Output the speciman sheet on a laser printer.

   b) Using your type specimen sheet and the marked up copy, create and print a copy of the flyer. Use your type scale to measure the dimensions of the flyer.

6. TYPE AESTHETICS

When you finish this chapter you should be able to:

- *Determine an appropriate line length for a text-intensive document.*
- *Distinguish between word spacing and letter spacing and discuss the importance of each in page layout and design.*
- *Discuss the merits of justified and ragged-right text and give examples of publications in which each would be most appropriate.*
- *Use display type to add contrast to the printed page and to give cues to designated levels of importantance.*
- *Use decorative type to enhance the design of a publication.*
- *Position headings and subheadings in text-intensive documents so as to provide cues to the hierarchy of the content while expanding visual interest.*
- *Combine typefaces in a single document so that they complement one another yet add contrast to the ideas presented.*

IN THE PREVIOUS CHAPTER YOU WERE INtroduced to the basics of typography, or *what type is*. In this chapter, you will gain an understanding of the function of type — that is, *what type does*.

Type is more than just letters on a page—it is the medium that carries your message. Type can speak quietly or it can shout. It can create a mood, awaken interest, and suggest action. Type has unique characteristics that are powerful vehicles for influencing the reader (see Figure 6.1.) Appearance, tone, goodness of fit, readability, legibility, line length, word and character spacing, as well as the selection of type face, style, and sizes, all contribute to the aesthetics of your final pages. The control of these elements is where desktop designers display their design skills and artistic judgement. This chapter contains guidelines that will help you create readable, attractive publications.

READABILITY AND LEGIBILITY

Readability of the body text should be one of your major considerations when you first start to design page layouts for a printed piece. If your publication consists mainly of text, the readability and legibility of the typefaces you use is particularly critical. Moreover, you can't count on illustrations to attract interest on those occasions when type is all you have to work with.

LEGIBILITY

Legibility and readability are often confused. *Legibility* is the term that describes whether or not the type is actually decipherable by the reader. Legibility is concerned with whether or not the type is large enough to actually be read as well as how clean and well-defined the letters are. Small type that is legible to the average reader may not be legible to the very young or the elderly, or to the visually handicapped even with glasses. Type that is large enough but is printed on absorbent paper may also be illegible if letters are smeared or filled in. If you know that your publication will be printed on newsprint or other absorbent stock, choose type faces with large open counters (the enclosed areas of o's, b's, e's, etc.) and make sure that letters are not set too close together (see Figure 6.2.)

Type that contrasts poorly with the background can be illegible to the reader. If your text is printed in color, or on a colored background, allow enough contrast between them for the type to stand out. Pale gray or light yellow type on a white background, or, a dark green type on a black background will be barely legible to most readers.

Type running over an illustration presents another problem in legibility; you must make sure that the type stands out clearly from an illustration background by choosing the right color, size, and contrast (see Figure 6.2.) If you can, select an illustration that has relatively flat contrast tonalities in the areas where you plan to run the type. Avoid the use of hairline rules wherever possible, since these are usually swallowed up by the illustration. If you are working with body text, enlarge it by several points or run it in bold to increase its legibility. Type used in a shade of gray or a color is discussed in more detail further in this chapter.

a b c d e f g

Figure 6.1: Some typefaces used for publication design. Reading from left to right: Century Schoolbook; Bodoni Bold; Futura Bold; Garamond Light; Futura Light Condensed Italic; Palatino; Helvetica Light.

A.

Legibility describ es whether or no tthe type is decipherable by the reader.	4 point New Century Schoolbook
Legibility describes whether or not the type is decipherable by the reader.	8 point New Century Schoolbook

B.

Legibility	80% tint of black
Legibility	10% tint of black

C.

10 pt. Avant Garde is a type face with large counters (set normal)

10 pt. Avant Garde is a type face with large counters (set tight)

10 pt. Avant Garde is a type face with large counters (set very tight)

12 pt. Garamond is a type face with small counters (set normal)

12 pt. Garamond is a type face with small counters (set tight)

12 pt.Garamond is a type face with small counters (set very tight)

Figure 6.2: Factors for ascertaining type legibility. A. (top) compares legibility according to letter size. B. (center) compares legibility according to background/foreground contrast. C. (bottom) compares typefaces according to their x-height and to their setting — tight or normal.

Adobe Garamond
Berthold Bodoni Antiqua
Optima
Helvetica Condensed
Adobe Caslon
Goudy 1
Futura Condensed
TRAJAN, CHARLEMAGNE
Univers
Gill Sans I
Univers Condensed

Traditional letter forms

ADOBE WOOD TYPE 1
Mistral, Reporter No. 2
Park Avenue
ITC Benguiat
Friz Quadrata
COPPERPLATE GOTHIC
Arnold Bocklin
Wilhelm Klingspor Gotisch
VAG Rounded

Mannered letter forms

Figure 6.3: Traditional letter forms compared to mannered and exotic type faces.

READABILITY

Readability describes the ease with which you can comprehend a document, as well as the speed with which you can read it. Naturally, text legibility affects its degree of readability. Other ingredients that aid or hinder readability depend on how much text you have, how long the lines of text are in relation to the size of the type you have chosen, and how easy the type form itself is to read. Most readers find that a traditional type face is the easiest to follow when reading long settings of body text. Basically, it is a good idea to stay away from those faces whose shapes are mannered or exotic. Those are best used in headlines or other places where you want to catch the reader's eye before he or she starts to read (see Figure 6.3.)

Readability and legibility are the most important requirements for text type, especially in documents that have little or no illustration, such as photographs, drawings, and charts and graphs.

A publication that is meant to be read but is hard to read is badly designed, no matter how clever or fashionable the layout might appear.

Readability doesn't equate with dreariness, though. On the contrary, the more attractive and interesting your body text is in feeling and tone, and use of color and space, the more readable that design will be.

SERIFS AND READABILITY

Chapter 5 described the structural differences between serif and sans serif type. Whether you should choose one or the other for your text copy has to do with the kind of material you are working with. Serifs guide the eye along the line of text. Sans serif text does not share this ability, although you can use the white space or leading between the lines as a substitute. When your copy is set in sans serif, add one or two more points of leading between the lines to act as a guiding channel of white space to replace the nonexistent serifs. This is particularly important when ascenders and descenders are short in proportion to the x-height in the font you have chosen (see Figure 6.4.)

Sans serif type is more contemporary in design; it works well with numerical text and tables, as captions and callouts for photographs and illustrations, and for shorter blocks of text in any document. When there are many successive pages of text to be read, a serif face is less tiring for the reader to scan. When text segments are shorter, a sans serif type face works just as well, especially if you remember to add one or two more points of leading.

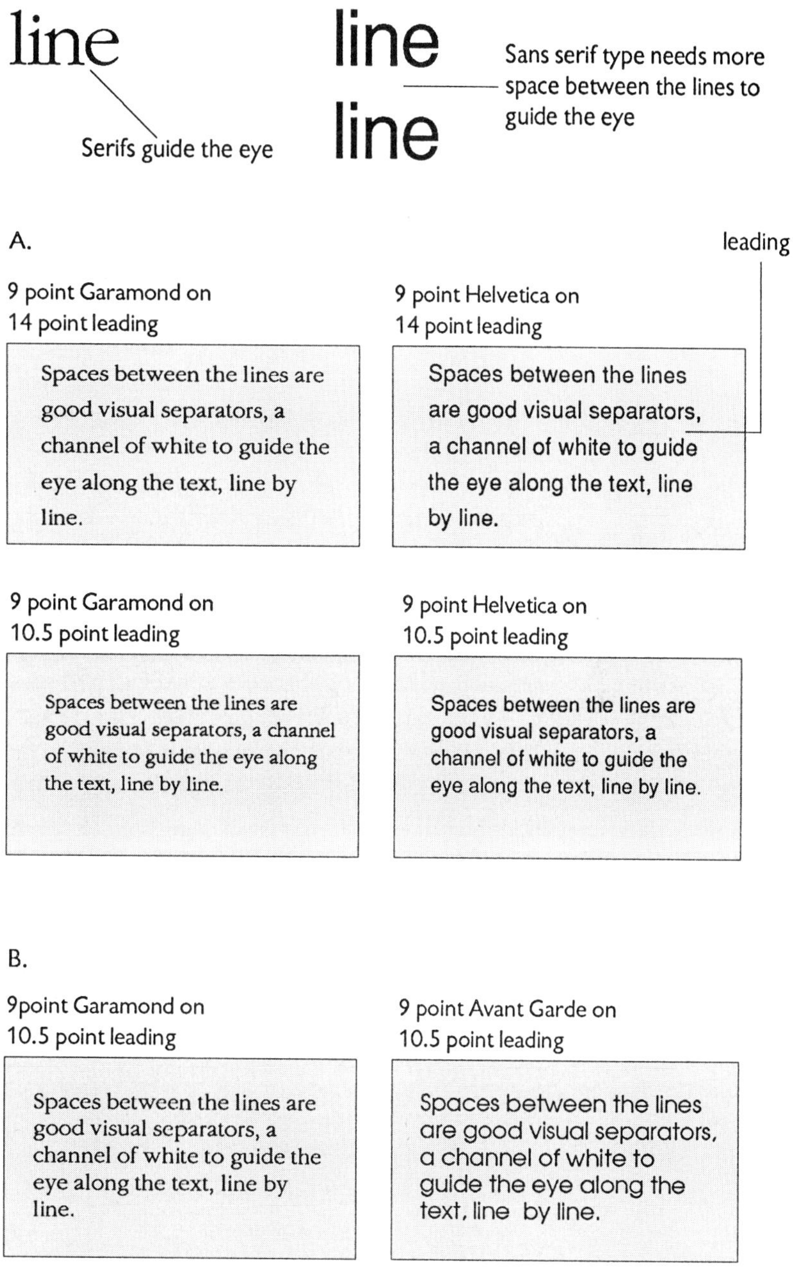

Figure 6.4: (top) The use of leading for serif and sans serif typefaces is demonstrated. A. Leading for Garamond and Helvetica are compared. (bottom) B. Leading is compared between Garamond with a small x-height, and Avant Garde with a large x-height.

COLOR AND READABILITY

When we talked about type and legibility, color was discussed in terms of legibility. Good use of color not only controls the legibility of your type elements, but also how readable they are. The color you have chosen will, in itself, communicate moods or ideas beyond the printed word. Since this book is limited to black and white, we will limit our examples to shades and tints of gray, but both color and black and white will be discussed as part of the text.

Hue is the term used for naming colors. If you are working with black ink on white paper, the color or hue you are using is black. *Saturation* or *value* is the amount or percentage of color that is being used. When you are using a gray tone in a tint block, the amount or percentage of black is the degree of color saturation that is present. Shades and tints are descriptions given to tonal values of colors other than black. A percentage of the pure color is called a *tint.* When a percentage of black is added to the color tint, it is called a *shade. Contrast* is the degree of tonal or saturation difference between one hue and another, or between percentages of one color.

WORKING WITH SHADES OF GRAY

A poster called "Type is to Read" was distributed several years ago. One section was devoted to showing how different faces of the same size look when printed in black over a range of gray percentages from white to black, and how those same faces looked appearing in white, over those same tones of gray. Typefaces in white are called *reversed type.* When you choose to reverse type out of the background, the typeface will be "white" or the color of the paper, while the background prints the gray tone that surrounds and outlines the type. If the background color is pale, the type will not stand out. In this poster, it was obvious that low contrast levels — dark gray with black, or light gray with white — were very hard to read, regardless of which typeface was used. Nonetheless, some faces were easier to read than others, based on their weight and structure (see Figure 6.5.)

Another aspect of readability and tonal value has to do with the weight or thickness of the letterform.

If for one reason or another, you need to work with colors that do not show enough contrast for good readability, you can increase the readability factor by making the type larger or by setting it in bold face.

By doing so, the contrast value appears to be greater because the type area is increased. For example, if you want your typeface to appear as a medium gray tint instead of black, choosing a sans serif bold for this purpose will read better than a Bodoni with hairline serifs (see Figure 6.6.)

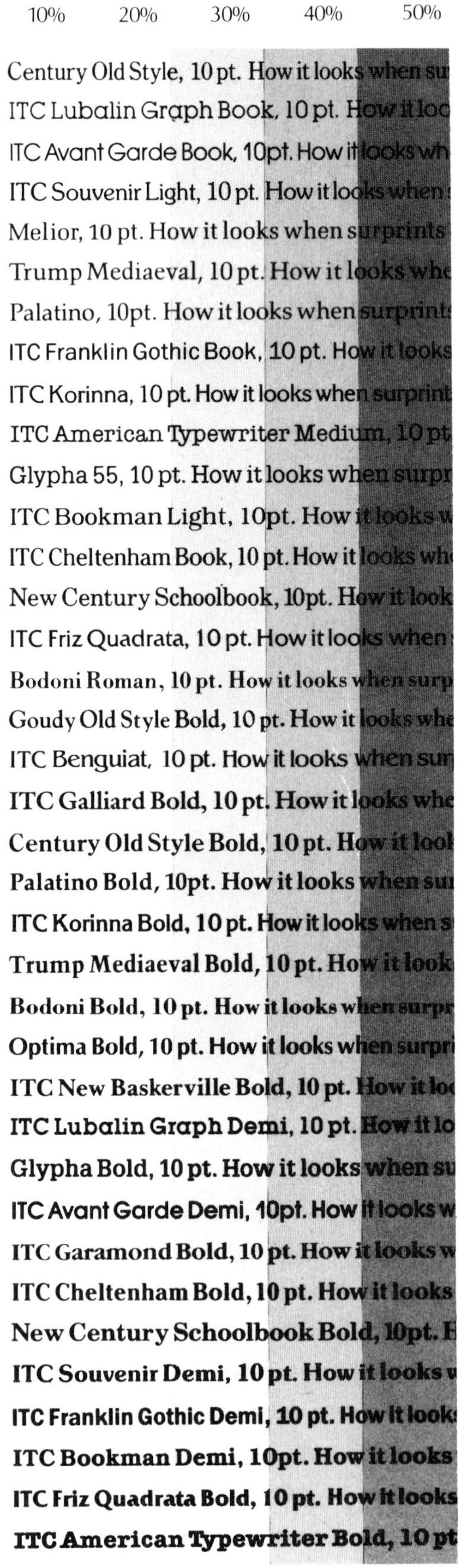

Figure 6.5: This type chart will help you choose an appropriate tint for a background box or page. (Courtesy Adobe Systems, Incorporated.)

60% 70% 80%

rprints over 133 line screen, f
ks when surprints over 13
en surprints over 133 line sc
surprints over 133 line screen
over 133 line screen, from
n surprints over 133 line sc
over 133 line screen, from
when surprints over 133 li
s over 133 line screen, from
How it looks when surpr
ints over 133 line screen, f
hen surprints over 133 li
en surprints over 133 line sc
s when surprints over 133 l
surprints over 133 line scree
rints over 133 line screen, fr
n surprints over 133 line scr
prints over 133 line screen
n surprints over 133 line sc
ks when surprints over 13
prints over 133 line screen
urprints over 133 line screen
s when surprints over 133 l
ints over 133 line screen, f
nts over 133 line screen, fro
oks when surprints over 13
oks when surprints over
rprints over 133 line scre
hen surprints over 133 line
hen surprints over 133 li
when surprints over 133 l
low it looks when surpri
vhen surprints over 133 li
s when surprints over 133 li
when surprints over 133
when surprints over 133
. How it looks when su

SOLID 90% 80% 70% 60% 50% 40% 30% 20%

Century Old Style, 10 pt. How it looks when reverses out from 133 line screen,
ITC Lubalin Graph Book, 10 pt. How it looks when reverses out from
ITC Avant Garde Book, 10 pt. How it looks when reverses out from 133 line
ITC Souvenir Light, 10 pt. How it looks when reverses out from 133 line scre
Melior, 10 pt. How it looks when reverses out from 133 line screen, fro
Trump Mediaeval, 10 pt. How it looks when reverses out from 133 line
Palatino, 10 pt. How it looks when reverses out from 133 line screen, fro
ITC Franklin Gothic Book, 10 pt. How it looks when reverses out from 133
ITC Korinna, 10 pt. How it looks when reverses out from 133 line screen, fro
ITC American Typewriter Medium, 10 pt. How it looks when reverse
Glypha 55, 10 pt. How it looks when reverses out from 133 line screen,
ITC Bookman Light, 10 pt. How it looks when reverses out from 133
ITC Cheltenham Book, 10 pt. How it looks when reverses out from 133 line
New Century Schoolbook, 10 pt. How it looks when reverses out from 13
ITC Friz Quadrata, 10 pt. How it looks when reverses out from 133 line sc
Bodoni Roman, 10 pt. How it looks when reverses out from 133 line screen,
Goudy Old Style Bold, 10 pt. How it looks when reverses out from 133 line sc
ITC Benguiat Book, 10 pt. How it looks when reverses out from 133 lin
ITC Galliard Bold, 10 pt. How it looks when reverses out from 133 line
Century Old Style Bold, 10 pt. How it looks when reverses out from
Palatino Bold, 10 pt. How it looks when reverses out from 133 line scre
ITC Korinna Bold, 10 pt. How it looks when reverses out from 133 line scr
Trump Mediaeval Bold, 10 pt. How it looks when reverses out from 13
Bodoni Bold, 10 pt. How it looks when reverses out from 133 line screen
Optima Bold, 10 pt. How it looks when reverses out from 133 line screen,
ITC New Baskerville Bold, 10 pt. How it looks when reverses out from
ITC Lubalin Graph Demi, 10 pt. How it looks when reverses out fro
Glypha Bold, 10 pt. How it looks when reverses out from 133 line sc
ITC Avant Garde Demi, 10 pt. How it looks when reverses out from 133 l
ITC Garamond Bold, 10 pt. How it looks when reverses out from 133
ITC Cheltenham Bold, 10 pt. How it looks when reverses out from 13
New Century Schoolbook Bold, 10 pt. How it looks when reverse
ITC Souvenir Demi, 10 pt. How it looks when reverses out from 133
ITC Franklin Gothic Demi, 10 pt. How it looks when reverses out from 13
ITC Bookman Demi, 10 pt. How it looks when reverses out from
ITC Friz Quadrata Bold, 10 pt. How it looks when reverses out from 13
ITC American Typewriter Bold, 10 pt. How it looks when reve

COLOR AS A COMMUNICATOR

Design principles for readability and contrast when using color are very much the same as those for black and white. Type in pale colors needs to be printed on dark color backgrounds, while dark colored type reads best on a lighter ground. If you choose to use a lighter color for your type against a light ground, readability is enhanced (up to a point) by increasing the size or weight of the type. Another item to consider regarding readability and color: Colors will always be less contrasty than when black and white are used. The lightest color will still be darker than white, and the darkest color will be lighter than black. To provide the best contrast, it is best to bold the face you are using when it appears in color or make it a point or two larger in size.

If you are using reversed type in a color tint block or on a full-color illustration, the type will appear smaller than the actual size you have chosen. To ensure that your message will be read or have the impact you desire, specify the type to be larger or bolder than similar copy appearing in black on white.

Earlier, we defined the saturation or value of a color as the amount or percentage of color that is being used. The degree of color saturation or value in a given color will affect the degree of contrast it will have with another color. For example, two very different colors of equal saturation, such as red and green, will not contrast well enough to read clearly. You can change the saturation or value of a color you have chosen by adding black to make it darker and white to make it lighter. When working on a computer, the white of the screen is what you add to the color. This is executed electronically by using only part of the fully saturated color, specified by a percentage. For example, if you specify a 50% red, it will appear as a rose color. If you specify a 15% red it will appear as a pale pink and will contrast well when used on a green background. A bright clean 100% red used on a very dark black-green will read quite well, especially if the type is a bold sans serif of 14 points or larger.

Colors can also be used for cueing purposes by applying an easily-seen color to a particular category of text or headline consistently throughout a document or publication. Using color in this way will alert the reader whenever it appears.

If you are using color as a cue, don't overdo it by splashing so much color all over the page that its value as a signal is lost. Keep in mind that if you decide to use that same color for anything else, you may confuse the reader as to which element has been selected for cueing.

READABILITY AND LINE LENGTH

During the design process, when you make decisions regarding line lengths for the text page, remember that a readable line is just long enough for the eye to scan without getting tired.

For good readability, a guideline that typographers follow is for the text line to be about one and one half to two times the length of a lowercase alphabet from 'a' to 'z.'

Using this guideline, a small typeface with a short alphabet length will be set proportionally shorter than a large typeface.

Another rule of thumb is that the appropriate line length (measured in picas) is two times the point size. In other words, if you are using a 24-point typeface, the line would be 48 picas long. When using large text type, remember, too, that the eyes also find it tiring to read very short lines, say three to four words from line to line, and finds hyphenated or broken words even harder to scan (see Figure 6.7.) The important thing to remember when considering line length is legibility. If you use a clear and easy-to-read type, the rules described earlier work well. However, if the type is small or somewhat harder to read, you may want use a slightly shorter line length than the formula suggests.

You can increase the readability factor by setting lighter colored type in a bolder face.

Increase the readability factor by setting lighter colored type in a bolder face.

Figure 6.6: A forty percent tint is used for both 12 point Bodoni Roman and Bodoni Poster. Readability is increased by bolding the type face when it is run in a light color.

JUSTIFIED, RAGGED RIGHT, OR LEFT OR CENTERED RAG?

Whatever style or size of typeface you choose, you need to decide whether to set the text in perfectly rectangular blocks, or blocks in which the line endings at either the right or left margins are uneven (see Figure 6.8.)

ABCDEFGHIJKLMNOPQRSTUVWXYZ
abcdefghijklmnopqrstuvwxyz

ABCDEFGHIJKLMNOPQRSTUVWXYZ
abcdefghijklmnopqrstuvwxyz

Figure 6.7: Alphabet lengths for 10 point and 16 point Bodoni Roman are compared.

Ragged right:

"Gutenberg's invention of movable letters convulsed an epoch and – from the Renaissance till the 20th century – left its stamp on a new one ... Gutenberg's method created the portable book which men could read in privacy and in isolation from others."
—Marshall McLuhan

Ragged left:

"Gutenberg's invention of movable letters convulsed an epoch and – from the Renaissance till the 20th century – left its stamp on a new one ... Gutenberg's method created the portable book which men could read in privacy and in isolation from others."
—Marshall McLuhan

Justified:

"Gutenberg's invention of movable letters convulsed an epoch and – from the Renaissance till the 20th century – left its stamp on a new one ... Gutenberg's method created the portable book which men could read in privacy and in isolation from others."
–Marshall McLuhan

Centered:

"Gutenberg's invention of movable letters convulsed an epoch and – from the Renaissance till the 20th century – left its stamp on a new one ... Gutenberg's method created the portable book which men could read in privacy and in isolation from others."
–Marshall McLuhan

Centered:

Mr and Mrs. John Jones

Mrs. Adele Smith

Request the honour of your presence

at the Marriage of their Son and Daughter

which will take place on Saturday, November17, 1991

a Reception will follow the Ceremony

Figure 6.8: Examples of text settings in 10 point Futura Light. The wedding invitation, centered and set boxed, is in 10 point Futura italic.

Figure 6.9: (top) Alternating tight and loose word spacing are a typical problem when text is set justified in a narrow text column. (bottom) A pull-quote set justified shows rivers of wide spaces between words.

depending on the desire and need for its power. These have included: price (it was always significantly more expensive than any competitor); the program's strange indifference to certain conventions of interface and usage, which might simply be intolerable to those versed in established ways; and finally, blizzards of features and labyrinths of precision inspiring fears of a steep learning curve.

These reasons don't exist anymore with the appearance of QuarkXPress 3.0. Quark hasn't raised its program's price, whereas its competitors have,

forces in yesterday's melee are being

The mounting political consciousness of Islamic peoples is spreading in both of these unions of highly diverse ethnic groups.

treated, a handsome Kashmiri youth dis-

JUSTIFIED

Traditionally, long passages of text such as those in books or lengthy magazine articles, have been set justified. *Justified* text appears as rectangular blocks with lines starting at the left margin and ending at the right. The reason for using justified text has to do with the way the eye behaves when reading (see Figure 6.9.) We scan text line by line, and mentally set a measure by which our eyes know how far to go from the beginning to the end of each line down the page.

As illustrated in Figure 6.9, the page layout program justifies text by distributing equal amounts of space among words in a line to make each line exactly the same length as all others. Justification also uses hyphenated words at line endings. Most page layout programs have hyphenation dictionaries that allow the computer to perform this task automatically. However, good page makeup suggests that you shouldn't have more than two hyphenated words in sequence at the right margin. Should this happen, either rewrite the text or use the automatic override in your software to break words manually.

If you decide to use justified text, be on the lookout for awkward white gaps that may appear. These white gaps in the text show up when a line is short and the next word cannot be hyphenated, causing word spacing to be increased abnormally. If this happens in several consecutive lines, a vertical "river" of white space develops, creating a distraction and causing the reader's eye to wander. These rivers can be seen easily by squinting at the text or holding the page upside down (see Figure 6.9.) Here, too, you can improve the look of poor typography by rewriting text or breaking words using your program's manual override.

Another problem that occurs in justified text, especially in narrow measures, is uneven character spacing. Some lines are spaced out to fill up the line, while others pack in as many characters as will fit into the space. Visually, a text column set this way looks like an accordion of letters, with some lines loose, and others open. Not only is this harder to read, but the gray tone of the text block varies unpleasantly to the eye (see Figure 6.9.)

RAGGED RIGHT

While justified text is often used for long documents, *ragged-right margins* are generally used for shorter documents. There is, however, no agreement on the merit of using justified text over ragged-right text. When ragged-right margins are used, the uniformity of spacing between words assists the reader in identifying word shapes. On the other hand, when text is ragged, the eye's scan line varies from line to line. It slows down the reading and tires the eye while doing so over many continuous pages. Rags can be set loose or tight, depending on the amount of space you allocate to the rag margin area, and also whether you choose to hyphenate or not. If the rag is too tight, with line endings almost, but not quite lined up, it can look like poorly set justified text. Very loose rags can look good when text is short, but are difficult to read in long settings. In addition, automatic ragging by computer may not always be visually pleasing. Good typographers generally proof the rag-set material and adjust unattractive line end shapes manually.

So, when choosing the text format, decide whether the text is long or short, and design accordingly.

RAGGED LEFT, FLUSH RIGHT

With flush right alignment, the text rags on the left with the extra white space set at the left margin (see Figure 6.8.) Flush-right text should be used only in small blocks and in a contoured shape as around a graphic since it is difficult for the eye to read long passages set in this alignment.

CENTERED RAG

When a more formal look is needed, such as for wedding announcements and advertising where elegance is featured, text may be set centered, and ragged at both the right and left margins. This text is not very readable except when a few lines are used, set wide apart. It is the most formal and elegantly traditional of typographic arrangements, but also the one most limited in use (see Figure 6.8.)

PARAGRAPH AESTHETICS

Paragraphs have always been given some kind of visual signal that lets the reader know when a new thought has started. There are several different kinds of markers you can use as cues. The most common is the indentation—a white space at the left margin of each new paragraph block.

When no indentations are used, the paragraph is referred to as a *block paragraph.* The use of additional leading (white space) between each paragraph block acts as the visual separator. This style is generally used in brochures, pamphlets, business reports, and often in manuals and textbooks.

A third separator is a typographic one, popularized by William Morris at the turn of the century. This style doesn't use any white spaces, but indicates a new thought through the use of a paragraph symbol or other graphic device. Typographers throughout this century have used variations of the typographic paragraph marker for article openers in magazines and brochures (see Figure 6.10.)

INDENTATION

Paragraph indentation is usually measured in em and en spaces. An *em space* is as wide as the point size of the type; an *en space* is one half an em space. For example, if 12-point type is being used, an em space is 12 points wide and an en space is 6 points wide. The most common indentation is the *first-line indent*, where a 1 em or 2 em space is placed at the beginning of the first line of each paragraph, with subsequent lines running flush left. When a paragraph follow a heading, it is generally set flush left, without an indent, since the head already acts as a visual marker. Stylistically, this treatment is cleaner and more decisive (see Figure 6.10.)

A hanging indent is the opposite of a first-line indent. The first line of a hanging indent is set flush with the left margin, and subsequent lines are indented 1 em or 2 em spaces (see Figure 6.10.) Hanging indents are often used for bibliographies, indexes, and numbered lists.

WORD SPACING

Word and letter spacing give the page visual texture. *Letter spacing* is the degree of closeness letters have to each other, based on the amount of space allotted to each character in the font. *Word spacing* deals with the amount of space between words (see Figure 6.11.)

Lines of text hold together better when word spacing is not too open in proportion to the leading—the space between the lines. Ideal word spacing dictates that the space between words should be wide enough so that words are clearly distinct from one another and do not run together. On the other hand, the spacing between words should not be so wide that the eye does not read the line of text as an unbroken flow. Ideal spacing uses the width of the letter "n" or "i," depending on the width, style, and word spacing of the type face you are using (see Figure 6.12.)

LETTER SPACING, TRACKING, AND KERNING

Letter spacing is concerned with the spaces between letters as an overall function of the

Figure 6.10: Examples of paragraph aesthetics. Text is shown set in 10 point Futura book in four different settings: a block paragraph style, a symbol used to mark paragraphs, a first line indent, and a hanging indent.

Block paragraph style:

"Gutenberg's invention of movable letters convulsed an epoch and – from the Renaissance till the 20th century – left its stamp on a new one...

Gutenberg's method created the portable book which men could read in privacy and in isolation from others."

— *Marshall McLuhan*

First-line indent paragraph style:

    "Gutenberg's invention of movable letters convulsed an epoch and – from the Renaissance till the 20th century – left its stamp on a new one...
    Gutenberg's method created the portable book which men could read in privacy and in isolation from others."

— *Marshall McLuhan*

Block style using a symbol:

"Gutenberg's invention of movable letters convulsed an epoch and – from the Renaissance till the 20th century – left its stamp on a new one... ❧ Gutenberg's method created the portable book which men could read in privacy and in isolation from others." ❧

— Marshall McLuhan

Hanging indent style:

"Gutenberg's invention of movable
    letters convulsed an epoch and –
    from the Renaissance till the 20th
    century – left its stamp on a new
    one...

Gutenberg's method created the
    portable book which men could
    read in privacy and in isolation
    from others."

— Marshall McLuhan

type face. The type designer allocates specific widths to each character as part of the original font design. Some page makeup programs allow you to change the widths inherent in the type font globally or in individual letter pairs.

TRACKING

Tracking and kerning are often confused by the person who is just starting to learn about type. Tracking refers to the setting for overall spacing relationships for all the characters in the alphabet set. Its characteristic is global. Some software will not allow you to change tracking, but more robust applications will allow you to specify tracking to be tight, normal, or loose. A tight setting means that characters are set very close together, but not touching.

Tight settings are very popular in advertising typography. Be careful that, in an attempt to be stylish, you have not destroyed the readability of the type and the aesthetic spacing intended by the type designer.

"Normal" is generally the way lengthy text is set — it is the way the font has been designed for best readability. Loose settings have a lot of space between characters and are hard to read in a text setting.

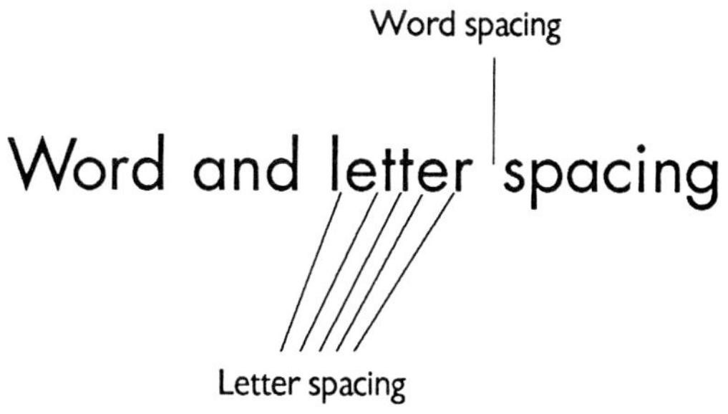

Lines of text hold together better when word spacing is not too open in proportion to the leading. Ideal word spacing dictates that the space between words should be wide enough so that words are clearly distinct from one another and do not run together.

Lines of text hold together better when word spacing is not too open in proportion to the leading. Ideal word spacing dictates that the space between words should be wide enough so that words are clearly distinct from one another and do not run together.

Figure 6.11: Loose and normal word spacing, compared. The text is set in 10 point Futura book.

Word spacing using an i

Word spacing using an n

Figure 6.12: Word spacing using an "i" space and an "n" space are compared.

Normal Tracking
Tracking refers to the all over character spacing used in setting type. Its characteristic is global. Some software will allow you to specify tracking to be tight, normal or loose.

Loose Tracking
Tracking refers to the all over character spacing used in setting type. Its characteristic is global. Some software will allow you to specify tracking to be tight, normal or loose.

Very Loose Tracking
Tracking refers to the all over character spacing used in setting type. Its characteristic is global. Some software will allow you to specify tracking to be tight, normal or loose.

Tight Tracking
Tracking refers to the all over character spacing used in setting type. Its characteristic is global. Some software will allow you to specify tracking to be tight, normal or loose.

Very Tight Tracking
Tracking refers to the all over character spacing used in setting type. Its characteristic is global. Some software will allow you to specify tracking to be tight, normal or loose.

Type sample set overlapping

Figure 6.13: Text tracking from very loose to very tight is compared in 10 point Bookman. At bottom is an example of 24 point Bookman set overlapping.

AT AW

AT AW

Figure 6.14: The top row of type is set without kerning. Type below has been kerned for better spacing.

Display type is generally set differently from the body text for a design objective. It may be letterspaced — that is, it may contain as much as 8 to 10 points between characters. It may be set very tight, even overlapping. A specification for tracking will depend on the face you have chosen and how it will be used (see Figure 6.13.)

KERNING: THE RELATIONSHIP BETWEEN LETTER PAIRS

Even with the best of care in font design, there will always be some letter combinations that are set too wide or too tight while the rest of the text looks good. When adjustments in spacing are made to specific pairs of letters, it is called kerning, particularly when taking out space between letters. This practice goes back to times when type was set using metal elements. If two letters did not look well together, the typesetter literally cut or kerned the metal on which each of the two letters were formed, to adjust the spacing.

The spaces between the letters in the pairs AW and AT are typical examples of what we call "negative kerning" today. Letters that looked visually tight, such as in the word "hill," were opened up by inserting thin leads between the type pieces. Today we call this practice positive kerning or letter spacing, although the description "letter spacing" is generally reserved for opening up the spaces equally between all the letters of a word or a line of type (see Figure 6.14.)

If you are fairly knowledgeable about type and its arrangements, you might be interested in using one of several type design programs that allow you to redesign the type spacing of a font you plan on using regularly. Fontographer and Font Studio on the Macintosh, and Type Foundry and Arts and Letters on DOS machines allow you to change both word and letter spacing for a font family fairly easily. Kerning pairs can also be adjusted to your personal preferences. These altered fonts can be saved under a different name and accessed as you would any other font. Such programs are intended for a more sophisticated user.

INTERLINEAR SPACING AND READABILITY

Text readability also depends on the interlinear spacing – the amount of leading to be used. Choosing the right amount of leading depends not only on the size of type and the leading you need for easy-to-read text. It can also affect the look you want (i.e., open and spacey, tight and authoritarian, or loose and flowing.) Most of the page makeup programs currently available will give you an automatic leading space.

When you are deciding on what text type to use, print out your choices in the size and width you have chosen. Include samples of several different leadings to look at.

You may find that for your particular design, the "auto" specification used by your page makeup program may not work as well as the selections made by your own eyes (see Figure 6.15.)

USING TYPE

A full page of body text, without cues to designate levels of importance, no matter how well planned, usually looks like a flat sea of gray. If you are designing a novel, solid text pages are the rule, but larger or display type is used to add visual contrast and variety at the beginning of each chapter. Other kinds of publications use display type for headings of different sizes. Headings not only break up and enliven the text, they also cue the reader as to levels of text importance.

CONSISTENCY AND RELEVANCE

CONSISTENCY

The grid arrangement of the page, body text, headings and other elements, provide the reader with information beyond that of the

Helvetica 10/12
Choosing the right amount of leading depends on the size of type you are using in proportion to the leading space alloted between the lines.

Helvetica 10/14
Choosing the right amount of leading depends on the size of type you are using in proportion to the leading space alloted between the lines.

Helvetica 12/14
Choosing the right amount of leading depends on the size of type you are using in proportion to the leading space alloted between the lines.

Helvetica 12/16
Choosing the right amount of leading depends on the size of type you are using in proportion to the leading space alloted between the lines.

Figure 6.15: Text leading examples.

BANNER HEAD

Major Heading or 1-Head

Sub-Heading or 2-Head

Sub-Heading or 3-Head

The Most Important Material:

The most important topics can be introduced in a headline and set in a bold large face that goes with the main text. It can be set in the same family as the main text, or else set in a contrasting face that works with it.

THE SECONDARY HEADING:

The secondary heading is used to introduce all those topics that are one level down from the main topic — like it says. A reader can tell just by looking at a page, the relationship scheme of the material.

The Third Head: A third level heading can be a run-in to the text, to identify a third level of importance, if your publication requires it.

Figure 6.16: (top) A hierarchy of headings, as follows: banner head, set in 30 point Helvetica regular; 1-head set in 14 point Helvetica bold; 2-head set in 14 point Helvetica regular; 3-head set in 12 point Helvetica regular.
(bottom) The paragraph example is set in Garamond 10/12 point.; The 1-head at the top of the text is set in 16 point Garamond Bold upper and lower case; the 2-head is set in 10 point Garamond bold small caps; the 3-head is set run-in in 10 point Garamond bold.

written word. High on the list is that of organizational consistency.

Do the reader a favor and place similar elements in the same spaces or location on a page throughout your publication.

For example, page numbers should always be placed in the same location, spread to spread, so that your reader will not have to search to find the page they are seeking. The same is true for type styles for each element. Once you have designed the text page and its headings, make sure that the design style for each element remains consistent throughout the publication. When you do this, readers unconsciously know what they are looking at, even before starting to read.

The size and style of headings at each level of editorial importance help the reader understand the logic of the sequences. Minor variations in the size of equivalent level headings are easily noticed, so avoid the temptation to increase or decrease the size of typeface in order to make the heading fit an available space. If you need to change a heading size, do so for all the heads of that particular level. If you are using style guides, style sheets, or a style palette, such as those provided by Ventura, FrameMaker, Design Studio, PageMaker and Quark, making a change throughout the entire document is very fast and easy (see Figure 6.16.) Review Chapters 3 and 4 for help with document structure and format.

RELEVANCE

Relevance refers to communication through visual emphasis. If your document contains a number of heads and subheads, the size and style of each level must be carefully chosen so as to maintain the relationship of the head to the hierarchy of the information. Logic, too, dictates that you don't place a large head in a document without a good reason. The size of the heads must be appropriate to the subject matter. Large heads, no matter how interesting they may appear, would be inappropriate if they make the copy look "padded" to fill more space than required.

Whatever decisions you may make regarding the selection of text and display type, the primary rule guiding your design should be that of relevance. Your ingredients include style, size, color, and area that the type element occupies. The particular kind of publication you are designing will guide you as to the mood of the document and its rules for readability (see checklist for typographic design, Figure 6.17.)

USING DISPLAY TYPE

Typographers usually divide type into two different use categories: text type and display type. Text type is set for readability, and occupies most of the space on the pages of the typical publication. Display type is larger and is used more sparingly — to attract attention, to break up long entries of text, and to provide a text outline for quick scanning. Display type can belong to the same type family as the body text, if it contrasts or stands out in some way. The designer can use either uppercase (capital) letters for contrast, or upper and lower case letters as long as they stand out from the body text. Size is one way to make a display type distinct from the body text. Other choices include the use of bold or italic, or a contrasting color or style.

UPPERCASE LETTERS FOR DISPLAY TYPE

Most body text typefaces can be set in solid capital letters (upper case) and used for emphasis, headings, or subheadings. Small caps are capital letters set at the x-height of the font. As shown in Figure 6.18 on the following page, capital letters used with small caps can be used and treated much as all upper case lines.

Care must be taken when using solid lines of upper case letters because they are more difficult to read than lowercase type. In type, the upper half of the x height, called

CHECKLIST FOR TYPOGRAPHIC DESIGN

✔ Type of document:

- ☐ Long *(serif typeface is suggested)*
- ☐ Short *(serif or sans serif typeface can be used)*

✔ Mood of document:

- ☐ Serious ☐ Conservative ☐ Traditional
- ☐ Light ☐ Humorous ☐ Contemporary
- ☐ Elegant ☐ Other ________________

✔ Nature of document:

- ☐ Primarily for information access *(avoid use of exotic type faces)*
- ☐ Many numerical tables *(use a sans serif type face)*

✔ Amount of text in relation to illustrations:

- ☐ 25% to ☐ 50% *(serif or sans serif typeface, ragged or block text)*
- ☐ 75% to ☐ All text *(serif typeface, with block text)*

✔ If there are illustrations, will they require captions and callouts?

- ☐ Captions ☐ Callouts

✔ Number of different levels of headings:

- ☐ 1 ☐ 2 ☐ 3
- ☐ 4 ☐ 5

✔ Required headings:

- ☐ Banner or very large ☐ Text 1
- ☐ Text 2 ☐ None

Figure 6.17

UPPER CASE

CAPS WITH SMALL CAPS

Figure 6.18: (top) 18 point Baskerville bold, all upper case. (bottom) The same face set in caps with small caps.

Figure 6.19: Capital and lower case letters demonstrating the "skyline" effect.

BOLDFACE FONTS

Boldface fonts are a heavy or darker weight of a typeface. Bold letterforms are usually about twice the thickness of the normal style, although different typefaces have different proportions.

Boldface Fonts

Boldface fonts break up large amounts of body text quite effectively. Boldface fonts are a heavy or darker weight of a typeface. Bold letterforms are usually about twice the thickness of the normal style, although different typefaces have different proportions.

Figure 6.20: Test setting using Baskerville 10 point text with Baskerville bold 12 point heading and subhead.

Italics are normally used with the body text to highlight foreign words and *to give special emphasis to selected words* or phrases.

Figure 6.21: 12 point Baskerville with italic.

the *skyline*, is what conveys most of the letterform information. In lower-case settings, there is more information gathered with less effort. Tests have shown that the upper half of the x-height has greater readability. Figure 6.19 illustrates the skyline effect.

BOLDFACE FONT

Boldface fonts are a heavy or darker weight of a type face. Bold letter forms are usually about twice the thickness of the normal style, although different type faces have different proportions. Boldface fonts, like those used in this text, break up large amounts of body text quite effectively. They do this when used to emphasize words or when used as headings or subheads. Care must be taken, however, not to use so many boldface headings or subheadings that they loose their effectiveness because the contrast between elements is reduced (see Figure 6.20.)

ITALIC FONT

Italic letter forms are characterized by light strokes inclined to the right, as in handwriting. Italics are normally used within the body text to highlight foreign words, to provide contrast for quoted sections, or to give special emphasis to words or selected phrases. Italic is less insistent than bold and may not be as effective as boldface for headings and subheadings (see Figure 6.21.)

UNDERLINING

Underlining was a popular method of providing variety and emphasis to body text when business documents were typewritten. Traditional underlining not only looks old-fashioned today, but when formatted from the computer, the underline rule is placed too close to the descenders for good typographic usage. Underlining should be avoided unless you set the rules graphically with the line or graphic tool in your page makeup program and place them at least 2 to 3 points away from the bottom of the descenders. Using the graphics tools in your page makeup program, you can vary the weight of your underlines from hairline rules to 2 points, 6 points, or even 12 points. If you like, you can place the rule *over* the type, as a design for a heading. See Figure 6.22 for examples of over and under rules made in page makeup programs. Try several combinations using different point sizes for rules and type and print them out for evaluation with your text.

FONT SIZE

All the popular desktop publishing programs allow you to set type in a variety of sizes. Mixing upper case and lower case letters of a size larger than the body text, as illustrated in Figure 6.23, can be more effective than using solid upper case letters.

SPACING DISPLAY TYPE

LINE SPACING

Headings and subheadings should be set off from the body text to break up the text blocks and to create interest on the page. All headings should be spaced for continuity of reading as well as for consistent line spacing.

> *As a rule of thumb, use less space below a heading than above it. With this arrangement, the heading is visually closer to its related text.*

Spaces above and below the heading should equal some multiple of the line spacing used in the body text. For example, if 10 point body text with 10 point headings is set with 12 points of leading (10/12), you might put points of space above the head and 3 points below (as shown in Figure 6.24) to demonstrate visually that the heading is attached to the body text it refers to.

You should keep in mind that more white space is generally better than less. If the spacing you have specified is unpleasing to you visually, try other settings.

LETTER SPACING IN HEADINGS

Spacing for major headings is often adjusted to attract the eye in ways that are unsuited

Example of a Heading Using a Rule Above the Text

Heading Using a Rule Set Below

Figure 6.22: (top) 14 point Baskerville bold with a 4 point rule placed above the first line of the heading. When two lines are used in a heading, the rule is placed above the first line only. (below) 14 point Baskerville bold with a hairline rule placed below the descenders in the text.

Upper and Lower Case Heading

"Gutenberg's invention of movable letters convulsed an epoch and – from the Renaissance till the 20th century–left its stamp on a new one.

Gutenberg's method created the portable book which men could read in privacy and in isolation from others." Today the "Gutenberg Galaxy" is approaching its end. A new age, the "Electric," is dawning. —*Marshall McLuhan*

Figure 6.23: The text is set in 10 point Baskerville while the heading is set in 16 point Baskerville upper and lower case.

"Gutenberg's invention of movable letters convulsed an epoch and – from the Renaissance till the 20th century–left its stamp on a new one.

Headings and Line Spacings

Gutenberg's method created the portable book which men could read in privacy and in isolation from others." Today the "Gutenberg Galaxy" is approaching its end. A new age, the "Electric," is dawning.

Total space base to base: 36 points

space above: 8 points

Heading: Futura Extra Bold 10/10

Space below: 4 points

Figure 6.24: Baskervill text set in 10 point on 12 point leading, with a Heading set in 10 point Futura Extra Bold.

Heading set tightly spaced

The Portable Book

Heading set letterspaced

T h e   P o r t a b l e   B o o k

Figure 6.25: A comparison of headings set tight and set letterspaced. Futura Bold condensed is used.

Flush Left Heading

Gutenberg's invention of movable letters convulsed an epoch. Gutenberg's method created the portable book which men could read in privacy and in isolation from others."

A.

Flush Right Heading

Gutenberg's invention of movable letters convulsed an epoch. Gutenberg's method created the portable book which men could read in privacy and in isolation from others."

B.

A Centered Heading

Gutenberg's invention of movable letters convulsed an epoch. Gutenberg's method created the portable book which men could read in privacy and in isolation from others."

A Centered Heading

Gutenberg's invention of movable letters convulsed an epoch. Gutenberg's method created the portable book which men could read in privacy and in isolation from others."

C.

A Centered Heading Set in Two Lines

Gutenberg's invention of movable letters convulsed an epoch. Gutenberg's method created the portable book which men could read in privacy and in isolation from others."

D.

Figure 6.26A, B, C, and D: Examples of various headline and text alignments.

to body text. Very tight spacing — spacing that results in letters touching, or even overlapping—is often used. On the other extreme, very open letter spacing — "extra" space between letters — is also used, with white space acting as the emphasizer. If you haven't had much experience working with type, it is best not to use exaggerated spacing, as there is a fine line between good and poor use of letter spacing. If you are a beginner in this area, start a scrapbook of headings that you find interesting from magazines, newspapers, and desktop design articles. Use these as examples for experimentation (see Figure 6.25.)

ALIGNMENT OF HEADS

While there are no hard-and-fast rules as to where titles and headings are to be positioned relative to its accompanying body text, there are some conventions that apply, depending on the situation and your choice of typeface.

FLUSH-LEFT HEADS

The most common position of all headings, or heads as they are more commonly referred to, is flush-left. This is true whether the body text is set justified or ragged and applies to heads set in all upper case, upper case and lower case, or all lower case. As illustrated in Figure 6.26A, there is an informality to body text set ragged-right, and the flush-left head appears most at home above such body text. Notice, too, that the less formal upper case and lower case type complements this look.

RAGGED-LEFT HEADS

As shown in Figure 6.26B, heads may also be set ragged-left or flush to the right-hand margin. Heads set ragged-left work well with informal ragged-right body text. However, care must be taken when using ragged-left headings. As you may recall, the eye relies heavily on returning to a common left-hand margin to make reading flow, so a ragged-left setting is best used only with heads or short lines of text.

HELLO MEGAN!

CENTERED HEADS

The formality of the centered head works well with the formality of justified text. You should not attempt to combine a centered heading over text set ragged-right, because the right hand margin is too variable to allow for accurate centering (see Figure 6.26C.)

The grouping of the lines in a centered, multiple-line heading is an important consideration. If the lines are too nearly the same length or staggered too radically, the grace of the symmetry is lost. However, staggered lines with a loose rag at each end adds a pleasant look to formal business reports where a traditional look is wanted (see Figure 6.26D.)

SIZE OF DISPLAY TYPE

The first rule here is to use what fits. Make the available space work for you. If you only have one available line for the heading, your options are a bit more limited. When determining the size of type to use for a heading, consider the factors of relationship and consistency. In flyers and covers, the design of titles is usually a major part of the job. Large size type works well here.

TYPOGRAPHIC AESTHETICS

The practice of elegant, knowledgeable typographic usage does not necessarily limit you to a few typefaces.

If you are just starting out as a desktop typographer, confine your use to a few basic type families and master as much as you can about their visual characteristics.

Review the overall look of the face, the design of the serifs, its weight in relation to its structure, its weight in relation to other faces, the nature of its thicks and thins and their relationship within the letterform. When you understand a type face on this level, you will know how to choose two or three fonts that will work well together on a page. As you gain confidence with typographic mastery, you will be free to play with type aesthetically, adding new visual interest and excitement to your work.

STARTER GROUP OF TYPE FACES

Getting to know the basic characteristics of several font families will help you to design more varied and interesting publications.

Below are a list of type faces suitable for both text and display. Become familiar with these or similar faces. Learn to handle them with ease, in their entire families of weights and stresses. Make samples for yourself in several sizes and leadings (see Figure 6.27.)

STARTER GROUP OF TYPE FACES

Serif Faces	Sans Serif Faces
Baskerville	Futura
Bodoni	Gill Sans
Caslon	Helvetica
Century Schoolbook	Optima
Garamond	Univers
Lubalin Graph or Memphis	
Palatino	
Choose one decorative face:	
Americana or Tiffany	
Eras	
Korinna	

Figure 6.27: A starter group of type faces.

THE 26 LETTERS: USING TYPE AS AN ACCENT

THE SINGLE LETTER

INITIAL LETTERS IN TEXT

The single letter can be used to "punch up" a visual design. Traditionally, a single large capital letter has been used at the beginning of a paragraph as a beautiful decorative element. In medieval manuscripts they were combined with illustrations, colored, and embellished with gold leaf to decorate the page and impress the reader. Today, initial capitals are used to draw the reader's eye to the place where the text begins, and to decorate the page (without the gold leaf, though.)

Like all decorative type elements, large initial capital letters should be used with care and applied sparingly, at the beginning of a document, a chapter, or an article in a magazine. As illustrated in Figure 6.28, there are several ways of using large capital letters, all of which take time to create and position. While large capital letters add a decorative element to the publication, a poorly placed large capital can make the first word of the paragraph difficult to read, thus detracting from its message.

THE SINGLE LETTER AS A HEADLINE ACCENT

The single letter can also be used within a headline as an added accent to catch the eye or to add a light touch to the page. To use this technique, pick out one letter in a word or heading and set it large, in relation to the other type used in the line. See how it adds snap to a headline, or punches up the opener for a magazine story or a chapter in a book (see Figure 6.29.)

Bolding a single letter within a word gives the word it is attached to visual importance. It adds interest to the page when it is well done — but be careful not to overdo it. This technique can be applied to one level of heading that will be used consistently throughout a publication. Letter spacing, too, can be used in conjunction with the large or bolded letter to design special headlines.

USING ONE TYPEFACE FOR ELEGANCE

As a basic rule of thumb, the novice designer should stay with a single type family. When using a single type family to design your pages, you simplify the task of visually analyzing type structures to see whether two different type faces will work together. For

Figure 6.28: (left) A contemporary example of an initial cap letter used as a paragraph opener. A sans serif type is used — the capital letter is italic bold used with a small letterspaced roman light text. (right) A traditional cap initial letter in a version by Adobe.

DESIGN WITH TYPE

Figure 6:29: A single letter is used here as an accent within a line of serif text.

an **a**pple a day

example, if you select 10 point Century Schoolbook for your main text, your major heading could be a larger Century Schoolbook — a 16 point bold upper and lower case. Your second head could be a 10 point Century Schoolbook bold all caps. A third heading, should you need one, could be a 10 point Century Schoolbook bold, run in to the text (see Figure 6.30.)

The use of a single typeface throughout a publication is a safe path for the novice designer to take, but not always the easiest when attempting a truly eloquent design. Using only a single typeface requires a good visual balance among all the typographic elements. Where appropriate, an exciting use of accent elements such as large single letter treatments and interesting spatial arrangements are needed to complete the image.

COMBINING TYPEFACES WITH PANACHE

As you have seen in Figure 6.30, the use of a single typeface with variations in size, weight, italics, and capitals letters, lend variations in shape and tone; it doesn't, however, add any contrast of visual ideas. The use of a companion typeface for headings can provide that diversion by adding another stylistic dimension to the publication and furnishing a different emphasis or tone beyond that of the single face. Moreover, the use of a complimentary pair of typefaces is the easiest for the first-time designer to work with.

One of the most traditional use of companion faces is that of a serif type such as the Garamond, Century Schoolbook, or the ubiquitous Times Roman for body text and a sans serif like Futura, Univers, or Helvetica for heads. By combining two typefaces that are so different in structural style, the distinction between the two is clear.

Use good judgment when combining typefaces so as to avoid a mixture of color, tone, and letter shapes that is unpleasant to the eye or is visually confusing. One of the most important rules of thumb is to use no more than two typefaces in a publication.

There are occasions where you can use more than one secondary display face, depending upon the project. Newsletters, for example, can accommodate a variety of type styles if the text and picture material to be presented

Typography

is the basic medium we present our ideas with.

It is necessary that we treat type with great care in communicating these ideas. Typographic style needs to be straight foreward to be easily read. However, the page needs to have style to give it visual appeal for the reader which can also add to the effectiveness of the message.

Figure 6.30: Use of a single type face for a heading with a variation of the same type for the body text.

is complex. Manuals, too, may require several different type styles. Formal reports and other business documents, on the other hand, tend to look cluttered if too many different typefaces are used (see Figure 6.31.)

When selecting companion typefaces, be sure your intent is clear. A typeface might fit nicely with your layout, but contradict the text's message. A typeface normally associated with computer automation would not be too attractive to factory workers in the garment industry! Likewise, a fancy or very contemporary typeface won't carry the proper message to the board of directors for a major corporation. There is no substitute for good judgment. Bad combinations tend to look bad. You will recognize them easily.

It's much less common to see Helvetica or some other sans serif typeface used for text, and Times or other serif typeface used for display type. One can argue that since every piece of visual language is different, the unusual typographic combinations are usually those we haven't seen or thought of yet. Figure 6.32 shows you a number of typeface combinations; good, bad, and middling. Follow it for suggestions on which face to use with which.

Type can be chosen to make words stand out or to set a mood. Figure 6.33 shows some examples of type that expresses a mood or a word picture.

If you are unsure of choosing good typeface combinations, you might be interested in packages for specific desktop publishing use, where the selection has been made for you. Several type companies including Adobe and Monotype have provided packages of

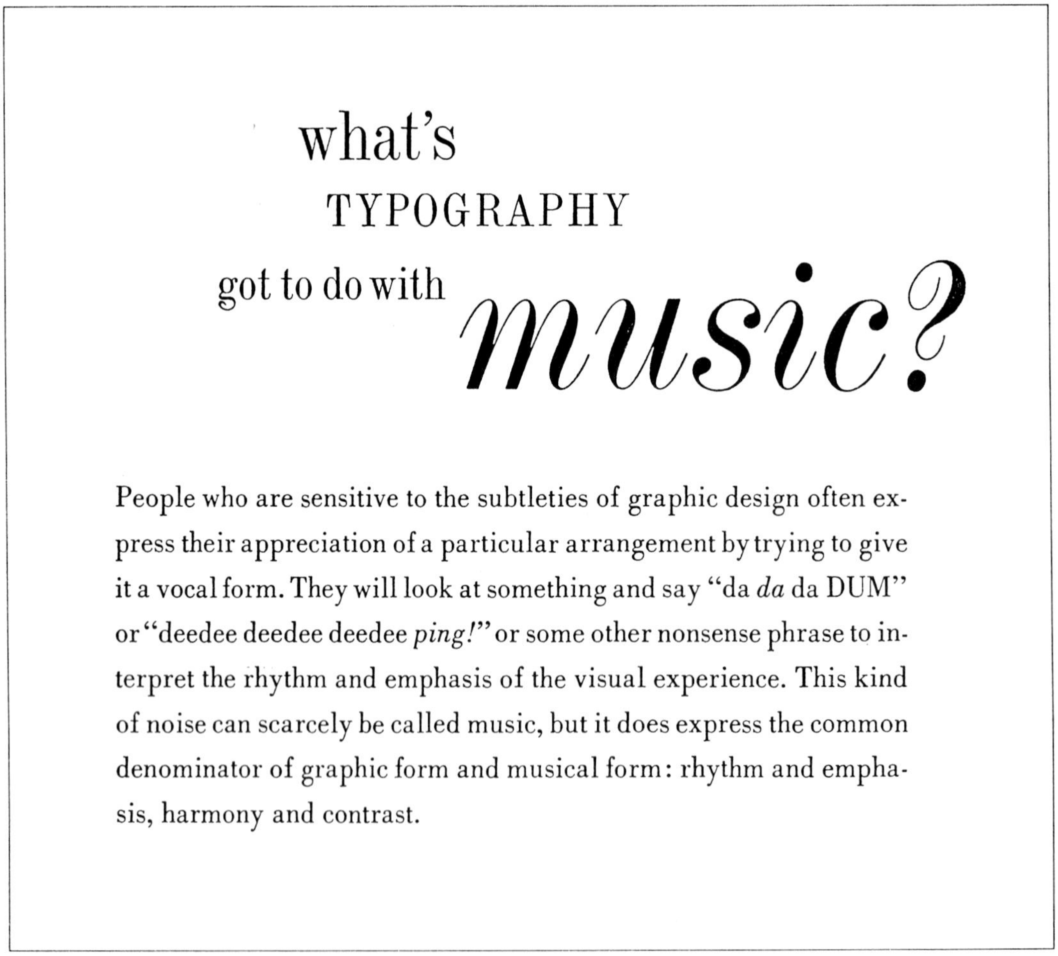
what's
TYPOGRAPHY
got to do with *music?*

People who are sensitive to the subtleties of graphic design often express their appreciation of a particular arrangement by trying to give it a vocal form. They will look at something and say "da *da* da DUM" or "deedee deedee deedee *ping!*" or some other nonsense phrase to interpret the rhythm and emphasis of the visual experience. This kind of noise can scarcely be called music, but it does express the common denominator of graphic form and musical form: rhythm and emphasis, harmony and contrast.

Figure 6.31: Example of three different type faces used in one document (courtesy Westvaco, Inc.)

TYPEFACE COMBINATION CHART

● OK
◍ Caution
○ Don't Use

TEXT \ DISPLAY	Americana	Antique Olive	Baskerville	Bembo	Bodoni	Bookman	Caslon	City	Copperplate Gothic	Cheltenham	Eurostyle	Franklin Gothic	Fritz Quadrata	Futura	Garamond	Gill Sans	Goudy Old Style	Helvetica	Lithos	Lubalin Graph	Minion	New Century Schoolbook	Optima	Palatino	Perpetua	Times Roman	Trump Medieval	Univers	Zapf Book
Americana	●	●	◍	◍	○	○	◍	○	●	○	◍	●	●	●	○	●	◍	●	●	○	◍	◍	●	◍	◍	○	●	●	○
Antique Olive	●	●	●	●	●	●	●	●	●	●	○	○	○	◍	●	◍	●	○	○	●	●	●	○	●	●	●	●	○	●
Baskerville	○	●	●	○	○	◍	○	●	●	○	◍	●	◍	◍	○	●	◍	●	●	○	◍	○	●	○	○	○	○	●	○
Bembo	○	●	○	●	○	○	○	○	●	○	◍	●	◍	◍	○	●	◍	●	●	○	○	○	●	○	○	○	◍	●	◍
Bodoni	○	●	○	○	●	◍	○	◍	●	○	◍	●	◍	●	○	●	○	●	●	○	○	○	●	○	○	○	○	●	○
Bookman	○	●	◍	○	○	●	◍	●	●	○	●	●	●	●	○	●	◍	●	◍	◍	◍	◍	●	◍	○	◍	◍	●	◍
Caslon	○	●	◍	○	○	○	●	◍	●	○	◍	◍	●	◍	○	●	○	●	●	○	○	○	●	○	○	○	○	●	○
City	◍	○	◍	○	◍	◍	○	●	○	◍	○	◍	○	○	◍	◍	○	◍	○	○	○	○	◍	◍	◍	◍	◍	●	◍
Copperplate Gothic	●	○	●	●	●	●	●	○	●	●	○	○	○	○	●	○	●	○	○	○	●	●	◍	●	●	●	●	○	●
Cheltenham	○	●	○	○	○	●	◍	●	●	●	●	●	●	◍	◍	●	●	●	●	◍	◍	●	●	◍	◍	◍	●	●	◍
Eurostile	◍	○	●	●	●	●	●	○	○	●	●	○	○	○	●	○	●	○	○	◍	●	●	●	○	●	◍	●	○	●
Franklin Gothic	●	○	●	●	●	●	●	○	○	●	○	●	○	○	●	○	●	●	○	●	◍	●	●	●	●	●	●	○	●
Fritz Quadrata	●	○	◍	◍	○	◍	◍	○	◍	●	○	○	●	○	◍	●	●	●	○	◍	◍	◍	◍	◍	◍	◍	●	●	●
Futura	◍	○	◍	●	◍	●	●	●	○	◍	◍	◍	●	●	●	○	●	○	●	◍	●	●	○	●	●	●	●	○	●
Garamond	○	●	○	○	○	○	○	◍	●	◍	◍	●	◍	●	●	●	○	●	●	○	◍	◍	●	○	○	○	●	●	◍
Gill Sans	◍	○	●	●	●	●	●	◍	●	◍	○	○	●	○	●	●	◍	●	●	●	●	●	●	●	●	●	●	●	◍
Goudy Old Style	○	●	○	○	○	○	○	◍	●	○	◍	●	◍	●	○	●	●	●	●	◍	○	○	●	○	○	○	◍	●	○
Helvetica	◍	○	●	●	●	●	●	◍	○	◍	○	○	◍	○	●	○	◍	●	◍	◍	●	●	◍	●	●	●	●	○	◍
Lithos	●	○	●	●	●	◍	●	○	○	○	○	○	○	○	●	●	◍	○	●	◍	●	●	●	◍	◍	●	◍	○	◍
Lubalin Graph	◍	○	◍	○	◍	●	◍	●	○	◍	◍	●	●	◍	◍	◍	○	●	◍	●	●	●	○	●	●	●	●	◍	◍
Minion	○	●	○	○	○	◍	◍	●	●	◍	◍	●	●	●	◍	●	◍	●	●	○	●	●	●	◍	◍	○	◍	●	◍
New Century Schoolbook	◍	●	○	○	○	◍	○	●	●	○	◍	●	◍	●	○	●	○	●	●	◍	○	●	◍	○	○	○	●	●	◍
Optima	●	○	●	●	◍	◍	●	●	●	◍	◍	●	●	○	●	◍	◍	●	●	◍	●	●	●	●	●	◍	●	●	●
Palatino	○	●	○	○	○	○	○	●	●	○	◍	◍	●	◍	◍	●	○	●	●	◍	◍	◍	●	●	○	○	○	●	○
Perpetua	○	●	○	○	○	◍	○	◍	●	◍	◍	●	●	●	○	●	○	●	●	◍	○	○	●	○	●	○	○	●	○
Times Roman	○	●	○	○	◍	◍	○	●	●	◍	◍	●	●	●	○	●	◍	●	●	◍	○	○	●	○	○	●	◍	●	○
Trump Medieval	○	●	○	○	○	○	○	◍	●	◍	●	●	◍	●	○	●	○	●	●	◍	○	○	●	○	○	○	●	●	○
Univers	●	○	●	●	●	●	●	●	○	●	○	○	○	○	●	○	◍	○	○	◍	●	●	◍	●	●	●	●	●	●
Zapf Book	○	●	○	○	○	○	○	◍	●	◍	●	●	◍	●	○	●	○	●	●	○	○	◍	●	●	○	○	◍	●	●

Figure 6.32: A typeface combination chart to help make better typeface choices.

Figure 6.33: Experimental typographic arrangements. (Top, by Rod Clarke, London; bottom left, courtesy Toni Hollander, The Design Works; bottom right, courtesy René Sheret Design.)

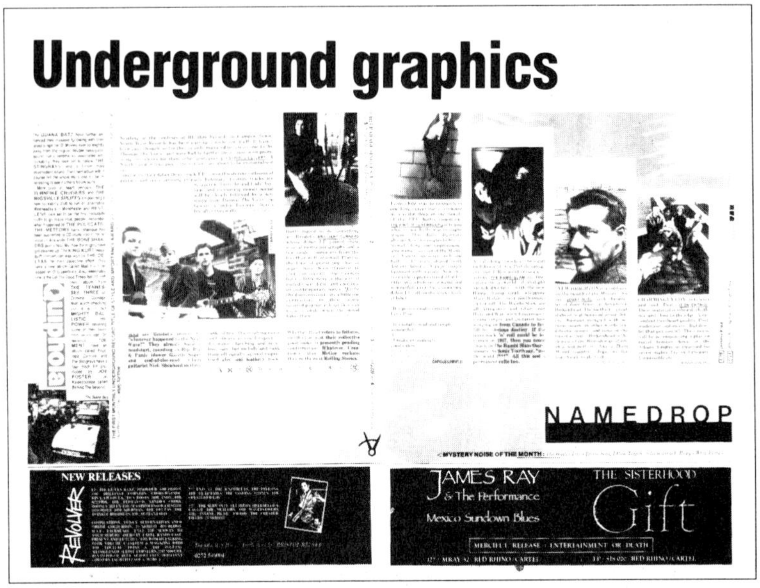

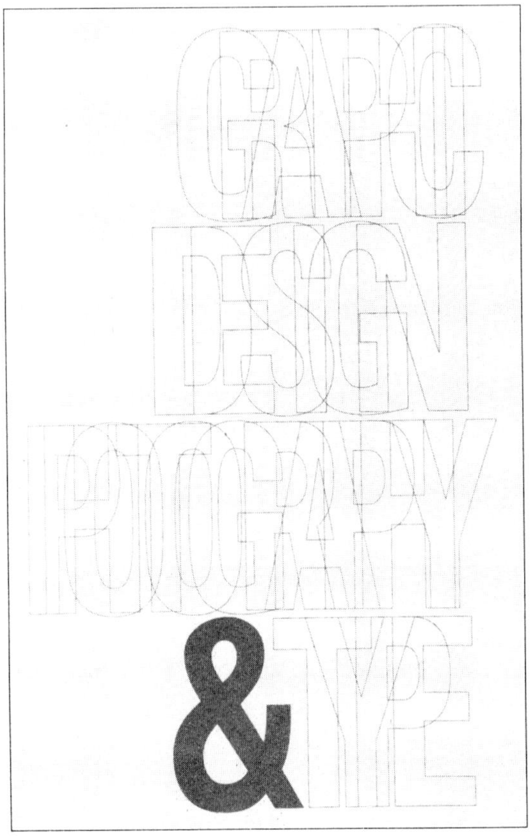

two or three type families that combine well together, for several different purposes. These include combinations selected for newsletters, business reports, forms, presentations and catalogues.

EXPERIMENTAL TYPOGRAPHY

The eclectic designs seen in contemporary publications can be interesting to look at, explosive, or on the edge. They can also be impossible to read. This use of type is experimental, and more concerned with communication using images rather than language. The new wave or experimental designer works with type almost as the illustrator uses paint and brushes to create a visual image (see Figure 6.33.)

Experimenting with type can also include the use of layering — each layer designed to blend with the whole, but also as an individual piece of text that could be read separately. Other methods include setting some or all of the type on a page at different angles, and in different sizes. Results can be exciting, interesting, chaotic, or a visual mess, depending on your abilities as a graphic designer.

CHECKING YOUR UNDERSTANDING

1. Distinguish between readability and legibility.

2. As a rule of thumb, what is the appropriate line length as measured in picas?

3. Distinguish between word spacing and letter spacing, and indicate when each should be used.

4. Distinguish between tracking and kerning, and explain what is meant by tight, normal, and loose track settings.

5. Identify and describe four types of alignments for body text in terms of where the line endings appear.

6. Describe five types of display type and indicate an appropriate use of each type.

7. Identify the two factors that must be considered when determining the proper size type to use and indicate why each is important.

8. Identify two guidelines that need to be considered when combining typefaces in a single publication, and indicate the reason for each one.

9. What are the typographical units used to measure indentation, and how do they relate to font size?

10. Identify four ways of using large capital letters as a decorative feature.

BUILDING YOUR DESKTOP PUBLISHING DESIGN SKILLS

1. Obtain or photocopy a page from a publication with a two-column format and one with a three-column format.

    a) Compare the typefaces used for the body text and the headings and any display type used in these publications. Write a one-page critique of these sample pages.

    b) Comment on whether you think the designer selected appropriate typefaces and used the display type to best advantage. If you feel better choices could have been made, explain why and give your suggestions for improvement.

2. Select a one-page, text-intensive publication with a design and layout you feel you can improve upon, and do the following:

    a) Keyboard the text from the publication using your word processor, or use the GREEK.TXT (DOS) or GREEKED TEXT (Mac) on your data disks.

b) Using your desktop publishing program, redesign the page using type faces, line space, word spacing, and alignment you think will improve the readability, tone, and appearance of the document.

c) Save and print a copy of your publication.

DESKTOP DESIGN WORKSHOP

The purpose of this section is to provide you with opportunities to develop and/or improve your desktop publishing design skills. The worksheet pages have been placed at the back of the book, and are designed so they can be removed and you can write, draw, or place your responses directly onto the pages.

WORKSHEETS 6.1 AND 6.2

Worksheets 6.1 and 6.2 contain the unformatted test for two sections of an annual report that is being designed for Worthington Corporation, an international manufacturer and marketer of goods and consumer products. Since the company's founding in 1942, it has operated in over 30 countries and markets its well-known brand-name products in more than 145 countries around the world.

1. Look at the headings used in the two worksheet pages. Then, using what you have learned about type aesthetics, do the following

    a) Design an appropriate Mission, Financial Goals and Strategies section using the typefaces, line spacing, word spacing, leading, and alignment available in your desktop publishing program. Use the GREEK. TXT (DOS) or GREEKED TEXT (Mac) on your data disk and create the appropriate headings.

    b) Design an appropriate layout for the Financial Performance section (assume it will be five pages in length) of the report, using the typographic features described above. Assume the shaded boxes are charts and graphs. You may adjust the length of the greek text to fit the sample page design.

2. Save and print a copy of your pages.

7. GRIDS: WORKING WITH STRUCTURE AND SPACE

When you finish this chapter you should be able to:

- *Understand reasons for standardizing publication designs.*
- *Identify the use of modularity and repeatability in publications.*
- *Design a basic formal grid for your publication.*
- *Use the basic formal grid for thumbnailing your design ideas.*
- *Execute intuitive grids.*
- *Understand how to use grids to emphasize horizontality and verticality in your designs.*
- *Use the Golden Mean as a basis for design proportions.*

ONE EFFECTIVE WAY TO ORganize document pages using grids was described in Chapter 3, *Document Structure.* This chapter will show you how to design a grid that will give your publication a planned, cohesive look. It will also allow you to place text and graphics quickly, especially for ongoing publications such as company reports and newsletters.

THE SENSE OF ORDER

The notion of grids should not be new to you — they are part of our natural world. Think about the repetitive curves of sea shells, the multifaceted faces of mineral crystals, and the symmetries of living things including plants, birds, fishes, and mammals. They are all based on some form of gridded or repetitive structure, as shown in Figure 7.1.

Many cognitive psychologists believe that people are sensitive to experiencing orderly, arranged patterns in nature; using it as one of the biological mechanisms for functioning in the world. For example, if you were given the sequence of numbers *1, 2, 1, 2, 1, 2,* wouldn't you expect that the next number in the sequence would be a *1*? It is a form of mental economy not to have to rethink the sequence once it is understood. The way elements are arranged and balanced on a page evokes a

Figure 7.1: Examples of orderly patterns found in nature.

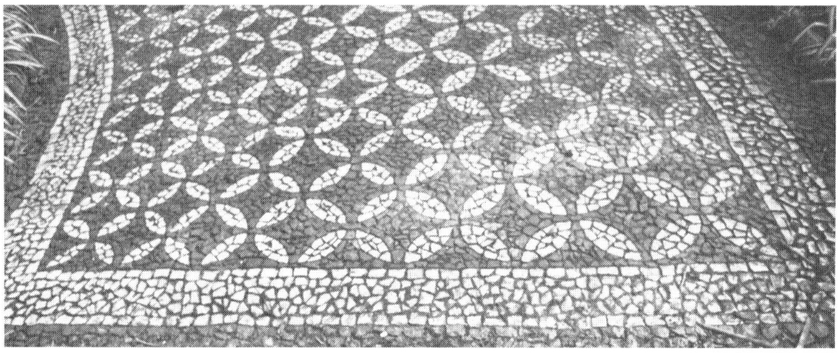

Figure 7.2.A repeated pattern using tiles.

Figure 7.3: Use of repeated patterns with changes and variations in architecture.

similar template for pattern recognition and creates the expectation that the pattern will continue (see Figure 7.2.)

People have used repeated patterning for centuries, in everything from wallpaper patterns to city plans. E. H. Gombrich, a noted art historian and psychologist, has said that "the arrangement of elements according to similarity and difference and the *enjoyment* of repetition and symmetry extend from the stringing of beads to the layout of the page in front of the reader, and, of course, beyond to the rhythms of movement, speech, and music."[1]

According to Gombrich, another reason for pattern recognition is because perception requires an orderly framework against which change can be viewed as a contrast to regularity. The *break* in the order is what arouses the viewer's attention. This sensitivity to orderliness, and breaks from it, is thought by some art historians to manifest itself in the creative arts such as music, painting, and graphic design (see Figure 7.3.)

Publication designers use a grid to give their publications a planned, cohesive look, and to help ensure consistency from one page to the next.

GRIDS: THE UNDERLYING STRUCTURE OF PAGE COMPOSITION

There are many advantages to using repetition and symmetry in designing page layouts for books, magazines, brochures, and business documents. Apart from the innate enjoyment of and comfort in repeated patterns described by cognitive psychologists, repeated patterns such as those imposed by a grid make text easier to read. They are also an aid to understanding complex information. Businesses that use standard, uniform styles and spatial arrangements for letters, reports, shipping labels, and the company logo transmit a distinct company image that implies efficiency and consistent reliability (see Figure 7.4.)

A page grid is made up of a series of non-printing vertical and horizontal lines that divide the page into units and sections. The elements making up the document are placed within the grid in a consistent and orderly fashion. Some of these elements are visual, such as type and illustrations. Others elements are spatial, marking locations for placing text, illustrations, and margins — the outer framework for the page. The grid is the underpinning or skeleton of the document. It may be compared to the staff used in a music score. The lines of the staff represent a formal structure, but within this structure there is a seemingly limitless freedom of expression. In much the same way, the structure of lines representing a grid is merely the basis for creative expression in your page designs.

For a review of document structure, look at Chapter 3, and Chapter 4, *Designing Form With Content,* in which the structural elements that compose a document are discussed.

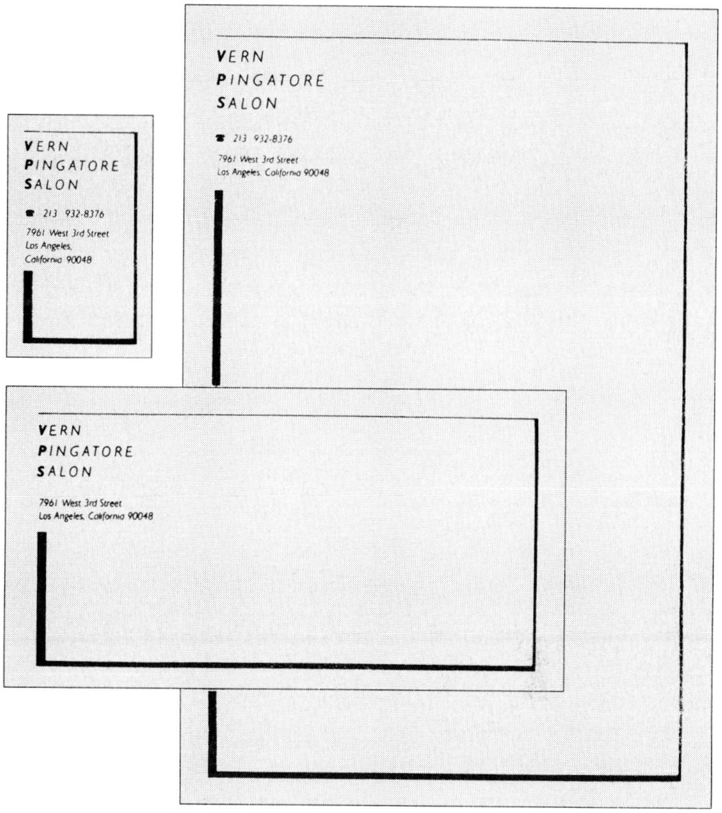

Figure 7.4: Business letterheads and cards are a form of uniform arrangements.

TYPES OF GRIDS

Grids may be of two types, formal and intuitive. The *formal grid* is the easiest one to use. As shown in Figure 7.5, the formal grid's basic design does not vary from one two-page page spread to another; it remains constant. The positioning for every element in the document is planned in advance and is continued from one page to the next in a publication. This type of grid is ideally suited to computer page layout programs, since automated repeatability is one of the things a computer is expert at.

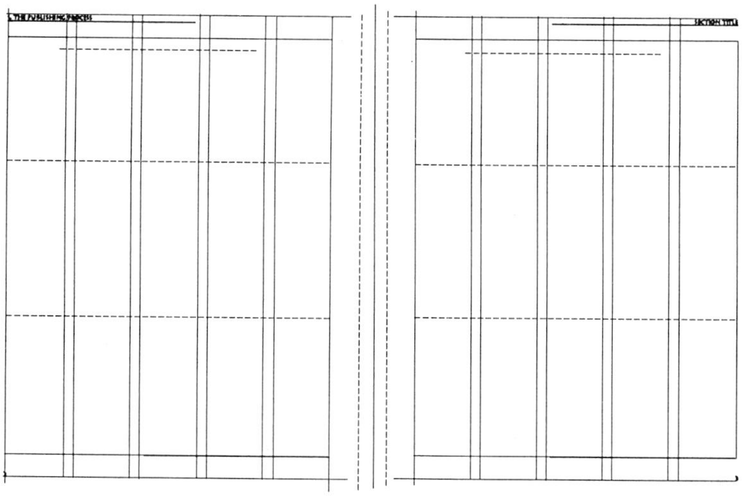

Figure 7.5: A formal structural grid for a five column publication.

The *intuitive grid* can be used to invoke a more interesting arrangement than that of the formal grid. As shown in Figure 7.6, the intuitive grid permits an arrangement of the elements based on some pleasing set of visual relationships in the mind's eye of an experienced designer. In using an intuitive grid, the designer arranges the elements according to their visual content in order to emphasize a desired communication. Generally, the intuitive grid is used for one to several pages.

Not all graphic designers use just one type of grid. Formal and intuitive grids can be combined in one publication to produce a more interesting overall design. For example, a formal grid can be used for the major portion of a magazine or manual and an intuitive grid used for certain parts, such as a photo essay or the section openers. As illustrated in Figure 7.6, you provide a visual break in the regular arrangement of the formal grid by incorporating an intuitive grid to place photographs or headlines that will catch the reader's eye.

The exclusive use of an intuitive grid is not for lengthy reading material such as novels or textbooks.

The variable arrangement of the intuitive grid is generally difficult to follow for more than a few pages at a time. Using a formal grid will help you to design material that avoids unwanted surprises for your readers. Your design should be one that keeps the reader's attention focused on the consistent text flow that a formal grid supports. Brochures and flyers and some magazines, on the other hand, often benefit from the surprise emphasis of intuitive arrangements. If your experience as a graphic designer is limited, you will do better to stick to stricter grid arrangements. Keep in mind too, that complex page design is based on content and editorial concept along with the taste, talent, and experience of the designer.

If the focus of the publication is on its text message, the page design should not distract the person from reading the text.

Figure 7.6: (left) Pages and art arranged within a formal grid. (right) Photographs arranged in an intuitive grid (courtesy B.T. Glenn)

GRID ARRANGEMENTS IN NEWSPAPERS, MAGAZINES, BROCHURES

Even when your page layout design is a formal grid, you will find that you can sketch thumbnail arrangements that become more interesting, visually, with practice. It will help your design if you keep the following rules in mind:

- ✔ *Balance the elements*
- ✔ *Provide a dominant element*
- ✔ *Direct the reader's eye movement*
- ✔ *Use white space wisely*

Strive for imaginative well-ordered arrangements with good continuity and flow. Place the elements in your publication so that they lead the eye from one part to the next on each page or spread, and from one page to the next as the text continues. Chapter 4 discussed some of the techniques you can use to direct the reader's attention. You can emphasize vertical or horizontal stresses, depending on how you place and crop graphics and photographs. If a grid is made up of several column widths, you will have more flexibility for making different graphic arrangements than with a grid using just one or two columns.

ONE-COLUMN GRIDS

The number of columns you decide to use is usually related to the size of the page of your publication, its margins, and the size of your text type. A simple one-column grid requires relatively little planning and allows you to place text and graphics quickly. If you are designing a 5 x 7 page, a one-column grid is generally pleasing and will provide a readable line length (see Figure 7.7.) If you recall from Chapter 6, *Type Aesthetics,* the optimum text line for good readability measures from one and a half to two times the alphabet length of your chosen text type.

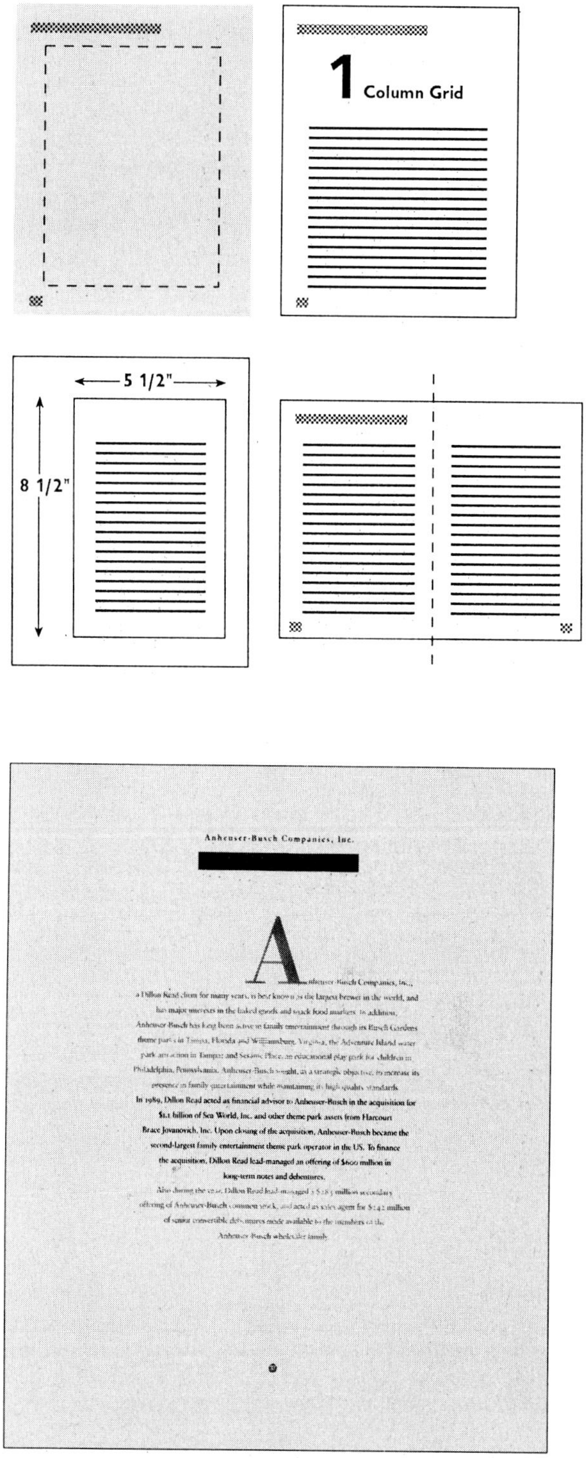

Figure 7.7: (top) A one column grid for an 8 1/2 x 11 size page. (center left) example of a one column grid for a 5 1/2 x 8 1/2 page. (center right) A reader spread for 5 1/2 x 8 1/2 facing pages on a landscape 8 1/2 x 11 page. (bottom) A page based on a one-column grid.

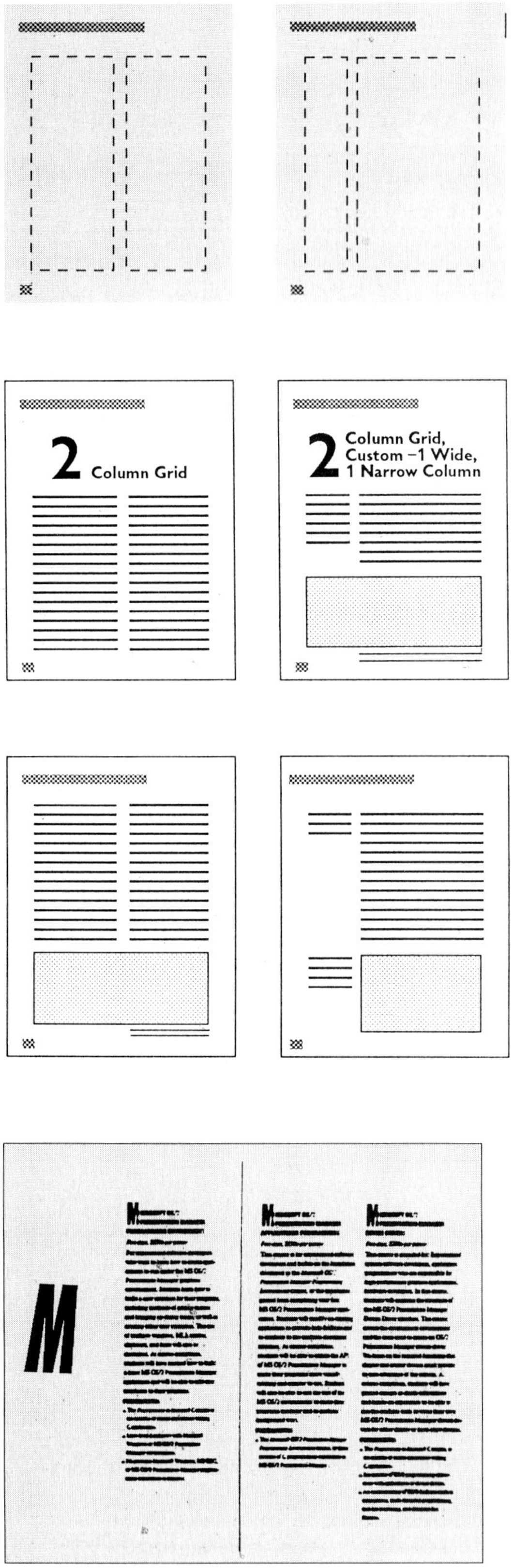

Figure 7.8: Several versions of a two-column grid

If your page size is 8-1/2 x 11, the most common business size, a one-column grid can present readability problems, unless you make sure that your text area is no more than twice the alphabet length of the type you are using. Increasing the size of your text, or using wider margins can help keep your text pages within suitable proportions. An advantage to using wide margins is that diagrams, subheadings, short quotes, or small photographs can be placed in this margin space.

Better solutions may be available in a two or more column grid. As illustrated in Figure 7.8, when you increase the margins, you can choose to put all of the extra space in the left and/or right hand margins, or in the gutter margin if you are using a spread of facing pages. If you are using facing pages and put all your space into either the inside or outside margins, the text on the reverse side of the page will occupy the same space as the front side. In the trade, this is called *backing up.* Backing up will reduce the possibility of any text showing through the page from the back side.

TWO-COLUMN GRIDS

Many variations are possible when you use a two-column grid. This format works for many different kinds of publications, including brochures, newsletters, annual reports, price lists, and bulletins. The standard solution is that of using two columns of equal size. While this grid is easy to work with, it can look stodgy or boring. Another solution that is frequently adapted is that of a narrow column for headings and captions, and a wide column for text as shown in Figure 7.8. A useful proportion is for the narrower column to be half the size of the wider one. When these proportions are used, the wide column can be subdivided into three columns and used quite effectively for a glossary or index.

While the two-column grid allows the use of a lot of text per page, don't try to fit in too much. You may find yourself creating unwieldy and monotonous pages that are hard to read.

Be creative in the way you choose to break up a two-column text mass:

- ✔ *Choose type for your heads that contrasts well with the text mass in its size and density.*
- ✔ *Position your heads to break up categories and sections of the text information.*
- ✔ *Aim for effective use of charts and graphs, illustrations and photographs.*

THREE-COLUMN GRIDS

A three-column grid can also provide many interesting layout variations. A grid made up of three columns of equal width can be used for three-column text. You can place headlines, art work, boxed copy, and other elements across any one, two, or three columns. Since you have a short line length due to the narrow columns, you can use a smaller type face for the body text—anywhere from 8 to 10 points, depending on your choice of typeface and the size of its x-height. Figure 7.9 shows several spatial variations that you can adapt using the three-column grid.

FOUR-COLUMN GRIDS

The four-column grid can be used with several variations, similar to those described for a three-column format. Four columns of equal width or two equal double-width columns can be used. The narrow column and a wide column made up of three widths is another

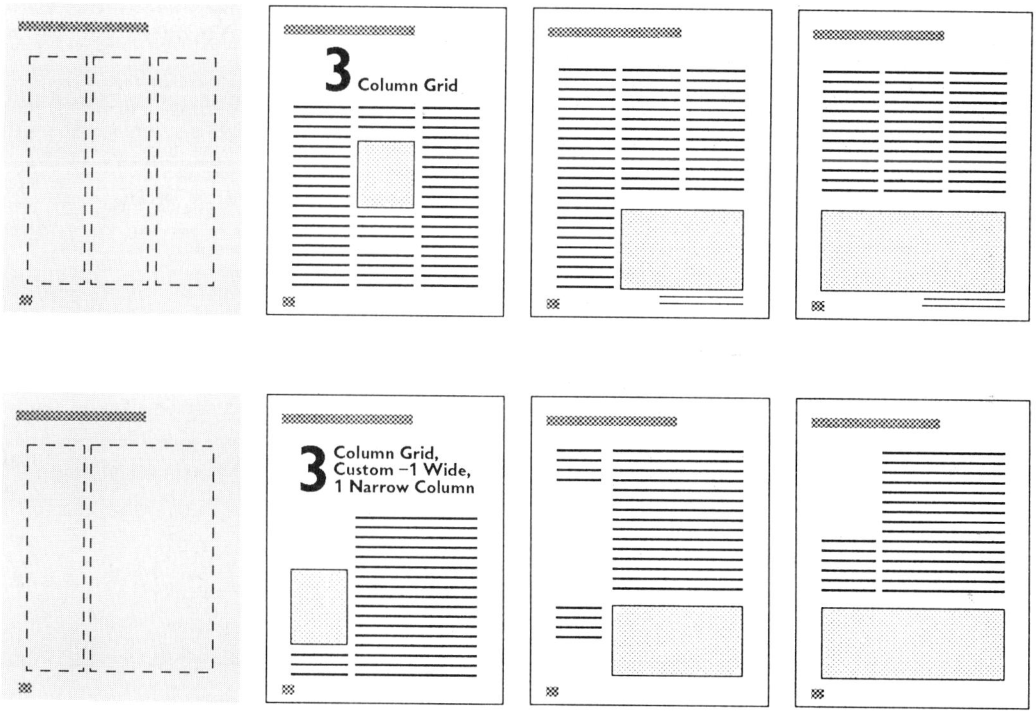

Figure 7.9: Examples of a three-column grid.

Figure 7.10: Examples of a four-column grid

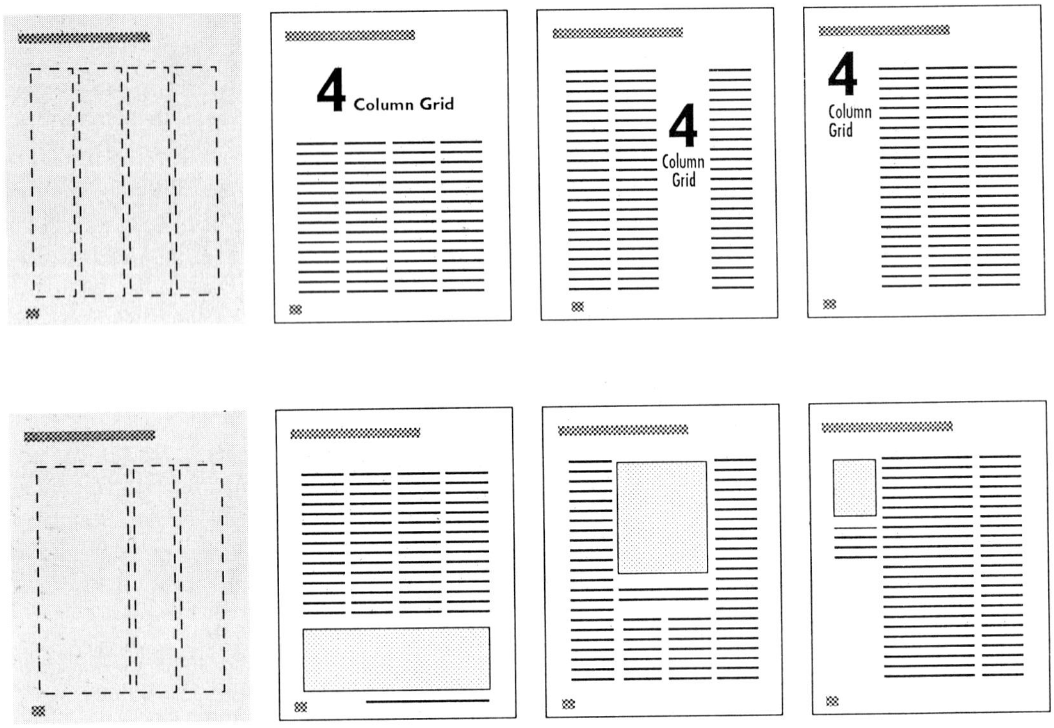

Figure 7.11: Examples of a five-column grid

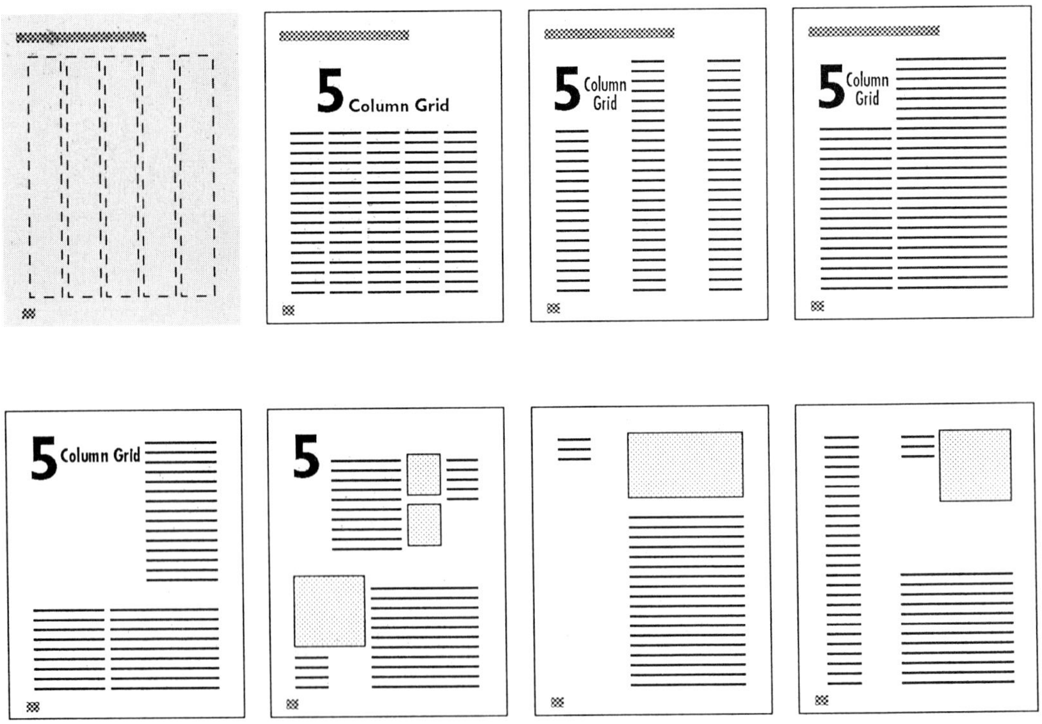

variant for text and illustrations. Figure 7.10 shows several possible arrangements.

Here again, this format permits you to use rules, boxes, and headings to break up the text. The four-column layout also allows you to design visuals in a variety of sizes, since a photo or illustration can be placed in one column or run across two, three, or four columns without looking awkward on the page.

FIVE-COLUMN GRIDS

As the number of columns are increased, many more variations are possible. In the five-column format, using five equal column widths allows you to use many interesting asymmetrical arrangements. As shown in Figure 7.11, the five-column format can also be used to support a two-column page text format by combining two narrow columns to form each text column, leaving a narrow single-width column for heads and captions.

REQUIREMENTS FOR COMPLEX GRIDS

Each structural element in a publication needs to have its place in the grid plan. Both the visible and invisible elements as described in Chapter 3 need to be included. In order to construct the grid, you will need to have a fairly complete design worked out typographically, using thumbnails and full-size roughs of all the elements in your publication. In the process of constructing the finished grid, you will be completing the final design for your publication.

To construct a grid, provide the information for each of the items on the Grid Planning Worksheet shown in Figure 7.12. The following paragraphs are a review and tutorial to help you fill out the Grid Planning Worksheet. The items listed below are for reference only; you do not have to fill them out. Document elements have been covered in Chapter 3, should you want to review them.

Margins: Although margins themselves are not made up of elements of type and are considered as white space borders on a page,

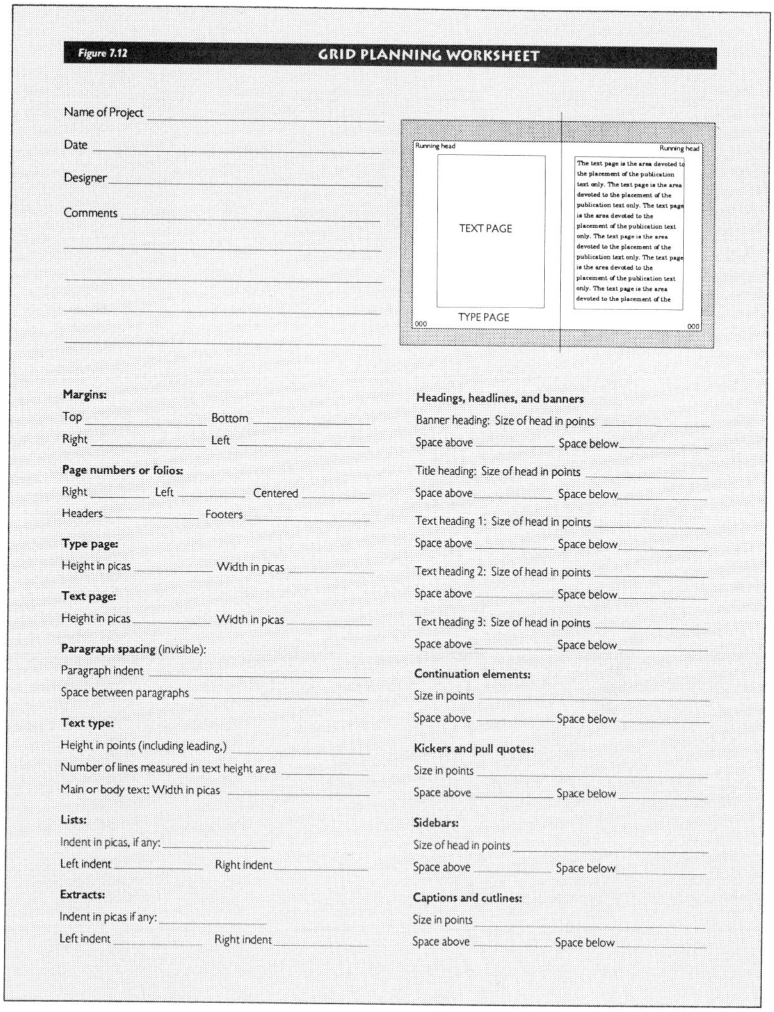
Figure 7.12 GRID PLANNING WORKSHEET

Name of Project ____
Date ____
Designer ____
Comments ____

Margins:
Top ____ Bottom ____
Right ____ Left ____

Page numbers or folios:
Right ____ Left ____ Centered ____
Headers ____ Footers ____

Type page:
Height in picas ____ Width in picas ____

Text page:
Height in picas ____ Width in picas ____

Paragraph spacing (invisible):
Paragraph indent ____
Space between paragraphs ____

Text type:
Height in points (including leading.) ____
Number of lines measured in text height area ____
Main or body text: Width in picas ____

Lists:
Indent in picas, if any: ____
Left indent ____ Right indent ____

Extracts:
Indent in picas if any: ____
Left indent ____ Right indent ____

Headings, headlines, and banners
Banner heading: Size of head in points ____
Space above ____ Space below ____
Title heading: Size of head in points ____
Space above ____ Space below ____
Text heading 1: Size of head in points ____
Space above ____ Space below ____
Text heading 2: Size of head in points ____
Space above ____ Space below ____
Text heading 3: Size of head in points ____
Space above ____ Space below ____

Continuation elements:
Size in points ____
Space above ____ Space below ____

Kickers and pull quotes:
Size in points ____
Space above ____ Space below ____

Sidebars:
Size of head in points ____
Space above ____ Space below ____

Captions and cutlines:
Size in points ____
Space above ____ Space below ____

Figure 7.12: Grid Planning Worksheet form, reduced. The full sized version is in the forms section of the Workbook/Forms Appendix.

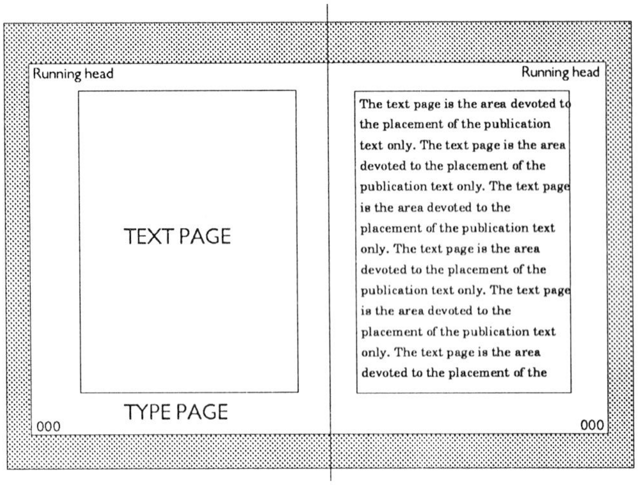

Figure 7.13: A type page and a text page, compared.

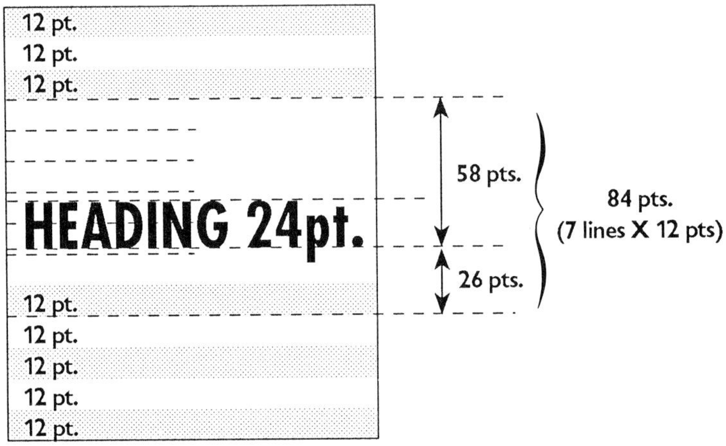

Figure 7.14: Section of a grid indicating a major heading.

they usually include running headers or footers and page numbers.

Top__________ Bottom__________

Right__________ Left__________

Page Numbers or **Folios:**

Right______ Left______ Centered______

Headers__________ Footers__________

Type Page: The type page is the total area for type placement on a page. It is measured from the top of the header or page number (in the margin above the text area) on the page to the lowest text element, usually a folio or a footer, depending on the design.

Height in picas______ Width in picas______

Text Page: The text page is the area devoted to the placement of the publication text only. Text page measurements differ from those of the type page in that only height and width of the text area is measured. Page numbers outside the text area, headers, and footers are not included. Printers usually ask for measurements for both text and type pages, especially if you are doing longer publications. Figure 7.13 shows a comparison between text and type pages.

Height in picas______ Width in picas______

Text Elements: You will need to create styles for your text elements.

Paragraph Spacing (invisible)

Paragraph indent________________

Space between paragraphs________________

Main or body text: Width in picas__________

The size of the text page should be a multiple of the height of the text type. If the body text is 10 points on a 12 point measure, base to base, then the height of the text page should be 12 points or 1 pica times the number of lines needed to fill the space between the top and bottom page margins.

Text type height
including leading, in points ____________

Number of points
measured in text height area ____________

The number of points in the text height divided by text type height equals number of lines per page. If the result is not a whole number, adjust the margin or text height to the closest number of points that will result in a whole number.

Lists: Lists are often indented from the main text margins. They may be indented from the left margin only, or from both margins.

Lists: Indent in picas, if any:

Left indent ________ Right indent ________

Extracts: Like lists, extracts can be indented from the left margin only, or from both margins.

Extracts: Indent in picas if any:

Left indent ________ Right indent ________

Headings and Headlines and Banners: The space for each heading or headline, including the space allowed above and below it, measured baseline to baseline, should be a multiple of the text plus its leading height. For example, if you have a main heading measuring 24 points and your text height with leading is 12 points, you could fit your heading into a space measuring 84 points measured baseline to baseline, as shown in Figure 7.14. The spaces above and below the head do not each have to be multiples of 12 points, as long the total measurement is. In the example shown in Figure 7.14, space below is 26 points, baseline to baseline. Space above is measured from the baseline of the headline to the base of the previous line of text is 58 points. 26 points plus 58 points equals 84 points, or 7 times 12.

Banner Heading: Size of Head in Points

Space above________ Space below________

Title Heading: Size of Head in Points________

Space above________ Space below________

Text Heading 1: Size of Head in Points

Space above________ Space below________

Text Heading 2: Size of Head in Points ________

Space above________ Space below________

Text Heading 3: Size of Head in Points ________

Space above________ Space below________

Continuation Elements: You may need to allow space in your grid for continuation elements, particularly when you are designing newsletters and magazines.

Continuation elements: Size in Points________

Space above________ Space below________

Kickers and Pull Quotes: Indicate in your grid the lines within which they will be placed, if it is not the same as the standard text areas.

Kickers and Pull Quotes: Size in Points ________

Space above________ Space below________

Sidebars: Indicate in your grid the lines within which they will be placed, if it is not the same as the standard text areas.

Sidebars: Size of Head in Points____________

Space above________ Space below________

Captions and Cutlines: Indicate in your grid the lines within which they will be placed in relation to the graphics.

Captions and Cutlines: Size in Points________

Space above________ Space below________

Illustrations: Illustrations are often placed intuitively on special spread pages, depending

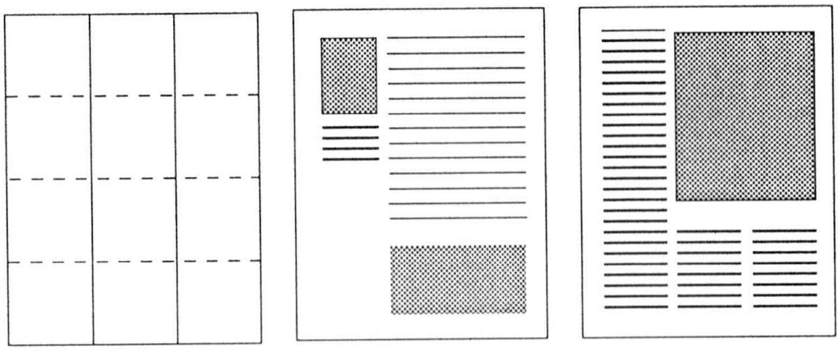

Figure 7.15: Examples of a three-column grid with horizontal divisions for illustration placement.

on their visual content. However, other elements in the text generally will follow the grid. For publications that require a consistent look, such as most business documents or documentation and training manuals, visuals follow a grid design in keeping with the other elements on the page, as shown in Figure 7.15.

Horizontal column placement

1 ____________________________________

Horizontal column placement

2 ____________________________________

Describe vertical restrictions, if any:

____

____

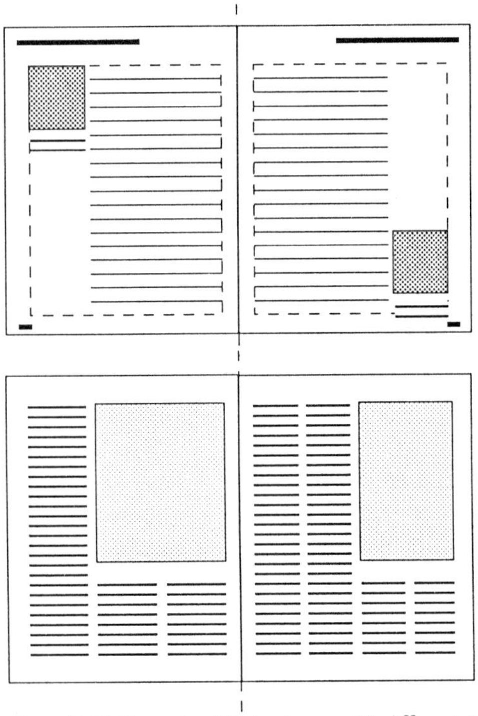

Figure 7.16: Example of facing pages with different right and left page grids.

In addition to the column and text arrangements described above, pages can also be organized horizontally, in thirds, quarters, eighths, or whatever the design requires. These breakdowns are useful when placing graphics and major headlines.

CONSTRUCTING COMPLEX GRIDS

By the time you are ready to complete your final grid on the computer, you should have sketched your preliminary designs and tried out a number of full-size variations on the computer. You should have experimented with different type faces and different column widths, using actual text or greeking if your program supplies it. When you have created a design that appeals to you, make a list of all the elements your document will need. If right and left pages have different margins or column arrangements, be sure that your grid shows facing pages (see Figure 7.16.) Check all your figures, and make sure you haven't forgotten anything. Using a page makeup program, specify the margin measurements and lay out your columns as needed. If your program allows you to set up master pages or spreads, the grid will be repeated on every page you will be using.

Unfortunately, most programs will not allow you to print a hard copy of your grid design directly, since it is composed of nonprinting lines (lines such as margins and ruler guides are supposed to be invisible in the final printed copy.) It is useful, though, to have some grid printouts for experimenting away from the computer. To make up "printable" grid pages, save a copy of your master grid file naming it "Print Master Grid." Select the rectangle or line tool in from your graphics component, and place a graphics line over all the nonprinting lines as shown in Figure 7.17. Many programs will allow you to vary line thicknesses and to use different kinds of dashes. If your grid is very complex, dashed lines may clarify the arrangement. When you are finished, print out the grid to see that it is correct, and has all of the elements for which you will need spatial indicators.

Some programs, such as PageMaker and Quark, will allow you to print out your "Print Master Grid" as thumbnails. If you want to do this, first copy your entire grid page, and paste it on the appropriate number of pages. If you have spreads using different left and right page grids, be sure that you paste your copies on the appropriate pages. Large thumbnails will print out four to the page; small thumbnails print out sixteen to the page. You will need to copy and paste a total of four pages if you want four thumbnails to the page, and sixteen pages if you want a printout with sixteen thumbnails to the page. Once your thumbnail pages are printed out, you can make photocopies of them to use for quick pencil sketches when planning your layouts. Sketching thumbnails this way is usually easier to do by hand than by using the computer (see Figure 7.18.)

You may find that design solutions are usually more interesting and varied when your original ideas are sketched quickly, away from the computer.

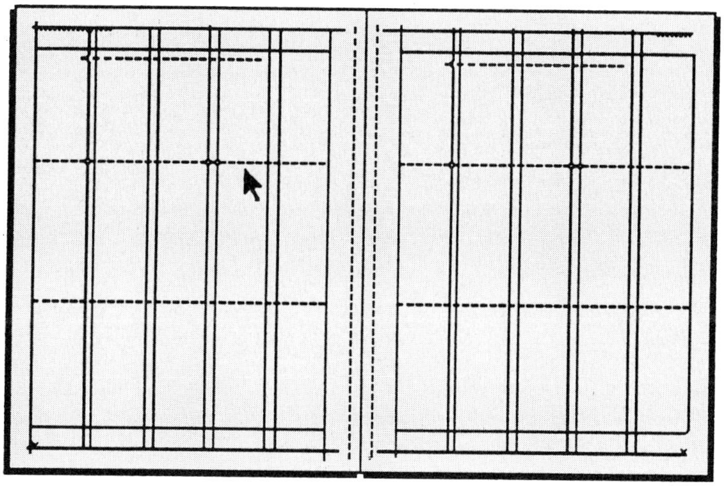

Figure 7.17: Example of graphic lines placed on the invisible grid in your page layout program.

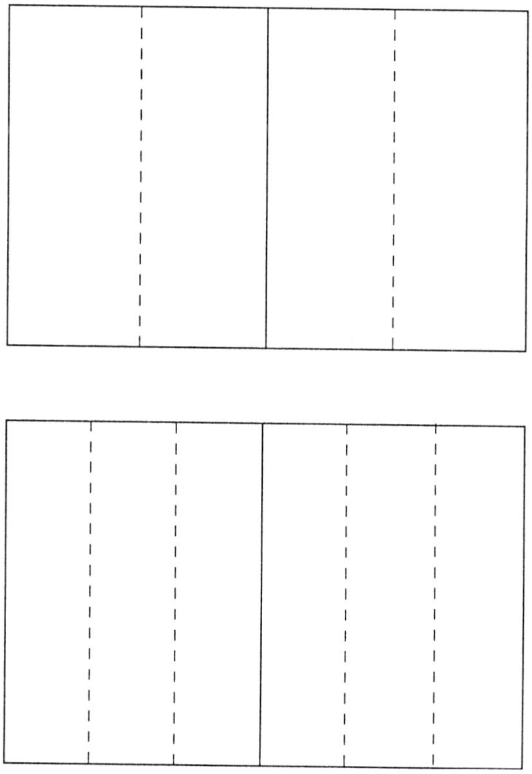

Figure 7.18: Examples of printed grid pages in thumbnail size.

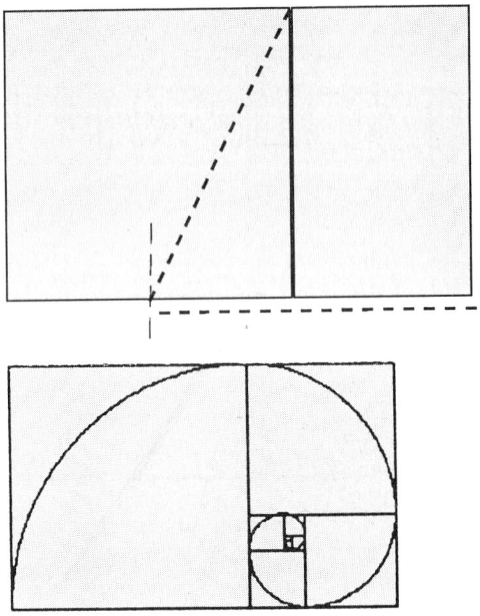

Figure 7.19: Geometric diagram showing the proportions for a golden rectangle used in many visual arrangements.

COMPUTERS AND DESIGN

It is not necessary to go through the work of creating a formal grid when you are planning a flyer that will be used only once. Designs for flyers and posters are often best handled using an intuitive layout. However, if you are preparing documents that will be used over and over again, such as business reports, newsletters, or price sheets, spending the time to make up a formal grid will save you much effort in the long run. The grid you make can be saved as a template, incorporating a typographic style sheet for all the elements you have designed. Not only will you save time in working on repeated similar publications, but other people can use your template for their projects without needing to reinvent the wheel.

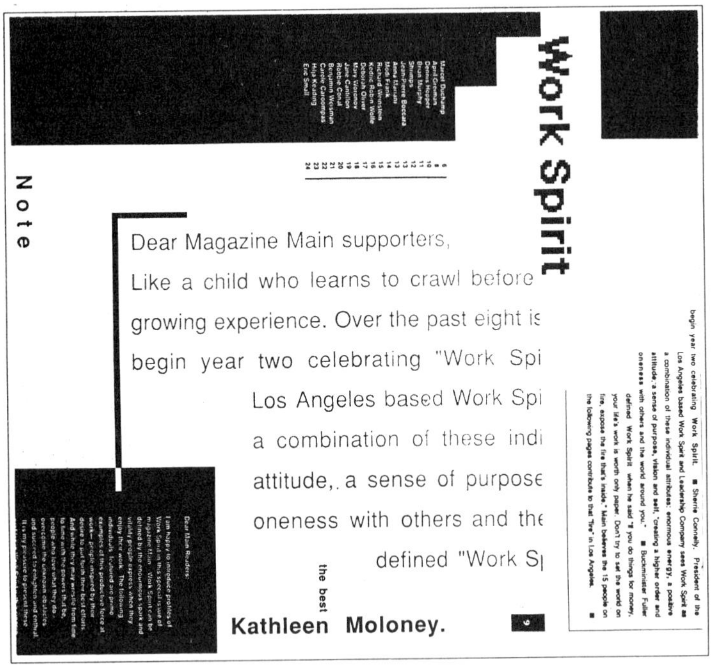

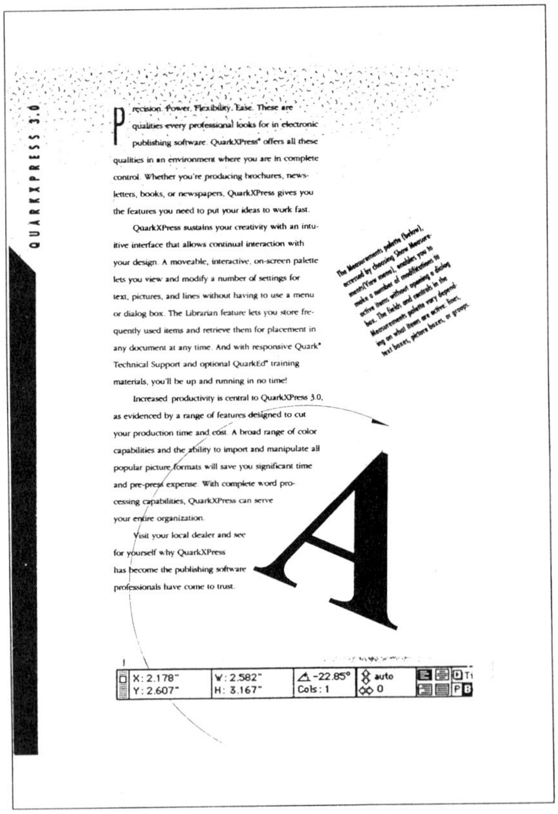

Figure 7.20: (left) a page based on a use of dynamic symmetry, designed by April Greiman for MAIN, a magazine targeted to merchants on a fashionable Main Street. (right) A page from a brochure by Quark.

THE INTUITIVE GRID

Once you have become familiar with the numerous formats that are possible using a formal grid, you can start looking at other arrangements used by graphic designers. Many of these arrangements rely on proportions based on the Golden Mean and other visual arrangements that go back to ancient Greek and Roman architecture. The Golden Mean is based on geometric proportions that form a rectangle. Figure 7.19 illustrates the geometry used to construct a Golden Mean rectangle.

PATTERNED SEQUENCES USING DYNAMIC SYMMETRY

Other visual arrangements are based on a concept called *dynamic symmetry*. You have probably used some of these concepts intuitively within the standard grid (see Figure 7.20.)

TRANSLATION

The simplest symmetry is that of *translation*. In translation, the visual image is repeated as is in a new location. It is visually the most restful pattern, and one that a viewer can follow almost automatically.

REFLECTION

Reflection is another form of symmetry that you will probably used frequently within the grid structure, particularly in page spreads. In reflection, the image or grid format is repeated as you see it in a mirror—everything viewed in a left-to-right grid on one page of the spread is viewed right to left on the other page (see Figure 7.21.) Reflection, too, is a simple patterning device, and one that is also understood and followed routinely by the viewer.

ROTATION

Rotation is somewhat more 'free-swinging' than either translation or reflection. It does, however, do what it says. In rotation, you take

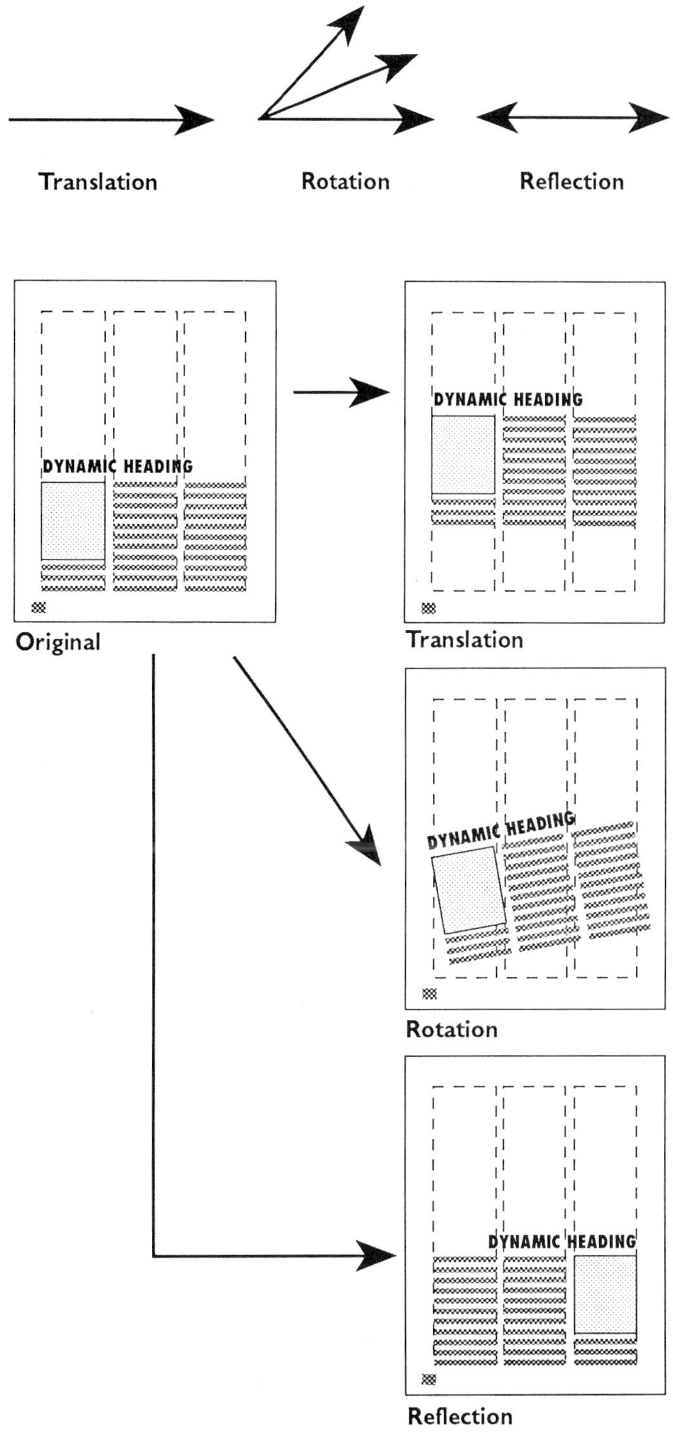

Figure 7.21: Grid using dynamic symmetry based on translation, rotation and reflection.

a segment of the grid, without changing any of its internal elements, and turn it to a different angle The break in regularity is visually interesting when well done. Grid segments can also be rotated and reflected, or rotated and moved to another location on the grid.

GRIDS AND VISUAL METAPHOR

Strict spatial discipline can look rigid, expected and easy to read, or classic, depending on how the grid has been constructed and how you as the designer have chosen to place the elements. When you reposition elements to include more and more disorder—or change from the rigid ordering in the grid, your design can change its look moving from playful to chaotic, depending on what you want to convey to the reader.

If you are designing an annual report, a rigid grid is a benefit. If you are designing a flyer that is an invitation to a party, a more dynamic grid may convey more of your intent. Even in a party invitation, though, you still need to make it clear where and when it will take place, who is giving it, and the theme (see Figure 7.22).

1. Gombrich, E.H. (1979, 1984) *A Sense of Order: A study in the psychology of decorative art.* 1984, Phaidon Press Limited, Oxford.

CHECKING YOUR UNDERSTANDING

1. Discuss what is meant by the statement, "grids are a part of our natural world."

2. Identify three advantages to using an underlying grid structure when designing page layouts.

3. What is a page grid?

4. Name the two types of grids and briefly explain how they differ.

5. Explain how the two types of grids can be combined in one publication to create a pleasing publication design.

6. List four rules to keep in mind when using a grid to design visually interesting layouts.

7. Give one advantage each for using the one-, two-, three-, and four-column grid layout.

8. Briefly describe the process for constructing a complex grid as presented in this chapter.

9. Define the Golden Mean and give one example of how it can be used as a basis for design proportions.

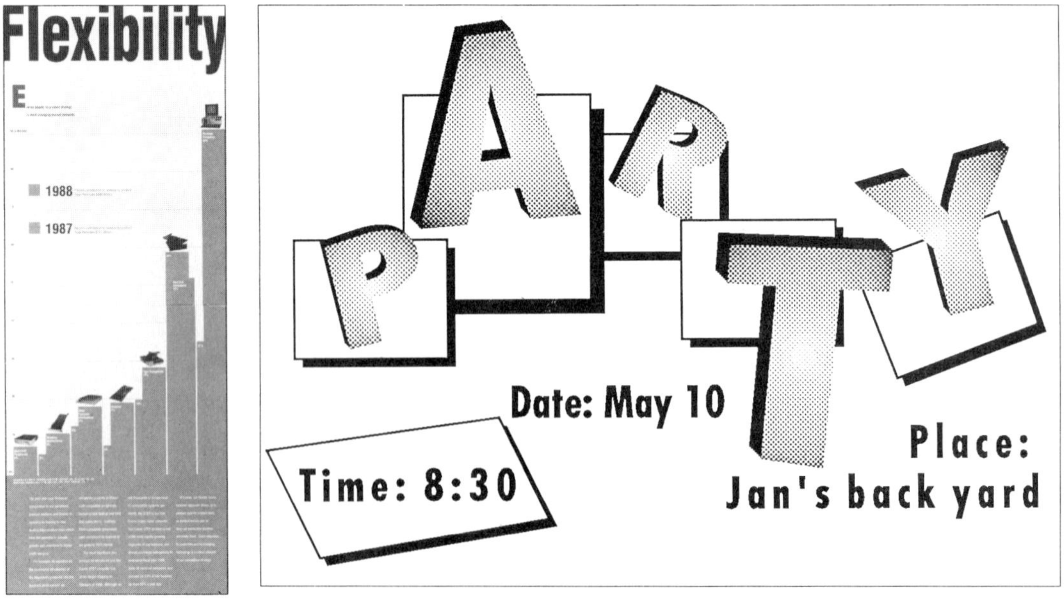

Figure 7.22: (right) a rigid grid used in an annual report. (far right) a dynamic grid used for a party invitation.

10. Identify and briefly describe each of the dynamic symmetry concepts as they relate to the page layout grid.

BUILDING YOUR DESKTOP PUBLISHING DESIGN SKILLS

1. Using the concepts you have learned in this chapter, sketch at least four thumbnails for a two-page (one page, two-sided), text-only company bulletin. Show several arrangements based on a four- or five-column grid.

    a) Indicate how you would place heaings and text.

    b) Include the masthead, "Company Messages," and issue and date information.

    c) In addition to the general news, provide spaces for the following sections: Personnel Issues, Wellness Program, and President's Message.

2. Assume you are to design a page layout for an 8-1/2 x 11 vacation advertisement flyer using a formal grid concept. Do the following:

    a) Provide for the heading, "Asian Capitals," as the dominant element. Allow space for a description and itinerary of the 15-day tour, departure dates, price, and listing of the available hotels. Do not include any art work in your layout.

    b) Prepare at least four thumbnail grids illustrating your ideas. The grid pages can be organized bilaterally, in thirds, quarters, eighths, or whatever the design requires.

3. Pick up a formal annual report with a pleasing layout design from a corporation, a stock brokerage, or a public library. Do the following:

    a) Complete the grid planning sheet presented in this chapter, using the annual report as your reference.

    b) Replicate the grid using your page layout program.

    c) Create a printable copy of your grid layout.

    d) Print a sixteen-thumbnail-to-the-page printout of your grid.

4. Design a sample two-column page layout grid for a catalogue page that provides for the following:

    a) One column that contains a table with the following headings: Description, Order #, Model #, Unit Price, and List Price; and one column that contains appropriate artwork to illustrate one or more of the items listed in the table.

    b) A minimum of four products listed per page with a maximum of eight descriptions under each item.

DESKTOP DESIGN WORKSHOP

The purpose of this section is to provide you with opportunities to develop and/or improve your desktop publishing design skills. The worksheet pages have been placed at the back of the book, and are designed so they can be removed and you can write, draw, or place your responses directly onto the pages.

WORKSHEETS 7.1 AND 7.2

Assume you have decided to enter the design competition for a club newsletter sponsored by the Burton Holmes Travel Club, to which you belong.

Using the design competition information shown on Worksheet 7.1, do the following:

1. Complete the grid planning sheet on Worksheet 7.2.

2. Develop a formal grid for your proposed newsletter design.

3. Save and print a copy of your grid.

8. WORKING WITH PHOTOS AND ILLUSTRATIONS

When you finish this chapter you should be able to:

- *Place graphic material on the page in relation to the text.*
- *Use graphic elements, including tint blocks and rules, in your publications.*
- *Distinguish between the line and halftone method of reproducing artwork.*
- *Choose the best method for reproducing photographs and illustrations.*
- *Crop art work for greater visual impact.*
- *Describe the concept and use of position prints.*
- *List various sources for artwork, including inexpensive sources such as the Library of Congress.*
- *Use photo release forms and permission-to-use forms.*
- *Adhere to copyright law restrictions.*

NEARLY ALL PUBLICATIONS produced today depend on a lively use of visual material to enhance and emphasize their content. In contrast to readers of the past, the present generation, nurtured on the television picture screen, is not drawn instinctively to a gray-looking document that is heavy with text. Typical readers tend to scan text-intensive material when they need to, not because they are drawn to it. Most people prefer to read documents whose text is reinforced with *artwork* — nontypographic elements that are also referred to as art, graphics, or visuals. Well-designed publications use these elements to enlarge the scope of communication, to grab the reader's attention, and to create a mood.

Artwork for publication can take many forms. It can be a *photograph* taken with a camera; a *diagram* drawn by hand; or a line, box, or chart created directly on the computer. You can use images to explain, to decorate a page, or to make people laugh. Artwork can influence the way people buy things or affect the way they read a magazine or newsletter. As you work out the final design for your publication, you will find many opportunities for using art to add interest.

When you use art that is appropriate, you can make text information easier for the reader to understand, which in turn will affect the way your publication is read.

Most desktop publishers are not illustrators or photographers. They are not professionally trained art directors who select and place artwork in order to make the most impact on the page. This chapter will not help you to become an illustrator. Rather, the material it covers will acquaint you with the various forms of artwork used in desktop publishing. Also included are guidelines to help you make intelligent decisions about how to create and obtain artwork and where to find it in the marketplace.

CHOOSING ARTWORK

In Chapter 2, *Communication: Visual and Verbal,* you learned about target audiences and how the look and feel of your publication affects its readership. Nowhere is this more true than in choosing artwork for your publication.

Primarily, you need to know what you expect the artwork to do and why you are using it. For example, as shown in Figure 8.1, you would select a different type of art to jazz up a flyer (possibly a drawing), to create a memorable business logo (perhaps a graphic design), to illustrate an event (generally a photograph), to indicate a set of sales figures (most likely a chart), or to simply elicit a giggle from your readers (a cartoon.)

COMPUTER-GENERATED NONTYPOGRAPHIC ELEMENTS

All desktop publishing software programs allow you to create graphic elements along with the text information. These graphic

Figure 8.1: Artwork for use in a publication; (top) a photograph; (center) a line drawing; (bottom left) an illustration from a clipart catalogue; (bottom right) a chart from an annual report (courtesy Sheret Design.)

A.

B.

Figure 8.2: (A., top) Futura light is used with 4 point rules. (A., center) Helvetica black is used with hairline rules. (B., bottom) Times Bold is used with Oxford rules.

elements include lines, or rules, as they are more accurately called; boxes and borders; and decorative characters.

RULES

Rules are lines that you can place anywhere on a layout for emphasis or decoration. They are one of the simplest kinds of artwork. All desktop publishing programs are supplied with an assortment of rules in varying styles and weights. Their menus usually allow you to select from a hairline rule to a thick one; from a single rule to dashes or parallel thick and thin rules. The length and weight of the rule can be changed with a click of the mouse.

While rules are easy to make, you will find that using them well requires visual judgement and attention. In Chapter 6, *Type Aesthetics,* you learned that the mood of the typeface should match the mood of the message transmitted by your document. To retain a consistent mood throughout your document, the artwork it uses should echo the flavor of its typography as well.

For example, if you are designing a flyer set in a Helvetica typeface (which has uniform horizontal and vertical strokes), the message can be set off attractively using rules of a weight equal to that of the Helvetica typeface. If your typeface is bold or heavy, hairline rules can be used as an effective contrast, and conversely, if your choice is Helvetica light, a heavy rule can be used as a contrast (see Figure 8.2A.) Can you see how the traditional Oxford rule (parallel thick and thin lines) compliments the Times typeface, a traditional serif face? Note the pronounced contrast between the thickness of vertical strokes and the thinness of horizontal strokes as illustrated in Figure 8.2B.

Apart from complimenting the typography in your document, rules should match the character of any other artwork you are using. If you plan to use rules around a fine line drawing, a hairline rule would be appropriate. On the other hand, you would use a thicker rule if the illustration consisted of dark, bold strokes.

It is easy to overuse line elements because they are so easy to make.

While there are no hard-and-fast principles as to when rules can be used, it is best to use them whenever they make sense. That is, if you can give a good reason for its use, a rule is probably appropriate.

Rules can be used to define areas on a page, to provide emphasis, or to reinforce the character of a publication. For example, magazines often use rules to separate ads from the articles, and newspapers place hairline rules between columns of text. Pull quotes in an article use rules to separate the decorative quote from the main text.

BORDERS

Borders and boxes are nothing more than rules that enclose an area (a square, circle, etc.). Borders that enclose a square or rectangle can have square or rounded corners. Many desktop publishing programs offer the same menu choice for border styles as line styles (hairline, Oxford, dotted, etc.). Like rules, border styles communicate. Plain borders isolate their contents, drop-shadowed borders give a three-dimensional effect, and filled borders spotlight. The border style should compliment the graphic and typographic elements. A square-corner border looks good with most typefaces. A rounded corner border tends to be traditional or art deco in its flavor and is harder to use successfully. Rounded corners work best with rounded typefaces (see Figure 8.3.)

Borders can be used to highlight text or graphic elements, to provide variety to an otherwise gray page, and to provide borders for photographs, line drawings, and other forms of artwork.

While borders emphasize, they can also trap; that is, completely surround an element. This makes the element stand out, so be sure that this is the effect you want to create. When type is placed within a border, at least one half to one pica should be left between the inside edge of the border and the type (see Figure 8.3.)

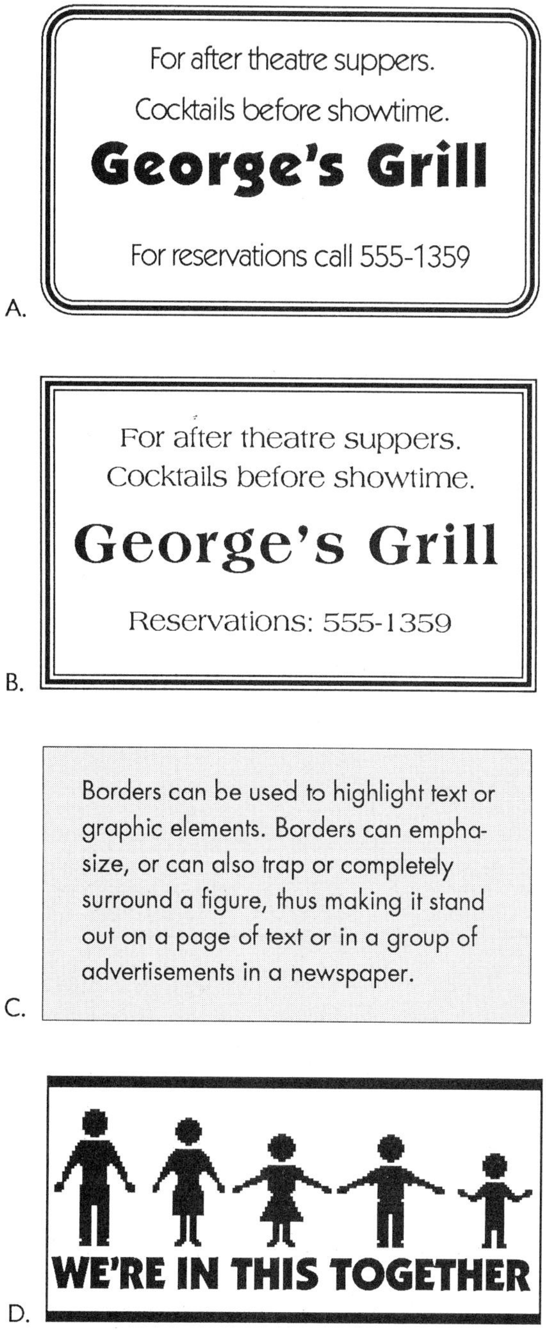

Figure 8.3: (A., top) Use of a rounded Oxford border combined with Kabel, a rounded Art Deco typeface that echoes the shape of the border. (B., center) A square border, using the same Oxford rule as A. Here it is combined with Americana, a decorative but traditional typeface. (C., center) A border used to accent a type block on a page. In this example it also traps a 10% tint overlay. Note that there is a pica space from the border to the type area. (D., bottom) A border is used to outline a graphic.

HOLIDAYS

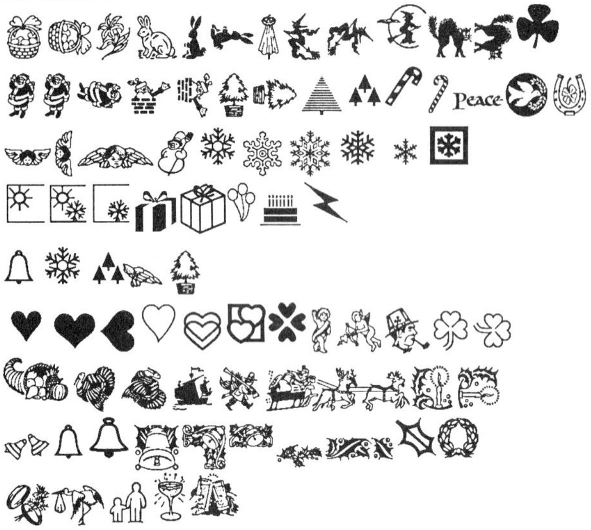

ECOLOGY

Figure 8.4: Examples of graphic fonts by AGFA

DECORATIVE CHARACTERS

Decorative characters are easily made using "graphic" typefaces. They are used for embellishment and emphasis. Zapf Dingbats, a popular graphic typeface by Adobe, and other graphics typefaces (see Figure 8.4,) offer bullets, boxes, arrows, stars, flowers, and other symbols. Some of the decorative elements can be repeated to form fancy borders. If you are using a PostScript printer, your desktop publishing software probably supports a graphic typeface.

Because decorative characters are easy to create, you can easily be lured into sprinkling your pages with them. Resist the temptation! Decorative characters can add character to a design, but only when used with a purpose.

Keep in mind that the purpose of artwork is to communicate, not to decorate!

Encircled numbers can be used as a design element in a listing or a set of instructions. Arrows can be used to draw attention to a special phrase or sentence. Bullets and boxes can be used on checklists like those inserted throughout this text. Oversize quote marks

Figure 8.5: Examples of several different illustration types and styles. (left top and bottom) computer drawings. (right) an illustration done by hand.

can be used to set off pull quotes, and the scissors along with a dotted or dashed line traditionally designate a tear-off or coupon. Like all artwork, decorative characters should be chosen and used to compliment the other elements of your layout.

PICTORIAL IMAGES

When people think of pictorial images, they usually think of illustrations or photographs that represent people, places, and things. Pictorial images done by hand or by computer are called illustrations; those done with a camera are called photographs.

There are many kinds of illustrations, as shown in Figure 8.5. Some are so realistically rendered that they almost appear to be photographs. Abstract design renderings are another illustration category. Other illustration styles include images drawn with a light touch, cartoons, and satirical illustrations.

REPRODUCING PICTORIAL IMAGES

Many people are not aware of how pictorial images are reproduced in print. Technically, there are two major image categories that apply regardless of what kind of artwork you are working with. The two categories are halftones and line art.

Artwork whose tonal values graduate from white highlights through a range of grays from light to black are reproduced on the computer and in print as *halftones.* All photographs are reproduced as halftones. Halftone art scanned for the computer can reproduce as many as 256 separate shades of gray. Line drawings have no gray tones; they are made up of lines and areas of black or white. Because line drawings do not use shades of gray, they are also called high-contrast art (see Figure 8.6.)

HALFTONES, LINE ART, AND TINTS

HALFTONES

Black-and-white photographs, the kind desktop publishers use most often, appear to be a continuous gradation of gray tones. It is important to keep in mind that these tonal values, as they appear in the original photograph, will not reproduce on a printing press. In order to reproduce a photograph, its gray values must be replaced by very small dots of varying sizes and distances from each other.

Figure 8.6: (left) A half-tone photograph. (right) a line drawing by June Rubin.

These dots represent the various gray tones in the original photograph and make up what is called a *halftone reproduction*. Areas in which the halftone dots are relatively large and close together look dark; the smaller and farther apart the halftone dots are, the lighter the area will appear. Figure 8.7 shows a portion of a photograph in its original size for reproduction, and an enlargement showing the halftone dots that will be used to print the photograph.

Some types of illustrations show gradations of tone similar to those in a photograph. Images of this kind also need to be reproduced as halftones in order to maintain the range of values.

Traditionally, halftones were made by using a camera and shooting through a screen that converted the continuous tone of an image into dots. Today, quality halftones are prepared by craftspeople who scan the image electronically, using high-precision equipment. The clarity of the halftone image is directly related to how well the craftsperson has interpreted the tonal range, as well as how fine the halftone dots are and how many of them there are per inch. More detailed information on working with halftones is covered in Chapter 14, *Working With Service Bureaus and Print Shops;* and Chapter 15, *Preparation of Camera-Ready Art*.

> *When your budget is tight, use line drawings in preference to photographs since reproducing photographs can be a problem when making low-cost multiple copies.*

LINE DRAWINGS

Line drawings can be drawn on the computer or by hand, using pen and ink. These can be reproduced simply and need no transformation. Drawings done in dark pencil can be reproduced either as halftones or line art. If they are reproduced as halftones, the delicacy of the pencil line will be retained but the background will have a light gray tone of about 5 percent due to halftoning. If a pencil sketch is reproduced as a line drawing, the lighter tones of the pencil sketch will disappear since the lines only can be either black or white. The resulting art is a black-and-white rendition, similar to but less delicate than a halftone reproduction of the same artwork. The line drawing will be crisper, because the background will be the white of the paper. Another option is to use the line drawing over a background that is a single tone of gray or other color, called a tint.

Figure 8.7: Portion of a photograph in original size and an enlargement showing halftone dots.

TINTS

Frequently, an area of a page will be printed with a lighter tone of the basic color or hue that is being used. This area is referred to as a *tint* or, more appropriately, a *tint block.* Each shade of a tint block is specified by a percentage, as shown in Figure 8.8. A 20 percent tint of black will be a fairly light gray, while an 80 percent tint will be closer to pure black. Tints can be used with colors as well as with black. For example, a 20 percent tint of red will print as pink.

Tint blocks are related to halftones in that they are made up of little dots placed close together, but different from halftones in that all the dots of a given tint are the same size as well as equally distant from each other. Tint blocks can be used to provide background color for type or for drawings, or shaped in irregular patterns to enhance a drawing.

Figure 8.8: A line drawing overlaid with a 10% tint block.

FINDING AND USING PICTORIAL IMAGES IN A PUBLICATION

CLIP ART

The easiest way to get art for your publication is through the use of *clip art* — the generic name for libraries of electronic drawings and illustrations on disk. Clip art — electronic art software libraries — is available with illustrations in many subject areas whose contents can be used freely upon purchase of the package. Clip art images are placed on the page by importing them into your page layout and printing them out with the text.

A wide variety and price range of clip art is readily available in both Mac and DOS formats, in both line and halftone formats. Clip art libraries include logos, symbols, holiday motifs, classic images, borders, and cartoons — virtually everything you can imagine or have ever seen (see Figure 8.9.) Art services such as the Designer's Club sell "generic art" on disk and give you permission to use these images in your publication. CompuServe, local electronic bulletin boards,

Figure 8.9 Clip art: (top) a bit mapped drawing. (bottom) a Postscript illustration.

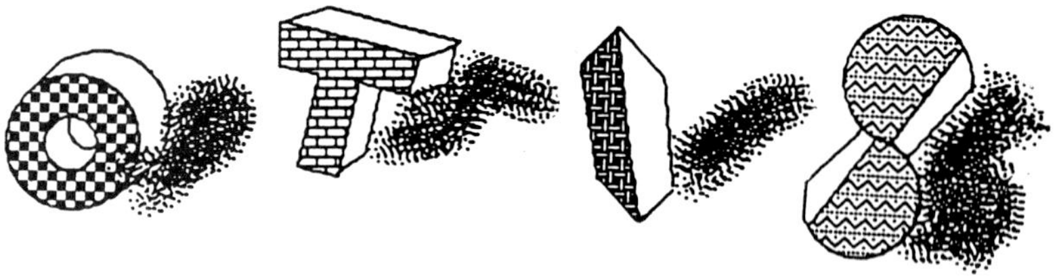

Figure 8.10: An image rendered in a paint program.

Figure 8.11: (top) A paint image, enlarged, showing jagged edges. (bottom) another paint image, same size, showing jagged edges.

and user groups also provide clip art available as public domain software. You should always check with the provider or the source of your clip art to determine its status for permission to use.

Because there is so much good clip art around, it is easy to fall victim to the beginner's temptation to overdo. One of the tell-tale signs of a novice desktop designer is a page filled with unrelated art. Drawings, like any other graphic elements, should not be used solely for ornamentation; they must always serve a purpose.

COMPUTER GRAPHIC PROGRAMS

If you want to make your own illustrations for your desktop publishing documents, there are a number of computer graphic programs that can help. These programs are classified as paint, draw, or illustration software. Each type of program relies on the use of a computer graphics monitor.

PAINT PROGRAMS

Paint programs operate by literally painting the screen with colored or black dots, usually called *pixels* (from the words "picture element"). The image created by this array of pixels is called a *bit-mapped image.* When you "paint" a computer screen, you are turning on pixels in color or black and white to make an image, as shown in Figure 8.10.

Although paint programs can replicate oil paint, watercolor, pencil, and pen with ink, the format they all use is that of pixels arranged on the screen. The fineness of the graphic image that is produced is called its *resolution*, and is based on the number of pixels per square inch on the screen. The resolution of the graphic depends directly on the computer screen resolution, the paint program producing the graphic, and how your printer will reproduce the bit-mapped screen image. Paint-type graphics usually have a screen resolution of 72 dots per inch. While this resolution is adequate for many types of images, it can create printouts with rough, jagged edges, especially on curves.

This phenomenon is known as *aliasing*, or, more familiarly, "the *jaggies*." (See Figure 8.11.)

Paint programs can be quite simple, or elaborate enough for the professional illustrator. Some examples of simple programs for the Mac are MacPaint and SuperPaint; Windows Paint is an example of a simple paint program for DOS-based machines. Complex paint programs enable you to edit art on a pixel level and often permit choices for higher bit-map resolutions. Such complex programs include PhotoShop, Studio 8 and Pixel Paint Professional on the Mac and PC Paintbrush+ and Arts and Letters on the DOS-based machines. Jag, a software application for the Mac removes "jaggies" on many bit-mapped images.

DRAW PROGRAMS

Draw programs, unlike paint programs, are geometrically based, operating on what is called *object-oriented programming*. This means that the program uses geometric shapes defined as objects by the program (Figure 8.12.) Objects such as circles, lines, and rectangles, are made up of *vectors* (lines with width and direction) with instructions for their location on the screen. Each object is rendered on the screen through the use of mathematical calculations and formulas, called *computer algorithms*. Once an object is made by a draw program, you can select it and group it with other objects; you can choose to have the program copy your object, move or enlarge or reduce it, or rotate and reflect it. These manipulations are called *transformations*; they are the strength of the draw program category.

Draw-type graphics can be used for higher quality documents because they do not produce the jagged edges that paint-type graphics do. Examples of draw programs are MacDraw for the Mac and GEM Draw for DOS machines.

ILLUSTRATION PROGRAMS

Illustration programs make up the third category of computer graphic software. They enable you to create finer illustrations — those with a high printout resolution. Illustration programs are similar to ordinary draw programs, but are more powerful in that they work with PostScript curves and lines. PostScript, as described in Chapter 5, *Type Basics,* is a language that communicates a typographic description to a printer capable of printing PostScript output. PostScript can be used to describe any graphic image, illustrations as well as type.

Illustration programs manipulate graphic images described by the PostScript language. PostScript graphics (also called EPS or Encapsulated PostScript Graphics) are actually very high-resolution line drawings with tint blocks, and can be thought of as filling in a gap between ordinary line drawings and photographs. Illustration programs on the Mac include Adobe Illustrator and Aldus

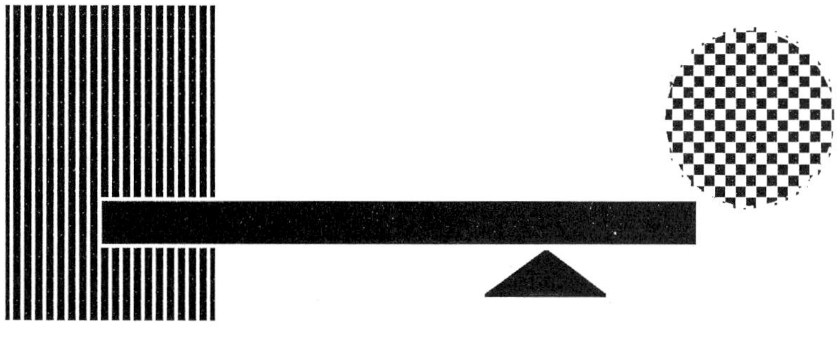

Figure 8.12: Illustration using a draw program.

Freehand. Those for the PC include Corel Draw and Micrografx Draw. Some illustration draw programs allow you to make typefaces and to manipulate type characters for logo design. These have been mentioned in Chapter 6.

PostScript graphics are of a much higher resolution than that of most computer screens. For that reason, desktop publishing programs have two options for viewing PostScript graphics on screen. One option is a low-resolution viewing mode, in which the on-screen graphic contains less detail than it will have when printed; the other is a shaded box without the graphic.

GRAPHICS FORMATS

Graphics for computer representation come in a number of different formats. We have discussed paint, draw, and PostScript programs and how the printed output format is controlled by the graphics program in which the image was constructed. Many graphics programs will format graphic output according to several different menu choices you can choose from when you are saving the file.

The format for your graphic must be compatible with the software in order to be able to use it.

Some graphics programs will accept a number of different formats to work with, and will allow you to convert to other formats you can select when saving the file. Not all software, though, will convert to all the available graphics formats.

Hotshop, in DOS, is a graphics converter that handles a large number of formats. Figure 8.13 lists graphics formats for both Mac and DOS, along with a brief description.

PHOTOGRAPHS

Photographs are used in a publication to portray a diversity of imagery, ranging from pictures of people, to products, to objects in nature. Photographs recording sporting events, family occasions, or corporate events are often used in newsletters, catalogs, and annual reports. Photographs are also used for documentation and training manuals to illustrate a process or document a procedure.

Photographs can be used individually on a page, or grouped together for additional impact. When many pictures are grouped together on a page or spread, the assemblage is called a *photo montage*. Newsletters as well as magazines use photo montages for article openers or page spreads. When photos are used as the main information element for an entire story, with limited text

BITMAPPED GRAPHICS FILE FORMATS		DRAWN GRAPHICS FILE FORMATS	
Application/Platform	**File Format**	**Application/Platform**	**File Format**
GEM bit map files	GEM	Autocad	PLT, DXF
Macintosh paint file	Apple/Claris	Computer Generated Metafiles	CGM
DOS picture files	PIC	Corel Draw files	CDR
Macintosh PICT files	PICT, PICT2	Desktop Color Separation files	DCS
Macintosh Paint files	Paint	Encapsulated PostScript	EPS
DOS bit format	PCX	Hewlett-Packard plotter files	HPGL
Tag Image File Format	TIFF	Microsoft Windows	WMF
Microsoft Windows bit map format	BMP	Pixar	RIB

Table 8.1: Graphic File Formats

accompanying the pictures, the story is called a *photo essay*. Magazines often use photo essays as part of their editorial content. Figure 8.13 shows examples of different ways in which photographs can be used.

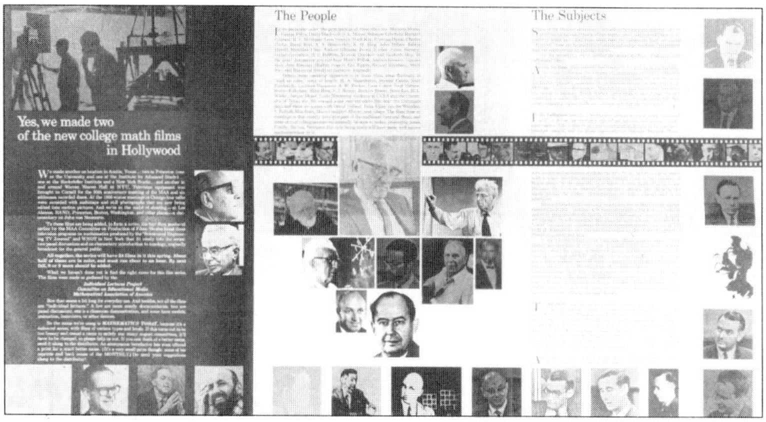

Figure 8.13: Examples of different ways in which photographs can be grouped and used

SELECTING GOOD PHOTOGRAPHS FOR REPRODUCTION

When selecting photographs for your publication, you want an image that is, of itself, a good composition. Figure 8.14 shows typical examples of good and poor composition.

BALANCE

First of all, make sure that the photograph is well-balanced and is not filled with extraneous detail. Make sure, too, that there are no disturbing elements in the image such as a tree that appears to be growing out of a person's head. Telephone wires in an otherwise pleasant landscape, or a hand or foot at the edge of the image, with the rest of the person cut off, are examples of typical disturbing elements.

Figure 8.14: (top) A poorly composed photo and (above) a good composition in a photograph.

FOCUS

Check the focus to make sure that everything within the photographic image is sharp rather than soft and fuzzy; examine edges, especially, to determine that they are sharp. Make sure, too, that there are no scratches or other flaws on your reproduction print.

TONAL RANGE

View the tonal range from black to white to verify that there is good contrast overall. Check to see that there is detail in the highlights and the shadows of your image, to insure that your photograph will reproduce well.

If your photograph is flawed in some way, determine if it is possible to retouch the image either by hand, or by using an electronic program such as Digital Darkroom or Photo Shop for Macintosh. It is best, though, to start out with good images

CROPPING

When you are laying out pages, it will help the design if you realize that you don't

Figure 8.15: Cropped photograph demonstrating how redundant or extraneous visual material can be eliminated to focus the reader's eye on what is important and visually interesting

have to use a photograph in its present size, shape, or composition. Photographs can be enlarged or reduced, or portions can be cropped. *Cropping* a photograph consists of cutting off portions of the image to concentrate on the content and communication you want to emphasize. Figure 8.15 illustrates how cropping can remove redundant or extraneous visual material and help the reader focus on what is important and visually interesting.

When cropping a photograph, be sure that you do not make any painful cuts. An example of a painful cut is a hand cut off at the wrist or a head shot that stops at the neck.

Photographs that are cropped in this manner are visually disturbing to the reader (see Figure 8.16.)

USING POSITION PRINTS

Once a photograph has been cropped, it can be resized to fit the space you have set aside for it. Chapters 14 and 15 have detailed information on preparing photographs for reproduction.

If you have a copying machine that does reducing and enlarging by single percentage increments, you can use it to try out different sizes for your page layouts. If a scanner is available, you can scan and size your photographs and arrange them on the pages electronically.

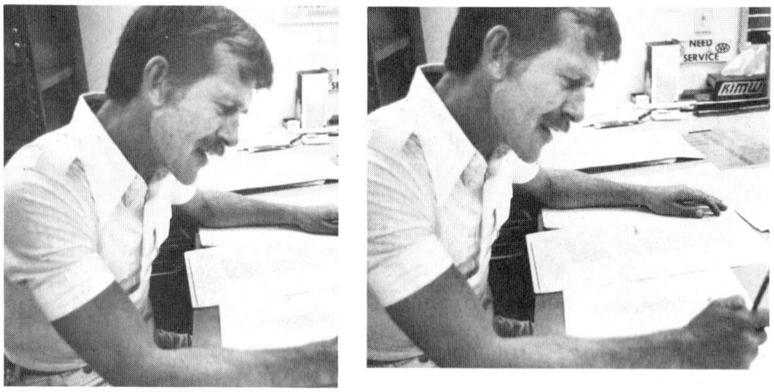

Figure 8.16: (left) A photograph cropped with a painful cut. (right) The appropriate crop for this image.

INFORMATION GRAPHICS

The last category of artwork to be discussed is *information graphics.* Information graphics are used to portray relationships visually between elements or data. Visual data is generally easier to interpret than the same data described by the written word. Information graphics include charts, tables, maps, and diagrams. Figure 8.17 illustrates a number of typical information graphics categories.

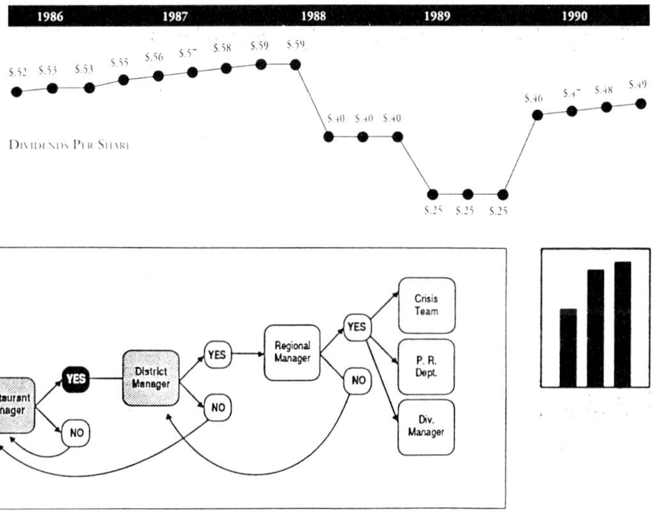

Figure 8.17: Examples of information graphics. (top) a line graph; (above left) a decision chart; (above right) a bar chart.

WORKING WITH CHARTS AND GRAPHS

These days, financial managers, statisticians, and others who work with numerical data don't have to rely on long columns of numbers to get their information across to the reader. There are a number of computer programs that produce charts and graphs directly from data. The data can be keyed in directly from within the chart software or exported to the chart software from spreadsheet files and other statistical programs.

As a desktop publisher, you can improve the usefulness of the data by knowing how to select the best format for representing the information that the figures represent. An excellent reference guide is *The Visual Display of Quantitative Information* by Edward R. Tufte, published by Graphics Press (1983). Programs for making charts and graphs include DeltaGraphics for the Macintosh and Harvard Graphics and Applause for DOS computers. In addition, many spreadsheet programs also have good charting abilities. On the Mac these include Excel, Full Impact and Wingz; Excel is a good DOS program.

The following suggestions will help you clarify your information by making the data representation obvious:

- ✔ In a graph, eliminate extraneous grid lines. Or, make them lighter in tone than the graph lines or bars.
- ✔ Label your information clearly, and large enough to be read. Make sure that your choice of typefaces is consistent both within the graph or table and for all similar graphics in your publication. Maintain a consistent hierarchy for graphics labels such as the figure number and title, table headings, the legend, data labels, and axis information (see Figure 8.18.)
- ✔ In general, avoid the use of serif typefaces for numbers wherever

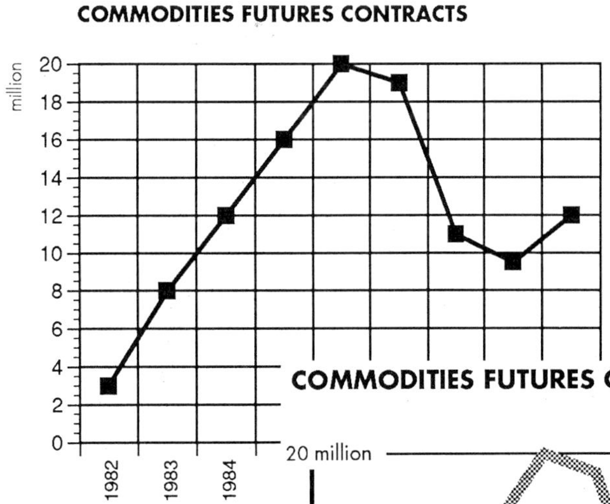

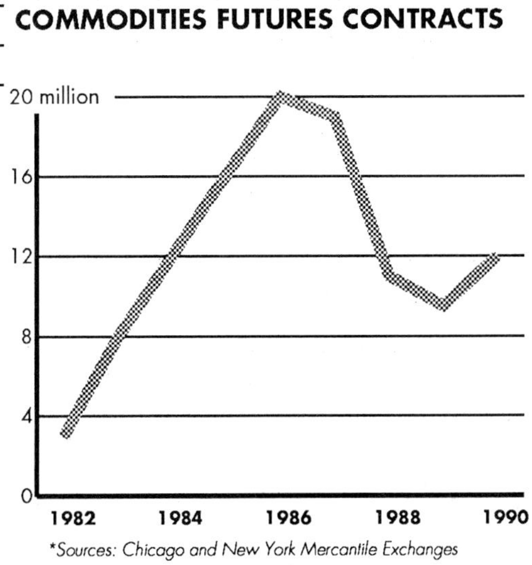

Figure 8.18: (right) a line graph showing simplified grid lines, consistent use of information text, and family resemblance in line weights and types of lines, as compared to the graph above.

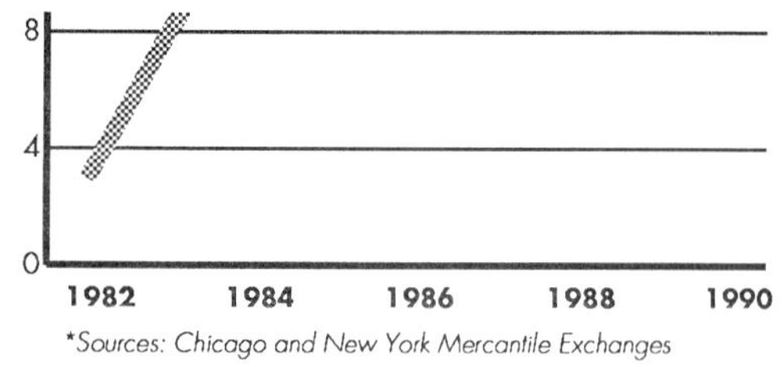

Figure 8.19: Placement of a data source at the bottom of the graph.

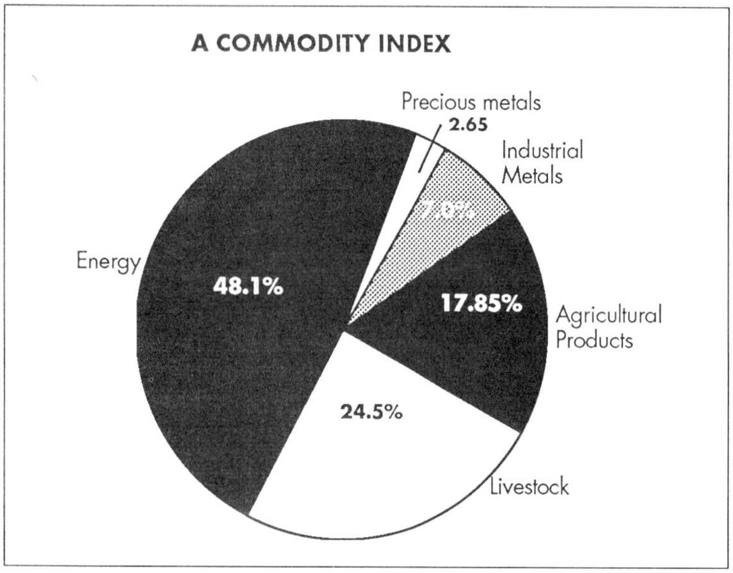

A

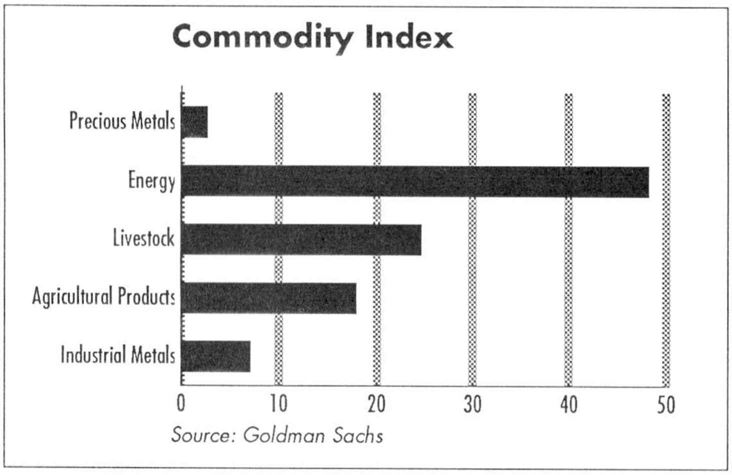

B

Figure 8.20A: A pie chart showing how just a few patterns can be used to differentiate the data elements. Figure 8.20B: A bar graph using the same data as Figure 8.20A. Note the simplified grid.

possible, as these usually tend to be more difficult to read in graphs or tabular form.

✔ On a chart, each plot in a data set should be different, through use of color, line weight, or line form (such as dashed or dotted lines). Maintain a family resemblance by using only one type of differentiation that can be either color, line weight, or line form. A graph can also benefit by labeling the curves if there is room.

— If you are using thick curves, these usually look better when specified in percentages of gray, while those of a thinner weight will read better in a solid black.

— When you are using color to differentiate between one graphic data set and another, choose colors that are obviously different from one another. Make sure, too, that the colors are contrasted from the background so as to be unmistakable and distinct.

✔ Indicate where your data has come from either in a caption, a footnote, or as a reference in small type as shown in Figure 8.19. If you do choose a serif face, use one in which the numerals all align at their base and cap height.

The number of data sets your chart is comparing is one of the factors that determine the type of format you should use. Pie charts compare items in only one data set. Moreover, a pie chart cannot adequately compare more than six to eight slices at one time, particularly in black and white.

In general, you should avoid using shading patterns. They distract visually from the data to be compared, and unless you handle patterns adeptly, they are unpleasant to look at. If your material will be printed in black only, choose gray values to represent data whenever possible, rather than shading patterns (see Figure 8.20A and 8.20B.)

TABLES

Tables, referred to by typographers as *tabular material,* are not, in the strict sense, artwork. When setting type, though, tables are set separately from the text and follow design specifications that are similar to those used for charts and graphs.

As shown in Figure 8.21, a heading should be placed over the table and horizontal and/or vertical headings should be placed over the table text. A table may also have an accompanying caption and footnotes.

- ✔ As in charts and graphs, be consistent in your use of typefaces, and observe the typeface hierarchy design of your publication.
- ✔ Using rules with two or three varying weights can help organize information; try to avoid using too many rules. Often a cleaner look can be gotten by using vertical rules with horizontal white space as separators; or conversely, horizontal rules with vertical white space separators.

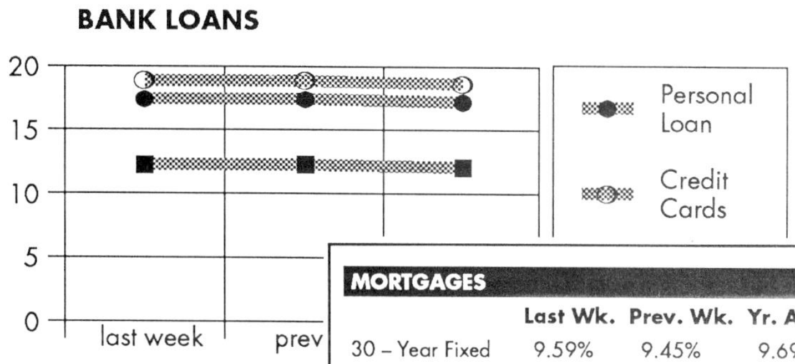

Figure 8.21: (right) Text information in a table. (above) For comparison, note the same information for the bank loan data set shown in a line graph.

	Last Wk.	Prev. Wk.	Yr. Ago
MORTGAGES			
30 – Year Fixed	9.59%	9.45%	9.69%
15 – Year Fixed	9.30	9.18	9.45
1 – Year Adj. Rate	7.85	7.87	8.40
BANK LOANS			
Personal Loan (2 Year)	17.40	17.40	17.18
Credit Cards	18.86	18.86	18.62
Automobile Loan	12.25	12.26	12.09
SAVINGS RATES			
Donoghue's Money Fund 7– Day Avg.	6.91	7.09	7.74
Bank Money Market Accounts	5.67	5.69	6.14
6 – Month CD's	6.87	6.95	7.66

Sources: Bank Rate Monitor, N. Palm Beach 33408; Donogue's Money Fund Report

DIAGRAMS

Organization charts and other simple diagrams follow many of the same rules of thumb for design as do charts and graphs. While rendering complex diagrams is best left to the technical illustrator, the following suggestions will help you to prepare simple diagrams. Refer to Figure 8.22 for illustrations.

- ✔ Be consistent in your choice of typeface for similar graphics. Develop a visual typeface hierarchy that reflects the importance of your graphics text labeling.
- ✔ Be consistent in your use of rule weights. All similar elements should use the same weight of rule and be the same in size. If you are using dropped shadows for some of your boxes, be sure that all boxes of that type drop their shadows in the same direction.

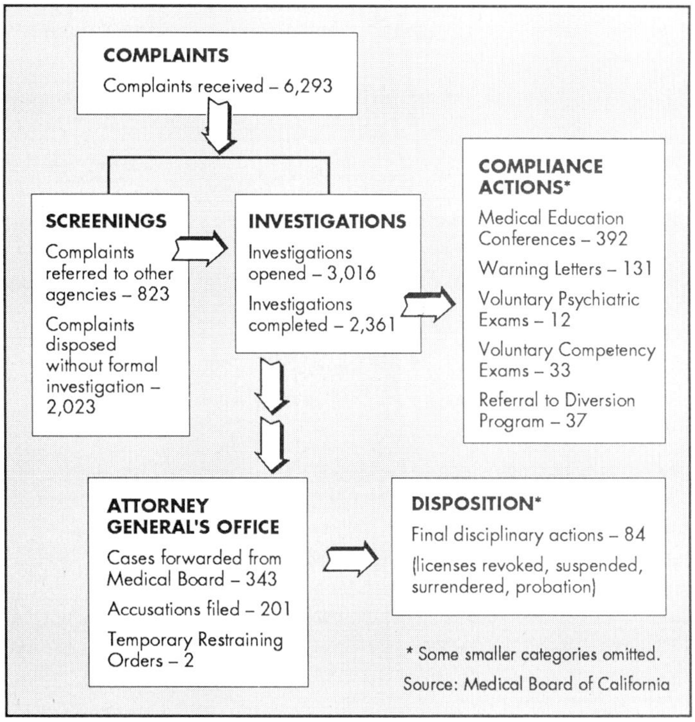

Figure 8.22: a diagram showing consistency of line weights and typeface choices.

- ✔ If you use a heavy outline for boxes, run it in a gray tone, or run your dropped shadow in a gray tone so as not to overpower the data. In an organization chart, if the organizational hierarchy and structure are more important than the individual line items, run the boxes in lightweight rules, and the connecting lines in a heavier weight.

MAPS

Drawing complex maps from scratch is best left to professional map makers, called cartographers. If your map needs are not complicated, you can probably find what you need in clip art maps from companies such as MicroMaps Software for both Mac and DOS, in PICT and EPS formats. With the use of a software graphics program, clip art maps can be embellished with decorative elements and gray tones and additional data can be added by the user. As with graphs, there are rules of thumb that will help you illustrate your publications with maps that contain clearly defined information.

- ✔ Maintain a hierarchy for the map title, labels, and legends. Follow the format for type styles used by cartographers (see Figure 8.23.)
- ✔ If you are using color or shades of gray, make sure that the callout text contrasts enough to be easily read. Use a legend to define the tinted or color areas if they convey information such as is given in weather maps or elevation maps (see Figure 8.24.)
- ✔ Include a scale showing the scale (distance to the inch), and an indicator for cardinal directions with north at the top. A simple cruciform with an arrow indicating north is generally used (see Figure 8.24.)
- ✔ If you need to point out specific areas on a map, labels and arrows will help clarify the information (see Figure 8.24.)

SYMBOLS AND INFORMATION GRAPHICS

Very often, information graphics are clarified through the use of visual symbols and icons. Make sure that these are simple and easy for the reader to identify quickly. If you are using a symbol to portray comparative data, don't enlarge the symbol to show growth.

MAJOR COUNTRIES,	***OCEANS***
CAPITALS OF COUNTRIES OR STATES	***LAKES***
MAJOR CITIES, ALL CAPS	***Major mountains and rivers***
Minor cities	*Minor mountains and rivers*

Figure 8.23: (above) A typographic hierarchy for maps, using Gill Sans. Bold face all caps are used for countries; a smaller size of bold face caps used for capital cities. Major cities are set in Roman all caps; upper and lower case of the same font for minor cities. Towns and villages are set in successively smaller sizes of the font used for cities. Oceans are set in bold face italic caps; lakes are set smaller, in the same typeface. Important mountains and rivers are set in bold face italic upper and lower case; other mountains and rivers set in italic upper and lower case.

Figure 8.24: Countries and cities are indicated in this map, along with labels and a callout. Grey tints are used to differentiate areas. (Courtesy MicroMaps Software.)

Information is portrayed more accurately if you use a proportionally larger quantity of the same size of symbol. Figure 8.25 shows how poor use of symbols can distort the data.

If you plan to use symbols, many drawing program and clip art libraries contain symbols appropriate to maps, charting, and diagram graphics. A type font that contains many cartographic symbols, called, appropriately, Carta, is available from Adobe.

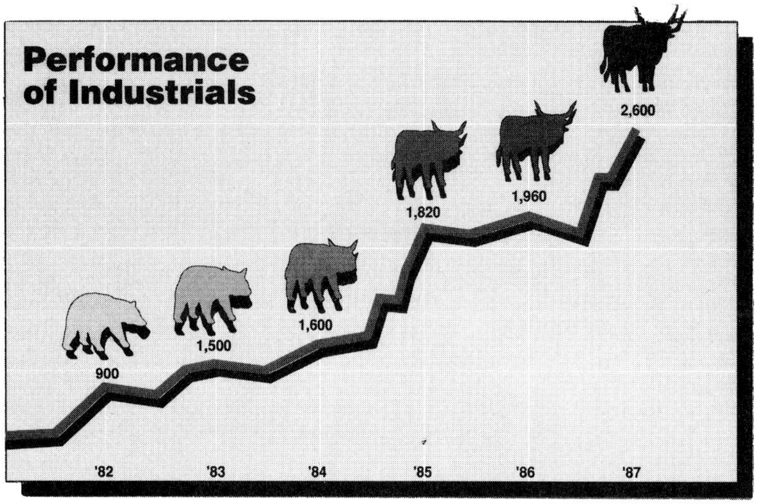

Figure 8.25: a chart with symbols. The line graph accurately reports the data, while the symbolic bear gradually turns into a bull.

ART WORK AND THE GRID

In Chapter 6 you learned about the various grid structures you can use to guide the placement of elements on a page. These same grid structures are used to place your artwork. Illustrations, photographs, and information graphics can be grouped together using either the formal or the intuitive grid. The intuitive grid is generally better when working with groups of graphics such as photo essays and montages. Figure 8.26 shows a photo montage using an intuitive grid.

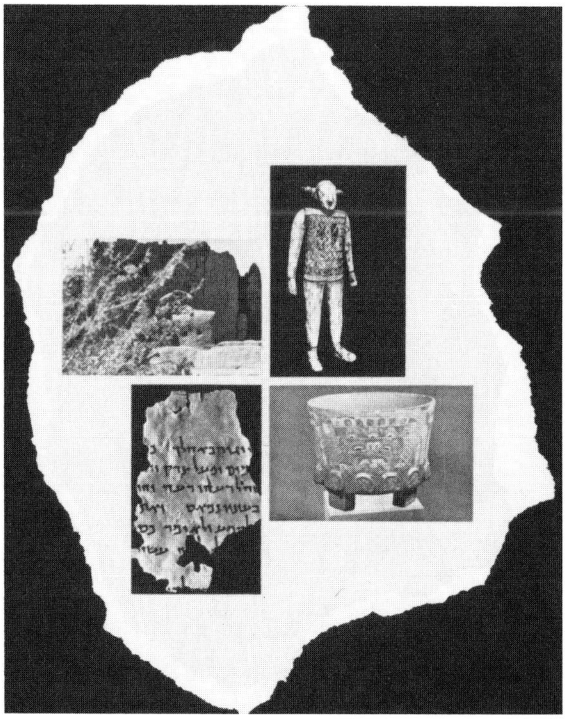

Figure 8.26: Photo montage using an intuitive grid.

VERTICAL AND HORIZONTAL EMPHASIS

You can emphasize the direction or flow that the elements take by the way in which you arrange artwork on a page or a spread. Part of that decision lies with the kind of artwork you have available. Other factors have to do with your grid and how you choose to arrange your visuals. If you are working with charts and graphs, you are limited as to their size and arrangement. Graphs cannot be lengthened or made wider in one dimension only without distorting the information. You can, however, place your captions to emphasize the visual flow that you require (see Figure 8.27.)

Page flow also has to do with continuity. It is more interesting to vary the visual flow from spread to spread while maintaining the same underlying grid.

You can get a visual picture of a layout's flow by printing out a thumbnail version of

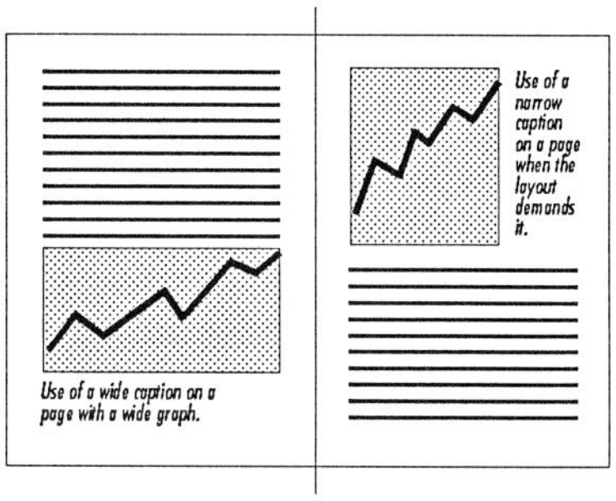

Figure 8.27: Example of how caption can be placed on a graph to emphasize the visual flow.

Figure 8.28: Pages can be designed to flow either vertically or horizontally, depending on the art used, the typeface chosen, and the text placement.

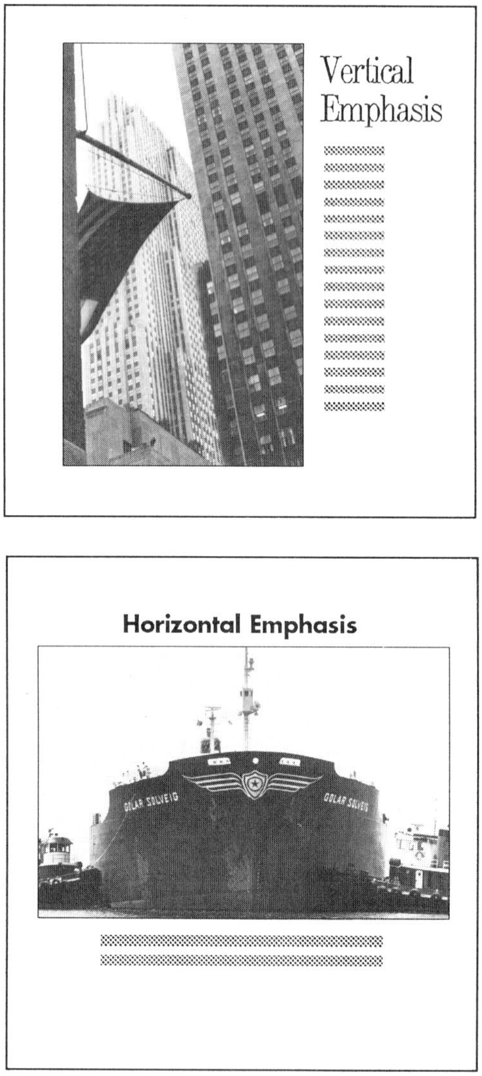

your publication after you have placed all the illustrations, photographs, and information graphics. When checking the flow, make sure that all the pages hold together as a single entity. You want them to look as if they all belong together as a design family. You also want to see that flow changes every so often (see Figure 3.28.)

Illustrations of people and the direction in which they are looking affect the flow of a layout. The power of optical direction is so strong that it can ruin the layout of a page, even when all other objects are in balance.

When placing a portrait, make sure that the eyes are facing inward toward the inside margin, especially if the image is placed close to the outside margin. If your image is close to the inside margin, have the eyes face outward (see Figure 8.29.)

Still another way to maintain visual flow is through contrast and emphasis. Vary the size of your illustrations. Using a large photograph with several smaller ones or interspersing a cartoon or drawing in a photo grouping give contrast and emphasis to your visual flow.

WORKING WITH CAPTIONS

When you are working with photographs or information graphics, you usually need to tell the reader something about the image: the name or title of a person, the location of a landscape, a description of an event, etc. Information graphics often have additional information about the data and the conclusions that can be drawn from it. Captions are the publication element that covers this information. Since illustrations vary in size and can be wide or narrow, it is a good idea to design captions so that they, too, can be used in a wide or narrow format, depending on the design of the page or spread. Figure 8.30 shows both uses.

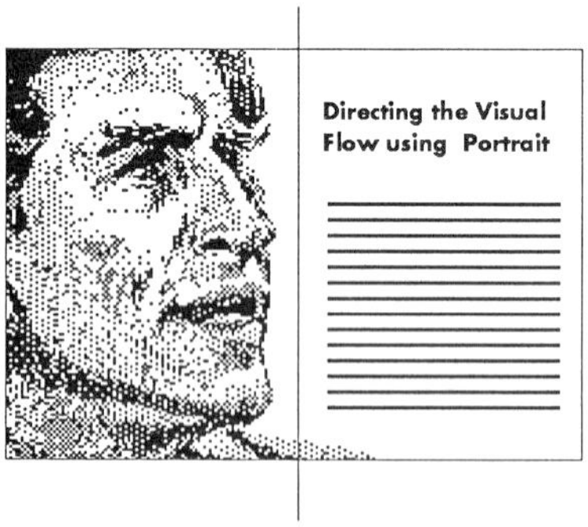

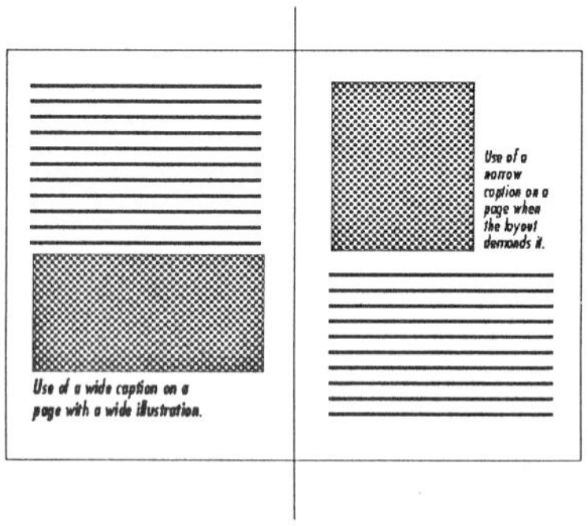

Figure 8.29: (left) You can control visual flow by insuring that eyes, whether human or otherwise, face in from the margin on a page.

Figure 8.30. (right) Captions can be designed to be used in both wide and narrow formats, depending on the images to be used.

ACQUIRING ARTWORK FOR YOUR PUBLICATION

When you need artwork for a publication and you can't create it on your own, you will need to purchase it. Artwork can be bought by hiring a professional to create the art for you personally or by selecting from an inventory of ready-made art.

BUYING ILLUSTRATIONS

When you purchase artwork from an illustrator, you can use either traditional or computer-rendered work. Price-wise, at the lowest end, students or talented amateurs can supply you with material, often for free, in order to get their work published. If your needs are for more sophisticated material, art organizations such as illustrators and art director's clubs in your city can generally recommend people who specialize in the kind of artwork you are seeking.

When interviewing an illustrator for a project, be sure you review his or her portfolio of work done in the past. If the project you have is a large one or involves tight deadlines, check with previous clients about the illustrator's reliability. Be explicit in describing your needs—the kind of visuals you need and the area the work is to occupy on the page, as well as your time schedule and deadlines. Make sure that your illustrator understands clearly what you require. Provide the illustrator with a purchase order that includes the above information and the agreed-upon price. You should expect to be furnished with two or three roughs for preliminary approval, to make sure that you and your illustrator are on the same track.

ACQUIRING PHOTOGRAPHS

You can pick up pictures for your publications by taking them yourself, by working with talented amateurs, or by hiring a professional after reviewing his or her portfolio.

HIRING A PHOTOGRAPHER

Hiring a photographer is very much like hiring an illustrator. Many photographers specialize in different branches of work; portrait photography, industrial, food, and sports are some of the categories. Photographers are usually paid by the day or half-day, plus materials. Provide your photographer with instructions comparable to those you would give to an illustrator. Your photographer will provide you with a number of pictures that are made at the same size of the negative and printed on an 8 x 10 sheet called a *contact sheet,* as shown in Figure 8.31. You will be asked to look at the contacts through

Figure 8.31: A photograhic contact sheet (courtesy Brittany Busché.)

Figure 8.32: A typical photo release form, reduced. A full sized version will be found in the Workshop/Forms Appendix.

Figure 8.32 **PHOTO RELEASE FORM**

Remove the header and paste this form on your letterhead

MODEL RELEASE AGREEMENT

To: ____________________ Date: ____________

____

____

____

I, ____________________,
Model Name

hereby grant to ____________________ a nonexclusive license to use my photograph or
Your Name

likeness for the following purpose ____________________

☐ for unlimited use

☐ for a one time use

for a term of

☐ unlimited amount of years

☐ ______ years

for the amount of

☐ gratis

☐ $ __________.

This agreement constitutes the entire agreement between the parties hereto and shall not be modified, amended, or changed in any way except by written agreement signed by both parties hereto. This agreement shall be binding upon and shall inure to the benefit of the parties, their successors, and assigns.

____
Model Signature

A copy of this letter is enclosed for your files. Please return this form to me by ____________
Date

Sincerely,

____
Name

Figure 8.33: A sample permissions form, reduced. A full sized version will be found in the Workshop/Forms Appendix.

Figure 8.33 **PERMISSIONS FORM**

Remove the header and paste this form on your letterhead

PICTURE REQUEST

To: ____________________ Date: ____________

I am preparing a ____________________

to be published by ____________________

on or about ____________________

May I please have your permission to include the following: ____________________

in my publication and in future revisions and editions thereof, including:

☐ nonexclusive distribution rights in the U.S.A. and its possessions and Canada in English

☐ nonexclusive distribution rights throughout the world in English

May I also have your permission to include the material cited above in the following publications and/or formats: ____________

These rights will in no way restrict other publication of your material in any form by you or by others authorized by you. Should you not control these rights in their entirety, please let me know to whom else I must write.

Unless you indicate otherwise, I will use the following credit line: ____________________

I would greatly appreciate your consent to this request. Please complete and return the release form below. A copy of this letter is enclosed for your files.

Sincerely,

____
(Name)

(Address)

I (we) grant permission for the use requested above. Date: ____________

Name/Title ____________________

Company ____________________

Address ____________________

Please fill in your Social Security # ____________ or Employer Identification # ____________

a magnifying glass to choose those you want enlarged. The photographer will help you make the selection, including cropping for best effect. A description of the project, with the space and direction (vertical or horizontal) allotted to each photo, plus the deadline, should be part of your purchase order. Also include the description of ownership and a permission-to-use statement.

BUYING STOCK PHOTOGRAPHY

Occasionally you find photographers who have a file of pictures you can purchase individually at a per-print rate. Your purchase is generally for a permission to use one time only, but it can be defined by mutual agreement.

Photographs can also be purchased from companies that sell images out of a large library devoted to many subject areas. This is called *stock photography*. Travel, foreign countries, political figures, special subjects, sports, can be purchased for one-time use from companies who maintain such files. Some companies are starting to provide stock photographs on disk; these have been scanned electronically and do not need additional processing for reproduction in low resolution. Use rates can vary substantially, depending on who the photographer is, whether you want black and white or color, the size you will be using, the quantity you are planning to purchase, and what the photos will be used for (a national magazine cover or a local nonprofit organization). Most stock agencies require a credit for the photograph in small type next to the photograph, as part of the caption, or in an acknowledgments section in the publication.

PHOTO RELEASE FORMS

Using a person's picture without permission can constitute an invasion of privacy, so make sure that you are protected. If the photographs you are using have people in them, verify that you have gotten a release from every individual that has been photographed prior to publishing your document. Photographs from a reliable stock company or news service will be covered by releases, but it is a good idea to confirm that fact when you make your selections. Figure 8.32 shows a typical photo release form, reduced. An actual sized version of Figure 8.32 is found in the Worksheet/Forms Appendix.

INEXPENSIVE SOURCES FOR ARTWORK

Illustrations and photographs can be purchased at fairly low rates from a number of sources. Art schools are one source, especially when purchasing from senior students and recent graduates. An excellent source for historical line engravings and photographs is the Library of Congress in Washington, D.C. Historical societies and museums also have large files of photographs that they rent out at low fees—often for the cost of the photograph and mailing. The news services such as Associated Press and UPI will sell you photographs of news events, including a print, with permission for one-time use. You will find that local newspapers usually have photo files devoted to local events that they supply at little or no charge. You are generally required to credit the source when you publish the piece.

THE COPYRIGHT LAWS

The copyright laws in this country have been designed to protect the original creator of a work. These laws cover authors, photographers, and illustrators among others. The producer of a creative work owns the work for a given number of years, unless it was done while under someone's direct employ, or if the creator has sold the ownership rights to another person or company.

Most clip art carries with it a permission to use, generally in any form. Any other art that you may pick up cannot be used without permission, even if you change it considerably. If you are not sure about ownership, get permission from the original creator or you may find yourself in a lawsuit! Figure 8.33 shows a typical sample permissions form, reduced. An actual sized version of Figure 8.33 can be found in the Workshop/Forms Appendix.

Copyright protection means that you cannot use someone else's artwork unless you have an agreement with the original creator or the present owner for permission to use it.

CHECKING YOUR UNDERSTANDING

1. Define the term "artwork" and give three forms of artwork discussed in this chapter.

2. List at least three suggestions for the appropriate use of each of the following graphic elements: rules, borders, and decorative characters.

3. Briefly explain the difference between line and halftone production of pictorial images.

4. Explain what a line drawing is and why line drawings are so popular in desktop published documents.

5. Contrast between the ways paint programs and draw programs produce a graphic image.

6. Identify and discuss three elements that must be considered when selecting a photograph with good composition.

7. List four categories of information graphics.

8. Discuss how the placement of graphics can emphasize the visual flow of a page layout.

9. Briefly discuss the various methods that can be used to obtain artwork for your publications.

10. Explain how copyright laws are designed to protect the owners of creative works.

BUILDING YOUR DESKTOP PUBLISHING DESIGN SKILLS

1. Through a visit to a software store or from a desktop publishing or computer magazine, identify the names of at least one paint and one draw program that are compatible with your computer and do the following:

   a) List the features of each program.

   b) Indicate any graphic libraries the programs have or that can be purchased separately.

2. Assume that you have been asked to design an employee newsletter for a local office furniture manufacturing firm, and do the following:

   a) Identify four different clip art library disks that would be appropriate for your newsletter.

   b) Using the local telephone book, obtain the name and address of at least one photographer you could hire to take any photographs you may need.

   c) Indicate three sources of free or inexpensive artwork for your publication.

   d) Describe what uses you may have for stock art in your newsletter.

3. Using a draw program and/or clip art and your desktop publishing program, create a simple logo for your friend who has just started his own building construction company.

4. Collect or photocopy a one-page layout that illustrates a photo essay and one that illustrates a photo montage, then do the following:

   a) Examine the photographs and evaluate their appropriateness for the publication and their composition (balance, focus, and tonal range).

   b) Indicate which of the photographs could be enhanced by cropping; then comment on how cropping would enhance those photographs.

5. Collect or photocopy one example of each type of information graphic discussed in this chapter. Identify and label each of your graphics.

DESKTOP DESIGN WORKSHOP

The purpose of this section is to provide you with opportunities to develop and/or improve your desktop publishing design skills. The worksheet pages have been placed at the back of the book, and are designed so they can be removed and you can write, draw, or place your responses directly onto the pages.

WORKSHEETS 8.1 AND 8.2

1. Assume you have been retained by a large travel service to produce a brochure that promotes their upcoming European tours. Prepare a thumbnail sketch of the brochure; using the sample photographs shown on Worksheet 8.1 and a broad tipped marking pen, indicate which portion of each of the photographs you would use.

2. Using the proof sheet and thumbnail sketch shown on Worksheet 8.2, select three action shots you would use for a story in a college alumni magazine. The title of the story is We Won! Mark your selections directly on each photo. Consider the following when making your selection.

The thumbnail sketch indicates a size and location for a large story lead-in photograph, and for two smaller ones. Select one photograph that you think will enlarge to work with the title to best convey the excitement of the game. Select the two smaller photographs considering the space that each one will fill, and how well all three photographs work together to tell the story visually.

PART THREE

DESIGN WORKBOOK APPLICATIONS

9. BUSINESS PUBLICATIONS

When you finish this chapter you should be able to:

- *Identify nine categories of business publications.*
- *Discuss the purpose and use of a corporate graphics standards handbook.*
- *Identify the elements to consider when planning a business publication grid.*
- *Discuss the purpose of business reports and give at least one example of a commonly used business report.*
- *Identify the basic items found in an effective business proposal.*
- *Contrast between the elements that make up a price/product specification sheet and those in a catalog.*
- *Define and distinguish between the different categories of analytical business graphics.*
- *Design overheads or 35mm slides to accompany a report or proposal.*
- *Design attractive business publications such as reports, manuals, directories, proposals, and catalogs.*

MOST BUSINESS PUBLICATIONS are documents that consist mainly of text with supportive graphics. The purpose of a business publication is the display of information that is easy to read and understand. Business publications include letters, memos, newsletters, reports, manuals, directories, proposals, catalogs, and product specification sheets. Reports and proposals are often augmented with matching overhead and 35mm slides containing material extracted from the text.

Some business related publications (i.e., newsletters, manuals, and catalogs) will be covered in separate chapters devoted to that particular category. Newsletters are covered in Chapter 10, *Newsletters and Newspapers;* short illustrated catalogs are covered in Chapter 11, *Flyers, Folders, Brochures, and Other Short Documents;* manuals and long catalogs are included in Chapter 12, *Long Documents.*

DESIGN STANDARDS FOR BUSINESS PUBLICATIONS

Design principles for business publications are the same as those covered in Chapters 1 through 8. As with all publications, design consistency is important. Business publications, particularly, benefit from a standard "look" that identifies the firm and its message. Large companies spend a great deal of time and money to design all their business print and graphics, from the company letterhead to the signage on their trucks, to a given corporate standard. The design standards for every single graphic element used by the company are generally recorded in a corporate graphics standards handbook. When a corporate graphic standards handbook is used, all members of the organization are expected to produce documents that conform to these standards.

The handbook is nothing more than an elaborate set of style guides, similar to, but more complex than style sheets used in your word processing and page layout programs.

Style sheets are one way to maintain consistency throughout all the publications produced by a business. They also help newcomers to get started quickly when preparing various type of documents.

STYLE SHEETS AND BUSINESS DOCUMENTS

Style sheets, covered in Chapter 3, *Document Structure: Organizing Your Publication,* are a collection of typographic and structural formats you as a designer can specify and name. Once you define a style sheet, you will have a new level of control over the documents that will be produced. To make a style sheet, you will need to define all the text and graphic elements to be included.

Since most page layout programs use style sheets to automate the layout and design decisions, you will first need to define all the text and graphic elements in your business design projects so they can be included in a style sheet. While business publications differ in content and format, they have some basic elements in common. These elements are shown in the business publication grid checklist illustrated in Figure 9.1.

DESIGNING A BUSINESS PUBLICATION

When designing a business publication, make sure that the text and visual language carry the message you want to the intended audience. The interior pages should be designed with consistency. Pay attention to titles, headings and subheadings, paragraph indentations, and text alignment, and make sure that they are uniform throughout the document. Rule lines, running heads, and folios should always appear in the same place on the page or spread and be set in the same font, page to page.

Before you start to design your layouts, confirm the purpose of the document and its audience with your client or the person in your organization who has ordered the design.

✔ BUSINESS PUBLICATION GRID CHECKLIST

- ☐ Page size and orientation
- ☐ Column
- ☐ Placement of Art
- ☐ Type specifications (typeface, size, and attributes)
    - ☐ Alignment (left, right, justified)
    - ☐ Subheadings
    - ☐ Running heads
- ☐ Margins
- ☐ Folios and page numbers
- ☐ Headings
    - ☐ Chapter or Section Titles
    - ☐ Figures and captions
    - ☐ Paragraph indentations

Figure 9.1: Business Grid Checklist

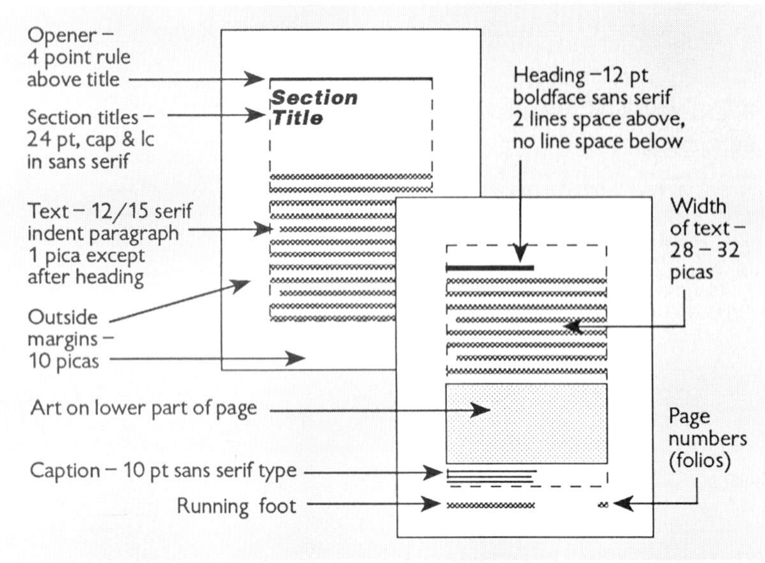

Figure 9.2: A grid for a sample publication.

Figure 9.3 **BUSINESS PUBLICATION SPECIFICATION WORKSHEET**

Publication: ____________

Designer: ____________ Date: ____________

SPECIFICATIONS:

Page size: ____________ Orientation ____________

Margins: Top ______ Bottom ______ Inside ______ Outside ______

Columns: Number ______ Width ______

New Sections: Begin with ☐ Next page ☐ Right page ☐ Left page

TYPE:

BODY TEXT: Font ______ Style ______ Point size ______

Line spacing: Alignment ______ Paragraph indent ______

HEADINGS: Font ______ Style ______ Point size ______

Subheading 1: Font ______ Style ______ Point size ______

Subheading 2: Font ______ Style ______ Point size ______

Folios: Font ______ Style ______ Point size ______

BOXED TEXT: Font ______ Style ______ Point size ______

Line spacing: Alignment ______ Paragraph indent ______

Rules: Size ______ Shade ______ ☐ Reverse out rule ☐ Tint boxed area

ILLUSTRATIONS/TABLES:

ART PLACEMENT: ☐ Full page ☐ Half page ☐ Quarter page ☐ Other ______

Boxed rule: Size ______ Shade ______ ☐ Reverse out rule ☐ Tint boxed area

Figure caption: Font ______ Style ______ Point size ______

Line spacing: Alignment ______ Paragraph indent ______

Table titles: Font ______ Style ______ Point size ______

Line spacing: ☐ All caps ☐ Caps and lowercase ☐ Caps and small caps ☐ Initial cap only

Table Text: Font ______ Style ______ Point size ______

Line spacing: Alignment ______ Paragraph indent ______

Figure 9.3: Business Publication Specification Worksheet; actual size found in Workshop/Forms Appendix.

Before you start to work on your preliminary thumbnail layouts, list all the elements needed in your publication.

As you polish the design layout, include specifications for every element you have listed. This way, your design will be consistent on every page of the document.

Business documents may be either 8-1/2 x 11 single sheets or double-sided publications. If your publication is double-sided, do your thumbnails as spreads. Show all the elements as illustrated in Figure 9.2. A specification sheet similar to the one illustrated in Figure 9.3 is completed so the design elements can be shared with others, as well as saved for future use when you need to design comparable documents.

BUSINESS REPORTS

Many different types of reports are used in business. In spite of their variety, the main goal for all reports is that of channeling information. There are no set rules for the format of business reports other than that they be easy to read and orderly in design. Depending on the company, you can chose from a wide range of styles.

In the average office, reports are typically a low-budget item. They are usually produced either on an office copier or on an offset press, depending on the quantity needed. Standard 8-1/2 x 11 paper stock is used; the text is set in a clean, straightforward typeface and includes one or two levels of headings. Charts and graphs are frequently part of financial and marketing reports. Occasionally, line drawings or photographs are used. Reports are traditionally laid out using a simple one- or two-column grid — a format that is all too easy to design poorly, in terms of clarity and readability. Recall the guidelines described in Chapter 7, *Grids: Structure and Space,* regarding length of line, margins, and the use of headings to break up the text. If you are designing a report with a one-column format, use wide margins, so that your line lengths are not too long. Most well-designed reports use a two-column format, with a wide column for text, and a narrow one for headings and illustrations. If you must use a format with two equal columns, avoid packing the pages full of solid text. Use headings, graphics, and white space as described in Chapter 7. Figure 9.4, a report makeover, illustrates some examples.

For all their simplicity, business reports are important documents. Make sure that the message carried by your design reinforces the company's image!

Most business reports include numerical or statistical data. Your design should not only make these data easy for reader to understand, but the style of data presentation should fit into the overall graphic style of the report (see Figure 9.5.)

Although most business reports are low-budget items, there are exceptions. Business reports that are made for clients and for the general public are usually attractive, expensive publications. Annual reports rank among the most attractive, "slickest" publications produced by businesses. Annual reports are required legally by the SEC (Securities Exchange Commission), but corporations also use them for public relations with their present and potential stockholders. Many annual reports are printed in full color. They include photographs of company personnel and products, along with charts and graphs showing company progress in the marketplace. They also include tables of financial data that, by

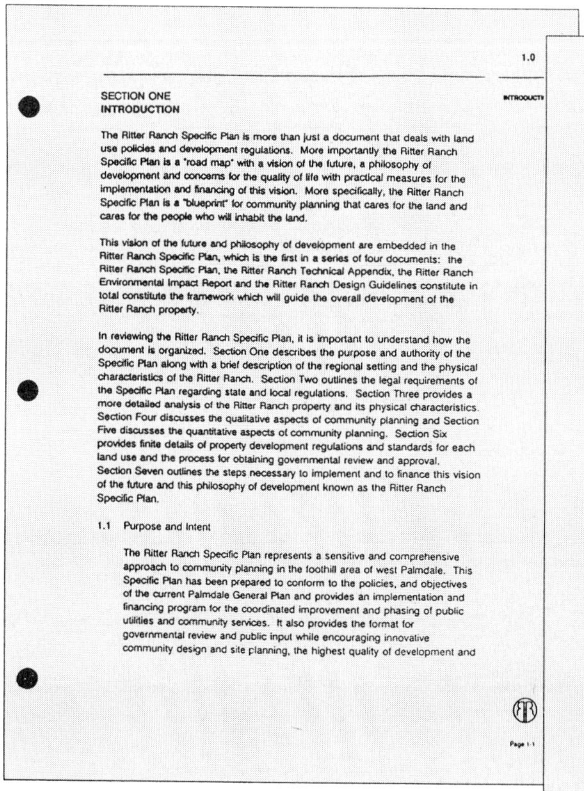

1.0

SECTION ONE
INTRODUCTION

The Ritter Ranch Specific Plan is more than just a document that deals with land use policies and development regulations. More importantly the Ritter Ranch Specific Plan is a "road map" with a vision of the future, a philosophy of development and concerns for the quality of life with practical measures for the implementation and financing of this vision. More specifically, the Ritter Ranch Specific Plan is a "blueprint" for community planning that cares for the land and cares for the people who will inhabit the land.

This vision of the future and philosophy of development are embedded in the Ritter Ranch Specific Plan, which is the first in a series of four documents: the Ritter Ranch Specific Plan, the Ritter Ranch Technical Appendix, the Ritter Ranch Environmental Impact Report and the Ritter Ranch Design Guidelines constitute in total constitute the framework which will guide the overall development of the Ritter Ranch property.

In reviewing the Ritter Ranch Specific Plan, it is important to understand how the document is organized. Section One describes the purpose and authority of the Specific Plan along with a brief description of the regional setting and the physical characteristics of the Ritter Ranch. Section Two outlines the legal requirements of the Specific Plan regarding state and local regulations. Section Three provides a more detailed analysis of the Ritter Ranch property and its physical characteristics. Section Four discusses the qualitative aspects of community planning and Section Five discusses the quantitative aspects of community planning. Section Six provides finite details of property development regulations and standards for each land use and the process for obtaining governmental review and approval. Section Seven outlines the steps necessary to implement and to finance this vision of the future and this philosophy of development known as the Ritter Ranch Specific Plan.

1.1 Purpose and Intent

The Ritter Ranch Specific Plan represents a sensitive and comprehensive approach to community planning in the foothill area of west Palmdale. This Specific Plan has been prepared to conform to the policies, and objectives of the current Palmdale General Plan and provides an implementation and financing program for the coordinated improvement and phasing of public utilities and community services. It also provides the format for governmental review and public input while encouraging innovative community design and site planning, the highest quality of development and

Page 1-1

Figure 9.4: A traditional business report, designed for a looseleaf binder (courtesy The Design Works.)

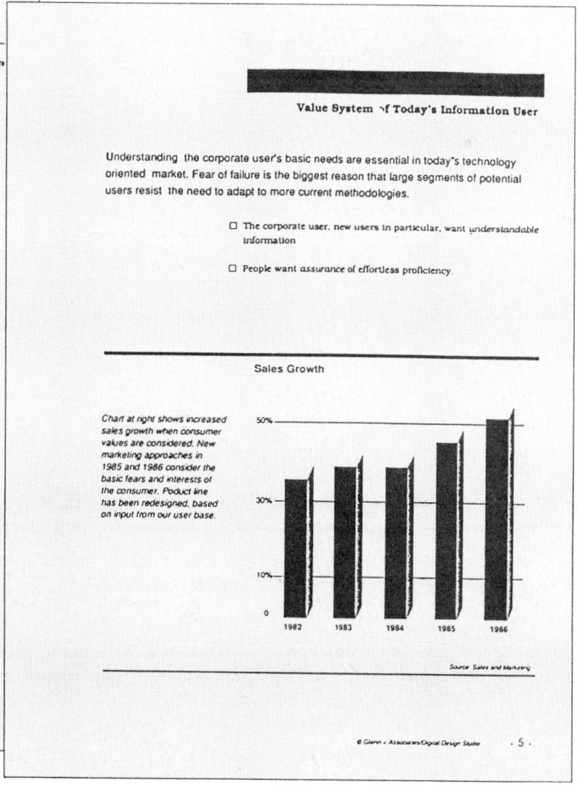

Value System ~f Today's Information User

Understanding the corporate user's basic needs are essential in today"s technology oriented market. Fear of failure is the biggest reason that large segments of potential users resist the need to adapt to more current methodologies.

☐ The corporate user, new users in particular, want *understandable* information

☐ People want *assurance* of effortless proficiency.

- 5 -

Figure 9.5: A business report incorporating graphics.

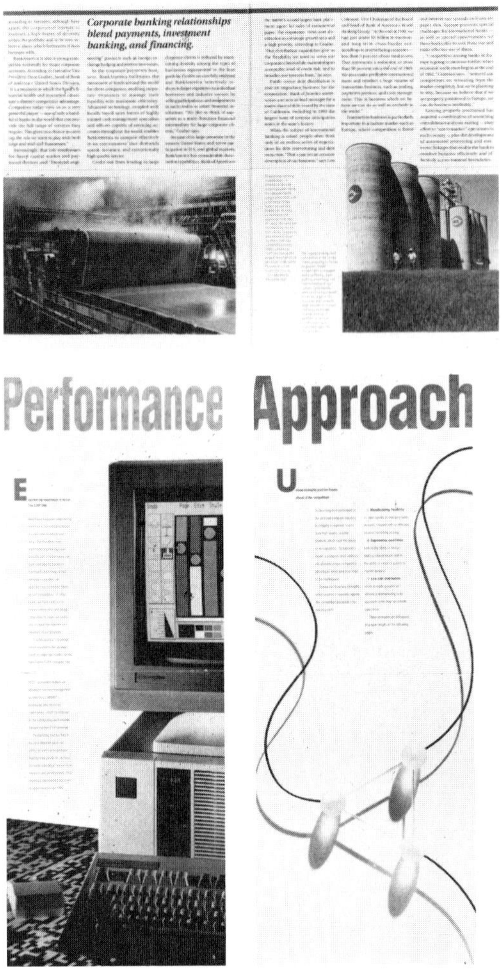

Figure 9.6: Pages from two annual reports; (top) a conservative layout for a bank and (bottom) a dynamic grid layout for a computer company (courtesy Vinje Design, Inc.)

law, must conform to SEC specifications. Figure 9.6 illustrates pages from a typical company annual report.

The annual report, like all business reports, consists of four basic elements: an introduction (a message from the president), a message (statement of goals and objectives), supportive data (financial reports), and graphic elements (artwork illustrating company activities and products.)

PROPOSALS

Proposals are business publications used to sell a product or service. Proposals are always customized for an intended audience, so they are produced in a limited quantity. As illustrated in Figure 9.7, a one- or two-column grid with an easy-to-ready typeface gives the proposal a professional look.

An effective proposal will contain the items listed in Figure 9.8.

DIRECTORIES

Directories are a special type of business publication. They are reference publications, but unlike reports and proposals, directories do not explain, they *present* information.

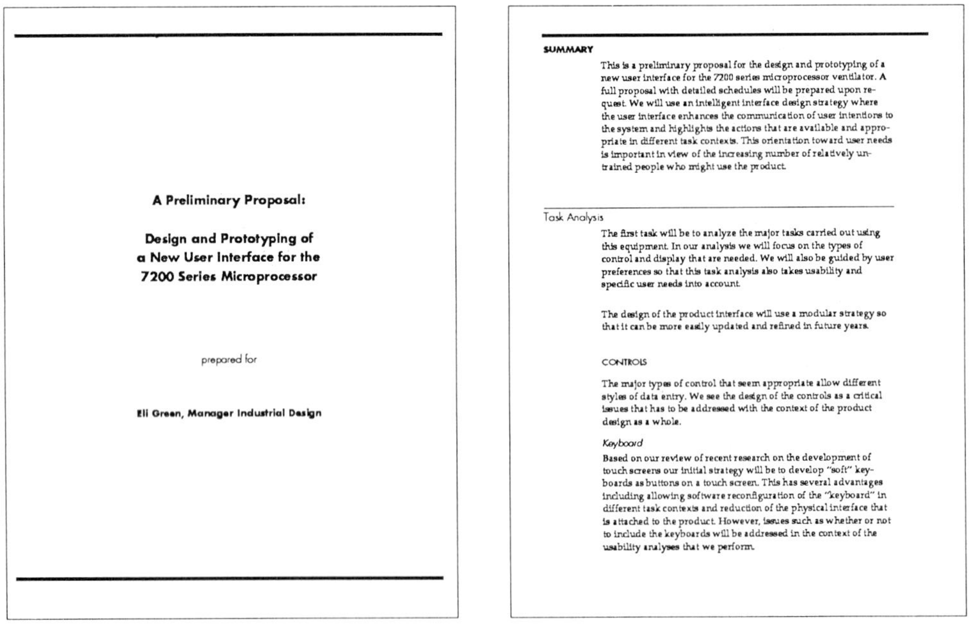

A Preliminary Proposal:

Design and Prototyping of a New User Interface for the 7200 Series Microprocessor

prepared for

Eli Green, Manager Industrial Design

SUMMARY

This is a preliminary proposal for the design and prototyping of a new user interface for the 7200 series microprocessor ventilator. A full proposal with detailed schedules will be prepared upon request. We will use an intelligent interface design strategy where the user interface enhances the communication of user intentions to the system and highlights the actions that are available and appropriate in different task contexts. This orientation toward user needs is important in view of the increasing number of relatively untrained people who might use the product.

Task Analysis

The first task will be to analyze the major tasks carried out using this equipment. In our analysis we will focus on the types of control and display that are needed. We will also be guided by user preferences so that this task analysis also takes usability and specific user needs into account.

The design of the product interface will use a modular strategy so that it can be more easily updated and refined in future years.

CONTROLS

The major types of control that seem appropriate allow different styles of data entry. We see the design of the controls as a critical issues that has to be addressed with the context of the product design as a whole.

Keyboard

Based on our review of recent research on the development of touch screens our initial strategy will be to develop "soft" keyboards as buttons on a touch screen. This has several advantages including allowing software reconfiguration of the "keyboard" in different task contexts and reduction of the physical interface that is attached to the product. However, issues such as whether or not to include the keyboards will be addressed in the context of the usability analyses that we perform.

Figure 9.7: A cover and summary page for a business proposal.

For example, a company telephone directory lists the name and telephone number of the firm's employees. An organization membership directory lists the name, address, and phone numbers for its members. Since directories contain text information in a list format, many directories are produced using entries directly from a computer database.

Directories are the least demanding of the business publications in terms of quality of layout and appearance. As you can see from the examples in Figure 9.9, a directory is a good example of a publication designed to fit a basic grid. As a text-intensive document, a directory fits nicely into a two-, three-, or four-column grid format. The two-column grid also works well for the design of those directories that include a limited amount of artwork.

✔ BUSINESS PROPOSAL CHECKLIST

An effective business proposal contains a:

- ☐ Title page
- ☐ Executive Summary
  - – All points covered in the report are summarized
- ☐ Table of Contents
  - – Shows organization of proposal
- ☐ Goals and Objectives
- ☐ Rationale for the Proposal
- ☐ Description of the Project
  - – Project phases
  - – Charts, graphs, timetables, and illustrations used to clarify points
- ☐ Proposed schedule
- ☐ Cost and Terms of Payment
- ☐ Assumptions
- ☐ Acceptance Form

Figure 9.8

CATALOGS AND PRICE/PRODUCT SPECIFICATION SHEETS

Catalogs and price/product specification sheets are publications that provide information about a firm's products and prices. Short illustrated catalogs are covered in detail in Chapter 11. Longer catalogs, those that list many items and parts, are covered in Chapter 12. Price/product specification

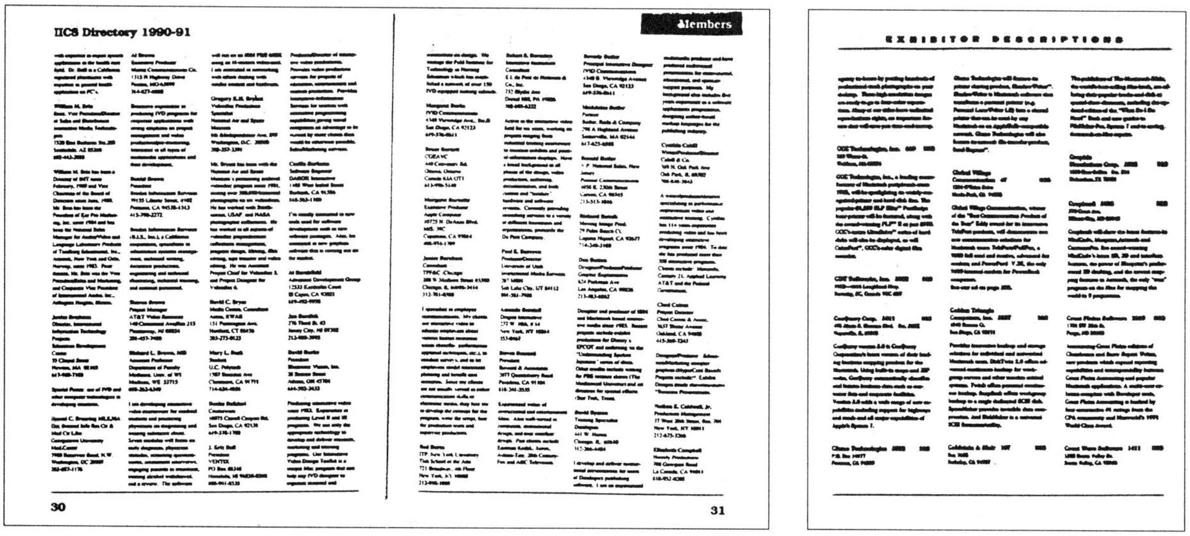

Figure 9.9: Sample business directories

Figure 9.10: A price/product specification sheet. (top) the front side, with an illustration. (bottom) the back, containing specifications (courtesy The Design Works.)

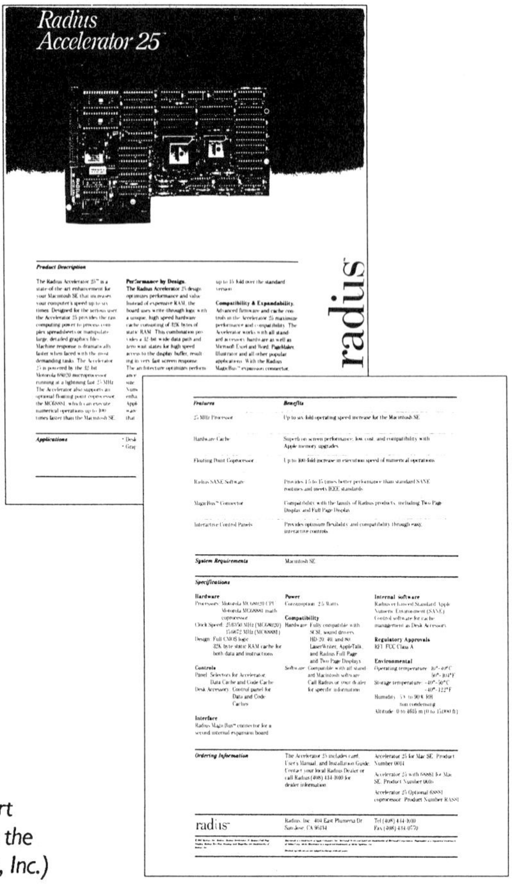

Figure 9.11: A business report with a bar chart to illustrate the text. (Courtesy Vinje Design, Inc.)

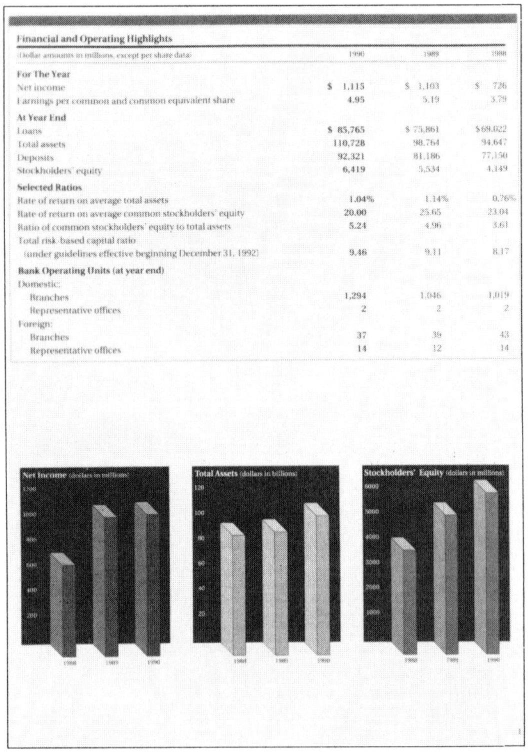

Financial and Operating Highlights

(Dollar amounts in millions, except per share data)	1990	1989	1988
For The Year			
Net income	$ 1,115	$ 1,103	$ 726
Earnings per common and common equivalent share	4.95	5.19	3.79
At Year End			
Loans	$ 85,765	$ 75,861	$ 69,022
Total assets	110,728	98,764	94,647
Deposits	92,321	81,186	77,150
Stockholders' equity	6,419	5,534	4,149
Selected Ratios			
Rate of return on average total assets	1.04%	1.14%	0.76%
Rate of return on average common stockholders' equity	20.00	25.65	23.04
Ratio of common stockholders' equity to total assets	5.24	4.96	3.61
Total risk-based capital ratio (under guidelines effective beginning December 31, 1992)	9.46	9.11	8.17
Bank Operating Units (at year end)			
Domestic:			
Branches	1,294	1,046	1,019
Representative offices	2	2	2
Foreign:			
Branches	37	39	43
Representative offices	14	12	14

sheets are single 8-1/2 x 11 sheets containing information on a single item or several closely related items. They are used when a company has only a few items for sale, or if the products or prices are updated frequently.

As illustrated in Figure 9.10, the front side of a specification sheet consists of a good-quality photograph or line drawing of the product, whichever will show it off in best detail. The front page also contains a headline, a short descriptive paragraph, and the company name and phone number. The reverse side contains detailed pricing information and specifications. Tables are often used for descriptive information, especially if there are several products displayed. The company name, address, and telephone number appear on the back side as well. If several specification sheets are to be shipped to prospective buyers, they are often put into special company-styled folders. Specification sheets are also used in loose-leaf binders, and are three-hole punched when designed for this purpose.

CREATING GRAPHICS FOR BUSINESS PUBLICATIONS

Most business publications contain financial or other business data. Often a variety of charts and graphs are used to make these data visually more understandable. Graphics used in business are commonly called analytic graphics because they are used to summarize the analysis of business data. There are three categories of analytic graphics, explained in the following paragraphs. Page designs incorporating analytic graphics are shown in Figure 9.11; examples of charts and graphs used in business publications are illustrated in Figure 9.12.

TEXT CHART

A text chart is a simple table in which text rather than numeric information is organized and presented for the reader. Text charts are rarely used in written documents because the text of the report takes the place of the chart.

FLOW CHART

This chart shows the form of an organization or a process. Flow charts are word charts supplemented with boxes, circles, lines, and arrows to indicate flow. These charts are often used in annual reports and procedures manuals.

GRAPH CHART

A graph chart presents information based on numbers that are plotted on a graph or represented with pictures. There are three types of graph charts: bar, line, and pie. Bar graphs show relationships between items. Line graphs show comparisons over a period of time. Pie charts show the relationship of parts to a whole.

Charts and graphs can be created with special business graphic software programs or with your page layout programs. If you create a bar graph and a pie chart using the graphic tools in your layout program, you will have to plan the graphic by estimating the size of the overall graphic and the bars and segments to be used.

You can enhance graph charts in several ways. The bars of a bar graph can be created with pictures instead of rectangular bars. Furthermore, bar graph data can be arranged to appear as comparative, stacked, or three-dimensional.

The visual appearance of the data in a pie chart can be highlighted by filling in each area with a different shade. Additional graphic interest can be added to a pie chart by exploding (showing a piece removed). Since charts and graphs are used to present information visually, use these enhancements only to clarify the data.

It is all too easy to fall into the trap of elaborate graphics that can look terrific but can also confuse the information.

Refer to Chapter 8, *Working with Photos and Illustrations* for additional help when producing information graphics.

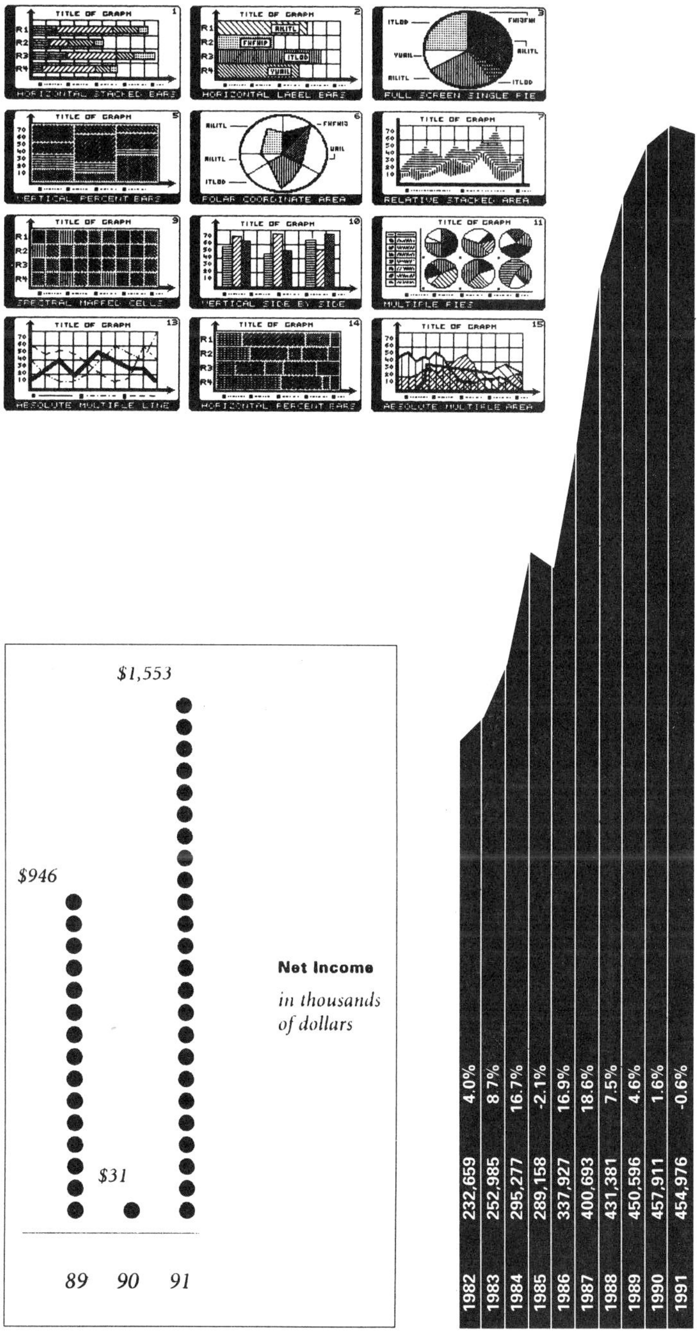

Figure 9.12: Charts and graphs used in business publications. (top) a screen dump showing a variety of formats in a graphics program (courtesy Three D Graphics); (bottom left) a bar chart from an annual report and (bottom right, a composite bar and line chart,(both courtesy René Sheret Design.)

PRESENTATION GRAPHICS TO ACCOMPANY A REPORT OR A PROPOSAL

When a report or a proposal is presented at a meeting, the power of the written document is enhanced through the use of presentation visuals such as overheads and 35mm slides. Material extracted from the published document is used to create these items. Text outlines are based on headings in the document. Information graphics are usually enlarged and presented as individual slides. (See Figure 9.13.)

OVERHEAD SLIDES

Overhead slides, or *overheads* are 8-1/2 x 11 transparent acetate sheets containing text and/or graphics. These are projected by an overhead projector onto a screen or light-colored wall. The presenter can write on the acetate sheet to make a point, or can point to it for special emphasis. Overheads are easily made using a desktop layout program. Merely laser print your material on clear plastic sheets especially made for that purpose. Overhead slides can be designed in either the portrait or landscape orientation, depending on the text and graphics.

It is equally important to follow the sequence of your written report. Your audience may want to take notes on their written copy handouts, which they can keep for reference after the presentation. The speaker is free to emphasize and expand on particular issues during the course of the presentation.

Don't overload your slides with too much text. For overheads to communicate with clarity, select only the most important material for your audience to focus on.

When preparing overhead slides, use no more than three or four main items, and set in 16 point type or larger. Bullets or dingbats can be used to set off each item in the list. Your main heading should be bold and larger than the text items; it can be set in white letters reversed out of a black area. As with any printed document, be consistent in your design from slide to slide and maintain a look that is similar in feeling to the printed document you are using. Use the same typefaces and graphics, but set larger for projection purposes. (See figure 9.14.)

When preparing overheads that present information in a graphics format, use only

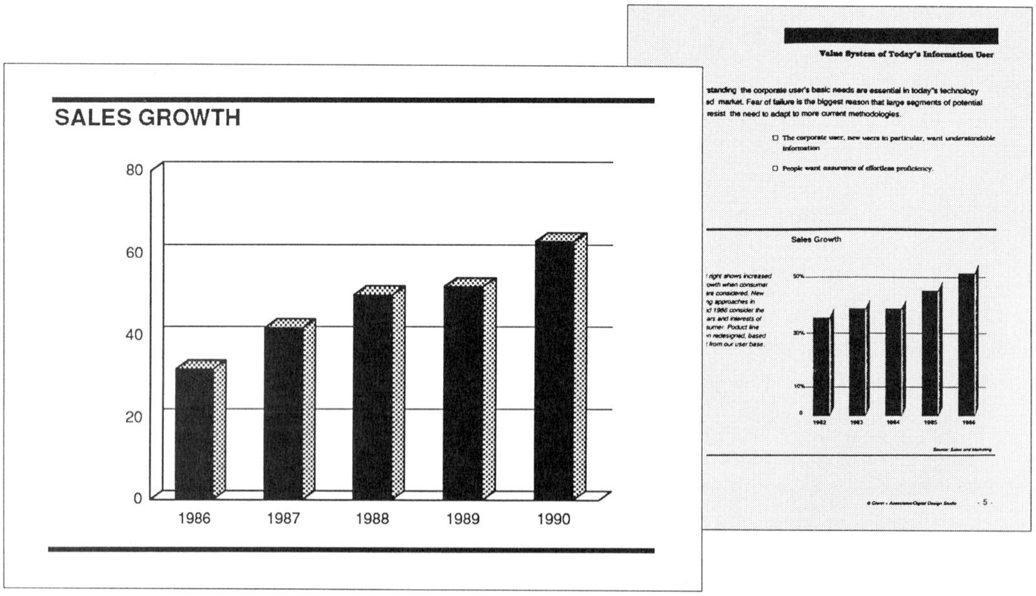

Figure 9.13: Overhead slide with an accompanying handout sheet.

one or two charts or diagrams per sheet, depending on how complex they are.

35MM SLIDES

Presentation-quality 35mm slides are just like the color slides made using a camera, but they are designed using a desktop presentation graphics program. If your audience is a large one and the presentation requirements are more formal, you might want to look into using presentation graphics to enhance the report.

In a presentation graphics program, you key in the text and place graphics much as you do in paint or draw programs. The rules for content are the same as those for black-and-white overheads; the main difference lies in the use of color. The background you choose can be in a range of colors, rather than white or clear. Text and graphics elements can be in color as well. When selecting color combinations, you should follow the rules for color contrast as outlined in Chapter 6, *Type Aesthetics.* Some programs allow you to use digitized photographs, drawings or elaborate graphics made in your paint programs. If you find that there are jagged or aliased edges in your screens, software programs are available to allow you to eliminate them in a process called anti-aliasing.

After you have completed your slides in the presentation graphics program, you will need to take the disk or communicate the file to a service bureau for processing.

Presentation graphics can also be shown directly on a computer screen, if your audience is limited to just a few people. If you are presenting computer screens to a crowd, systems are available that project the computer image on to a large screen.

For more information on producing 35mm slides with a desktop presentation graphics program, read the documentation that comes with your software package. Persuasion and PowerPoint are two programs for Macintosh. Applause, Harvard Graphics, and Power Point are presentation program for DOS-based machines. Jag is a software program for the Mac that eliminates "jaggies" on many kinds of graphic images, and is compatable with a number of paint programs.

CHECKING YOUR UNDERSTANDING

1. Briefly define the purpose of a business publication and list at least four different types of business publications.

2. Why should you consider all of a business publication's elements when designing a business publication?

3. Compare and contrast the layout and design of in-house company reports with the design of an annual report.

4. Which part of an annual report needs to conform to government specifications?

5. Distinguish between a business report and a proposal.

6. Give three elements on which the design of a business price/product specification sheet will depend.

7. Give two examples of a directory used in business.

8. List and briefly define the different types of analytic graphics used in business publications.

9. Indicate three ways in which an analytic graphic can be enhanced. Include a small sketch illustrating your answer.

10. What are two important features of an overhead slide?

11. What are the design considerations for text elements on a slide?

12. When should 35mm slides be used in preference to overhead slides?

BUILDING YOUR DESKTOP DESIGN SKILLS

1. Secure a copy of a business report; perhaps one issued by your firm or school. Select one page of the report, and using what you have learned from this book and your page layout program, redesign the selected page. Submit a copy of the original

report page with your "makeover" and a brief description of your changes and why you made them.

2. Secure a recent issue of a price/product specification sheet. Using the layout of the specification sheet, draw a design grid for its front and back pages.

3. Secure an annual report. (Most public libraries maintain a file of such reports).

   a) Review the charts and graphs used in the report and discuss whether the format that has been chosen shows the information in the best possible form.

   b) Discuss the overall layout of the report and describe whether the page design and photographs do a good public relations job in presenting the company to its stockholders.

   c) Review the financial tables at the end of the annual report and sketch an alternate design that you think will present the data more clearly.

4. Use the following statistics to create a simple pie chart and a comparative bar chart. Sketch your graphs or create them using your page layout program.

   a) Pie Chart

   Title: Desktop Publishing Uses
   Subtitle: Year-1991
   Data Elements:
   - Newsletters, 25%
   - Business Publications, 15%
   - Brochures and Flyers, 50%
   - Books, 5%
   - Magazines, 2%
   - Other Uses, 3%

   b) Bar Chart

   Title: Desktop Publishing Uses
   Subtitle: (by Computer Platform)

Data Elements:	DOS-based	MAC
Newsletters	130	300
Business Publications	70	35
Brochures and Flyers	101	450
Books	30	10
Magazines	5	25

DESKTOP DESIGN WORKSHOP

The purpose of this section is to provide you with opportunities to develop and/or improve your desktop publishing design skills. The worksheet pages have been placed at the back of the book, and are designed so they can be removed and you can write, draw, or place your responses directly onto the pages.

WORKSHEET 9.1

Use the thumbnails on Worksheet 9.1 to create the layout for a simple business report. The text of the report is stored on the data disk that accompanies this book ("9Report.DOC" for DOS or "9 Report" for Mac) and can be printed so you can see the copy that will be used.

1. On page 1, design a cover using text and rules only (no graphic).

2. Create a table of contents on page 2.

3. Create a layout for pages 3 and 4.

4. Produce a hard copy of the report using the layout you have just created as a guide. Use your page layout program along with the appropriate text file on the data disk.

WORKSHEET 9.2

Using the area provided on Worksheet 9.2, design two overhead slides in portrait orientation to accompany the report you designed on Worksheet 9.1.

1. Design the first slide as a cover or title slide, based on your report cover design.

2. Design the second slide as a text slide, using bullets or dingbats to emphasize some point(s) in the text of the report.

3. Print out copies of your overhead slides.

10. NEWSLETTERS AND NEWSPAPERS

When you finish this chapter you should be able to:

- *Distinguish between a newsletter and a newspaper.*
- *List the typical dimensions and formats for newsletters.*
- *List and briefly describe the four categories of newsletters.*
- *Discuss principles of newsletter layout and design.*
- *Discuss the grid elements common to all newsletters.*
- *Distinguish between a nameplate and a masthead.*
- *Distinguish between the balance layout and the modular layout in newspaper design.*
- *Distinguish between display ads and classified ads.*
- *Explain how newspaper ads are sold by the column inch.*
- *Discuss why the placement and position of newspaper ads is important to the advertiser.*

NEWSLETTERS AND NEWSPAPERS are publications issued at regular, repeated, intervals such as weekly, monthly, or quarterly. They fit into a category known as *periodical publications*. Newsletters and newspapers are grouped together in this chapter because they share many of the same features. They also include features that are distinctly different, such as size and budget. These similarities and differences are discussed here.

NEWSLETTERS

A *newsletter* is a publication directed toward a well-defined audience. Its content is usually limited to specific information aimed at the chosen audience. Newsletters are meant to inform rather than entertain. Unlike newspapers, newsletters generally do not contain advertisements. They are usually short documents — about ten pages or less — and are written and produced on a limited budget. Newsletters are one of the most common desktop publishing projects.

TYPICAL NEWSLETTER DIMENSIONS AND FORMATS

Dimensions	Format
8-1/2 x 11	one-side
8-1/2 x 11	two-sided
8-1/2 x 14	one- or two-sided
8-1/2 x 14	two-sided, folded at center (7 x 8-1/2) and stapled
17 x 11	two-sided, folded at center (8-1/2 x 11) and stapled
17 x 25-1/2	two-sided, folded at center and trimmed to 8-1/2 x 11
14 x 22	two-sided, folded at center (11 x 14)

Table 10.1

McGraw-Hill InfoPlus

the newsletter for healthcare information managers

1991 Issue 1

The Impact of Severity of Illness on Hospital Utilization and Outcomes

John G. Christoffersson, M.B.A., M.S.E., Jonathan E. Conklin, M.S., Joseph Gonnella, M.D.*

Professionals

DECEMBER

Real Estate

Decision Support Software for DOS

Griffin's Signature

A NEWSLETTER FOR THE PUBLISHING INDUSTRY

Book Publishing is Serious Business

Do Your Homework!

by Robert Erdmann

It was exactly two years ago that I wrote the first of many articles for *Griffin's Signature*. In that first article, I stressed the importance of strategic planning for every book published. I feel even stronger about that position now.

The advent of the personal computer and desktop publishing has made it ever so easy for nearly anybody to publish a book. Industry statistics point out quite vividly to us by telling that over 53,000 new titles are published annually. How many of these are successful by any definition? Very few!

Publishing is a very cost- and labor-intensive business, with little guarantees that rewards for such expenditures will ever be fully realized. Unfortunately, I encounter many publishers only after they have taken the deep plunge, printed several thousand copies of a book, and find themselves in trouble.

How do they get themselves into such desperate situations? Because quite often, they haven't done their homework. Oh sure, they have attended some seminars and read materials on how easy it is to self-publish. Unfortunately, they have responded emotionally to poor advice. When they finally face the realism of the situation, they find that they are alone in the very serious business of publishing. Thousands of hard earned (or worse, high-interest loaned) dollars are spent with no ROI (return on investment in sight). Not much attention, realistically speaking, has been spent on the basics of cash flow. Most have simply felt that their great idea for a book becomes real simply by getting it printed. Getting it to the stores or other channels of distribution will be easy. Wrong!

The greatest advice I have heard for the small publisher was given to me some months ago. It came from Mr. Jim Chandler, General Merchandise Manager at B. Dalton Booksellers home office in New York. Quite simply, he stated, "Tell them to do their homework BEFORE anything else". Just think of all the problems you will avoid and money you will save if you only follow that sage advice... DO YOUR HOMEWORK.

Yes, publishing has changed a great deal in recent years. Everything has. And believe me, al-

(Cont'd page 2)

INSIDE THIS ISSUE

THE SIX DEADLY SINS IN MAIL-ORDER Page 6

PUBLISHERS' CHRONICLE OF EVENTS Page 3

PUBLISHERS' SPOTLIGHT NAT BODIAN Page 5

VOLUME 4, NO. 2 MARCH/APRIL 1989

Figure 10.1: Three typical newsletters. (top) McGraw Hill, for health professionals, courtesy Edward Smith Design, Inc.; (center) by the Boston Computer Society; (bottom) by Griffin Printing.

NEWSLETTER CATEGORIES

Newsletters can be placed into one of four basic categories: subscription, organizational, franchise, and public relations newsletters.

As the name implies, a *subscription newsletter* is produced for an audience that buys a subscription to the newsletter, or receives it as part of the organization's membership dues. Subscription newsletters contain news that is specific to an area of personal or professional interest, to a product, or to consumer-related issues. Club, group, and institutional publications are included in this category. There are probably more subscription newsletters than any other type.

Organizational newsletters are directed and distributed to employees, volunteers, or members of business firms, nonprofit organizations, and governmental agencies. The content for newsletters in this category is based on a comprehensive coverage of news and trends related to the purpose of the business or organization.

Franchise newsletters are prepared by the head office and sent to local franchise stores or offices to complete and distribute. In a typical example, the head office of a real estate sales franchise will prepare a newsletter for its franchisees. The newsletter is complete, except for a space called the nameplate, where each local office can place its name and address. When the local office receives its newsletters, they are sent to a print shop that imprints the local office nameplate. The personalized newsletters are usually distributed free of charge within the local community.

Public relations newsletters are produced and distributed for the express purpose of building goodwill. The public relations newsletter contains articles that appeal to the interests of the intended audience. It also includes product information specific to the sponsoring organization.

DIMENSIONS AND FORMAT

The biggest difference between newsletters and newspapers is the size of the finished publication. While the most common newsletter size is 8-1/2 x 11, there are other sizes and formats. Some of the more common formats are listed in Table 10.1 and illustrated in Figure 10.1.

The dimensions and format of your newsletter will depend on its target audience and publication goals. For example, a monthly newsletter for a local computer user group might use a single 8-1/2 x 11 page printed on both sides, while a newsletter for the fund-raising foundation of a local hospital would be more likely to use an 11-1/2 x 17 layout featuring high-quality paper, folded and stapled into a multipage publication.

NEWSLETTER GRID

Newsletter design, like all publication design, begins with a plan. First you must decide if the newsletter is to be a *self-mailer* (a publication that is mailed without an envelope). As illustrated in Figure 10.2, a self-mailer newsletter has one outside panel that folds over and is used for the mailing address label and other post office requirements. Check with the post office to find out what the requirements are for your publication and the mailing method you have chosen.

After distribution plans for your newsletter have been determined, you start planning the design by sketching rough thumbnails. When you have gotten an approval for your rough design, you will be ready to prepare your final design and page layout grid. The grid is important in maintaining a consistent look to your newsletter from issue to issue. A sample newsletter grid is shown in Figure 10.3. As you can see, this grid is similar to those prepared for any other publication in that it includes specifications for margins and columns, rules and borders, folios, and type. A newsletter grid will also include specifications and positions for two elements specific to newsletters and newspapers: the nameplate and the masthead. These and other newsletter elements are discussed in this section.

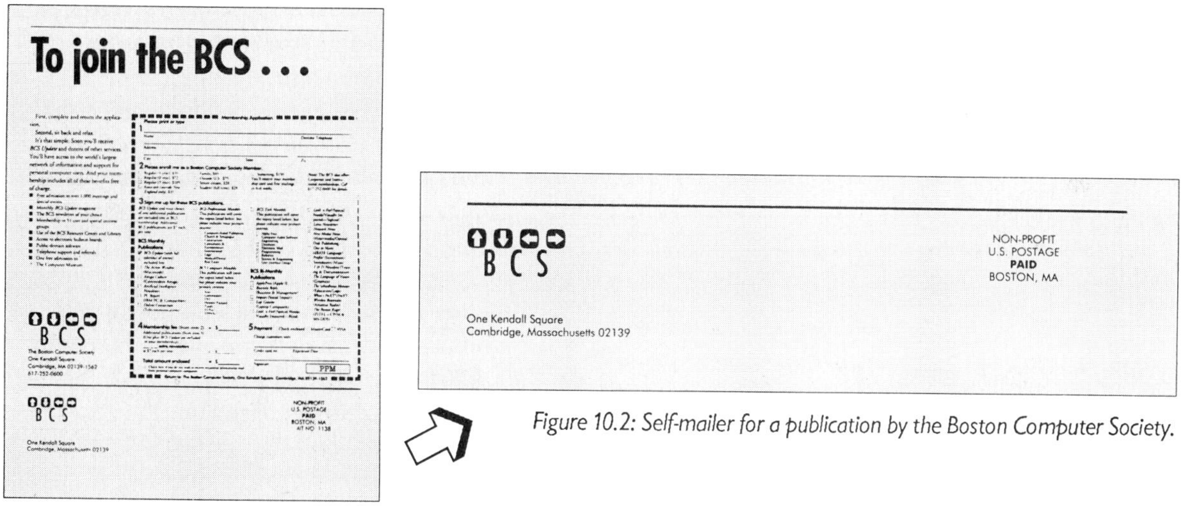

Figure 10.2: Self-mailer for a publication by the Boston Computer Society.

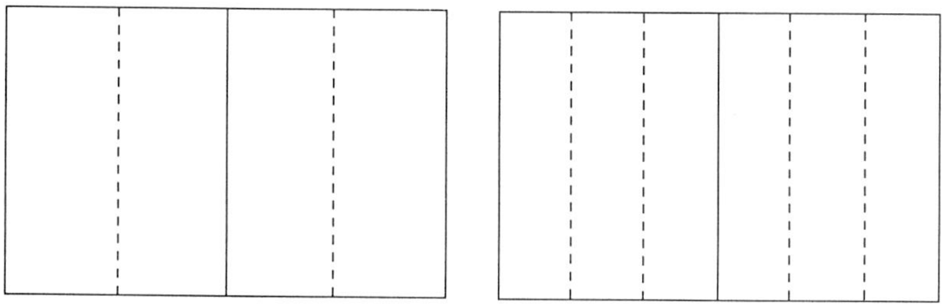

Figure 10.3: Grid layout for a two- and a three-column newsletter

NUMBER AND SIZE OF COLUMNS

There is no set rule regarding the number of columns that should be used; follow the guidelines discussed in Chapter 7, *Grids: Working with Structure and Space.* Most newsletters use a two- or three-column format. A popular technique is to vary column widths. For example, if you are using a two-column format, you can have one column that is two-thirds of the page wide and one column that is one-third of the page wide.

If you are using a three-column grid and don't want to vary column widths, you can create interest by occasionally spreading an article across two columns.

TEXT ALIGNMENT

Except for consistency, there are no hard-and-fast rules regarding text alignment. Ragged right columns of text result in fewer hyphenated lines; therefore, there is less of a chance for readers to lose their place. Although ragged text makes the spaces between the columns appear wider than they actually are, it also requires more space between the columns as a visual separator. If you need wider columns and have set the column gutter space to no narrower than 1-1/2 picas, a hairline rule between the columns will make the visual separation more clear.

Justified text works well for a more formal newsletter, but, because of the narrow column width you may run into the danger of overly wide word spacing and rivers. Try to avoid wide word spacing by selecting a body type face with a high character count per pica. If your page layout program allows it, selecting an appropriate body type and setting it on a tight normal track will also help. Columns of justified text can be set with as little space as 1-1/2 picas between them and still appear comfortably separated without the use of rules.

RULES AND BORDERS

Rules help set off the page and column boundaries and they are often placed in the column gutters. Rules act as visual breaks, helping to return the reader's eyes to the left rather than allowing them to accidentally move over into the next column. Experiment with the style and thickness of the rules you plan to use to see which works best with your design. For example, a hairline rule is usually used between columns because it will not overpower the space as a heavier rule would. A wide rule used at the top of an article title will pull the reader's eye to the beginning of a story and add sparkle to the page.

NAMEPLATE

The nameplate and masthead on a newsletter are often confused. The nameplate is the

Figure 10.4: A nameplate for a newsletter. Note that it contains the name of the publication and the sponsoring organization.

area that names and identifies the newsletter. A nameplate includes the following:

- ✔ *Name of the publication*
- ✔ *Name of the organization producing or sponsoring the newsletter*
- ✔ *Graphic(s) associated with the nameplate*

The nameplate is usually placed at the top of the newsletter, but it may be placed along one side (see Figure 10.4.) Be consistent in its placement, issue to issue.

MASTHEAD

A masthead is a box listing editorial information about the newsletter. The masthead can be placed at the top or bottom of the page or along the left side. If a masthead is placed on the first page, it is usually fitted in at the bottom. If it is placed on the editorial page, the masthead is usually placed at the top left. Mastheads are also placed on the same page as a table of contents, at the side or on the bottom (see Figure 10.5.) All mastheads include the following six elements, as well as any other information the publisher wants to include.

- ✔ *Name of the newsletter*
- ✔ *Name and address of the sponsoring organization*
- ✔ *Name of the editor*
- ✔ *Circulation*
- ✔ *Frequency of the publication*
- ✔ *Date of issue and volume number, if there is one*

HEADER OR FOOTER

Most multipage newsletters contain a header or footer that includes the page number or folio, the name of the publication, and the date or issue number. This information is grouped as a unit, and is placed uniformly on each page of the newsletter.

TYPE FAMILY AND FACES

The type family and faces used for all elements should compliment your design (see Chapters 5, *Type Basics*; and Chapter 6, *Type Aesthetics,* for a full discussion of typographic possibilities.) In a single-column 8-1/2 x 11 newsletter design, 12-point type is generally used for main text. Three-column

EL PAIS

PRESIDENTE DE HONOR
José Ortega Spottorno

PRESIDENTE
Jesús de Polanco

CONSEJERO DELEGADO
Juan Luis Cebrián

DIRECTOR
Joaquín Estefanía Moreira

DIRECTOR GENERAL
Javier Díez Polanco
DIRECTOR GERENTE
José Mariano Martín

EDICIÓN INTERNACIONAL

DIRECTOR GENERAL
Carlos Mendo
REDACTOR JEFE
Ángel Luis de la Calle

Figure 10.5: a masthead from the international edition of a well-known European newspaper.

8-1/2 x 11 pages works well with a 9 or 10 point main text, depending on the typeface you have chosen.

NEWSPAPERS

Newspapers are periodicals printed on large unbound sheets and are generally issued at least once a week. Newspapers carry both news and advertisements. From the standpoint of design and layout, newspapers differ from newsletters in terms of their scale or size. They are similar in the way that they assign stories to pages. As you can see in Figure 10.6, the same basic design components that are used in newsletters are found in newspapers.

LAYOUT AND DESIGN

Newspapers generally have more columns than newsletters because they are printed on larger sheets. Newspapers tend to have four or five column grids. A five-column format is more popular because it offers more design flexibility. When a five-column design is used, a story may be from one to five columns wide or any combination: (one column and four columns, two columns and three columns, and so on.) A four-column layout only allows one column and three columns, two columns and two columns, and a full four columns wide. See Chapter 7 for more information regarding layout options.

Newspaper stories are placed into the columns according to one of two patterns: balanced layout or modular layout. When a *balanced layout* is used, stories are placed in the columns according to their relative importance as news. That is, the most important story is placed in the top of the right-hand column. Other stories are placed in sequence down and across from this starting point. The importance of a story is also indicated by the size of its headline. The larger the headline, the more important the story (see Figure 10.6.)

NEW YORK FORUM

Johnson Asks 10% Income-Tax Surcharge

Lindsay Prods Banks: Aid Stores in Slums

'Hate' Unit Said to Get U.S. Funds

45,000 More U.S. Troops Will Go to Vietnam

ANALYSIS

Between the Lines, Indicators of a Wider War

INSIDE

Priceless Gems Stolen In Jerusalem Shrine

EL PAIS

EDICIÓN INTERNACIONAL

González pide a Bush que mantenga su ayuda a Europa

La documentación incautada en Francia demuestra la lucha entre grupos etarras

La caída de Artapalo desvela la crisis en ETA

El Rey sella la paz con los judíos

EN ESTE NÚMERO

Bérégovoy, nuevo primer ministro de Francia

Manifestantes libios asaltan embajadas en Trípoli

47 millones de italianos juzgan en las urnas el sistema partitocrático

Cultura

Memorias de Sefarad

La huelga general paralizó Galicia el jueves 3

Este año no se ha producido el agujero en la capa de ozono sobre el Polo Norte

Figure 10.6: Newspaper layouts. (right) Modular layout. (center) Modular layout. (Courtesy El Pais.) (far right) A contempory design using a modular layout. (Copyright © 1974, Courier-Journal & Louisville Times Co. Reprinted with permission.)

When the balanced layout is used, most stories will jump or will be continued to the inside pages. Newspaper editors do this to get readers to look at the inside pages.

The *modular layout,* the second arrangement for newspapers, also places the most important story in the upper right of the page. However, the importance of stories in a modular layout is based on their human interest value. This means that each story is rated according to its appeal to the readers' emotions, rather than the importance of the news. These stories are usually shorter and are completed on one page. See Figure 10.6 for sample newspaper using this layout.

Descriptive headlines cover the entire width of the layout module. Photos may be run within the same layout block as the copy. Headlines are designed so as to create a visual balance across the page. Photographs are often placed in central positions so that the headlines will balance on either side. Figure 10.7 shows a newspaper makeover including main text and headings.

State aid no gold mine
See story page 3

Studds at Middle School
Saturday, 3-4pm

Spinning straw to gold
See story page 4

Hull Newsweekly

US POSTAGE PAID BULK RATE PERMIT #94 HINGHAM, MA 02043

Vol. 1 No. 43 Thursday, January 29, 1987 Tel. 925-9266 25¢ Newsstand

Snow-bound

Nearly 80% of highway snow removal budget expended
By Susan Ovans

Just five weeks into winter and with more snow forecast as we go to press, the town's highway department has used nearly 80% of its $40,000 snow removal budget for the year.

Highway Superintendent Edward Parent said Wednesday that he's notified the selectmen, town accountant, and finance committee that the department's snow budget is nearly bust.

An average storm, Parent estimates, costs the town $4-$5,000 for sand, salt, overtime, equipment rental, unexpected breakdowns and an independent contractor who helps clear the streets. The highway department head said that this year is the first in several that his department will probably expend its entire snow budget.

"Keep in mind that the snow removal budget has been set at $40,000 for about 15 years," he added.

While the highway department is authorized to exceed its budget cap in snow emergencies, Parent said he wanted the town's fiscal agents to be aware of the situation so that they can determine where the extra money is to be found.

Parent said his department has 11 workers available for a storm, three of whom are "inside" people. During the 1960's, the highway department had 24 men. In a severe storm, Parent said he would have to hire more independent contractors.

While the town contracts to buy sand and salt at volume prices, Parent said the department's eight plows are unreliable, at best. His biggest complaint, though, is that people do not observe the winter

The Big Chill... (Richard Green photo)

Con com reviews Weir River ACEC
By Edward Lothrop

Hull resident Kevin Conway appeared before the conservation commission Tuesday night to review the state's recent designation of the Weir River

Edward McCabe and Kevin Conway were voted as "associate members" of the conservation commission at the meeting Tuesday night.

In seeking the ACEC application, Conway cited the area has having value as a scenic and historical site, as being a wildlife habitat, flood plain coastal estuary, salt marsh and coastal beach, among other reasons.

Inland from the Weir River itself is included land

Hull Newsweekly

U.S. Postage Paid
Bulk Rate Permit #94
Hingham, MA 02043

VOL. 2 No. 9 / 30 Cents Thursday, May 28, 1987 925-9266

Mirror Images - Graves Light in the background appears to be an illusory twin of Boston Light in the fore of this photo of Nantasket Roads.

Planners Urge Marina License Denial

By Susan Ovens
HNV Staff

The planning board Tuesday night unanimously voted to recommend that the state deny Waveland Marina a permit to increase its boat slips from the current 56 to 96.

Paragon Marine Services, owner of the A. St. marina, has applied for a chapter 91 license from the state Department of Environmental Quality Engineering (DEQE). As part of the chapter 91 process, the town's planning board and conservation commission have the right to provide comments to the state relative to any license applications within their jurisdiction.

The conservation commission has alrea' issued an order fo conditions to allow construction of the additional slips and last week voted not to comment on Waveland's DEQE application.

In moving to recommend denial, planning board members said they believe that expansion of the marina "at this time" would restrict public access to the A Street pier, launching ramp, and surrounding shoreline.

The planner noted that Waveland's new restaurant and lounge and plans for a health club and chandlery within the building hae caused selectmen to schedule a traffic study for the already congested area.

"Essentially, expanding the number of slips would have an adverse impact on the public's right to use and enjoy public tidelands and facilites," summarized planner Joanne Adduci.

The overriding criteria for issuance of chapter 91 liecnse is that the public benefit to be derived from a project outweigh the public detriment.

Several area residents attended the planners' meeting to give the board a letter signed by nine residents protesting the proposed marina expansion.

Saying that "a crisis situation" exists in the neighborhood with regard to traffic and parking concerns, B St. resident Gwen Saylan added that she believes Waveland should have to wait at least a year to expand its number of slips.

Sayland said use of the ramp and pier for boats and fishing, and public swimming lessons at A st., make more enforcement of boat speed limits a necessity this season even without marina expansion.

The residents' letter to the planning board, which will be submitted to DEQE with the board's recommendation, said residents also would like the area from A to F Sts. bayside to be a restricted parking neighborhood and that "no wake" signs be posted in the inner harbor. They also suggest the Kahn or another Waveland employee once again be made assistant harbor master with enforcement power over speeding boaters.

"With a new restaurant, health club, and more slips, the whole thing doesn't make sense anymore," said Emory LeBlanc of B St. " Someone has to say 'no' until we study the situation and come up with a solution." Planning board memhers said that they had scheduled to

(continued on Page 3)

News and Analysis

Con-Comedy of Errors

By Rod Young

At Wednesday's selectmen's meeting, selecmen Chariman Claudette Fitzsimmons skillfully gaveled the town's vital, but fractured, conservation commission back together.

The chairman had taken an apparently timely initiative to convene the con com with her board in order to reconcile its members, bitterly alienated over a fiasco of misunderstandings which occurred May 9. A conservation meeting posted for the date at 7:30 p.m. at Town Hall was not held, and two developers on the agenda, Leonard Hersch and the A.J. Lane corporation, were left in the lurch.

May 9 was the last session of this year's annual town meeting. Three conservation articles were due for consideration, including one that would have established the new position of conservation officer. Nancy Winget, the con com's secretary, had anticipated that the commissioners would want to advocate the conservation officer position on town meeting floor and attempted to relocate the committee's meeting to a vacant room at the Memorial School, site of town meeting.

She intended that the commissioners would convene first at Town Hall, as posted and legally required, but only for the purpose of adjournment to the middle school. There they could recess to participate in town meeting when the conservation articles were called.

Winget posted a confusing notification of the meeting's relocation on the doors of Town Hall, misleading at !east five of the commissioners, according to their stories Wenesday night. One, Jack Darcy, thinking no meeting was to be held at Town Hall, which was locked up by the time he arrived, decided not to attend the session at Memorial School, assuming the committee's meeting there would not be legal.

Indeed, the requried Town Hall meeting opening and transfer was never held.

At town meeting, Winget and, subsequently, Town Counsel James Lampke, attempted in vain to persuade commissioners Dennis Hollingshead and John Gould to return to Town Hall and convene with board Chairman Andrew (Nick) Genes and Commissioner Dianne Goode. Meanwhile Hersch and A.J. Lane had arrived at the school.

When Genes arrived from Town Hall, upon hearing Winget's story, he gave up in frustration and went home. The developers departed with their charts and paid staff. Only Goode remained to advocate the commission's supposed top-priority conservation officer position at town meeting. It failed passage.

With the unfortunate scenario thus related at the selectmen's meeting, Commissioner Daniel Neville stood up

(continued on Page 11)

Community Bulletin Board

Bottle and can collection,
St. Ann's Church,
Saturday and Sunday after Mass.

Hull Episcopal Picnic,
Fort Revere,
Sunday at 11am.

SOB meeting to save our beaches,
Hull Historical Society Hall (above Village Fire Station),
Monday, June 1 at 7:30.

Inside This Week

Beach cleaning schedule / *Page 3*

Veteran's Outreach / *Page 4*

Midge Solution / *Page 5*

SOB organizes / *Page 5*

Museum Discovery Program / *Page 7*

Senior Banquet / *Page 8*

Figure 10.7: A newspaper makeover by Kimberly Cleveland. (top) the original Hull Newsweekly, a small town newspaper. (above) a remake; the number of columns changed for more flexibility.

LOUISVILLE Times

SATURDAY EVENING JUNE 1, 1974 / 10¢

NEWS	SCENE	SPORTS
The news in brief...page A2	The world of Pucci...page 3	Tennis and tremors...page A7
More veteran benefits...page A2	How about this design?...page 5	Bench and the Reds roll...page A7
Artificial blood...page A2	Earning money at home...page 6	Baseball on a tightrope...page A8

Prisoners are exchanged by Israel and Syria in the 'first stage of the end of the war'

Trains that once flew now crawl along the tracks

Drinking on credit doesn't go down well with the state

Bluegrass festival brings downhome music to downtown

Sunday may really be sun-day

Where to look

ADVERTISEMENTS

A major difference between newsletters and newspapers is that newspapers are supported by the sale of advertisements. Newspaper advertising is either display or classified. A *display ad* consists of text and a graphic and is designed to sell or promote a product and/or service. Most display ads are provided in ready-to-print form by advertising agencies. A *classified ad* is designed to sell, advertise, promote, or announce through the printed word alone. Classified ads are usually placed in a special section in the newspaper. The size of a classified ad is usually limited by the number of lines or words that may be printed.

The design and placement of ads are major factors in newspaper design. As shown in Figure 10.8, ads are often sold by the *column inch*. A one-column-inch ad would be one inch deep by one column wide, a two-column-inch ad would be two inches deep by two columns wide, and so on.

The placement and position of ads are important to advertisers. Display ads are generally distributed throughout the newspaper, not grouped on one page. Ads placed above the center fold are believed to be more easily seen; therefore, this space is more desirable — and more costly. For more information on advertising in publications, see Chapter 13, *Magazine Layouts*.

Figure 10.8: One and a half-column inch and three-column inch advertisements in a small town newspaper. (Courtesy Hull Newsweekly, Hull, MA.)

CHECKING YOUR UNDERSTANDING

1. What are some of the differences between a newsletter and a newspaper?

2. Why are newsletters a popular project for desktop publishing?

3. Define the four categories of newsletters.

4. Give five common newsletter dimensions and formats.

5. Discuss at least five of the major newsletter design elements.

6. Discuss two ways in which newsletter or newspaper columns can be used to add interest to your publication design.

7. Give two reasons why you might want to put rules in the column gutters of a newsletter.

8. Distinguish between a nameplate and a masthead.

9. Discuss the major differences between display ads and classified ads.

10. What is a column inch?

BUILDING YOUR DESKTOP PUBLISHING SKILLS

1. Secure two newsletters, one with a two-column layout and the other with a layout using more than two columns, then do the following:

   a) Study the newsletters and using the four newsletter classifications discussed in this chapter, indicate the appropriate classifications of the newsletters.

   b) Comment on the typeface and size used for the various text elements. Indicate whether they are appropriate, and, if applicable, indicate what other typeface might be used.

   c) Compare the nameplate and masthead of each newsletter. Indicate whether they are appropriate for the newsletter on which they appear. If applicable, comment on how you would improve upon these elements.

   d) Comment on the placement of any graphic element. If rules and borders were used, indicate their purpose. If you disagree with the selection or placement of any graphic element, explain why.

2. Using the information below and your page layout program, create a nameplate and masthead for the newsletter. Include a logo in your work. If clip art or a graphic program is available, you may want to create a graphic for the logo; otherwise, create a logo using text only.

Newsletter:	The Happy Traveler
Organization:	Worldwide Tours, Inc. 3210 Valley Circle St. Louis, MO 63022 (314) 555-2374
Publisher:	Madeline Russo
Published:	Quarterly

3. Assume you are asked to develop a one-page public relations newsletter for your school or company. Develop a thumbnail design of an 8-1/2 x 11, front and back format. The purpose of the newsletter is to present news related to your organization's employees, products, and services, so be sure to include the appropriate headings. Include space for a feature article on page 1. Indicate each element: nameplate, masthead, columns, and type specifications.

4. Thoroughly examine the front page of a local newspaper. Develop a grid for this page. Label the grid elements appropriately.

DESKTOP DESIGN WORKSHOP

The purpose of this section is to provide you with opportunities to develop and/or improve your desktop publishing design skills. The worksheet pages have been placed at the back of the book, and are designed so they can be removed and you can write, draw, or place your responses directly onto the pages.

WORKSHEETS 10.1 AND 10.2

Assume that the Four-Wheel Club of Northern Arizona has asked you to develop a sample layout for their quarterly subscription newsletter. Use the grids on Worksheet 10.1 for your design thumbnails. You may need several copies of this sheet to complete your design sketches. Use Worksheet 10.2 for your final rough design for this four-page series publication.

1. Include a nameplate and a masthead in your design. Use the information given below in your design.

Newsletter:	The Four-Wheeler
Slogan:	Committed to ecologically compatible four-wheeling.
Editor:	Mark Edwards

Publication notice: The Four-Wheeler is published quarterly by the:

Four-Wheel Club of Northern Arizona,
P. O. Box 7268,
Flagstaff, Arizona 81647.
Phone: (618) 555-0988.

Subscriptions are $15 yearly.

2. Provide for the following departments and stories in your sample layout:

a) Front page: Feature article, "Copper Canyon, Mexico" by Peggy Dennis. The feature article always has a photograph. Include an "In this Issue" table of contents.

b) Pages 2 through 4: Stories, calendar, and editorial.

- "Scouting Trips are Fun" (provide for a "Who, What, When, and Fee" description of the following trips: Death Valley, Copper Canyon, Indian Rock, and The Baja Adventure.)
- "The Bureau of Land Management Report" (make this a two-page spread.)
- "The Calendar" (provide for a calendar of events for the period of time until the next newsletter issue.)
- Editorial and Letters to the Editor.

3. Use one spot color of your choice where appropriate.

4. Indicate all grid elements and mark your specifications in the area outside the grid.

5. If time permits, produce a full-size layout using your page layout software and the GREEK.TXT (DOS) or the GREEKED TEXT (Mac) files on the data disk, along with graphic boxes, to show the placement of these elements. Include the proper headlines and subheads.

11. FLYERS, FOLDERS, BROCHURES, AND OTHER SHORT DOCUMENTS

When you finish this chapter you should be able to:

- *List and discuss the elements needed in a design strategy statement for short publications.*
- *Identify and describe the purposes of a flyer.*
- *Give three basic design principles for flyers.*
- *Describe at least two different folding techniques to form a folder.*
- *Discuss why the flap panel of a folder is a design problem.*
- *List and discuss at least one design principle for each part of a folder.*
- *Distinguish between a booklet and a brochure.*
- *Lay out and design attractive flyers, folders, booklets, and brochures.*
- *Lay out and design a brochure type of catalog.*

FLYERS, FOLDERS, BOOKLETS, AND brochures are all relatively short documents that vary in format and intent. Flyers are generally quite simple in their format, while booklets and brochures are designed more elaborately. What these short publications all have in common is their size, one to sixteen pages long, and a message that is to the point.

Because these publications are limited in length, the message they carry should be limited in scope as well. Whatever you say in a short publication should be clearly focused and well-defined. Even when you don't have much room for text, remember that an effective visual format will allow even the simplest of folders or flyers to carry many implicit messages about the information that is presented.

DESIGN RULES FOR SHORT PUBLICATIONS

Before any of the copy is ever written, you will need to find out what your organization wants to achieve with the publication — its strategy statement. A strategy statement will determine what will be said in the text, the illustrations you will use, as well as the size, colors, and printing of the finished piece. Review the section, "Design as a Skill," in

Chapter 2, *Communication: Visual and Verbal,* for help in putting together your strategy statement. The strategy statement needs to include:

- ✔ ***Objective*** *of the publication.*
- ✔ ***Target*** *audience: Who are they and what is your chief appeal to them?*
- ✔ ***Benefits*** *to the reader: Make sure they are believable and meaningful.*
- ✔ ***Tone*** *and* ***manner:*** *Aggressive, soft-sell, upmarket, political. The tone that is decided on will establish what it said and what the publication will look like.*

Study the competition to find out what their strategy is. Your piece can be more effective if you can offer something the competition isn't including. If you can't offer something more, try to offer what you have by saying it better or by making it more believable than your competition does.

Concentrate on the most important area of what is being featured in your individual folder, flyer, booklet, or brochure. You can't be all things to all people, so limit your focus to convincing your target group to take a positive action.

FLYERS

A *flyer* is a one-page sheet whose main purpose is to persuade, educate, or announce something to a reader (see Figure 11.1.) Announcement flyers notify their readers about an event or happening. Educational flyers are intended to teach or inform. Persuasive flyers rally their readers around a cause or urge them to buy something. Everywhere you look there are thousands of flyers; flyers announcing a special event, introducing a new product, soliciting votes on a political issue, and so on. If you want to produce a flyer that will work for you, focus on the major reason for producing it and limit the message to that objective.

Flyers are one of the most popular publication types, probably because they are just one page long and they appear to be easy to do. For these very reasons, they present a bigger challenge to the designer than a longer document might. Flyers are essentially small

Figure 11.1: (right) a flyer for a conference on color by Davis, Inc.; (right, center) A restaurant uses this flyer (courtesy Susan Linville); (far right) Information for a photo stock agency (courtesy Glenn & Associates.)

posters. They need to grab the reader's attention, hold as much information as possible in a limited amount of space, and look good besides. If you try to include a lot of text, you will have to use a type size that is too small to be read easily. If you choose a large graphic, you may not have room for the text. Your problem as the designer is to find the happy balance!

BASIC DESIGN PRINCIPLES FOR FLYERS

The basic design criteria for flyers can be summarized in three words: Keep it simple. Flyers are usually read quickly. If the flyer is intended to be posted, it may be read from a distance. Because of this, use large type and spotlight the important facts using white space, bold type, and bullets. These points are illustrated in the Flyer Makeover shown in Figure 11.2. If the flyer is to be a self-mailer, leave enough space in your design for the mailing information block.

As illustrated in Figure 11.1, flyers are usually printed on the two most available paper sizes: letter size, 8-1/2 x 11 or legal size, 8-1/2 x 14.

Otis/Notice

Vol. 4, #14 Week of April 2, 1990

Student Sale Garners $50,000 ! ! !
Special thanks to Waynna Kato and Michael Fuller who really made this thing happen!

Congratulations to everyone on a very successful sale.

Dig It! Scheduled for April 19th – Hockney to Give Keynote Address
Otis/Parsons will break ground for the construction of its new 60,000 sq. foot studio building on April 19, 1990 at 11:30 a.m. The ceremony will feature a keynote address by David Hockney.

All students and faculty are invited to attend.

The new building complex will increase current studio space by more than one-third and will enable us to bring all students and faculty back to the Main Campus. The complex will also include a 450-seat multi-use auditorium (finally!) and a new two-story library and computerized media center.

Completion date for the new structure will be Fal 1991.

Jones Foundation Grant Announced
Dean Roger Workman announced recently that the Fletcher Jones Foundation has awarded Otis/Parsons a $100,000 grant for computer equipment for the new Media Center of the Library.

This is the second grant from the Jones Foundation in four years. The first grant of $150,000 was used to establish the current computer laboratory and its equipment.

Students, Faculty, Staff – Be a Part of History. Time Capsule Pieces Needed!
As a part of the building project, we are looking

NOTISE

calendar

OTIS/PARSONS MAIN GALLERY
December 14, 1991 - February 8, 1992
The Presence of Absence
A traveling exhibition curated by Nina Felshin for Independent Curators, Inc. N.Y. Featuring conceptual work from the 1960's - 1980's, the exhibition will be installed and interpreted by the Otis students who actually create the works of art anew by executing instructions from the artists. Participating students are:
Erik Adolph, Anne Bower, Mike Carrig, Randi Chaplin, Charlotte DeBlock, Michael Espinoza, Jeanie Frias, Michael Fuller, Paula Hammond, Craig Hawley, Carmine Iannaccone, Patty Johnson, Shari Lee, Amorisa Lynn, Kristin Morse, Amy Perez, Keith Pirlot, Arolyn Smith and Oliver Warden.

UPCOMING BOLSKY GALLERY STUDENT SHOWS

IMPORTANT DATES:
FALL SEMESTER LAST DAY OF CLASSES
Friday, December 20, 1991
SPRING SEMESTER FIRST DAY OF CLASSES
Monday, January 13, 1992

OPENINGS/EXHIBITIONS
"Addiction Show" at Santa Barbara Contemporary Arts Forum. November 2, 1991 - January 11, 1992 (805)966-5373.
Includes works by Scott Grieger, Chair of Fine Arts, Joyce Lightbody, Caroll Caroompas and Jeffrey Vallance, all of whom are Otis instructors.

"Alaboration" an installation by Phyllis Green, Otis/Parsons Alumni.

notise

IMPORTANT DATES

Fall Semester Last Day of Classes Friday December 20, 1991. Spring Semester First Day of Classes Monday January 13, 1992.

CONGRATULATIONS

Continuing Education Instructor, B.J. Krivanek, was the recipient of a recent Best of Design Award from the Art Directors Club of Los Angeles in recognition of his recent public work: The Commemorative Art Installation at Jefferson High School, Los Angeles.

CALENDAR

OTIS/PARSONS GALLERY

The Presence of Absence December 14, 1991 - February 8, 1992. A traveling exhibition by Nina Felshin for Independant Curators, Inc. N.Y. Featuring conceptual work from the 1960's - 1980's, the exhibition will be installed and interpreted by the Otis students who actually create the works of art anew by executing instructions from the artists. Participating students are: Erik Adolph, Anne Bower, Mike Carrig, Randi Chaplin, Charlotte DeBlock, Michael Fuller, Paula Hammond, Craig Hawley, Carmine Iannacconne, Patty Johnson, Shari Lee, Amorisa Lynn, Kristin Morse, Amy Perez, Keith Pirlot, Arolyn Smith, and Oliver Warden.

UPCOMING BOLSKY GALLERY STUDENT SHOWS

Pray for Sex December 1 - December 14. A Master of Fine Arts Student Curated Show of Undergratuate Student Works.

Dropping Bombs (part 1) A Photographic Installation by Mark LeRoy December 17 & 18, 12 noon-6 p.m. Opening Reception: Dec. 17, 7:00 p.m.

OPENINGS/ EXHIBITIONS

Addiction Show at Santa Barbara Contemporary Arts Forum. November 2, 1991 - January 11, 1992. 805.966.5373. Includes works by Scott Grieger, Chair of Fine Arts, Joyce Lightbody, Caroll Caroompas, and Jeffrey Vallance, all of who are Otis Instructors.

Alaboration an installation by Phyllis Green, Otis/Parsons Alumni. December 5, 1991 - January 24, 1992 at Pierce College Galler. Reception for the Artist Tueday, De-cember 10, 7-9 p.m. 818.719.6498.

Memorial an Installation at Mendenhall Gallery by Barbara Lee Furbush, November 25 - December 20, 1991. Reception on Tuesday, December 3 from 7-9p.m. Whittier College, Painter at Phadelphia in Whittier.

Sarah Perry, Otis Fine Arts Faculty, Koplin Gallery 213.319.9956, January 4 - February 3, 1992. Opening Reception - January 4 from 3:00-5:00 p.m.

Figure 11.2: A flyer makeover by Anne Cook for the Otis Parsons Art School. (top left) the original Otis Notice. (top right) Otis Notice, revised; (above) the makeover.

ILLUSTRATION OF THE FOLDER SIZES AND FORMATS

Paper Size	Format
8 1/2" x 11"	Vertical fold with 3 panels on each side. Because the flap panel folds into the center, it must be slightly narrower than the other two panels.
8 1/2" x 11"	Horizontal fold with 3 panels each side.
8 1/2" x 7"	Vertical or horizontal fold with 2 panels of equal size on each side.
8 1/2" x 14"	Vertical fold with 4 panels on each side.
17" x 11"	Folded once to form an "8 1/2 x 11" panel booklet.

Table 11.1

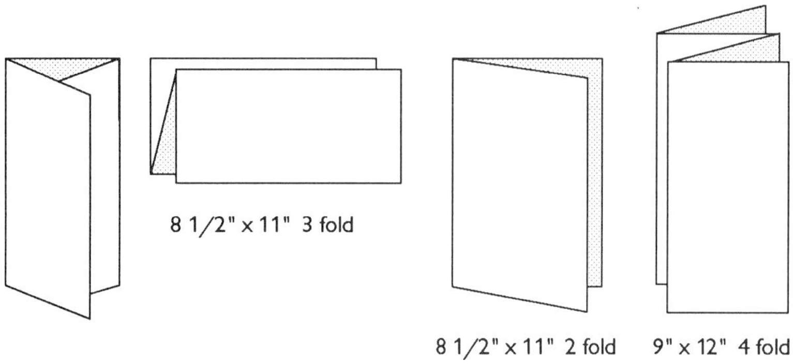

Figure 11.3: Folder examples.

COMMERCIAL & BOOKLET ENVELOPES

Name of Item	Size	Commercial	Booklet
7 3/4	3 7/8" x 7 1/2"	✓	
9	3 7/8" x 8 7/8"	✓	
10	4 1/8" x 9 1/2"	✓	
11	4 1/2" x 10 3/8"	✓	
12	4 3/4" x 11"	✓	
6 3/4	6 1/2" x 9 1/2"		✓
7 1/2	7 1/2" x 10 1/2"		✓
9 1/2	9" x 12"		✓
10	9 1/2" x 10 1/2"		✓
13	10" x 13"		✓

Table 11.2

FOLDERS

A *folder* is a publication that is printed on both sides of single sheet of paper and is folded to form two or more panels. Like flyers, folders are used by business and education to promote products and services. In business, folders range from those reproduced on an office copier to the elaborate color publications that open into clever layouts. Folders are also used to advertise trips to foreign countries, raise funds for organizations, and inform readers about political issues.

FOLDER STYLES

Folders can be designed in many sizes, depending on your needs and your budget. One popular folder style is a letter-size page (8-1/2 x 11) folded in thirds. This format is called a letter-fold, or sometimes a three-panel. Most print shops have paper, presses, and folding machines specifically tailored to this style because it is a popular low-budget format. Another popular size is a 9 x 12 sheet folded into a 4 x 9 final size. A 9 x 12 sheet can be designed with your page layout program, using a custom setting, but it will need to be printed at your local print shop, unless you have access to a tabloid size copier (see Table 11.1) This size, too, will fit comfortably into the ordinary #10 business-size envelope.

There are three restrictions that limit the final size of the folder. First, the paper size should be one that can be run on the printing press your print shop uses. Second, the final folder should fit into a standard mailing envelope, unless you plan to use it as a self-mailer (see Table 11.2.) Your print shop will help you select standard paper and envelope sizes. Third, the number of panels you want will depend on the size of your paper sheet and the number of folds that you plan for it. Five or six folds are the absolute limit; the number of folds you decide on will depend on the thickness of your paper stock. Figure 11.3 illustrates a number of popular folder formats from which to choose.

BASIC DESIGN PRINCIPLES FOR FOLDERS

Folders are always printed on two sides. That means you will need to design layouts on two pages: Side one, representing the front and side two, the back of your folder. Each side then needs to be divided into panels. If your folder is larger than 8 1/2 x 14, each side can be designed using a custom format. When printing out a custom format, you may find it easier to print out the panels individually, using the tiling feature in your page layout program. The printed panels can then be assembled in a two-page pasteup. If you want to do this, refer to Chapter 15, *Preparation of Camera-Ready Art*, for instructions on how to prepare a pasteup.

When you are designing a folder, treat the panels as separate pages or a spread, depending on how they are viewed when the folder is opened. The opening side of the folder is designed as a cover page while the back side is frequently used as a self-mailer or for response information. When panels appear next to each other in an opened folder, they are designed as panel spreads. Depending on how you arrange the panel spreads in your design layout, a folder can also be used as a poster.

The order of panels depends on how you fold the paper. Generally speaking, the front of the folder is the panel on the far right of one side. In a three-fold folder (Figure 11.4), the center panel of the outside is the back, and the panel on the far left is panel 4. The inside contains panels 1, 2, and 3.

Folders need to be carefully thumbnailed, not only for visual content, but to ensure that the folds are in the right places for your design. Once you have completed an approved design thumbnail, you should prepare a dummy folder in its final size. Use the dummy to verify the size of the margins for each panel, because the margin size depends on how the final piece will be folded. Use the paper stock that the folder will be printed on to test how the paper will fold.

COVERS

A basic rule for cover design is to put your selling message right up front. About 80 percent of your readers will never go past the folder cover, but you will have grabbed the attention of the 20 percent who will be interested in learning more. This group will be encouraged to open the folder and get the details.

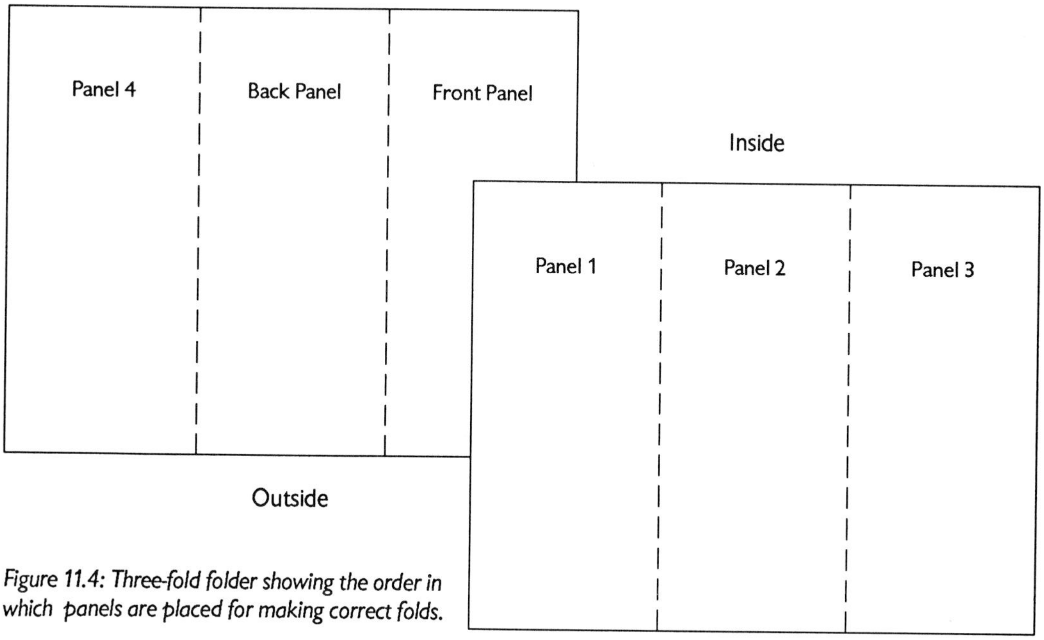

Figure 11.4: Three-fold folder showing the order in which panels are placed for making correct folds.

The front panel or cover design should include a dominant element. This element can be an illustration or a photograph used with a headline. Tests show that people respond most actively to visuals that have people in them. The cover text should not be too wordy, but it should include enough text to let the reader know who and what you are and what you offer. (See Figure 11.5.)

Use just enough text on the cover to help the reader grasp the message quickly.

If the folder is to be placed in a rack, place the title heading in the upper third of the front panel. (See Figure 11.5.)

INTERIOR DESIGN AND LETTER FOLD TECHNIQUES

Pages in a folder are seen as adjoining panels marked only by folds. Your design will need to move the reader from panel to panel in the order that they have been designed to be read. To do this, place the important points on the first panel that the reader sees upon opening the folder. Secondary points can be highlighted as succeeding folds are opened. Use the inside panels to carry the bulk of the message. Avoid using large blocks of text.

Graphic elements such as photographs and illustrations that tell a story can often give the reader more information than words alone. Choose them for their story-telling ability.

Figure 11.5: Folder covers; (right, courtesy The Design Works; far right, courtesy Sonsie Conroy.)

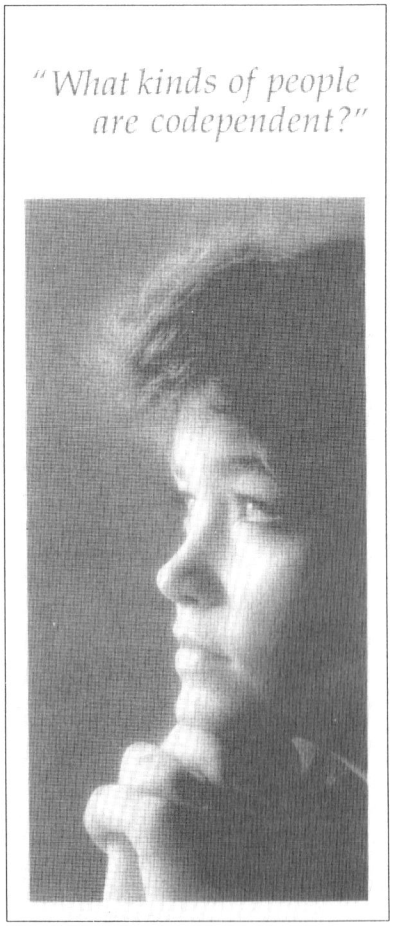

Focus your text by using subheads, large caps, pull quotes, bullets, and rule lines. White space, too, can be used to highlight your message. (See Figure 11.6.)

The second or flap panel in a three-fold folder can present a design problem. Because this panel folds to the inside of the folder, you can use it to begin the message or to end it. This may present a problem for the reader; i.e., not knowing where to begin. One way to overcome this dilemma is to place stand-alone material on this flap. Since the flap panel is folded in, it is slightly narrower than other panels.

The back panel should include the mailing information if the folder is to be a self-mailer. Make sure that the name, address, telephone number, and logo of the organization are easy to find to allow the reader to respond to the information. Invite the reader to use an 800 number if one is available, and include a coupon to be mailed in for more information.

Generally, each panel of a folder should be a single column of text, although two or even three columns may be used for bulleted or numbered lists in a small type size. The following type sizes are often used in folders, since they are restricted by the narrow column width: Title, 24 to 36 point; heads, 12 to 14 point; main text, 8 to 10 point.

BOOKLETS AND BROCHURES

Booklets and brochures look pretty much the same, with two essential differences. A *booklet* is a made up of interior printed pages with a self-cover. The cover stock of a booklet is

Figure 11.6 (top) A folder for a real estate developer; (left) the envelope in which it was mailed. (Courtesy The Design Works.)

the same as that used for inside pages. But, when you put a hard cover on the booklet and staple or stitch the pages together, it is called a *brochure*. Many people, including those in the business, confuse the two types, so in this book we will treat booklets as a type of brochure.

Brochures are multipage publications similar to, but shorter than, books. Because brochures are short, they focus on a single purpose or message, but they can carry more complex messages to their audience than other small publications. Highly illustrated short catalogs are a type of brochure.

BASIC DESIGN PRINCIPLES FOR BROCHURES

Many of the design criteria described for folders hold true for brochures as well (see Figure 11.7 for examples.)

- ✔ Refer to the strategy statement for purpose and tone.
- ✔ Put your selling message on the cover. A single large illustration usually has more impact than several small ones.
- ✔ State your benefits. Pictures describe benefits often better than words do.
- ✔ Use people in your illustrations wherever possible. They can be used to show benefits.
- ✔ Spotlight important facts using bold type, white space, bullets, and dingbats.
- ✔ Make sure that the organization's name, address, and telephone number are easy to find.

When you begin your brochure design, thumbnail several roughs that best represent the tone as presented in the strategy statement. Choose two or three document sizes, selecting those that will fit into a standard envelope. (See Table 11.2 for standard mailer envelope sizes.)

Brochures produced by desktop publishing methods are frequently printed on standard letter-size paper that has been folded to form four pages 8-1/2 x 5-1/2. Sheets can be stacked to increase the number of pages. If you plan to have your brochure printed, other standard sizes can be used. Check with

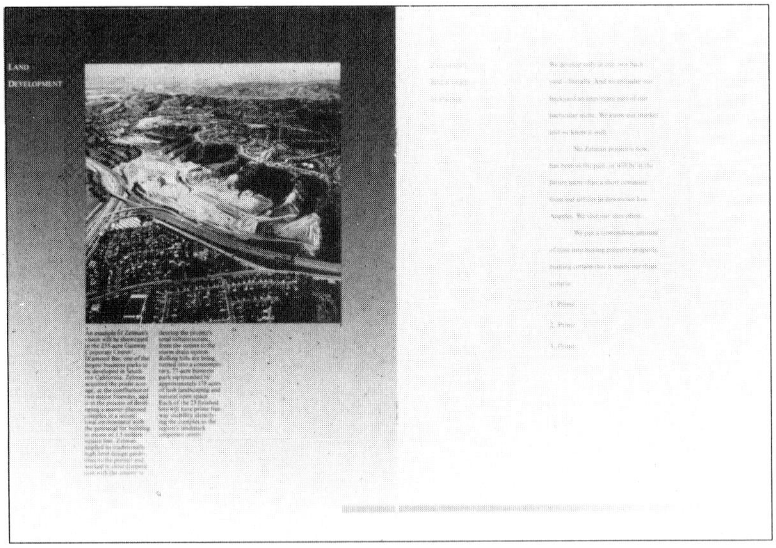

Figure 11.7: Brochure design examples; (above, The Design Works, right, Vinje Design, Inc., far right, René Sheret Design.)

your print shop to find out what sizes it can handle before you decide to work with a different format than that allowed by 8-1/2 x 11 or 11 x 17 sheets. For more information on typical paper types and sizes, refer to Chapter 14, *Working with Service Bureaus and Print Shops.*

Your brochure design will depend on several factors. For example, your grid and the number of columns you choose will depend on the size you have decided upon for the printed piece. The typefaces you choose will depend on the tone you want to project, the width of your columns, and the size of your illustrations in relation to the text. Magazine and book design techniques can be applied to brochures. For more information see Chapter 12, *Long Documents;* and Chapter 13, *Magazine Layouts.*

CATALOGS

Since the catalog information that readers generally use is in the pictures, catalog text is used to support the art. Type elements, therefore, can be smaller and more compact when they are used as a pictorial caption. Even when the type you choose is small, readability is always a major consideration. The reader needs to know prices, colors, and other pertinent information. Make sure that the typefaces you have chosen follow the rules for good readability and blend well with the images used in the brochure.

- ✔ *Refer to the strategy statement for purpose and tone.*
- ✔ *Put your selling message on the cover. A single large illustration usually has more impact than several small ones.*
- ✔ *State your benefits. Pictures describe benefits often better than words do.*
- ✔ *Use people in your illustrations wherever you can. They can be used to show benefits.*
- ✔ *Spotlight important facts using bold type, white space, bullets, and dingbats.*
- ✔ *Make sure that the name of the organization, its address, and telephone number are easy to find.*

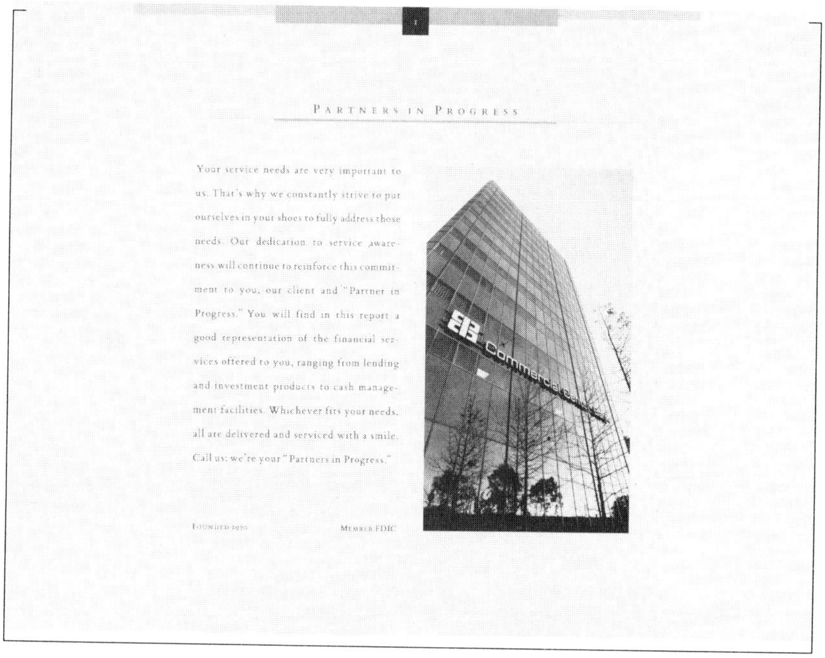

READER RESPONSE

Short publications like brochures are often used to promote a product or service. Since these publications are directed to readers who may not know too much about the product or service, you should make it easy for them to get back to you. Leave room for a telephone number and a mailing address, or better yet, a reader response coupon. Order blanks for merchandise may also be part of a brochure or a booklet (see Figure 11.8.)

If your booklet includes a coupon or an order form, you will need to design the response form as part of the page layout. Coupons, outlined with a dotted cutting line, are usually placed at the bottom or outside edge because you want the reader to be able to clip them without destroying the rest of the brochure. Order blanks are often placed in the center fold so that they can be removed or filled in without destroying the rest of the brochure or booklet. Order blanks may also be put on the last page of the brochure.

CHECKING YOUR UNDERSTANDING

1. List the four types of short publications discussed in this chapter.

2. What is the first thing you need to do when designing a short publication?

3. Why is designing a flyer a challenge to the desktop designer?

4. Identify the elements that should be placed on the cover of a folder and explain their importance.

5. Sketch the letter-fold technique to form a folder from an 8-1/2 x 11 piece of paper.

6. Name each of the different panels of a letter-fold folder and discuss one design technique for each panel.

7. List the three type sizes most often used in folders.

8. What points should you consider when choosing a typeface for a brochure?

9. What are the concerns to be aware of when designing a response coupon?

BUILDING YOUR DESKTOP PUBLISHING SKILLS

1. Select one flyer of each of the following types: announcement, educational, and persuasive. Compare and contrast between the purpose and the design of each flyer. Attach a copy of each flyer with your response.

2. Select two different-sized folders to examine and compare. Study the folders, then answer the following questions:

Figure 11.8: A reader response coupon.

LACPS
Los Angeles Center For Photographic Studies
1052 West Sixth Street
Suite 424
Los Angeles, California 90017

NON-Profit ORG.
U.S. Postage
PAID
Los Angeles, CA
Permit No. 34415

JOIN THE LOS ANGELES CENTER FOR PHOTOGRAPHIC STUDIES NOW!

Member's Benefits Include: Reduced admissions to LACPS exhibitions, screenings and lectures. Subscription to the Calendar and FRAME/WORK. Eligibility to show in LACPS' annual Members Exhibition. For more information call (213) 482-3566

Name ______________________

Address ______________________

City/State/Zip Code ______________________

Telephone Number (   ) ______________________

New Membership/Renewal. I would like to join a committee. Yes/No

Annual Student Membership	$20
Regular Membership	$35
Specia Membership	$100
PatronMembership	$250
BenefactorMembership	$500
Collector's Circle	$1000

a) What is the size and format of each folder?

b) How does the front panel of each folder present and highlight the message?

c) How is the flap panel used on each folder? Does it start or end the flow of text, or is it a stand-alone piece?

d) What graphic elements, if any, are used on the interior panels?

e) How has the back panel been used?

3. Select a booklet or brochure that is not in a catalog format. Study the publication, then do the following:

a) Write a short description of the publication. Include answers to the following questions:

- How many pages does the publication contain?
- Is the printing single- or double-sided?
- How are the pages kept together?
- What is the basic message of the publication?
- What graphic elements are used and how are they used?

b) Study the message of the publication, then design a new cover for the publication.

4. Obtain two catalogs, each with an obviously different tone, then do the following.

a) Identify each catalog by its target audience and tone: i.e., upscale, mass market, limited market (such as sporting goods), or education.

b) Compare and contrast the layout and design of each catalog and write a brief paragraph discussing your findings.

c) Redesign a page of one of the catalogs and write a brief paragraph discussing the reason for your changes.

DESKTOP DESIGN WORKSHOP

The purpose of this section is to provide you with opportunities to develop and/or improve your desktop publishing design skills. The worksheet pages have been placed at the back of the book, and are designed so they can be removed and you can write, draw, or place your responses directly onto the pages.

WORKSHEETS 11.1 AND 11.2

Assume that Donald Harper, owner of All-American Home Inspection, has given you a copy of the three-panel folder illustrated in Worksheets 11.1 and 11.2. Mr. Harper uses this folder to promote his home inspection business. He has been fairly successful in his local area and would like to have the folder redesigned to give it a more professional look. He plans to use the folder as a self-mailer to real estate brokers who are unfamiliar with his service.

a) Study the current folder for ways in which you may improve upon its layout and design.

b) Sketch your new layout on a separate piece of paper. Indicate the page elements and type specifications on your page.

c) Using your page layout program and the text files on the data disk that accompanies this text (see below), create a full-size model of your design.

11COVER.DOC (DOS) or 11 COVER (Mac)

11BACK.DOC (DOS) or 11 BACK (Mac)

11FLAP.DOC (DOS) or 11 FLAP (Mac)

11PANEL3.DOC (DOS) or 11 PANEL 3 (Mac)

11PANEL4.DOC (DOS) or 11 PANEL 4 (Mac)

11PANEL5.DOC (DOS) or 11 PANEL 5 (Mac)

12. LONG DOCUMENTS

When you finish this chapter you should be able to:

- *Discuss the purpose of a publication specification form and indicate the kind of information that is recorded on such a form.*
- *Distinguish between the various parts of a book and give examples of each, including the frontmatter, interior pages, and backmatter.*
- *Discuss ways in which the elements that make up a manual are different from those in a trade book.*
- *Identify the basic elements that make up a typical manual.*
- *Discuss why rules for using type in catalogs differs somewhat from other kinds of publications.*
- *Apply layout and design principles to the production of publications such as manuals, books, and catalogs.*

LONG DOCUMENTS INCLUDE TRADE AND text books, manuals and training guides, documentation, and lengthy catalogs. They are the most complex of all the different types of business publication to design. The difficulty lies in the fact that they contain so many different elements — not because they have more pages than brochures or reports. Although this chapter discusses only three types of long documents, the basic principles of layout and design discussed for these publications can be applied to other kinds of long documents.

THE LONG DOCUMENT SPECIFICATION FORM

So, you have a manual to design that is 192 pages long, and you are concerned that this project will never be completed on deadline because there are so many pages to design. If you remember how to do style guides (see Chapter 3, *Document Structure: Organizing Your Publication),* you can apply that knowledge to the design of any long document including manuals, books, and catalogs.

A designer does not literally design every page of a long publication. Instead, he or she considers the different elements that make up the long publication and designs each element as part of a set of *sample typical pages*. In order to design the sample pages, all the elements that make up your document need to be listed and defined. An editor will often provide you with this information. If this has not been done, you will have to skim through the entire manuscript and make up the list yourself. While you are designing the sample pages, record the specifications for all the elements that you are working with as part of your rough design.

When the final design for your sample pages is approved, you can use the rough specifications list to help fill out a long documents specification form. This form is similar to the simpler style sheet that defines all the typographic and structural formats for shorter, less complex publications. A publication specification form differs from a style sheet in that many more elements are defined.

Using a publication specification form for long documents will ensure that your design has consistency throughout the publication. It will also be useful when revised editions are made.

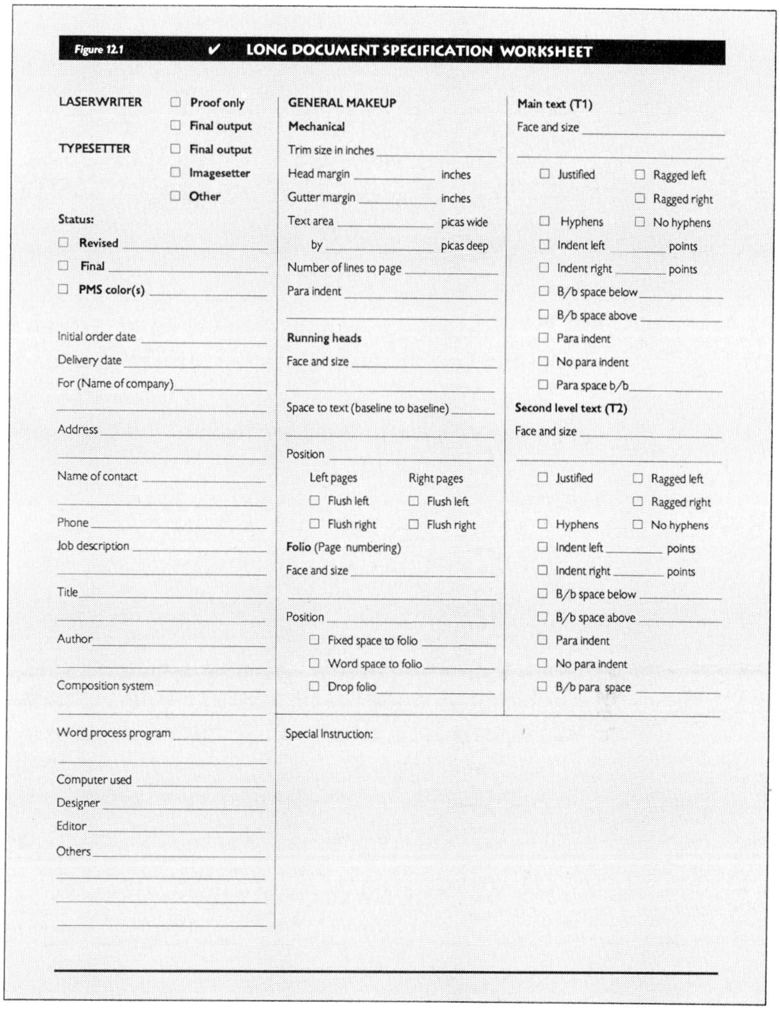

Figure 12.1 ✔ LONG DOCUMENT SPECIFICATION WORKSHEET

LASERWRITER ☐ Proof only ☐ Final output
TYPESETTER ☐ Final output ☐ Imagesetter ☐ Other

Status:
☐ Revised
☐ Final
☐ PMS color(s)

Initial order date
Delivery date
For (Name of company)
Address
Name of contact
Phone
Job description
Title
Author
Composition system
Word process program
Computer used
Designer
Editor
Others

GENERAL MAKEUP
Mechanical
Trim size in inches
Head margin inches
Gutter margin inches
Text area picas wide
by picas deep
Number of lines to page
Para indent

Running heads
Face and size
Space to text (baseline to baseline)
Position
Left pages: ☐ Flush left ☐ Flush right
Right pages: ☐ Flush left ☐ Flush right

Folio (Page numbering)
Face and size
Position
☐ Fixed space to folio
☐ Word space to folio
☐ Drop folio

Main text (T1)
Face and size
☐ Justified ☐ Ragged left ☐ Ragged right
☐ Hyphens ☐ No hyphens
☐ Indent left points
☐ Indent right points
☐ B/b space below
☐ B/b space above
☐ Para indent
☐ No para indent
☐ Para space b/b

Second level text (T2)
Face and size
☐ Justified ☐ Ragged left ☐ Ragged right
☐ Hyphens ☐ No hyphens
☐ Indent left points
☐ Indent right points
☐ B/b space below
☐ B/b space above
☐ Para indent
☐ No para indent
☐ B/b para space

Special Instruction:

Figure 12.1: *A simple long document specification form in reduced size. See Workshop/Forms Appendix for full-sized form.*

A simplfied Long Document Specification Form is illustrated in Figure 12.1. Frequently used trim sizes are shown in Table 12.1.

MARGINS

All pages have margins at the top, bottom, outside, and inside. Inside margins are always the narrowest on the page, but the combined gutter or inside margins on facing pages should be larger than a left-hand margin on single-sided text. The outside margins should be wider than the top margin, but narrower than the bottom margin.

COLUMNS

Generally one or two columns are used. If your layout is based on a two-column format, the columns may be equal or unequal in width. See Chapter 7, *Grids: Working with Structure and Space*, for further information regarding the number and use of columns.

SECTIONS AND CHAPTERS

The first section or chapter page is traditionally a right-hand (recto) page. This page is numbered at the top or bottom and does not carry a running head or foot.

FREQUENTLY USED TRIM SIZES

Hard Cover Books	Soft Cover Books
5 1/2 x 8 1/2"	5 1/2 x 8 1/2
6 x 9"	6 x 9 "
6 1/8 x 9 1/4"	6 1/8 x 9 1/4"
6 1/2 x 9 1/4"	6 1/2 x 9 1/4"
7 1/2 x 9 1/4"	7 1/2 x 9 1/4"
7 3/8 x 9 1/4"	7 3/8 x 9 1/4"
	8 1/2 x 11"

Table 12.1

TYPE SPECIFICATIONS

Generally only two or three typefaces should be used (see Chapter 5, *Type Basics*). When selecting typefaces and sizes, choose a face that looks good used in large areas of text. Type size should be between 10 point and 14 point.

INDENTATIONS

The first paragraph of each chapter is generally blocked (set flush left throughout) and all following paragraphs are indented. The first paragraph below each subhead is usually blocked as well.

QUOTATIONS AND EXTRACTS

Quoted passages or longer extracts from other publications need to be set off from the main text in some way. There are several ways in which this is done. The quoted text can be indented from one or both margins, set ragged right with an indented left margin, or set in a different typeface or size from the main text. Poetry is usually specified differently than long extracts.

PAGE NUMBERS (FOLIOS)

Page numbers (folios) may be placed at the top or bottom of the page. The preferred locations are flush with the outside margin or centered. Page numbers are frequently included as part of a running header or footer.

BOOK LAYOUT AND DESIGN

While many people think of books only as hard-bound volumes on a library shelf, most long publications actually are types of books. Biographies, travel books, and fiction are part of a book category called *trade books*. *Textbooks* constitute another category of books that includes training manuals and documentation as well as books used in schools. Lengthy catalogs such as those for tool and automobile parts are yet another category of books whose entries are essentially long lists of part descriptions and illustrations.

The main concerns of book design and layout are (1) the length of the manuscript and (2) the intended use of the book. In order for you to make suitable design decisions, assess both the intended use and the length of the book. For example, if the book is to be a school textbook or an information manual, an easy-to-read typeface and lots of illustrations would be important. If, however, the book is intended for trade, the typeface will also need to be easy to read, but a catchy title and slick cover will sell the book (see Figure 12.2.) Coffee table books are generally oversized and more expensive looking than other types of books. Books also are usually categorized by their content.

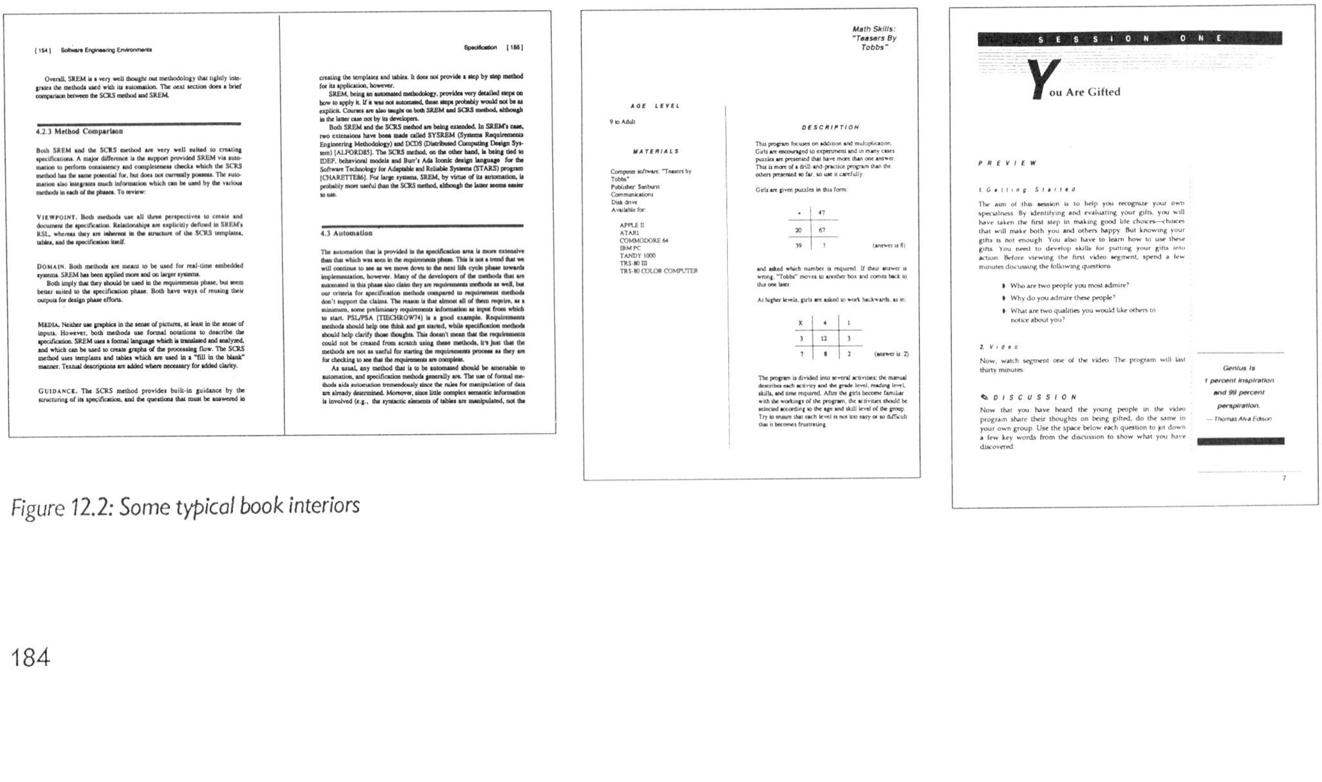

Figure 12.2: Some typical book interiors

ELEMENTS OF A NONFICTION BOOK

The elements in nonfiction books can be grouped into one of the following three divisions: frontmatter, interior pages, and backmatter.

FRONTMATTER

The elements, up to the first page of the main text are called the *frontmatter*, or preliminaries. As explained below and illustrated in Figure 12.3, many different elements make up the frontmatter. No one book contains all these elements, but every book will contain at least two or three.

Half title page: A page listing title and author in small type, placed before the more elaborately designed title page.

Advertisement page: A page that lists other books by the same author or by other authors under the same subject series or category.

Title page: A page on which the name or title of the publication is listed.

Copyright: A page containing the copyright notice. U.S. copyright law specifies that the notice must be on the title page or on its reverse side.

Dedication page: Notice from the author indicating that the publication is dedicated to a person or several people.

Table of contents: A page or pages that list the name and page numbers of publication elements (chapters, appendices, indexes, etc.)

List of illustrations: A page listing the names and location of all art in the publication.

Preface or foreword: The preface is an introduction written by the author; a foreword is an introduction to the work written by someone other than the author.

Acknowledgments: A page on which those who contributed to the work are recognized.

Introduction: A section of the publication that helps set the stage for the reader. Sometimes blank pages are inserted in the front matter so that certain pages will be either right- or left-hand pages. Lower case Roman numerals are normally used to number the front-matter pages.

INTERIOR PAGES

The interior pages contain the main text of the book. The main text is generally divided into parts, sections, chapters, or a combina-

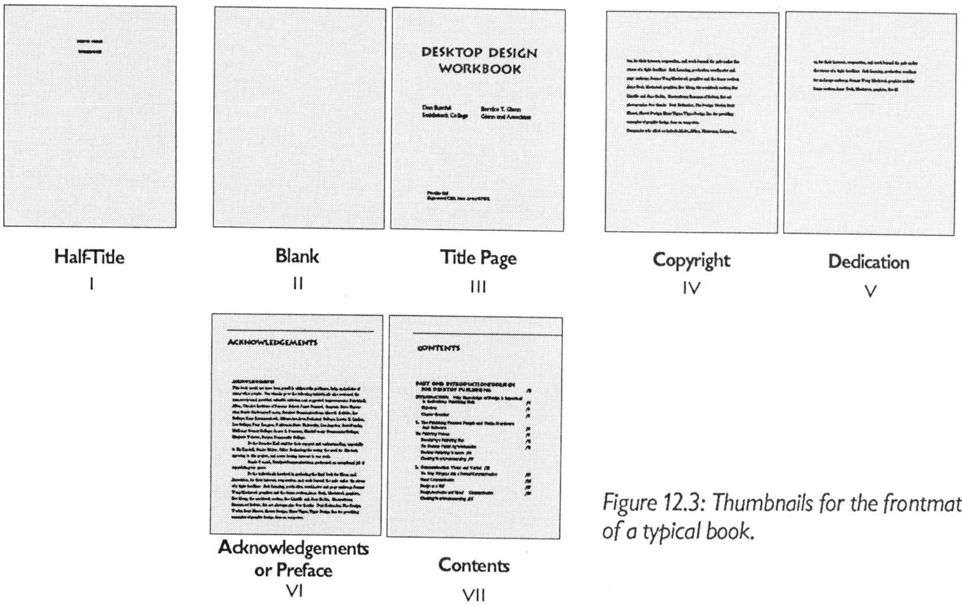

Figure 12.3: Thumbnails for the frontmatter of a typical book.

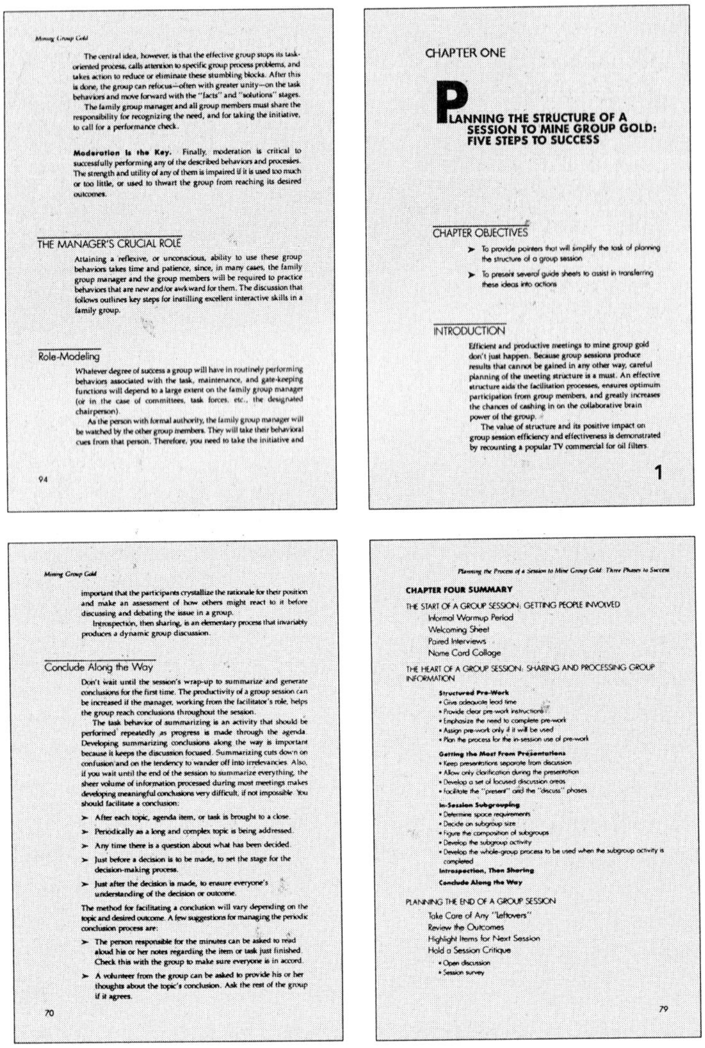

Figure 12.4: Typical book interior pages. Note top right, the opening of the first chapter, starts with page 1.

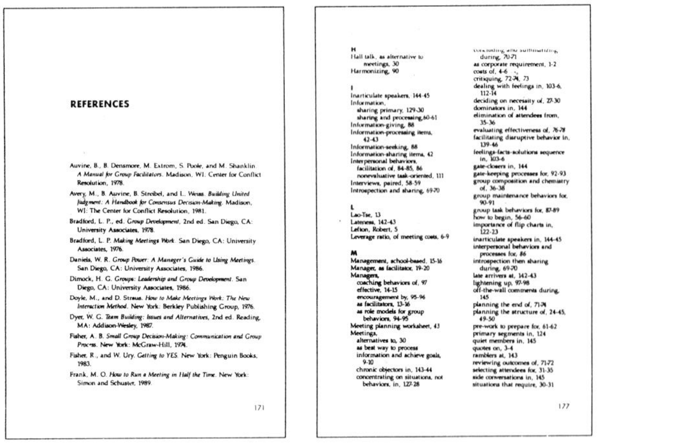

Figure 12.5: Backmatter pages.

tion of two or more of these elements. Unlike the text in fiction books, nonfiction text is broken up using one or more levels of subheads. These headings act as an outline of the information covered in the main text. Explanations for information and ideas explained in nonfiction text are often enhanced with illustrations and other graphics.

As illustrated in Figure 12.4, the first page of the first chapter is a right-hand page and is numbered page 1. The chapter numbers may be set in the same type size as the chapter title.

BACKMATTER

A number of elements are placed at the back of a book. These are not part of the main text, but support the content of the book. Typical reference matter elements are presented below and illustrated in Figure 12.5.

Appendices: Information that is thought to be useful to the reader, but not necessarily a part of the book.

Bibliography: A list of the works used in writing the book or a list of additional material relevant to the text.

Glossary: A listing of words that were used in the book, with their definitions. Glossaries are generally included only in technical books.

Index: A comprehensive listing of topics and individuals mentioned in the book.

MANUALS

Manuals are a kind of book used to document a procedure or to explain an operation such as processing a payroll or using a piece of equipment. User manuals are sometimes called *documentation*. Manuals are usually published to fulfill special needs by schools, companies, and product manufacturers. Manufacturers provide their customers with documentation and technical manuals to support the products they are selling.

Good documentation and technical support manuals need not be expensive to produce. They should contain the information that users need, in a language and a visual format that is accessible and easy enough for a beginner to follow. There are two different types of manuals: those used to document procedures for reference or training purposes, and those used by an institution as *position documents* for public image purposes. Many companies use manuals to improve customer relations. They provide their customers with well-written manuals, printed on good-quality paper, generally in a looseleaf format. Other companies take the view that a minimum amount of time and money should be spent on documentation, since the product they are selling is good enough to stand on its own.

LAYOUT AND DESIGN FOR MANUALS

As illustrated in Figure 12.6, the design of a manual varies according to its purpose and intended audience.

Manuals are seldom read from beginning to end, unlike nonfiction books or novels. They are used primarily for reference. To be of value to the reader, a manual should include a table of contents with subcategories and a detailed, cross-referenced index. Each section or part of the manual should be easily located in the table of contents and the index. The various sections of the manual should be easily identified, using color coding, numbers, or a graphic such as a picture or icon. If the manual covers a technical subject, you may want to include a glossary of terms.

Even more than most publications, the needs of the intended audience must be respected when designing any kind of manual. Many user problems can be solved by thoughtful design decisions using well-organized page layouts. If the manual is to be used for product assembly, the user may have both hands busy while following a set of written instructions. This means that the manual will have to open flat — a binding consideration. Special binding, in turn, has implications for page layout (such as a wider inside margin.) Space limitations may also dictate the overall size of the manual. Size, in turn, dictates the kind of grid you can use.

The kind of art you choose — its style, size, and placement on the page — is very important when designing a manual. Most

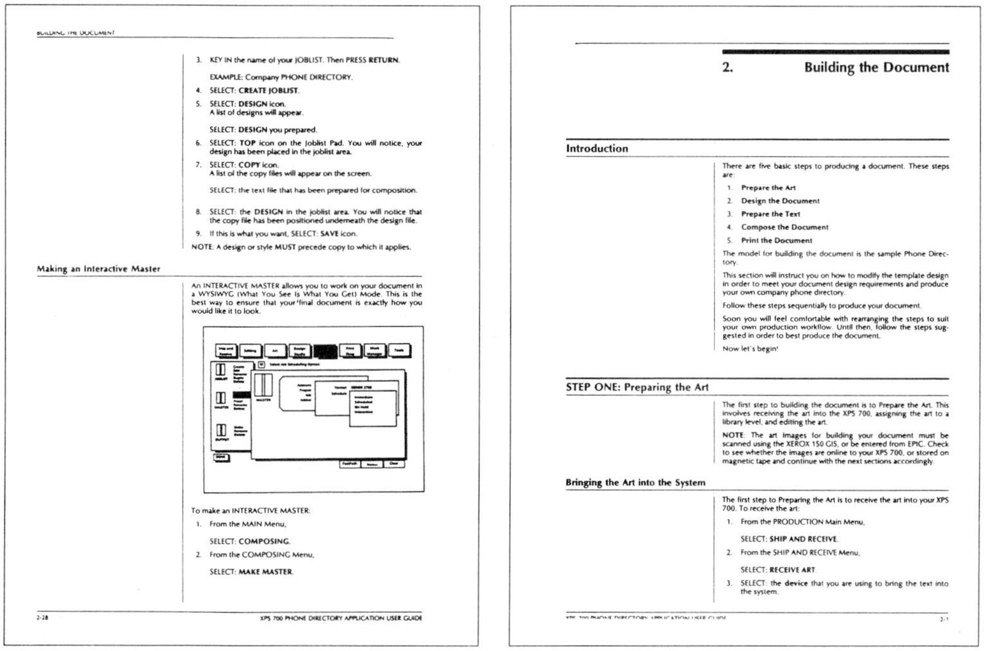

BUILDING THE DOCUMENT

3. KEY IN the name of your JOBLIST. Then PRESS **RETURN**.

   EXAMPLE: Company PHONE DIRECTORY.
4. SELECT: **CREATE JOBLIST**.
5. SELECT: **DESIGN** icon.
   A list of designs will appear.

   SELECT: **DESIGN** you prepared.
6. SELECT: **TOP** icon on the Joblist Pad. You will notice, your design has been placed in the joblist area.
7. SELECT: **COPY** icon.
   A list of the copy files will appear on the screen.

   SELECT: the text file that has been prepared for composition.
8. SELECT: the **DESIGN** in the joblist area. You will notice that the copy file has been positioned underneath the design file.
9. If this is what you want, SELECT: **SAVE** icon.

NOTE: A design or style MUST precede copy to which it applies.

Making an Interactive Master

An INTERACTIVE MASTER allows you to work on your document in a WYSIWYG (What You See Is What You Get) Mode. This is the best way to ensure that your final document is exactly how you would like it to look.

To make an INTERACTIVE MASTER:

1. From the MAIN Menu,

   SELECT: **COMPOSING**.
2. From the COMPOSING Menu,

   SELECT: **MAKE MASTER**.

2-28 XPS 700 PHONE DIRECTORY APPLICATION USER GUIDE

2. Building the Document

Introduction

There are five basic steps to producing a document. These steps are:

1. **Prepare the Art**
2. **Design the Document**
3. **Prepare the Text**
4. **Compose the Document**
5. **Print the Document**

The model for building the document is the sample Phone Directory.

This section will instruct you on how to modify the template design in order to meet your document design requirements and produce your own company phone directory.

Follow these steps sequentially to produce your document.

Soon you will feel comfortable with rearranging the steps to suit your own production workflow. Until then, follow the steps suggested in order to best produce the document.

Now let's begin!

STEP ONE: Preparing the Art

The first step to building the document is to Prepare the Art. This involves receiving the art into the XPS 700, assigning the art to a library level, and editing the art.

NOTE: The art images for building your document must be scanned using the XEROX 150 GIS, or be entered from EPIC. Check to see whether the images are online to your XPS 700, or stored on magnetic tape and continue with the next sections accordingly.

Bringing the Art into the System

The first step to Preparing the Art is to receive the art into your XPS 700. To receive the art:

1. From the PRODUCTION Main Menu,

   SELECT: **SHIP AND RECEIVE**.
2. From the SHIP AND RECEIVE Menu,

   SELECT: **RECEIVE ART**.
3. SELECT: the **device** that you are using to bring the text into the system.

XPS 700 PHONE DIRECTORY APPLICATION USER GUIDE 2-1

12.6: Example of a user manual showing placement of an illustration and important text elements.

✔ MANUAL CHECKLIST

- ☐ Foreword or preface
- ☐ Reason for the manual
- ☐ Overview of the manual
- ☐ How to use the manual
- ☐ Table of contents
- ☐ Chapters and sections
- ☐ Page numbers
- ☐ Interior pages (or chapters)
- ☐ White space
- ☐ Consistency of design elements
- ☐ Numbers used to list steps in a process where sequence is important.
- ☐ Bullets, check marks, and boxes used to set off important elements
- ☐ Appendix
- ☐ Relevant reference materials
- ☐ Design conforms to the grid used for interior pages
- ☐ Index
- ☐ Complete index
- ☐ Cross-referenced

Figure 12.7

require a liberal use of illustrations, using both line art and photographs. The kind of illustration you choose should clearly show users what needs to be done. All illustrations should be carefully placed so as to help readers understand the text and follow the flow of information from one idea to the next.

The typographic style in any manual or training guide should visually establish a clear hierarchy of information so that users will know the relative importance of the text components. Include main headings and subheadings, text, captions, and bullet points in your design specs. If there is no clear visual treatment of important information, users will be unable to find what they are looking for. The basic parts of a manual are shown in the manual checklist in Figure 12.7. The material in this section applies to both technical and job performance manuals.

Rules, screens, bullets, and boxes can be used in manuals to emphasize important facts. The layout and design treatment of manuals like the one illustrated in Figure 12.8 makes it easy for the reader to follow and find any reference. Figure 12.9 illustrates another design solution.

The solution was to design a manual that would facilitate quick scanning and retrieval of specific information. This was accomplished by employing a variety of "Filtering" techniques.

Highly visible titles create landmarks for chapter beginnings.

"Hanging" bullets enable the eye to pick out key points.

Use of bold heads, contrasting text typefaces and rules help the reader to scan the page and quickly find the specific information needed.

Color, typeface and graphic "flags" indicate procedures to be performed.

Second color helps to organize and differentiate types of information.

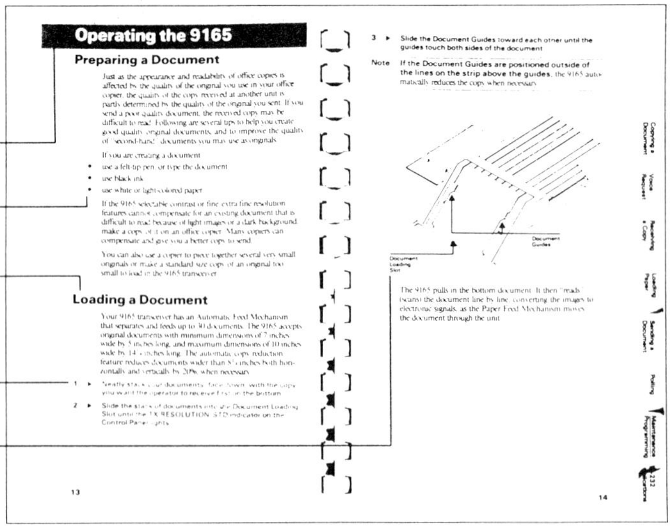

Figure 12.8: A manual page layout with callouts emphasizing some of the points mentioned in Figure 12.7. (Courtesy Suzanne Watzman, Watzman Information Design, Cambridge, MA, USA.)

However careful you are, you will undoubtedly need to clean the scanner glass occasionally. In addition, you will need to replace the lamp some day.

There is very little troubleshooting you can perform on the Apple Scanner itself. Most problems are the result of problems with your SCSI connections. Appendix A provides a SCSI troubleshooting guide.

Cleaning the scanner glass and case

Clean the glass with pure alcohol or with a glass-cleaning product specifically designed to evaporate completely. Commercial glass cleaners are usually ammonia-based and leave a film that interferes with the light reflection off the original. Clean with tissues that are designed for lint-free cleaning.

Periodically, wipe the plastic case of your Apple Scanner with a damp cloth to remove any dust.

Removing and reattaching the scanner lid

If you need to scan very thick originals, you can remove the scanner lid by following these steps:

1. Open the lid as far as it will go.

The lid makes a 90-degree angle with the scanner glass when it is fully open.

210 Chapter 5: Maintenance and Troubleshooting

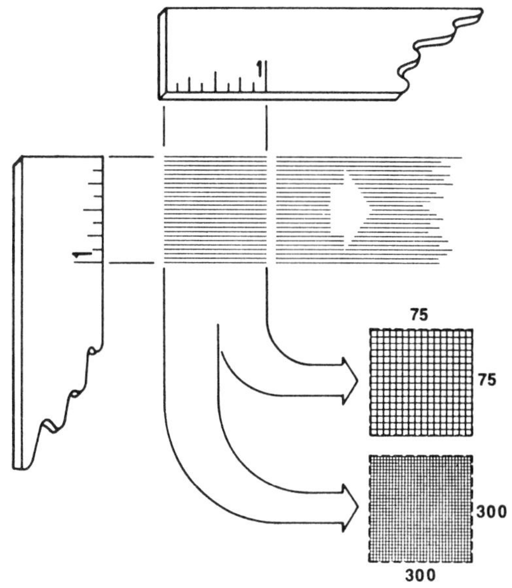

Figure 4-7
Scanning with different resolutions

Normally you choose the Resolution value to match as closely as possible the output device you will use to reproduce the image. A laser printer that prints at 300 dots per inch can reproduce images scanned at 300 dots per inch. If your printer prints 216 dots per inch, you will achieve most-satisfactory results with a resolution of 200 dots per inch. If you print an image scanned at 300 dots per inch on a printer capable of printing only at 72 dots per inch, AppleScan scales the image to achieve the correct actual size, but scaling can distort the image and reduce the quality of the reproduction.

AppleScan menus 171

Figure 12.9: A documentation manual by Apple Computer, Inc., that clearly outlines the features and instructional elements that a user needs to find quickly. The illustration is large enough to identify elements that are mentioned in the text.

CATALOGS

A catalog is a publication that provides a listing of a firm's products and prices. There are three different formats for catalogs. One form is the price/product specification sheet, described in Chapter 9, *Business Publications.* The second type of catalog is the brochure style, usually used for selling specialty or sale items. These are described in Chapter 11, *Flyers, Folders, Brochures, and Other Short Documents.* The third type of catalog is the long document form, as illustrated in Figure 12.10. This type of catalog includes all of a company's products for a given time frame, either a year or a season. Lengthy catalogs usually use short supplements to support changes in stock and pricing until a new catalog is printed.

Nothing takes the place of a thorough understanding of the company and its products, when designing a catalog layout.

If you are designing a lengthy catalog, your primary objective should be easy retrieval of information.

The graphic presentation of your catalog will depend on the company, the type of goods, and on the type of consumer to whom it is addressed. In addition, a company catalog should match the company's position in the market. If a company seeks an upscale image, its catalog should reflect the same image. On the other hand, if the organization wants to be known as a low-priced "bargain" company, a less elaborate catalog is in order.

The rules for typeface selection and text formatting are no different for catalogs than for any other business publications.

The grid is a major design tool for catalog design. Depending on the structure of the information in the catalog, one convenient grid is the three-column format that divides an 8 1/2 x 11 page into three columns. Other grid arrangements may be more suitable, depending on the nature of the products and their illustrations (see Figure 12.11.) Review Chapter 7, *Grids: Working with Structure and Space,* for more information on working with grids.

Many readers just browse through catalogs; others use them as references. A catalog should therefore include a detailed index so any product described in the catalog can be easily and quickly located.

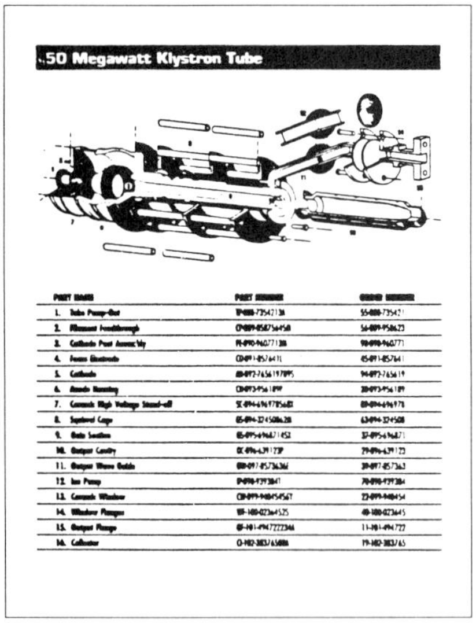

Figure 12.10: An item with many parts in a lengthy catalog.

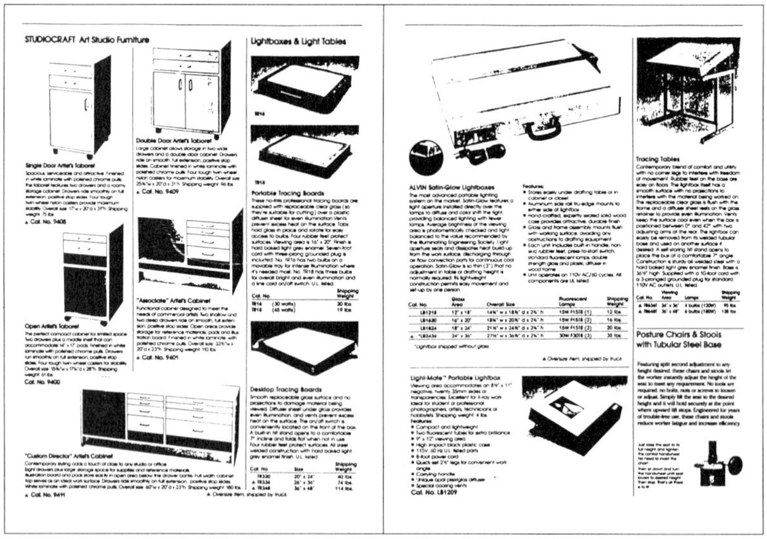

Figure 12.11: A three-column 8 1/2 x 11 catalog with many illustrations.

CHECKING YOUR UNDERSTANDING

1. What are some basic design considerations for books?

2. Define frontmatter, interior pages, and backmatter as they apply to book layout and design.

3. List and define at least six elements that might be found in the frontmatter of a book.

4. List the typical sizes for hardbound and paperback documents.

5. Compare and contrast the layout and design of trade books with textbooks and manuals.

6. What are some basic manual design considerations?

7. Discuss why it is important to know the intended audience before you begin the layout and design of a manual.

8. Explain why it is important for a manual to contain a table of contents and an index.

9. Explain why the organizational considerations for catalogs differs from those of most other business publications.

10. Why must you have a thorough understanding of the company and its products before you begin the layout and design of its catalog?

BUILDING YOUR DESKTOP DESIGN SKILLS

1. Secure a copy of a fiction book. Using the book you selected, along with this text, do the following:

   a) Review the frontmatter of both books, then prepare a three-column chart that lists the frontmatter elements common to both books in the first column. List the elements found only in the fiction book in the second column, and those found only in this text in the third column.

   b) Compare the following elements for the two books, then indicate how the differences are affected by the type of book:

      Trim size

      Top, bottom, inside, and outside margins

      Number and width of columns

      New chapter/section format

2. Secure a copy of two manuals (perhaps those that came with your computer hardware or software). Compare the design of the two manuals using the manual checklist in this chapter as a reference. Indicate whether you feel the designer made the appropriate decisions. If you disagree with any of the designer's choices, explain why.

3. Locate one section in a manual that has been designed to provide step-by-step instructions to the reader. Comment on the design features and elements used to support the written text.

4. Secure a recent issue of a long catalog. (Long catalogs are often available at the reference section of your local library.) Photocopy several typical pages to use for this assignment. Draw a design grid for one of the catalog's typical pages.

DESKTOP DESIGN WORKSHOP

The purpose of this section is to provide you with opportunities to develop and/or improve your desktop publishing design skills. The worksheet pages have been placed at the back of the book, and are designed so they can be removed and you can write, draw, or place your responses directly onto the pages.

DESIGNING A BOOK

Assume you have received a request for a quote (RFQ) for the layout and design of the book *Desktop Publishing in the Modern Office.* The RFQ requires that you submit sample pages with your quote. Do the following:

1. Output a hard copy of the files on the data disk that accompanies this book. Label your printouts so you can identify the file by name later.

12TITLE.DOC (DOS) or
12 TITLE PAGE (Mac)

12TOC.DOC (DOS) or
12 TABLE OF CONTENTS (Mac)

12SPREAD.DOC (DOS) or
12 PAGE SPREAD (Mac)

12INDEX.DOC (DOS) or 12 INDEX (Mac)

2. Sketch your ideas for each of the following pages on the thumbnails on Worksheet 12.1.

   a) Title page

   b) Table of contents

   c) First two pages of Chapter 1 as a two-page spread.

   d) Index

3. Using your page layout program, the appropriate text files, and any graphics you may wish to include, create and output a full-size copy of each of your sample page designs.

DESIGNING A MANUAL

Use the thumbnails on Worksheet 12.2 to create a sketch for a payroll manual for the Kawakami Motor Corporation. You might want to prepare a grid planning sheet (Chapter 7) before you begin.

1. Sketch your ideas for a title page on page 1.

2. Assume the second page is the copyright page and label it "Copyright."

3. Plan pages 3 and 4 for the introduction. Provide headings for the three sections: Introduction, Materials Needed, and Overview.

4. Assume the manual has six chapters and Appendix A through G. Allow two pages for the contents sections. Sketch a table of contents on pages 5 and 6.

5. On page 7, design a chapter title page for Chapter 4, "Payroll Reporting Requirements."

6. Design two sample interior pages. Use pages 8 and 9. Show where you will put elements on each page, then shown where you might place art.

7. Use page 10 to develop a sample appendix page for your manual. The appendix should conform to the interior page design you created in step 6 above.

8. On page 11, design a sample index page.

13. MAGAZINE LAYOUTS

When you finish this chapter you should be able to:

- *Discuss the purpose of a publication specification form and indicate the kind of information that is recorded on such a form.*
- *Discuss how magazines differ from books and newspapers.*
- *Discuss the principles involved in creating a distinctive, well-designed magazine cover.*
- *Distinguish between a logo and a logotype.*
- *Identify the interior pages of a magazine by name and discuss basic design principles for each.*
- *Distinguish between an editorial and a feature article.*
- *Display a working knowledge of common ad shapes and sizes.*
- *Produce a well-designed magazine layout.*

A MAGAZINE IS A PERIODICAL WITH A book-like format. Magazines furnish their readers with more timely information than books do and provide readers with more in-depth coverage than they are apt to find in newspapers. As with newsletters, there are magazines for every taste and interest. Some are aimed at a particular gender, others to a selected age group, or to distinct geographic regions. The contents may vary, but all magazines are designed based upon the same graphic principles.

When designing a magazine layout, you must keep in mind the purpose of the publication and its value to its target audience.

ELEMENTS OF A MAGAZINE

Not all magazines are made up of the same elements. All magazines do, however, include most of the five elements listed on the following page as part of their makeup. The way each element is designed will establish how your magazine looks and communicates to its readers.

- ✔ *Cover*
- ✔ *Contents page*
- ✔ *Departments*
- ✔ *Feature openers*
- ✔ *Editorials*

MAGAZINE COVERS

No element is more important to a magazine than its cover. The cover must identify the magazine, attract attention, and sell copies. A typical magazine cover includes a logotype (the name of the magazine), the date of the issue, price per copy (if warranted), and a dominant element(see Figure 13.1.) Since the cover is the first part of the magazine the reader sees, it must stand out from all the others on a newsstand. The following items have been used successfully to create a dominant element on a magazine cover:

- ✔ A photograph or illustration tied to a feature article. News magazines like *Time* and *Business Week* use this feature.
- ✔ Abstract art, a photograph, or an illustration that stands by itself.
- ✔ Type only. The type may be a title from a feature article or a table of contents. *Reader's Digest* is a well-known example of a magazine that includes its table of contents on the cover.
- ✔ A short article or the beginning of an article or editorial that continues inside. Some magazines like *Advertising Age* always have a few well-placed articles on their covers.

Once you have decided *what* you want to put on the cover, you must then decide *where* to put it. The placement of the cover elements is dictated in part by the way magazines are sold and distributed. If, for example, the magazine is sold on the newsstand, it is often placed upright in a metal rack with many other magazines. The prospective buyer sees only a small top portion of the cover. That's where you want to place the title and logo. On the other hand, paid subscription magazines arrive in mailboxes, so you have more freedom in placing the cover elements.

THE LOGO AND LOGOTYPE

The logo and logotype in magazines are very much like trademarks. The *logo* is generally a graphic while the *logotype* is the name of the magazine. The logotype is usually a very distinctive typeface — often one that is especially designed for the publication. When

Figure 13.1: Examples of well-designed, familiar magazine covers

selecting a logotype, choose a typeface that reflects the personality of the magazine (see Figure 13.2.) Avoid type or letterforms that will become dated.

A magazine's content changes from issue to issue, but the cover should adopt a consistent design for each succeeding release. The logo and logotype should be the same size and in the same position issue after issue.

Figure 13.2: Illustration of familiar logotypes.

INTERIOR MAGAZINE PAGES

A good cover design will induce your reader to pick up the publication and start flipping through it. Then, it will be up to your interior page designs to grab the readers' attention and induce them to focus on the text and pictures inside. The information in Chapter 4, *Designing Form With Content,* will help you do that.

Interior pages follow the same general design principles used in other publications, but there are some pages that are unique to the magazine format. Among these are the *functional pages,* which may include a contents page, various departments and feature sections, and the editorial pages.

Features, editorials, and other stories frequently do not end on the page they start on. Stories may run on for several pages, occasionally jumping over double spread advertisements. For this reason, it is important to design a signature block or a small dingbat that signifies the end of an editorial or other type of story. In conjunction with the end-of-story dingbat, you should also design a dingbat signifying that the text continues on the next page. If continuing text jumps a number of pages, be sure to use a jump page indicator. It is also helpful to your readers to include page numbers even on advertisement pages, so that all the pages are numbered (see Figure 13.3.)

Figure 13.3: End of story mark and continued story mark.

This is the end. ■

This story continues ☞

This story continues ➡

CONTENTS PAGE

There is no standard format for the contents page. You can place the table of contents on part of a page or expand it to fill an entire page. As illustrated in Figure 13.4, some magazines include photographs and illustrations to stimulate reader interest.

Like the cover, it is important to standardize your contents page so that readers recognize it from issue to issue. Standardizing the format also makes the production process easier. You can design the contents page once, using a style sheet, and save it on disk as a "Contents Format." When producing each new issue all you have to do is insert different text into the file to create a new but similar table of contents.

MASTHEAD

All magazines contain a masthead similar to those used in newsletters and newspapers. The masthead should be placed on one of the first five pages and should list the name of the publication, its address, date of issue, volume number, name of the editor and designer, and the frequency of publication. In some publications, an entire page is devoted to the table of contents and the masthead (see Figures 13.5 and 13.6.)

DEPARTMENTS

Many magazines contain standing matter or columns that appear in every issue. Frequently, magazines will include columns that are written by paid staff members. Together these columns are referred to as *departments*. The subject of the articles in the departments always discusses some aspect of the magazines subject matter. For example, *PC Computing* magazine runs a "Perspective" and a "Micro Mephisto" column as well as monthly columns by David DeJean, John

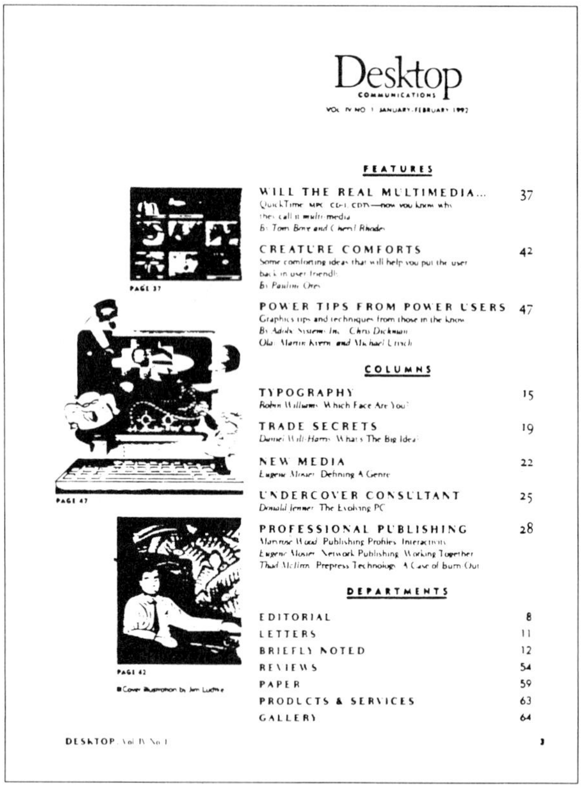

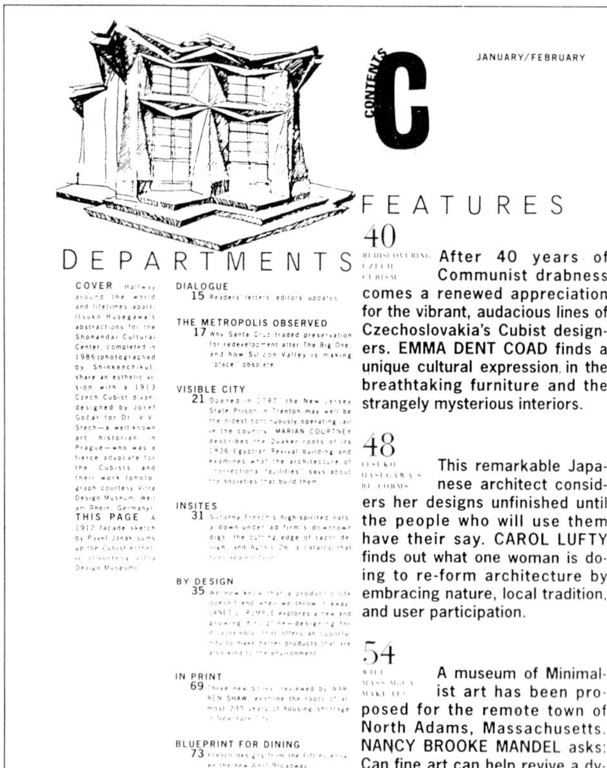

Figure 13.4: (left) A contents page with illustration for some articles from "Desktop." (right)A contents page from "Metropolis" set in type only; art is used to embellish the contents heading (reprinted by permission of Metropolis Magazine.)

Cover created by Steve Lyons in PixelPaint Professional.

Editor PETER GIFFEN
Art Director GEORGES HAROUTIUN
Contributing Editors DOUG DOLAN, LARRY GAUDET, SHONA MCKAY
Director of Marketing and Sales SHIRLEY M. SETO
Contributing Photographer GARY WHITE
Controller/Office Manager RITA HAROUTIUN
Distribution/Circulation Manager PATRICIA MERTENS
Western Sales Manager HAROLD S. WHITE (604) 943-3377
Production M.A.G. GRAPHICS

Applied Arts Quarterly (ISSN 0829-9242) is published four times each year (January, April, July, October) by Applied Arts Inc., 885 Don Mills Road, Suite 324, Don Mills, Ontario, Canada M3C 1V9.
Phone (416) 510-0909. Fax (416) 510-0913.
President: GEORGES HAROUTIUN. Vice-President: PETER GIFFEN.
Applied Arts Quarterly is a trademark of Applied Arts Inc. Copyright © 1988 by Applied Arts Inc. All rights reserved. Reproduction of any part of this publication without written permission of the Publisher is strictly forbidden.
Second Class Mail Registration No. 7104. Postage paid at Toronto.

ccab
SUBSCRIPTION RATES: $44 per year in Canada. For U.S. subscriptions, add $6 U.S. per year. For subscriptions outside Canada and the U.S., add $19 U.S. per year. (U.S. and foreign subscriptions payable only in U.S. funds.)
Printing by MATTHEWS INGHAM AND LAKE INC. Color separations by EMPRESS GRAPHICS INC.
Inside stock: Royal Classic 100 lb.text manufactured by PROVINCIAL PAPERS, A DIVISION OF ABITIBI-PRICE INC.
Cover Stock: Jenson Cover 100 lb. manufactured by PROVINCIAL PAPERS.
UNSOLICITED CONTRIBUTIONS: We encourage the submission of articles but cannot be responsible for their return. All material submitted for editorial consideration must include a self-addressed envelope and return postage.

NEWSSTAND DISTRIBUTORS
CANADA: C.M.P.A., 2 Stewart Street, Toronto, Ontario M5V 1H6 (416) 362-2546 Ron Sellwood.
U.S.A.: IPDDS, 2323 Woodlawn Street, Harrisburg, PA 17104 (416) 496-8444 John Lafranier (Disticor).
INTERNATIONAL: RotoVision SA, 9, route Suisse CH-1295 Mies, Switzerland, (22) 755-3055 Evelyne Chesaux.

Figure 13.5: A magazine masthead from "Applied Arts Quarterly."

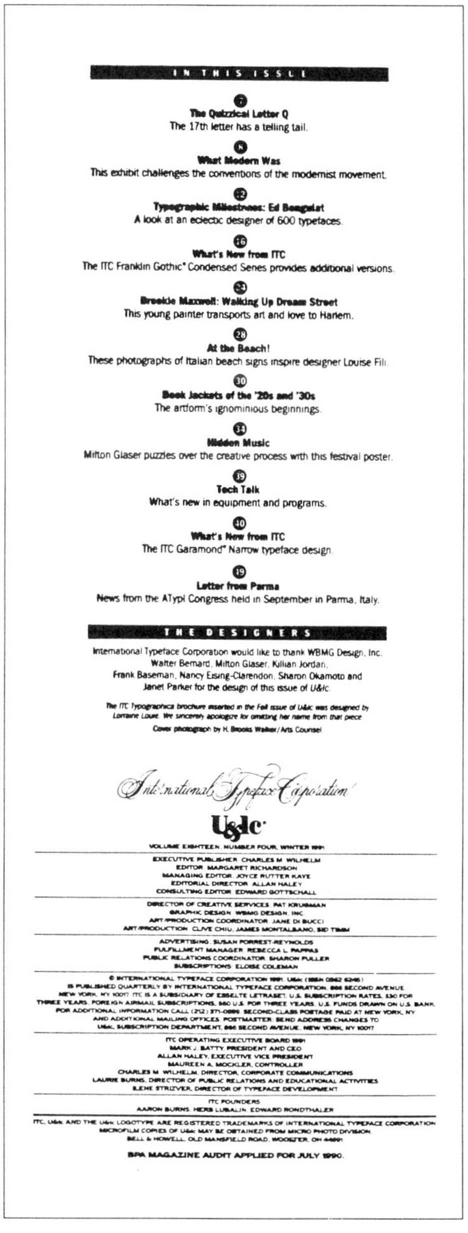
IN THIS ISSUE

7
The Quizzical Letter Q
The 17th letter has a telling tail.

8
What Modern Was
This exhibit challenges the conventions of the modernist movement.

12
Typographic Milestones: Ed Benguiat
A look at an eclectic designer of 600 typefaces.

16
What's New from ITC
The ITC Franklin Gothic® Condensed Series provides additional versions.

23
Brookie Maxwell: Walking Up Dream Street
This young painter transports art and love to Harlem.

28
At the Beach!
These photographs of Italian beach signs inspire designer Louise Fili.

30
Book Jackets of the '20s and '30s
The artform's ignominious beginnings.

34
Hidden Music
Milton Glaser puzzles over the creative process with this festival poster.

39
Tech Talk
What's new in equipment and programs.

40
What's New from ITC
The ITC Garamond® Narrow typeface design.

19
Letter from Parma
News from the ATypI Congress held in September in Parma, Italy.

THE DESIGNERS

International Typeface Corporation would like to thank WBMG Design, Inc. Walter Bernard, Milton Glaser, Kilian Jordan, Frank Baseman, Nancy Eising-Clarendon, Sharon Okamoto and Janet Parker for the design of this issue of *U&lc*.

The ITC Typographica brochure inserted in the Fall issue of U&lc was designed by Lorraine Louie. We sincerely apologize for omitting her name from that piece.

Cover photograph by H. Brooks Walker/Arts Counsel

International Typeface Corporation

U&lc

VOLUME EIGHTEEN, NUMBER FOUR, WINTER 1991

EXECUTIVE PUBLISHER: CHARLES M. WILHELM
EDITOR: MARGARET RICHARDSON
MANAGING EDITOR: JOYCE RUTTER KAYE
EDITORIAL DIRECTOR: ALLAN HALEY
CONSULTING EDITOR: EDWARD GOTTSCHALL

DIRECTOR OF CREATIVE SERVICES: PAT KRUGMAN
GRAPHIC DESIGN: WBMG DESIGN, INC.
ART/PRODUCTION COORDINATOR: JANE DI BUCCI
ART/PRODUCTION: CLIVE CHIU, JAMES MONTALBANO, SID TIMM

ADVERTISING: SUSAN FORREST-REYNOLDS
FULFILLMENT MANAGER: REBECCA L. PAPPAS
PUBLIC RELATIONS COORDINATOR: SHARON FULLER
SUBSCRIPTIONS: ELOISE COLEMAN

© INTERNATIONAL TYPEFACE CORPORATION 1991. U&lc (ISSN 0362 6245) IS PUBLISHED QUARTERLY BY INTERNATIONAL TYPEFACE CORPORATION, 866 SECOND AVENUE NEW YORK, NY 10017. ITC IS A SUBSIDIARY OF ESSELTE LETRASET. U.S. SUBSCRIPTION RATES, $30 FOR THREE YEARS; FOREIGN AIRMAIL SUBSCRIPTIONS, $60 U.S. FOR THREE YEARS; U.S. FUNDS DRAWN ON U.S. BANK. FOR ADDITIONAL INFORMATION CALL (212) 371-0699. SECOND-CLASS POSTAGE PAID AT NEW YORK, NY AND ADDITIONAL MAILING OFFICES. POSTMASTER: SEND ADDRESS CHANGES TO U&lc, SUBSCRIPTION DEPARTMENT, 866 SECOND AVENUE, NEW YORK, NY 10017

ITC OPERATING EXECUTIVE BOARD 1991
MARK J. BATTY, PRESIDENT AND CEO
ALLAN HALEY, EXECUTIVE VICE PRESIDENT
MAUREEN A. MOCKLER, CONTROLLER
CHARLES M. WILHELM, DIRECTOR, CORPORATE COMMUNICATIONS
LAURIE BURNS, DIRECTOR OF PUBLIC RELATIONS AND EDUCATIONAL ACTIVITIES
ILENE STRIZVER, DIRECTOR OF TYPEFACE DEVELOPMENT

ITC FOUNDERS
AARON BURNS, HERB LUBALIN, EDWARD RONDTHALER

ITC, U&lc AND THE U&lc LOGOTYPE ARE REGISTERED TRADEMARKS OF INTERNATIONAL TYPEFACE CORPORATION. MICROFILM COPIES OF U&lc MAY BE OBTAINED FROM MICRO PHOTO DIVISION, BELL & HOWELL, OLD MANSFIELD ROAD, WOOSTER, OH 44691

BPA MAGAZINE AUDIT APPLIED FOR JULY 1990.

Mirabella

advance word

...movies and theater

TRACEY ULLMANN has all the fun. She's just finished shooting opposite KEVIN KLINE and WILLIAM HURT in Tri-Star's *I Love You to Death*—billed as "an offbeat romantic comedy about a wife who almost kills for love and a husband who almost dies for it." The production was shot on location in Tacoma, Washington, and is scheduled for a Christmas release. This is yet another collaboration between Kline, Hurt, and director LAWRENCE KASDAN (Hurt was in his *Body Heat* and *The Accidental Tourist*; Hurt and Kline were both in his *The Big Chill*). In the new film Ullmann plays the wife of a pizza parlor owner (Kline) who gets so sick of his cheating on her that she plots his murder with the aid of his coworker (Hurt). The characters are based on a real couple who appeared on the *Oprah Winfrey* show last year—the wife never did quite kill her husband, and it seems the two are more in love than ever. Nothing like sticking to your guns—or not.

Mermaids, the CHER/EMILY LLOYD project for Orion, has been postponed until the fall. Originally set to shoot this spring with LASSE HALSTROM (*My Life as a Dog*) directing, plans went awry due to Cher's well-publicized flu/tonsillitis/ROB CAMILETTI troubles. Halstrom had another film scheduled, so next time around FRANK OZ (*Dirty Rotten Scoundrels*) will direct on location in Canada. *Mermaids* is a coming-of-age story about the daughter of an itinerant family (Lloyd) who is striving for sainthood. Cher plays her 'oddball' mother.

CARRIE FISHER's *Postcards From the Edge*, based on her semi-autobiographical book which recounted her escapades in drug addiction, is scheduled to start shooting in New York this summer with MERYL STREEP playing Fisher and SHIRLEY MACLAINE playing her mother. While MacLaine is certainly a contemporary of Fisher's real mom, DEBBIE REYNOLDS, Streep is almost six years older then Fisher and only seventeen years younger than MacLaine. This is one of those perfect Hollywood moments when nothing makes sense. But the inside combinations usually tell the story. Superagent Sam Cohn represents Streep and director MIKE NICHOLS. Nichols is good friends with singer PAUL SIMON (remember the score for *The Graduate?*) whose ex-wife is Fisher. Nichols and Streep worked together on *Heartburn*, the NORA EPHRON script; Fisher costars in Ephron's *When Harry Met Sally*... opening next month. The obvious question is: why isn't Fisher playing herself? The answer is also obvious. Meryl Streep would do it better.

an Allen, right, as *The Heidi Chronicles*' Heidi with Peter Friedman.

From left: A preppy Robin Williams; gloating Tracey Ullmann; Billy Crystal and Meg Ryan in *When Harry Met Sally*...; Meryl Streep, yet again; Carrie Fisher, just a little starved for attention.

Speaking of *When Harry Met Sally*...: this is yet another film in which women are whining about the lack of "good" men. In one scene a stereotypically predatory New York female earmarks a man's number in her Rolodex the instant he marries. The implication is that he is only worth knowing if he's available to save her from the sentence of being single. Are we supposed to laugh? Is it funny for a woman to see herself as a desperate lady-in-waiting? Are men only "good" when they're marching down the aisle? WENDY WASSERSTEIN'S Broadway kvetch, *The Heidi Chronicles*, is another example of this rotten phenomenon. Wasserstein's Heidi seems capable of having relationships offstage, while the sets change, but when the lights come back on we find that none of them worked out. Why? Because she wanted to pursue her nomadic academic career and he, all of those he -didn't want to be uprooted. Is Wasserstein saying that men should be the doormats now that women have refused the role?

Heidi is disappointed because the women's movement has let her down. I thought we were all in this together, she whines. Well, maybe it ot the movement that let Heidi down—maybe "together" is simply not one of her talents. She seems as distant from the women in her life as she is from the men. She condemns women for abandoning the herd behavior of a "movement" and finding their own solutions for their own problems. But confronting problems individually is too scary an option for Heidi. Criticizing others, as a group, is a much safer option for a woman so incapable of intimacy with men *and* women. And adopting a baby, as Heidi does in the play's last scene—without having given us even a glimmer of an indication that motherhood represents fulfillment to her—is too pat an antidote to her copiously listed complaints. There's certainly no indication that she'll be any better at being "together" with a child than she has been with anyone else.

What's the moral? Women need to develop a persona on film, stage, and in print that's positive without being so relentlessly, destructively self-indulgent. Men aren't here to fix women. Women aren't here to be fixed. Next?

Dead Poet's Society, the ROBIN WILLIAMS film opening this month, is set at a boy's prep school—and was shot at St. Andrew's in Middletown, Delaware. According to Steven Haft, the film's producer, the authenticity of prep ritual is guaranteed: Williams went to Detroit Country Day, Disney execs MICHAEL EISNER and JEFFREY KATZENBERG attended Lawrenceville and Fieldston, respectively; there were also staffers from Groton and Hotchkiss. The crowning glory is that Haft is married to none other than prep expert LISA BIRNBACH of *The Preppy Handbook* fame who seems to have had the film's most superfluous position: Technical Consultant. For the record, Haft graduated from Flushing High School in Queens.

—ALEX WITCHEL

Figure 13.6: (left) A page incorporating both the contents and the masthead (reprinted with permission from "Upper and Lower Case, The International Journal of Type and Graphic Design." ©1991 International Typeface Corporation.)

Figure 13.7: (above) A magazine department page from "Mirabella."

C. Dvorak, John Dickinson, and Stephen Manes (see Figure 13.7.) For many readers, these departments are as important, if not more important, than the feature stores.

As illustrated above, department pages often contain a department label, a byline, and a headline. Rules and other graphics may be part of the label design. Some magazines also include a photo or sketch of the columnist. Department pages may also contain ads.

FEATURE PAGES

The feature page should carry the feature articles and no advertising. An example of a two-page feature is shown in Figure 13.8. If you have a "feature page" with no ads, try to start it on a left-hand page, if possible. This will give you a two-page spread.

All features have an *opener*. An opener is the first right-hand page or first spread of a feature article. A *first right opener* is a single right-hand page. The page opposite a first right opener is usually sold to advertisers. Since this space is next to a feature article, this ad is generally more expensive than the others.

Every opener must be exciting visually to draw the reader into the story. A large illustration used with a compelling text headline, or a copy of the cover are used in the design of this page. A two-page spread opener is much more effective than a single page only.

EDITORIALS

Occasionally, you will find editorials classed together with departments, but they are different. *Editorials* are written expressions of opinion presented by the editor or publisher. Features and departments present factual information, not opinion. The editorial page should contain the following elements, illustrated in Figure 13.9.

- ✔ *A column title, such as "Editorial"*
- ✔ *A headline that indicates the subject of the editorial*
- ✔ *The editorial text*
- ✔ *The author's signature block*

Figure 13.8: (left) a feature page from "Metropolis (reprinted by permission of Metropolis Magazine; (right) a feature page from Mirabella.

The editorial page contains elements that are different from the other interior pages, and its design should reflect this difference. Using type and leading that is somewhat larger than the main text is one way to reflect the difference and importance of editorial content. Adding an extra margin of white space between the editorial and any advertising will also help to give importance to this element. Like other page elements, the location of the editorial page should not change from issue to issue.

BACK COVER

The back cover can present a design problem. If the magazine accepts advertising, the back cover is often used for this purpose. Since the back cover gets almost as much notice as the front cover, the ads are always more expensive. If ads are not used, you may design the cover by wrapping the art over to the back and treating the cover as one unit.

ADVERTISEMENTS

If your magazine accepts advertising, you may have as much as 70 percent of the magazine space devoted to the advertisements. The proportion of advertising to text is determined by the editorial policy of the magazine. Some magazines like professional journals have far fewer ads than monthly news and speciality magazines.

AD SHAPES AND SIZES

Most of the advertising that will be included in your magazine will be provided to you by advertising agencies. Although you will not prepare the ads, you must have a working knowledge of typical advertising shapes and sizes so you can place them on your pages.

Advertising is generally sold by the page, half-page, or column inch. The average magazine page is about 8 x 11-3/4 to 9 x 12. A popular size for desktop publishers is 8-1/2 x 11 with a live area of 7 x 10 in which to place ads. Many publications use a three-column format because advertisers prefer it. Some magazines will work with a six-column design for page layout, which will allow their advertisers to work with three columns. A three-column layout has 30 column inches of advertising available per page (three columns times ten inches).

Figure 13.9: Editorial pages from (left) "Gourmet" and from (right) "Communications of the ACM."

Figure 13.10 presents some typical shapes used for advertisements on an 8-1/2 x 11 page.

The smallest ad size is generally 1/6 page. A 1/6-page column ad may be one column wide by 5 inches deep or two columns wide by 2-1/2 inches deep. The 1/3-page ad may be vertical or horizontal. When the 1/3-page ad is placed in the horizontal position, it is two columns wide by 5 inches deep. This format is called an *island*, because text can be wrapped around the ad both vertically and horizontally. Notice that the 1/2-page and 2/3-page ads also can be placed horizontally or vertically. When placed vertically, they, too, form an island.

DUMMYING THE PUBLICATION

Magazines are lengthy, complex publications with many different kinds of stories and functional pages. The advertising, too, is made up of many sizes and shapes. Some advertisers may have paid extra for preferred positions next to feature articles in the magazine. You may need to change your page layout a number of times when you are designing the pages for a specific issue. Under these circumstances, it is a good idea to prepare a rough dummy of the publication before you design the spreads.

Full-page ads may be single-page ads or two-page spread (two-spread) ads. When a two-spread is used, care must be taken to ensure that the two pages line up properly.

Magazine advertisements follow some basic layout preferences.

- ✔ *Advertisers prefer right-hand pages and the front half of the magazine.*
- ✔ *Coupons should be on the bottom or outside edge; one coupon should not be placed directly behind another.*
- ✔ *Color ads should be placed on color pages.*

PREPARING A MAGAZINE DUMMY

The first thing you need to do when preparing a magazine dummy, is to get copies of all your advertisements, including information about preferred positions. Design the opening pages for your stories and functional pages, and run out all the text that the articles contain. You may want to use larger type and a different grid format for your story opening pages and spreads, and use a

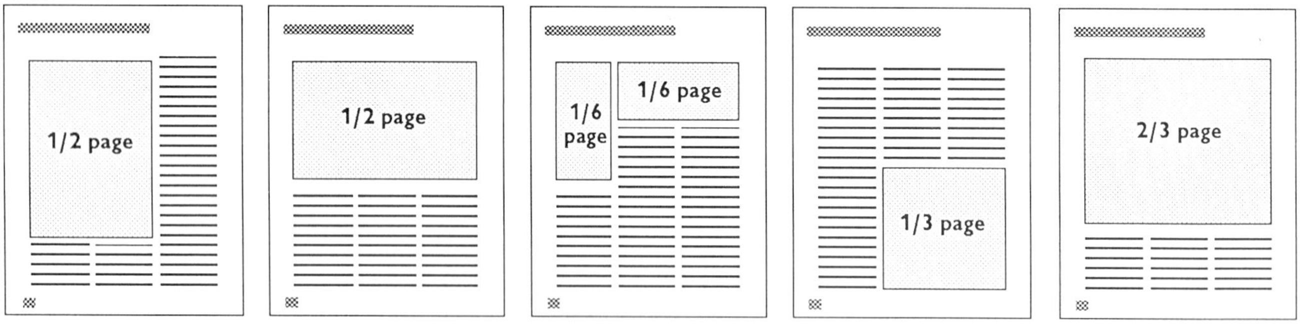

Figure 13.10: Common shapes and sizes for advertisements as shown on a 8 1/2" x 11" page, using a three-column grid.

smaller type size with a standard grid for story continuations. Include all the graphics you will need for each story together with the type (see Figure 13.11.)

Now comes the fun part. Estimate the final number of pages planned for the issue, based on all the text, graphics, and advertising that must be included. The final magazine length will need to be based on multiples of eight pages called *signatures*. If you absolutely must, a single four-page signature can be inserted, but this often creates problems when assembling the pages. For further information about signatures, see Chapter 14, *Working with Service Bureaus and Print Shops.*

After you have established the magazine page length, you will need to thumbnail all the elements to be used on each page in miniature, adjusting and readjusting to get all the elements to fit. You may find that some stories will need to be cut shorter, either by eliminating a graphic or cutting a paragraph. Other stories may be required to fill out a page by using an additional graphic or pull quote. When the workable dummy has been assembled, you can use it to produce the magazine using your page layout program.

CHECKING YOUR UNDERSTANDING

1. How does the purpose and value of a magazine differ from those of a newspaper and a book?

2. List the five elements that are common to most magazines.

3. Discuss three techniques you might use for creating an attractive magazine cover.

4. Distinguish between a logo and a logotype and give an example of each.

5. What is a masthead and what information must it contain?

6. What is a department and how does it differ from an editorial?

7. Discuss two methods of laying out a feature article.

8. What elements should be displayed on the editorial page?

9. What are some of the possible formats for the placement of advertisements on an 8-1/2 x 11, three-column page?

10. List three considerations that should be taken into account when dummying a magazine.

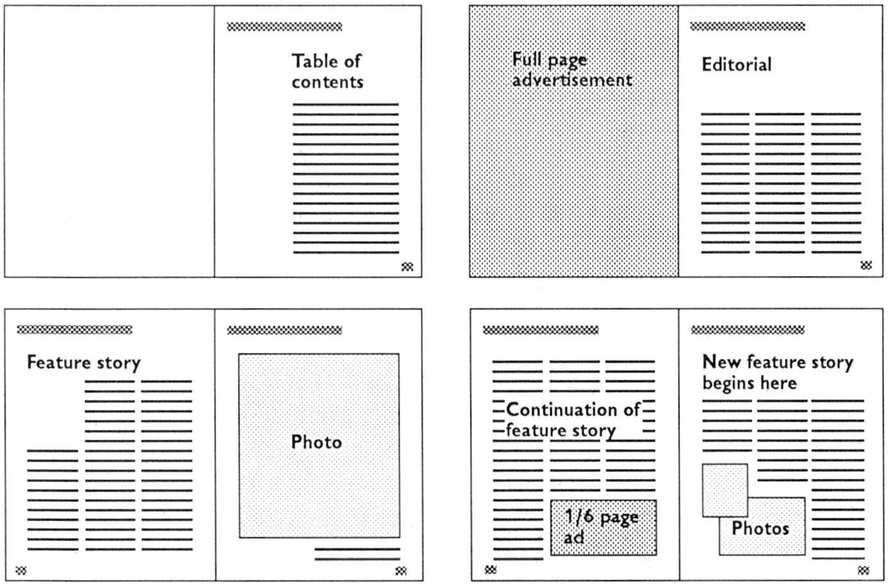

Figure 13.11: Thumbnails for a magazine dummy

BUILDING YOUR DESKTOP DESIGN SKILLS

1. Secure a copy of two different magazines, one that is sold on the newsstands (it may also be sold by subscription) and one that is available only by mail. Examine the issues, then do the following:

   a) Briefly describe how the magazines are similar in design and how they are different.

   b) Compare the following elements for the two magazines, then indicate how the differences are affected by the nature of the magazine:

      Cover

      Content page

      Logotype

      Department pages

      Feature openers

      Editorial pages

2. Using your page layout software, design a cover for *The Pampered Pet*, a monthly magazine designed to be mailed free to pet store owners and to pet groomers. Use any art or text you may choose.

3. Secure a recent issue of any magazine that contains advertisements. Open the magazine to a spread that contains feature or department text and at least two ads. Then do the following:

   a) Measure the size of each ad.

   b) Briefly comment on the shape, size, and position of each of the ads.

   c) Comment on the layout of the text and the placement of the ads on the page. If you disagree with the placement or the size or shape of any element, indicate what you would do to improve it.

DESKTOP DESIGN WORKSHOP

The purpose of this section is to provide you with opportunities to develop and/or improve your desktop publishing design skills. The worksheet pages have been placed at the back of the book, and are designed so they can be removed and you can write, draw, or place your responses directly onto the pages.

Assume you have been commissioned to design the layout for the "World at a Glance" department of a popular subscription travel magazine. The publication is a 36-page, 8-1/2 x 11 magazine with a three-column grid. Using the grid on Worksheet 13.1 and the advertisements on Worksheet 13.2, do the following:

   a) Design a layout that utilizes both the advertisements and the department text and thumbnail your design on the grid. Include all type and element specifications.

   b) Design a standing head for the "World at a Glance" column in the space provide on Worksheet 13.2. The head will always be one column wide. If you like, you may include any graphic you have available.

   c) Using your page layout software, your thumbnail layout, and a photocopy of the advertisements on Worksheet 13.2, create a full-size sample of your design. Paste or tape the advertisements in place on your printout and use one of the following text files for the department text: 13DEPT.DOC (DOS) or 13 DEPARTMENT (Mac).

PART FOUR

PLANNING, PRODUCTION, AND PRINTING

14. *Working With Service Bureaus and Print Shops*
15. *Preparation of Camera-Ready Art*
16. *Publication Planning, Budgeting, and Scheduling*

14. WORKING WITH SERVICE BUREAUS AND PRINT SHOPS

When you finish this chapter you should be able to:

■ *Know when to consult with a service bureau and a print shop.*

■ *Choose a service bureau and a print shop.*

■ *Know when to use paper or film for final imagesetter output.*

■ *List specifications for halftone reproduction.*

■ *Know the differences between process color and spot color.*

■ *Use your page layout program to do color separations.*

■ *Decide when to have color separations done by a prepress service.*

■ *Specify paper and understand its importance to the way your job will look.*

■ *Explain the different methods for folding and binding publications.*

YOU HAVE FINALLY COMPLETED your publication. Laser printed copies have been proofread and corrected through what seems like a never-ending cycle. Your final copy is ready for quantity duplication. But is it?

If you need just a few copies and the pages are standard bond 8-1/2 x 11 or smaller, and are to be printed in black and white, with line art only, you can duplicate your publication easily using a photocopier. If you use a photocopier to reproduce your document, keep in mind, though, that photographs will reproduce crudely and tint blocks will have coarse screens. Your type will be *almost typographic quality* — suitable for general use, but not meant for high-quality reproduction on quality paper stock. All you need to produce good quality copies using a photocopier is final copy of the highest quality output your laser printer can provide. Make sure that the laser printer is clean and its cartridge is still producing good blacks; the paper you use should be laser quality 24 pound stock with a smooth finish. Many paper companies now produce papers made especially for the laser printer.

Does your publication have tint blocks, photographs or other halftone art? Do you need many copies, say 250 or more? Does the publication have colors in addition to black? Does it have *bleeds* — art or tint areas that go to the very edge of the page? Is the page size of your publication larger than 8-1/2 x 11? Would you like to have it printed on rough or textured paper? If the answer is yes to any of these questions, you will need to use the services of a print shop. You may also need to rely on a reputable service bureau to prepare high-resolution output (see checklist, Figure 14.1.)

If you find that you will need to use a service bureau to complete your job, or if the job will be printed on a press, consult with the service bureau or the print shop *before* you start working on a project, especially if it a complex one. People who work for these facilities usually have suggestions to help you prepare the work correctly and can often save you money.

WORKING WITH A SERVICE BUREAU

Service bureaus vary in the extent of the services they can perform for you. Some service bureaus deliver high-resolution typographic output only. Others undertake full color proofing and separations, design, and other publishing services for the desktop publisher. The quality and degree of service varies as well. Some service bureaus, usually at the lower end of the per-page price scale, will take your disk(s) and print out final copy. These facilities may not always have the latest equipment and they may not be familiar with all the software people use, but, they may be doing just the kind of work that *you* need to get your work done. On the other hand, the high-end service bureau may have all the latest equipment but the people there may not have the time to go over your job with you to offer you the best solution.

HOW DO YOU FIND A SERVICE BUREAU?

As a start, ask friends and business associates who have worked with service bureaus for their recommendations. The rest is up to you. Interview the people at the bureaus

✔ SERVICE BUREAU & PRINT SHOP CHECKLIST

	In-house	Service Bureau	Print Shop
✔ How to many copies do you need?			
☐ 1 to 100		✔	
☐ 100 or More			✔
✔ Size:			
☐ 8.5 X 11 or small	✔		
☐ 9 X 12			✔
☐ 11 X 17			✔
✔ Colors:			
☐ B & W	✔		
☐ Color other than black		✔	✔
☐ Black and spot color		✔	✔
☐ 4 color process		✔	✔
✔ Scanned images:			
Do you have a scanner?			
☐ No		✔	
☐ Yes	✔		
Do you need high resolution output?			
☐ No	✔		
☐ Yes		✔	
✔ What printing method?			
☐ Copier	✔		
☐ Offset process			✔
✔ Does your project have halftones?			
☐ No	✔		
☐ Yes		✔	✔
Tint blocks			
☐ No	✔		
☐ Yes		✔	✔
Bleeds			
☐ No	✔		
☐ Yes			✔
✔ Paper quality:			
Standard			
☐ No	✔		
☐ Yes			✔
Heavy			
☐ No	✔		
☐ Yes			✔
Textured			
☐ No	✔		
☐ Yes			✔
✔ Binding:			
Stapled			
☐ No			
☐ Yes	✔		
Other			
☐ No			
☐ Yes			✔

Figure 14.1

✔ SERVICE BUREAU CHECKLIST

✔ Recommended source:

Name ____________________

Address ____________________

Phone # ____________ Modem # ____________

Contact ____________________

✔ Equipment:

Imagesetter printer or other model: ____________

Color printer: model ____________

Scanner: model ____________

Slide scanner: model ____________

✔ **Price per page**

☐ 1270 DPI ☐ 2540 DPI

		Number of Pages				
		1 – 10	11 – 25	25 – 50	50 – 100	100+
RC paper	8.5 X 11					
	8.5 X 14					
	11 X 17					
Film	8.5 X 11					
	8.5 X 14					
	11 X 17					
Color comps	8.5 X 11					
	8.5 X 14					
	11 X 17					

✔ What fonts do they use

☐ Adobe

☐ Other ____________

✔ Illustrations/Artwork

Scanning ☐ Yes ☐ No

Line art ☐ Yes ☐ No Cost ________

Half - tones ☐ Yes ☐ No

B & W ☐ Yes ☐ No Cost ________

Color ☐ Yes ☐ No Cost ________

Color separations ☐ Yes ☐ No Cost ________

Slides ☐ Yes ☐ No Cost ________

✔ Turn around time

Standard ☐ Same day ☐ Overnight ☐ 24 Hour

Rush charges ____________

Delivery charges ____________

✔ Other services

Waxed repros ☐ Yes ☐ No Cost ________

Accept files for modem ☐ Yes ☐ No Cost ________

Self-service ☐ Yes ☐ No Cost ________

Figure 14.2

that have been recommended to you and record their answers using a checklist similar to the one illustrated in Figure 14.2. Find out what the bureaus charge, and for what services. Prices go down with the number of pages you are running, and can be negotiable. Prices go up if you want high-resolution output—2400 dpi rather than 1270 dpi. Find out what fonts are used and if they are compatible with the ones you use. If not, service bureaus will usually provide you with screen fonts for the versions they carry. You won't be able to check proofs on your laser printer, though, unless you have the accompanying printer fonts as well.

If you work with photographs and other art at a low resolution on your scanner, you will need to know if the service bureau can output good quality halftones at higher resolutions. You will also need to get prices for halftone work; it is usually higher than straight output. Ask how long standard jobs take and what the rush charges are if you need it yesterday. It is better to allow extra time, especially when you are just starting out in desktop publishing, in case there is a foul-up. Find out, too, if the bureau can accept work by modem. Even if you don't work with one now, it is a convenience you may want to use in the future.

If you work with color, you will need to know if the service bureau has the equipment to handle color separations. Make sure that your service bureau is trained in the use of color separation and uses clean chemicals and carefully calibrated equipment. If you have a complex job, ask to see color samples of its work, and request client references.

Another option is to go directly to a color pre-print house whose personnel have had years of experience preparing images for print. You want to be sure that the firm handling your color work has the skilled craftspeople needed to run your job successfully to give you the help you will usually need when you are starting out, even with simple work. If your projects include the complex use of color, you will always need the advice and support of the service bureau to get it done properly.

When you have narrowed down your search for a good service bureau, try it out on a small job. Call first, to find out exactly what is needed from you and if the company is free to do the work in its normal turn-around time. Sometimes shops get overloaded, especially if they are small. Bring them your disk and a proofed copy of its laser-printed output. The shop will also need some specific information about your file, as shown in Figure 14.3.

A good service bureau will want to know what program and equipment you used to make the file. It will also want to know what fonts you used (including the name of the manufacturer; i.e., Adobe, Bitstream, Monotype, etc.), and what kind of graphics your job, might include. If you have used graphics in your job the service bureau will want to know what format they are in — EPS, TIFF, PICT, etc. — and if they are simple or complex. It will want to know your page size and how many pages there are in the job. The bureau will also need to know your deadlines.

Allow at least a day for turn-around time on simple projects, and add enough time for corrections on any large project.

PREPARING YOUR FILES FOR IMAGESETTER OUTPUT

Imagesetter printers can accommodate large page sizes and (unlike your laser printer), on 8-1/2 x 11 output, the image area can run almost to the edge of the paper. Check with the service bureau to see if you need to adjust your file page size to accommodate the new size options.

If you have tint blocks specified in your laser copy, the percentage you have allocated for the tint area will probably need to be made about 10 percent darker for the imagesetter printer. Imagesetters output lighter tint values than laser printers. Ask to see imagesetter tint percentage samples when completing your specifications.

WORKING WITH FILM

Output from a high-resolution imagesetter is usually in the form of photographic paper known as *RC paper*. If your job consists of type and line images and will be printed at a local print shop using less expensive paper plates, RC paper output will do just fine.

If your job incorporates high-resolution tint areas, halftones, or color, the higher resolution quality needed by this kind of

✔ JOB ORDER FORM CHECKLIST *

✔ Name of project ________		✔ Deliver to ________		
✔ Job # ________		✔ PO # ________		
✔ Due date ________		✔ Due time ________		
✔ Service bureau modem number		✔ Type of modem used		
✔ Operating system used – software and CPU		✔ Number of copies per page		
✔ File name ________		✔ File used – program name including version #		
☐ Adobe fonts		☐ B & W scans		
☐ Non-Adobe – list mfg.		☐ Color scans		
☐ Slides		☐ Color comps		
☐ Graphics formats	☐ EPS	☐ Tiff	☐ Pict	☐ Other
✔ Page size	☐ 8.5 X 11	☐ 8.5 X 14	☐ 11 X 17	☐ Other
✔ Imagesetter	☐ RC paper	☐ Film	☐ 1270 DPI	☐ 2540 DPI

** Make sure that your order form includes this information.*

Figure 14.3

document requires film negatives and metal plates for printing. Imagesetters can also output film for metal plates directly. Metal plates are a little more expensive than RC paper output but can save you quite a bit, especially if your job is a large one. Make sure that your service bureau calibrates its equipment properly for film; make sure, too, that you check with your print shop first to find out exactly what is needed in order to make good plates for your job.

REPRODUCING BLACK AND WHITE PHOTOGRAPHS AND ILLUSTRATIONS

There are several ways to handle halftone reproduction. The easiest, and the one that guarantees the highest quality, is to let the print shop provide screened halftones for you. It will cost a little more, but not by much if you have just a few photographs. You will need to provide the print shop with final output, camera-ready, including *windows* for placing your photographs and illustrations as shown in Figure 14.4.

A window is an outlined or solid black rectangle or other shape that represents the space the actual graphic will occupy. The window acts as a frame and provides the prepress service with a clear sharp outline within which the graphic will be placed. You can print the window outline to show as a black outline for your art, or you can include instructions not to print it; to *drop it out*. You will also need to indicate the size of your final image and show how you want it cropped. Chapter 15, *Preparation of Camera-Ready Art*, describes how this is done.

If you want to use a scanner to indicate position and sizing, scan your images at low resolution and place them, cropped and sized as desired, into your pages. The quality of these low-resolution images is not high enough to use for final reproduction, but the images show accurate size and cropping to the people preparing your halftones. Be sure to put the words FOR POSITION ONLY or FPO in large type on each positioned image, so that they will not be used as final art by mistake.

The second method involves the use of *PMTs* or *photomechanical transfers*. These are mechanically produced halftone prints that your print shop can make for you, ready for reproduction as line art in your publication. In order to make the PMTs, your original photographs will need to be sized and cropped as described in Chapter 15. The PMTs you get from your supplier should be pasted into position on your final art, a process also described in Chapter 15. The quality is not quite as good as conventional halftoning, but the cost is lower, especially if you have a lot of photographs in your publication. Costs can be lowered even more if you *gang* your

Figure 14.4: Final output on a board with keyline windows indicated. Solid black windows can also be used.

images — that is, resize several of them together, at the same percentage, as shown in Figure 14.5. You can find out more about ganging images from your supplier.

The third method, for creating output requires the use of a gray-level scanner. Your photographs need to be scanned twice. One scan is made at low resolution and placed in position on your pages for proofing. The second scan is made at a high resolution, to be printed out by your service bureau. The low-resolution scanner uses little memory, it takes up much less disk space, and also allows you to work more quickly when laying out pages. High-resolution scans are very memory-intensive, but of much better quality.

The quality of high-resolution scanned images, while adequate for some work, is not as good as conventional halftoning. Using digital scans can save both time and money, especially if you have many photographs of varying sizes and are printing on a softer finish paper. Digital halftones have imperfections that will be highlighted when running on coated stock or better quality papers.

SPECIFYING RESOLUTION FOR YOUR HALFTONES

If you are working with a scanner, your halftone image is reproduced digitally. The number of gray scale levels and the degree of resolution offered by your scanner will control the level of screen fineness that is possible. However, regardless of the degree of resolution your scanner offers, the output you get will correspond to the resolution capabilities of your printer. When you specify the degree of resolution that is required, your scanned graphic will be converted into digital information, usually as a Tagged Image Format (TIFF). With TIFF files, the dots will *approximate* those of a conventional halftone. Imagesetter output can vary from as little as 600 dpi to as high as 2400 dpi, depending on the degree of smoothness you need and the quality of the paper you will be printing on.

Conventional halftoning exposes the photograph through a fine screen that breaks up the continuous tone photographic image into dots. If you examine photographs in a daily newspaper, you will be able to see the dots making up the photographs with the naked eye. If you look at reproductions in an art book, you will notice shadings from light to dark, but the dots will not be visible unless you use a magnifying glass.

Screens come in varying degrees of fineness, running from 65 lpi (lines per inch) to 85 lpi for anything run on coarse paper such as newsprint. For general usage, 120 to 150 lpi is specified. For fine reproduction on high-quality paper, screen fineness can run

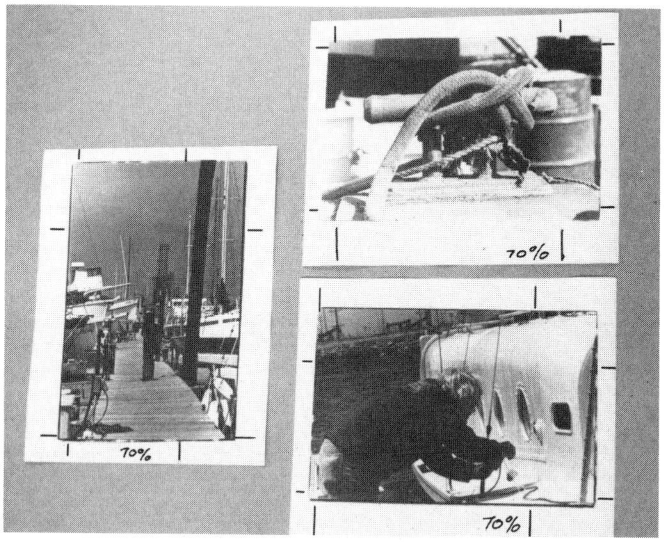

Figure 14.5. Ganging photos.

A.

B.

Figure 14.6A: (top) A photograph with a half-tone screen of 85 lines per inch: (center) The same photo screened at 120 lines per inch: (bottom) An extremely coarse halftone, showing individual halftone dots.

Figure 14.B: (above) A dot percentage scale from 0% to 100% in 10 steps. See how the size of an individual halftone dot affects the gray shade that is produced. (Illustrations for 14.6 A and B courtesy Linotype-Hell.)

anywhere from 175 to 300 lpi. (Figure 14.6A.) When halftoning an image, the number of lines to the inch remains constant; the size of the dot changes to accommodate areas from light to dark, as shown in Figure 14.6B.

Screen halftone specifications can vary depending on the surface and texture of your paper stock. Before specifying your final halftone screen resolution, select the kind of paper you will use for the job. Then check with your preprint house and your service bureau to make sure that your screen specifications are appropriate.

WORKING WITH COLOR

Color preparation can be as simple as using your page layout program to print a separate sheet or overlay for each color on your final output pages, or it can be as complex as preparing an intricate four-color process separation using color scanners and prepress software for your result.

Discuss color with your print shop and service bureau before you start any complex color project. Shop personnel will advise you about how to get the best possible results.

A printing press prints only one color at a time. For that reason printing plates are made for each separate color. Many page layout programs allow you to separate colors as part of the program. What this means is that each separate color you are using on a page will occupy a page layer that is separate from the part of the page that will print in another color.

When a color-separated page is printed by laser, you can choose to output it in one of two different ways. For proofing purposes, you can elect to print the page as a composite in which all the layers will print in position on a single sheet. This output is not meant for reproduction; its colors will appear in gray values so that you can judge whether everything appears as it is supposed to in the final printed piece.

For color that will eventually be printed on a printing press, you will need to laser print each color layer separately. If your final printed page is smaller than 7-1/2 x 10, most page layout programs allow you to select and laser-print *register marks*. Register marks help to ensure that each color will print exactly over the previous color; they consist of a circle with a centered cross. You will want to make sure that when you use register marks, they are accurately superimposed over each other layer by layer as shown in Figure 14.7.

SPOT COLOR

Color can be selected in two different ways. If you are using one or two colors as accents in addition to black, and you do not intend to mix these to produce many blended colors, you will be working with what is called *spot color*. With spot color, you can select the specific ink color you want to use from a book of printed ink samples. If you are using a color computer, you can select colors from numbered samples in your page layout program. Pantone™ PMS colors are the most frequently used standard samples, with matched sets of numbered colors for the computer and for the printing press. PMS colors have been selected by the manufacturer based on fashion and design interests and needs. They are not a standardized color system, based on equal measure percent changes for tints and shades.

CYMK: USING PROCESS COLOR

When you are preparing pages that will include full-color images, you will be working with *CYMK* color. CYMK stands for cyan blue, yellow, magenta, and black; the ink colors used in preparing full-color printing. Full color printing is also known as *four-color process*, because of the way the color is produced on the printed pages. When different percentages of cyan blue, yellow, magenta, and black are printed layer upon layer, they can support a wide spectrum of color tints and shades.

Individual PMS ink colors can also be specified as percentages of CYMK if you are doing four-color work, but process colors will rarely match well to a solid ink color sample in PMS ; some colors will not replicate at all to the printed colors based on cyan blue, yellow, magenta, and black.

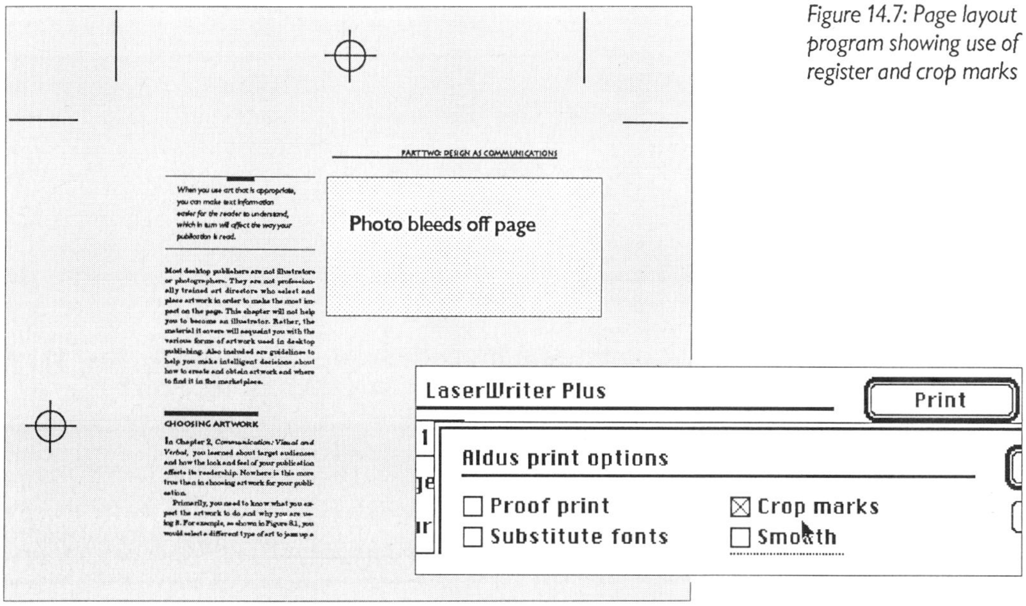

Figure 14.7: Page layout program showing use of register and crop marks

Trumatch™, a newer color matching system, is printed entirely in four-color process so that the Trumatch™ color can be replicated closely on the press. Unlike the Pantone™ PMS colors, Trumatch™ provides proportional gradations of tints and shades in as little as 6 percent increments. This allows you to choose colors for reproduction more precisely. Figure 14.8, a photo of the Trumatch™ color sample book, shows the gradations as replicated in black and white.

You can use a high-resolution color scanner to prepare your own four-color separations if you want to save money. But, unless you have lots of experience as a color separator and have the expensive equipment you need for high-resolution output, you will get much better results working with the experts.

If you are doing work that combines use of spot color with four-color process, you can do some of the work yourself and save some money in your prepress costs. Be sure that you prepare your pages indicating CYMK color percentages for all the areas that will appear as solid color tints and shades. Use crop marks and place windows using position prints for all your four-color images wherever they are to appear on your pages.

Your color service bureau or prepress house will separate four-color art and position it as needed.

Before you get too far into your project, discuss your color work with experienced, reliable craftspeople to find out what they will require in order to complete your project smoothly.

You can usually rely on an experienced color service bureau or prepress house or color print shop to give you good results without repeated corrections. Any color work is subject to problems from imagesetter output to final printing on a press. Some of the variables are:

1. The accuracy of the settings for imagesetter controls when creating tints.
2. The cleanliness of the chemicals used in processing imagesetter output, and how carefully they are measured.
3. The sharpness of the printing plates.
4. The sequence in which the different colors are printed on the press.
5. The density of the ink colors running through the printing press.
6. Color of the "white" paper, which can run from a bright white to cream.

Figure 14.8: Photo of the Trumatch™ color sample book

7. A condition known as *dot gain,* in which the amount of color applied by each dot in a halftone increases during the printing process.

Experienced craftspeople are aware of these conditions, and compensate for them when preparing and printing color work.

DO-IT-YOURSELF SEPARATIONS

If you do color separations yourself, use a scanner to digitize your four-color images in low resolution and put them on the pages as position only. Make your color corrections in low resolution first; do the final corrections and color balancing in high resolution, using a program such as PhotoShop or Color Studio on the Mac. Remember, you need not only a trained eye to do color balancing, but you also need to know how to compensate and adjust for good color balance on the printing press.

PROBLEMS IN COMPATIBILITY

Whether you will be using spot color or process color, the color on your computer monitor generally will not match that on another monitor because of differences in calibration and intensity. Several companies are offering devices that will calibrate monitors to the same setting if that is important in your work group.

Another problem is that at the present time most color printers do not accurately laser-print the PMS or CYMK colors you have selected for your document, as they appear on your computer screen. Unless you are fortunate enough to own a printer that calibrates its output to match the colors you have chosen, you will have to make adjustments to your file when preparing color proofs and comprehensives. One solution is to use software that will print out a range of PMS colors specific to the particular printer you are using. With this system, you select the PMS color samples you want to use from the printer output rather than the ones that the computer shows you on the screen. By choosing the PMS numbers from a color printer output and using them in your file, you will get colors that will be fairly close to those you want in the comprehensive. Some companies offer software that will print out PMS samples for you, specific to their printer.

The third problem in compatibility is that even when you have a great color proof from a color laser printer, the colors will not match those printed on a printing press. To get around that problem, use a recent edition of a PMS printers ink sample book when choosing your final colors for reproduction (see Figure 14.9.) Be sure you have chosen your paper first because that, too, affects the color image.

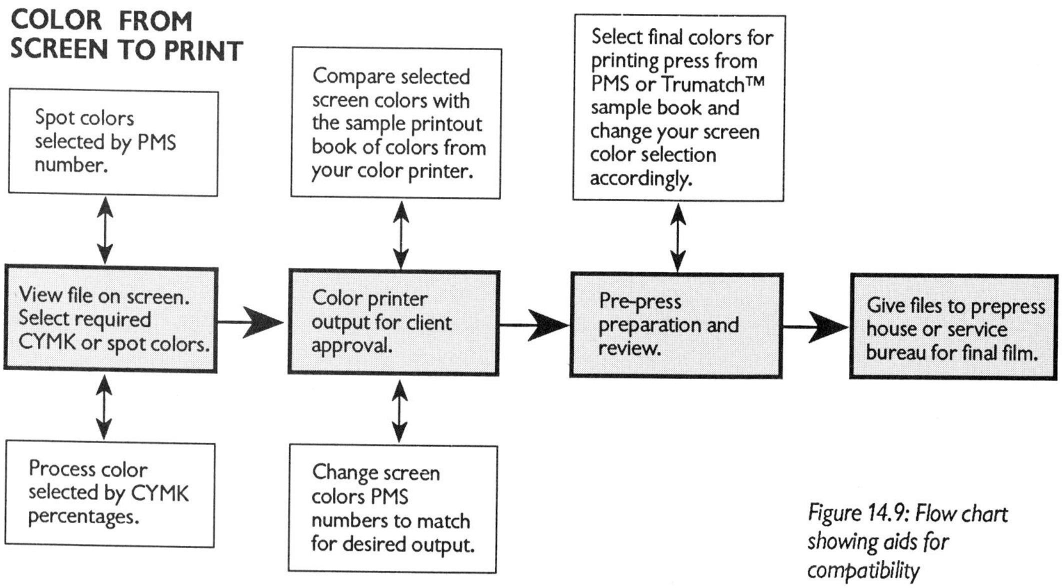

Figure 14.9: Flow chart showing aids for compatibility

Figure 14.10: Offset lithography

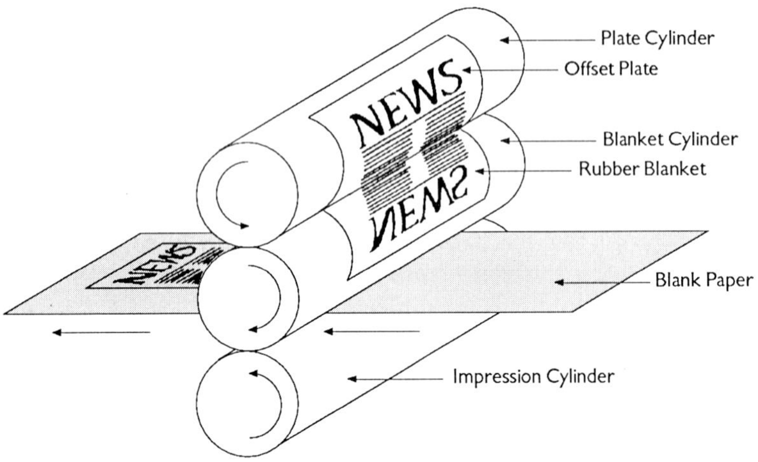

WORKING WITH PRINT SHOPS

Locating the right printer for the job to be run is similar in many ways to finding a good service bureau. Word-of-mouth is usually the best way to start out, along with the understanding that printing is a diverse industry and facilities vary from the neighborhood print shop to the large full-service plant. If your projects are fairly simple black and white with occasional use of spot color, the small print shop can handle your needs. If your publications are lengthy, if you use full color, and if your print runs are large, a larger shop will serve your needs better. Moreover, printing presses vary in size, and press size can affect the price of your printed work.

TYPES OF PRESSES

Most printing these days is done in offset lithography. This process requires printing plates that do not print directly on to the paper. The image is transferred to a series of rollers that print the image on the paper of your choice, as shown in Figure 14.10. There are two kinds of printing plates used for offset lithography: paper and metal.

Offset presses come in a variety of sizes to print paper stock of different standard sizes. There are two different kinds of presses, differentiated by the form of paper they use.

SHEET-FED PRESS

The sheet-fed press uses paper cut into a number of standard sizes. Lower priced presses are generally 11 x 17 and 17 x 22 inches, and use paper of that size. 17 x 22 paper will cut up into four sheets of 8-1/2 x 11 as illustrated in Figure 14.11. More expensive sheet-fed presses handle larger sheets of paper, and many can print two or four colors at one pass through the press. A two-color press has two sets of color rollers, each using a different plate. High-end sheet-fed presses are used for better quality color work.

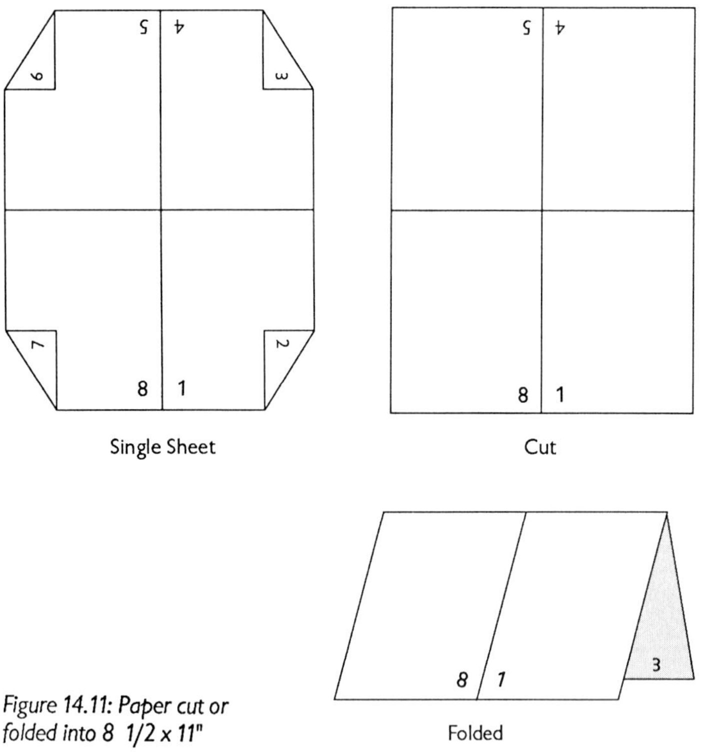

Figure 14.11: Paper cut or folded into 8 1/2 x 11"

WEB PRESSES

Web presses use uncut paper in rolls like those that are used to print newspapers. Newspaper presses are, in fact, high-speed one-color web presses. Most web presses print two- or four-color work, both sides at a time, at high speed. The final printed sheet is folded, ready for binding, at the end of the pass through the press.

A web press requires a crew of pressmen working together to run the job through its length. Some webs are as long as a city block. While most are made to handle large publications with lengthy print runs, there are smaller webs made for smaller print orders. Web presses offer work at medium quality. The advantage is high speed and quantity at lower cost. If you have four-color catalogues to print, or 10,000 copies of a 24-page brochure, a small web may prove to be your best bet.

PRINTING PLATES

Metal printing plates are positive images made from negatives of your final pages. Figure 14.12 illustrates items to be aware of when ordering negatives for your project. Review these with your pre-press source. Plates are used for all halftone and color work, and for any job that will be reproduced in quantity. Each separate color will use a separate plate. Plates may occasionally be saved for reuse if you need to reprint. Otherwise negatives are used to make new plates when needed. If you are printing letterheads, it is a good idea to work with a printer who will save both negatives and plates for reruns.

Paper plates do not use the negatives required for metal plates. They are inexpensive and are made quickly. Paper plates don't last through long runs on a printing press, but if your run is under 1000 sheets they work adequately. Paper plates can only run coarse halftones, 100 line screen or under, and are generally used for one color only, usually black.

CATEGORIES OF PRINT SHOPS

You may need the services of more than one printer. First, find a good shop for the basic work you do most of the time. What you need is good, dependable workmanship offering decent quality at reasonable cost.

Establishing a relationship with a print shop that does the bulk of your work will help you in many ways.

FILM QUALITY CHECKLIST

- ✔ *No streaking or scratches*
- ✔ *Base material is not fogged*
- ✔ *Tint/half-tone quality is good*
- ✔ *Dmax in proper range*
- ✔ *Negative*
- ✔ *Emulsion down/right reading*
- ✔ *Crop/register marks are lined up*
- ✔ *Dimensions are accurate*
- ✔ *Proper fonts are used*
- ✔ *Traps properly executed*
- ✔ *Moiré evaluated*
- ✔ *Dot percents are accurate*
- ✔ *Proper screen angle/ruling*

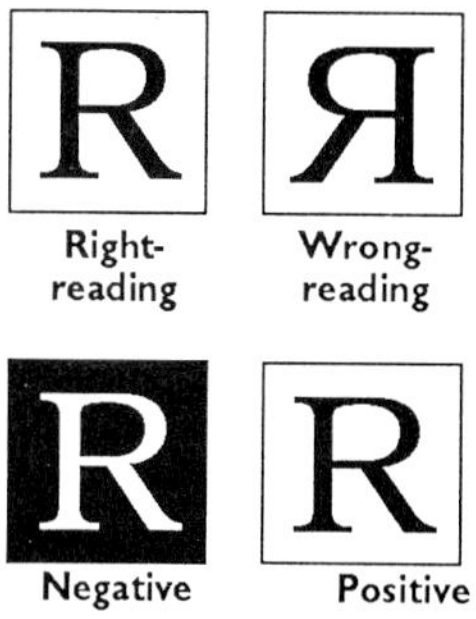

Figure 14.12: (far left) a craftsperson cleaning up a film negative; (center) a list of items to consider when reviewing film; (above) ways in which negatives can be produced. Right-reading is usually required.

When you have a good working relationship with a print shop, you will find that their staff will take the time to go over your job carefully, to ensure that you will be satisfied. Your regular printer will be more apt to get paper samples for you beyond the regular stocks the shop carries. When tight deadlines come up, your print shop will be more considerate about running your work than if you had just come in off the street. And, should you have a project that your print shop cannot handle for one reason or another, your regular printer will often recommend another shop that has the equipment to do the job properly.

QUICK PRINT SHOPS

Quick print shops offer low-end printing, specializing in short, inexpensive runs using paper plates on small presses. Their work is mainly single color without halftones. Some shops may only have one press on the floor, which can present problems when you need quick turn-around on a deadline project. Other quick print shops offer middle range print services as well. They will make metal plates from negatives, print halftones, and have a press equipped to do more elaborate two-color work. If you usually do short run black-and-white projects, a local quick print shop offering a range of services including preparation of camera-ready art can be your best bet. These shops can vary in quality, so check around for recommendations. Do some interviewing on your own, ask to see samples, and try out the likely prospect with a small job first.

SMALL TO MEDIUM PRINTING SHOP

The small to medium print shop or plant can offer a fairly wide range of standard print services. They generally have several sheet-fed presses on the floor, both black and white and two color. The small printing plant may work with both paper and metal plates, but the main emphasis is on the use of metal plates with negatives. Some small plants do four-color process in addition to spot color. These shops generally have their own folding equipment and simple bindery equipment. Larger shops may have more elaborate binding equipment, though many printers contract their work out to binderies who specialize in that kind of work.

LARGE PRINTING PLANT

Web printing presses are only found at larger printing plants. They will also have an assortment of sheet-fed presses in several sizes. The large plant is generally full-service, offering typesetting, color prepress, full bindery services, shipping, and storage. They may be expensive for short-run projects, but if you are printing long manuals, books, and catalogues, they may be advantageous for both price and quality.

DECIDING ON YOUR PRINTER

Figure 14.13 is a checklist you can use to help you find the best printer for your immediate needs. You will need to decide on what level of printing you require: "quick and dirty," average, good quality, or the best. Obviously the printing quality will reflect the cost; you won't get high quality at "quick and dirty" prices.

There are other questions you will need to answer before interviewing and deciding on a regular printer. Will you be working extensively in black and white line art? Will your projects use many halftones? Will you be using spot color, or does the job require full color? What size is your project — what size are the pages, and how many pages are there? How many copies will you need? Will the final job be folded or bound in some particular way? What kind of printed piece is it to be — a catalogue, a newsletter, letterheads and business cards, or a lengthy training manual?

When you find a good match between the kind of work you will be printing and the print shop, try them out with a small job at first.

Allow enough time for corrections, especially if you are working with a print shop for the first time.

You will need to get a cost estimate from the printer *before* the job is run.

PAPER STOCKS AND THEIR CHARACTERISTICS

The time to choose your paper is at the time you are designing your publication. Paper comes in different standard sizes; if the design of your publication does not fit exactly into the size of the paper stock as shown in Table 14.1, you may be paying for paper that will be wasted. Your print shop can advise you as to the sizes of paper that are available for their presses, and they can get you samples to look at. Paper comes in different finishes and weights, so you will need to choose one that is appropriate to your document.

Weight: The weight of paper is measured in pounds and is based on a weight of 500 sheets (1 ream) of paper measured in its basis size. Each paper type, reviewed in Table 14.1, has its own basis measurement that is used for weight calculation. Another paper characteristics is its bulk, or how thick the paper is.

Paper Bulk: Bulk is measured by how many sheets will measure up to an inch. The higher the number of sheets per inch, the lower the bulk.

Paper Grain: A third element to be aware of is paper grain. The direction of the paper grain determines the ease with which the paper can be folded. A fold made with the grain is smooth, while one running across the grain tends to crack the paper.

Opacity: Opacity is another important characteristic when choosing paper. It is the degree

✔ PRINT SHOP SERVICES CHECKLIST

Evaluating print projects to select the right printer

✔ Quality:

☐ Quick print ☐ Average ☐ Good ☐ Best

✔ Colors:

☐ B & W ☐ Color other than black
☐ B & W w/spot color ☐ 4-color process

✔ Artwork / Illustrations:

☐ Line art ☐ Half-tones

Project requirements	Catagory of print shop
✔ Number of copies:	
☐ 1 – 100	Quality copy shop, quick print shops
☐ 100 – 1,000	Small or medium print shops
☐ 1,000 – 5,000	Small or medium print shops
☐ 5,000+	Medium or large print shops
✔ Type of project:	
☐ Few pages, i.e. newsletters	Quick print or small print shops
☐ Many pages, i.e. manuals, catalogues, brochures	Medium or large print shops
☐ Letterheads	Quick print or small print shops
✔ Fast turn around time:	
☐ Depends on shop	
✔ Quality of printing:	
☐ Photocopies	Quality copy shop
☐ Paper plates	Quick print or small print shops
☐ Metal plates	Small, medium or large print shops
✔ Storage needs:	
☐ Large runs	Medium or large print shops
☐ Full color	Medium or large print shops
✔ Printing equipment and services:	
☐ Color separations	Large print shops & color houses
☐ Sheet fed presses	Small, medium or large print shops
☐ Web presses	Medium or large print shops
☐ Folding and binding	Small, medium or large print shops
☐ Embossing & foiling	Medium or large print shops & specialty
☐ Engraving	Large print shops & specialty
☐ Pick up and delivery	Small, medium or large print shops
☐ Shrink wrapping	Medium or large print shops

Figure 14.13: A checklist to evaluate your print project.

TABLE OF POPULAR PAPER SIZES AND WEIGHTS

Paper type	Size in inches	Weight in pounds						
Bond	17 X 22	16	20	28	36			
Book text	25 X 38	40	50	70	90			
Cover	20 X 26				50	60	80	90
Vellum bristol	22.5 X 28.5				57		100	
Index	25.5 X 30.5					90		140
Tag	24 X 36				90	100		150

Table 14.1

to which material printed on one side will show through to the other. More opaque papers are preferable.

BOND PAPER

The most commonly used paper in offices and schools is *bond paper.* This is the standard 8-1/2 x 11 stock you find in stationery stores, although its uncut or *basis* size is 17 x 22 inches. Bond paper comes in three weights: 16, 20, and 24 lb., with 20 lb. as the standard. Bond paper comes in several colors and finishes: *smooth, cockle,* and *laid.* Smooth finish paper has been run through rollers in the paper making process to give the sheet a slick finish. Cockle finish is fairly smooth with a slight dimple, due to the way the paper has been dried. Laid paper has narrow textured stripes running parallel to each other, replicating the surface on which the paper has dried. Your print shop can show you samples of each.

BOOK PAPERS

Book papers are the standard sheets used for brochures, catalogues, newsletters, as well as books. They come in a variety of sizes for different presses, and have different weights based on a basis weight for 500 sheets of 25 x 35 inches. Standard weights for book papers include 50, 60, 70 and 80 lb., with 60 lb as the most popular. They also come in different finishes and colors. Smooth finish is the same as that of bond. *Coated* finishes are very smooth. These papers are coated with a type of clay or with a plastic with an ultrasmooth finish suitable for quality black-and-white halftone and four-color process reproduction. Coated finishes come in a *glossy* or *dull* finish. While many people prefer the glossy finish because it looks expensive, dull coat is much easier to read because of the lower levels of reflection and glare.

COVER PAPERS

Cover papers are papers that can be used for covers, since they are heavier than book papers. Their basis size is 20 x 26 inches. Cover papers come in a very wide range of colors, with many different kinds of textured finishes as well as smooth ones. Their weight varies from lighter weights used for brochures, folders, and letterheads through to heavy-duty cover weights.

Paper companies supply samples of whole sheets of their papers for you to use when designing and preparing publication dummies. Your printer can get samples for you early in the design phase to help you complete your design decisions.

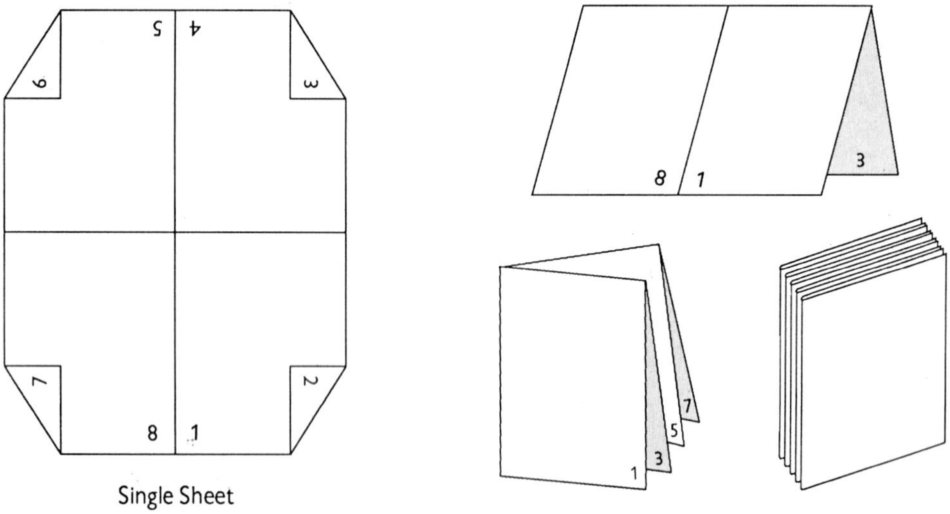

Figure 14.14: A large sheet of printing paper shown folded into a signature. (bottom right) Several signatures gathered together for a publication.

COMPLETING THE JOB

FINISHING

When your publication is printed, it will generally be done several pages at a time, as shown in Figure 14.14. It will then be folded and trimmed to its final size. When sheets are printed and folded, the result is called a *signature*. Signatures can vary from 4 pages, 8 pages, 16 pages, to 32 pages.

Your publication must fit into multiples of any of the above signature sizes, or you will have blank pages left over.

The way that the printer places your pages on a signature for printing is called the *imposition*. Some printers will ask you to prepare your final copy pages as they will appear in the imposition, or they will charge you a fee for doing it in their shop.

BINDING

Some publications will not need any kind of binding. Newsletters and folders are ready to go as is, but if your publication is a 24-page brochure or a lengthy manual, you will have to decide on how the pages will be held together. The simplest binding methods are those that can be done in-house or at your quick print shop.

LOOSELEAF AND SPIRAL BINDING

If your publication will be updated regularly, changing a few pages here and there to update prices or specifications, a *looseleaf punch* is generally the best way to go. It can be more expensive at first, since looseleaf books will need to be supplied, but changes can be printed independently, and distributed to users with instructions on updating.

Spiral comb binding, using punched holes with a plastic comb inserted to hold the pages, is offered by quick print shops. These, too, are expensive by the unit. But if your run quantity is low, the total price may be lower than other forms of binding.

An alternate to spiral binding is *velo bind*, also offered by most quick print shops. With velobind, a series of small holes are punched along the binding edge of the publication, and metal strips are inserted front and back through the holes. Figure 14.15A and B illustrates these binding choices, which can also be done in-house since the equipment is relatively inexpensive and easy to use.

A

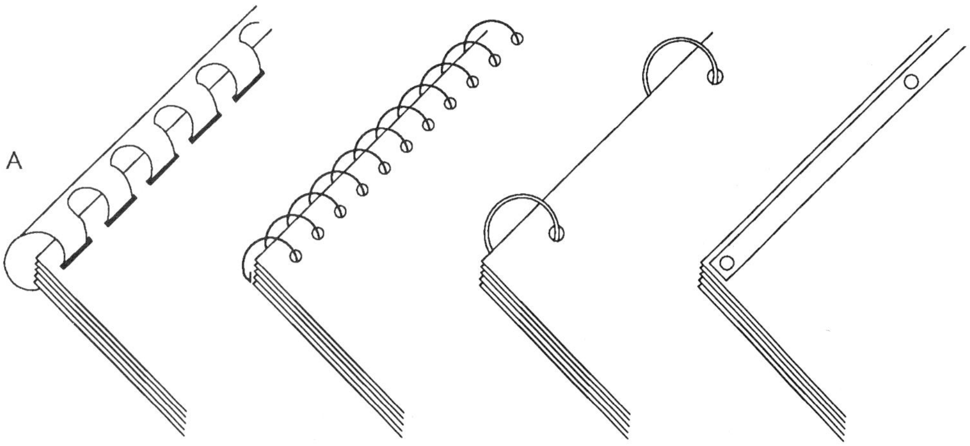

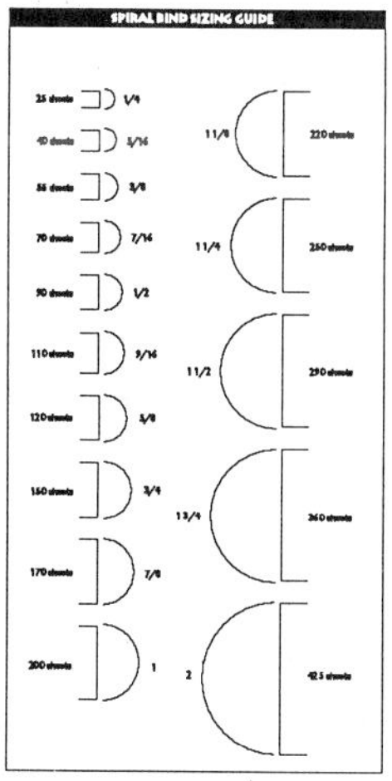

B

Figure 14.15A: Comb and wire spiral binding, looseleaf, and velo binding are illustrated. Figure 14.15B: A gauge for determining the size of a spiral comb binding. The full size scale is in the Workshop/Forms Appendix, page 328.

STITCHING AND STAPLING

Booklets and brochures of 12 to 16 pages or more will need to be stitched in some way to hold the pages together. *Stapling* consists of placing metal staples in the center of the booklet along the fold edge. *Stitching* is similar to stapling except that a loose sewing stitch is made instead of metal staples. It is used for larger books and booklets of 64 pages or more. *Side Stitching* or *stapling* consists of stapling or sewing along the edge of the publication when it is folded into its final state, as shown in Figure 14.16A.

PERFECT BIND

Perfect bind is the kind of binding used in paperback books. It consists of a flexible glue applied to the spine of the book after its signatures have been folded and gathered together. The *spine* is the thin edge of the book between its front cover and back, along the edge on which the folds occur. The spine is sanded smooth, glued, and the cover is applied as a single unit as shown in Figure 14.16B. When the glue is dry, the book is trimmed and boxed, ready for distribution. Perfect bind is used for books 64 pages and longer. It is costly to set up, but in quantity it is very inexpensive.

GETTING PRINTER PROOFS

Before a job is run on a printing press, you need to make sure that everything is correct and ready to go. Your printer can supply you with proofs made directly from the negatives of your final artwork.

Proofs for black and white work are usually submitted as *bluelines,* a blueprint image of your publication as it will appear printed in black and white. Occasionally proofs may be made as a *brownline* image. These are brown, as the name says, but are usually not as clear as the bluelines.

Check your proofs carefully, and try to get at least one other person to check them as well.

Make sure that nothing has been dropped out, that everything is properly aligned, that all the numbered pages do have numbers. Circle *everything* that appears to be suspicious or wrong to you. Mark all the little specks and blobs that should not be there. Your printer may tell you that they are just pieces of dust, but occasionally they will print, and *you* will be the one charged with the error. After you have approved the proofs the printer may show you a corrected set, or if there were few or no errors, plates will be made.

Color images require different kinds of proofs. The most common ones to be used are Chromalins, a full-color representation of your image using process colors. The color may be a little darker than the final printed piece because of the density of the layers used to compose the Chromalin. Make sure that all the colors appear in balance, and represent the original photograph overall. Point out areas that are questionable to your

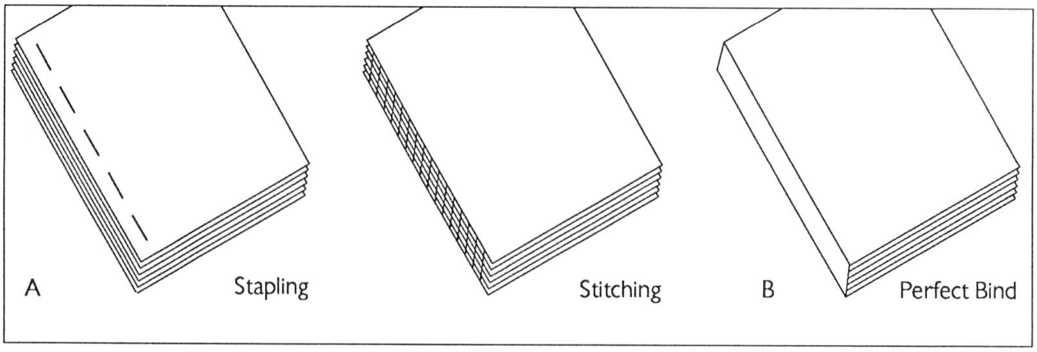

Figure 14.16.A: Signatures that have been stitched or stapled. Figure 14.16.B: Signatures that have been perfect bound.

color representative and have him or her advise you as to the corrections required. You should be working with skilled experts who can give you the best separations possible from your originals. If you have very many changes, you will be charged extra for them. On the other hand, if you don't get what you want in a Chromalin, you won't get it on your printed piece.

Chromalins come in "A," "B," and "C" qualities, reflecting the amount of time the color preparation house will spend on scanning and correction cycles. "A" quality is used for coffee table and art books, and expensive advertising pieces where color will be important. "B" quality separations are good for most work, while "C" quality is used for lower end work such as catalogues printed on inexpensive paper.

Be aware that any proof is just that. When a job is run on a press, the quality of the plates and the expertise of the press operator will affect the look of your printed job.

The paper you have chosen to print on changes the amount of ink that is laid down on the sheet, and thus affects the printed image.

A soft finish will absorb more ink and increase the size of the separation dot structure, while a hard finish will reduce it. An experienced press operator can control the flow of ink applied to the paper, adjusting for the paper being used and inconsistencies in the image density of your pages.

DELIVERY

You will need to discuss with your print shop how you want your job delivered on completion. Will you pick it up yourself? If it is a large, heavy order, will you want it shipped? In one large box, or in smaller units? Some printing plants have warehousing facilities to store the work for you, delivering a part at a time as you require. You need to specify all these possibilities at the time of your original order, and get estimates for delivery arrangements that will be convenient for you.

CHECKING YOUR UNDERSTANDING

1. Discuss the purpose and function of a desktop publishing service bureau.

2. Identify how you can locate a service bureau that will serve your desktop publishing needs.

3. Indicate the type of information a service bureau will need in order to complete your desktop publishing project properly.

4. List and briefly describe the three ways to handle reproduction of halftone art.

5. Briefly explain conventional methods of producing halftone images.

6. Distinguish between spot color and process color.

7. List and briefly describe each of the different kinds of print shops.

8. Identify and describe the kinds of printing presses usually found in commercial print shops and printing plants.

9. List three types of paper stock and point out their characteristics.

10. Briefly describe the different methods that can be used to bind a printed publication.

BUILDING YOUR DESKTOP PUBLISHING SKILLS

1. Using your local telephone directory and any other available resource, make a list of service bureaus and print shops. If the information is available, indicate the type of services each provides.

2. Visit two or three of the desktop publishing service bureaus you identified and secure a copy of the job order sheets or other forms used for incoming projects. Analyze the forms, then prepare a paper that discusses the type of information required by these service bureaus.

3. Locate four halftone reproductions in periodicals or brochures. Using a magnifying glass, examine the various tone values of the photographs and describe the dot patterns that you observe. Notice whether they are close together, far apart, lighter or darker toned, etc., and record your comments on a sheet of paper.

4. Locate four multipage publications that are bound differently. On a sheet of paper, describe each of the different methods used for binding and write a justification for each of the binding methods used. If possible, contact one of the print shops from the list you prepared earlier and obtain the cost for each binding method.

5. Visit two or three of the print shops you identified above, then prepare a reference sheet that indicates the name, address, telephone number, and service available. Include the following information as it applies:

a) Type of equipment used:
   Imagesetter
   Printing press
   Duplicating machine
b) Method for handling color jobs:
   Spot color
   Process color
   Color separations
c) Method for handling halftones
d) Paper stocks used
e) Binding methods used

DESKTOP DESIGN WORKSHOP

The purpose of this section is to provide you with opportunities to develop and/or improve your desktop publishing design skills. The worksheet pages have been placed at the back of the book, and are designed so they can be removed and you can write, draw, or place your responses directly onto the pages.

WORKSHEET 14.1

1. Assume that your quotation for the layout and design of the book *Desktop Publishing in the Modern Office* (see Desktop Design Workshop 12) was accepted and you have completed your layout and design. You now need a service bureau to assist you in finishing the project. Using the information below, complete the Service Bureau Work Order form on Worksheet 14.1.

   a. Create a name, address, and phone number for your fictitious company, and use your name as the Contact person.

   b. Complete the Application, Paper size, Pages to print, Graphic files, Graduated screens, and Fonts sections. Indicate the asked for information based on the files you created in instruction 3 of Desktop Design Workshop 12.

   c. In the Media section, indicate that you would like to have Negative film at 2400 dpi.

2. Using the information below, complete the second Service Bureau Work Order form on Worksheet 14.2 for the All American Home Inspection brochure you created in Desktop Design Workshop 11.

   a. Assume you work for the same fictitious company you created in response to the exercise above.

   b. Use the appropriate information to complete the Application, Paper size, Pages to print, Graphic files, Graduated screens, and Fonts sections.

   c. Ask for RC paper at 1200 dpi with spot color.

15. PREPARATION OF CAMERA-READY ART

When you finish this chapter you should be able to:

- *Know when to prepare camera-ready art.*
- *Describe the elements of a pasteup or mechanical.*
- *Describe the tools used for preparing a pasteup or mechanical.*
- *Prepare photographs to be made into halftones.*
- *Indicate spot color for the printer.*

THERE ARE OCCASIONS when the output from your computer may require some additional preparation in order to be ready for its final use. If your standard 8-1/2 x 11 publication will be printed in quantity at a print shop, your final paper copy, as it comes out of a laser printer or imagesetter, will be too flimsy to hold up. It must be pasted onto stiff boards and protected from dirt by a tissue overlay because it will be handled by a number of people during the printing process. Your print shop calls even this simple format camera-ready art.

PREPARING CAMERA-READY ART

Camera-ready art is the form your copy takes, from which the printing plates will be made. It is the final assembly of all of the elements of your document pasted on to pieces of firm white cardboard. This is why it is called a *pasteup*. It is also called a *mechanical* because all of the elements essential to the printed page are pasted down in accurate alignment, using mechanical tools described in this chapter. Feel free to use either the term "pasteup" or "mechanical," since they both refer to camera-ready art.

Figure 15.1

✔ **CAMERA-READY ART CHECKLIST**

Prepare camera-ready art if any of the following apply to your publication:

- ☐ Pages have photographs
- ☐ Pages have continuous tone illustrations
- ☐ Pages have tint blocks
- ☐ Large quantity needs to be reproduced on a press
- ☐ Pages with image area larger than 7.5 X 10, and you are using laser printer output
- ☐ Image area on page bleeds – image(s) print to the very edge of the page.
- ☐ Spot color areas on pages run very close together
- ☐ Publication uses four-color process.

The elements in your pasteup or mechanical include your final copy and drop-in art— all of the photographs and other halftone illustrations you may be using that have not been digitized as part of your final output. The pasteup also includes indications for color, and any instructions you may have for the printer.

Before you prepare a mechanical, it is a good idea to check with your print shop to make sure that you are providing them with all that they need. Guidelines for working with a print shop are covered in Chapter 14, *Working With Service Bureaus and Print Shops.* If you find that the pasteup requirements for any particular job are too complicated for you to handle, you can hire a pasteup or production artist who specializes in this kind of work. See Figure 15.1 for a checklist that helps you decide when to prepare camera-ready art.

TOOLS AND MATERIALS

The tools and materials you will need to prepare a pasteup are illustrated in Figure 15.2. First of all, you will need a drawing board or table at which to work. Before you start working on the drawing board, you should cover its top with cardboard or plastic to keep it clean and free of nicks and cuts. Your art supply store can show you samples of covering material. The right or left edge of

Figure 15.2: Tools of the trade. At bottom is the straight edge of a T-square, with a 30°x60°x90° triangle, and a 45° triangle resting on it. X-acto knife, pica ruler, rubber cement jar, scissors, and tape dispenser are also shown.

the board (the side opposite from the hand that you use) should be equipped with a *straight edge*, a metal strip that ensures even alignment up and down its length.

You will also need a *T-square* to ensure horizontal alignment and a triangle for vertical alignment. A T-square looks like a "T" laid on its side. The long side, made of wood or metal, parallels the front edge of the drawing board, as shown in Figure 15.2. The short side, equivalent to the T horizontal crossbar, rides up and down the side of the board, along your straight edge.

A *triangle* is used for vertical alignment. It is placed above and touching the long edge of the T-square, and can be moved along the edge from one end of the T-square to the other. Triangles come in see-through plastic, in different sizes and shapes, depending on your needs. Figure 15.2 shows the two triangle shapes: one with two 45° angles and one 90° angle, the other 30° angle by 60° angle by 90°. A 30°x60°x90° triangle with a long side measuring 12 to 14 inches is a convenient size for aligning most document pages.

In addition to the tools already described, you will need pasteup boards, cutting tools, adhesives, and pencils and pens in *nonreproducing blue.* A nonreproducing pen or pencil uses a particular shade of blue that will not be picked up when the printing plates are made.

Any light- to medium-weight boards can be used for pasteup, as long as it has a smooth surface that can be written on with black ink and with nonreproducing blue pens or pencils. Art stores also carry board that has been already been printed with a grid of nonreproducing blue lines for your convenience.

Good quality tracing paper, called a *tissue overlay*, is placed over your pasteup to indicate color areas and other information for the printer (Figure 15.3). Transparent sheets of acetate can be used for color placement as well. Tracing paper is also used to protect your mechanical from dust and fingerprints.

Cutting tools include a good pair of scissors with long blades, and one with short blades. You will also need a sharp knife; an X-Acto knife with #10 blades is excellent for cutting paper, using a metal ruler as a straight edge. A plastic board made specifically for cutting is convenient to use.

Rubber cement or wax is used to adhere your paper to your board. For occasional use, rubber cement is easy to apply, and excess cement can be picked up from the board when it is dry. Rubber cement will smear laser output, so be careful not to get any on your copy. A newer type of rubber cement, one that dries to a tacky finish, is also available. The tacky finish allows you to pick up and move your paper and reposition it on the board, should you want to do so. If you prefer to use wax, there are hand waxers available

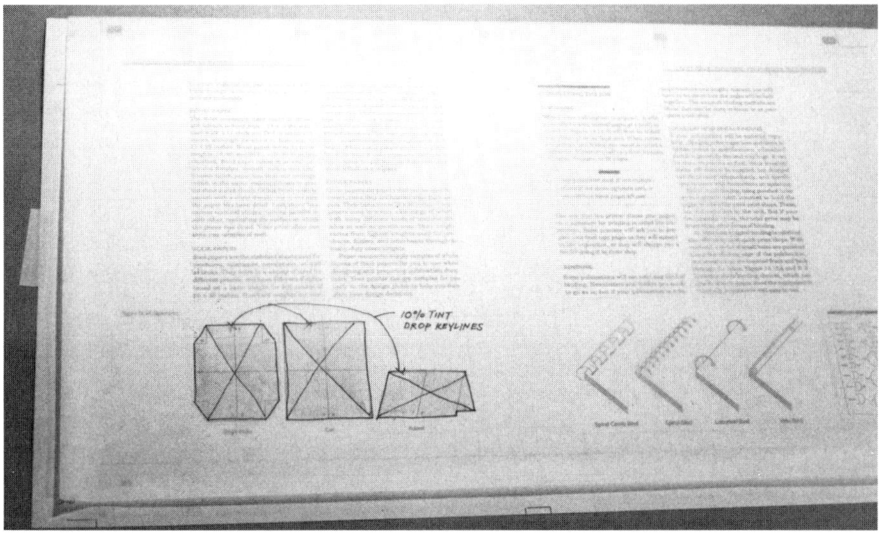

Figure 15.3: Pasteup board with tissue overlay.

Figure 15.4: The pasteup workstation.

Figure 15.5: The pasteup board with crop and fold marks indicated.

that heat the wax and dispense it using rollers. These plug into a standard electric socket. The waxed copy is positioned temporarily by rubbing it lightly. For permanent positioning, the copy is rubbed down firmly using a smooth plastic stick called a *burnisher.*

Plastic sprays are available to help keep your pages clean. These come in both matte and gloss finish.

Be careful not to breathe in any fumes when you are working with plastic spray. They are toxic.

Seating and lighting at your work table should be adjustable. You will also need a small table or cabinet at one side to hold your tools. Figure 15.4 shows a work station for the pasteup artist to work at.

You should be able to find all the materials described here at any good art supply store.

PRODUCING MECHANICALS OR PASTEUPS

Neatness and accuracy are the rules of the game when preparing your mechanical or pasteup. The simplest pasteup consists of your final copy pasted down neatly on a board, with *crop* or *corner marks* to indicate the outside edges of your paper sheet. These marks are black lines placed outside the edges of your final printed document, as shown in Figure 15.5, to indicate the outer edges or *trim* of your pages. If your final laser printed page is larger than 7-1/2 x 10, or if your page layout program doesn't provide crop marks, you will have to rule them in by hand using a pen and your T-square and triangle.

MARKING FOR ALIGNMENT

Crop marks not only show the print shop the outside edges of your publication, they are also used to ensure accurate alignment for any type and images that you may add to the pasteup. If your pasteup consists of adjoining pages that will be folded, the fold line is also indicated using a dashed black line outside the margin. If you want to indicate margin and fold lines within the print area, a nonreproducing blue pen or pencil is used, as shown in Figure 15.6.

Any elements that were not part of your laser or Imagewriter output are also pasted into position on your board. Line art and logos that are correctly sized fit into this category. If you have had the photographs you plan to use converted into accurately sized PMTs (as described in Chapter 14), these, too, can be pasted into position on the board as line art.

POSITION PRINTS AND WINDOWS

Any graphics element that is not actual final art pasted into position on the page is shown on the pasteup by a window—an outlined rectangle that represents the space to be occupied by the graphic (Figure 15.7.) Windows are easily made using the graphics capability of your page layout program.

If you are using graphics windows, you will need to let the print shop know which graphic goes with which window on your pasteup. To do so, mount each graphic carefully on heavy paper or light board using masking tape outside the image area. Label the graphic using a figure number and a brief description as shown in Figure 15.8. Each window on the pasteup should also contain the same information as appears on the graphic label. For further identification, a *position print* of the graphic is placed within its window for the printer to use as a reference. Position prints can be low-resolution scanned copies cropped to size and placed in the publication electronically. Or you can photocopy your graphic, reducing or enlarging it to size, and cropping it with scissors, before pasting it on the board in the exact position you intend for the final printed piece.

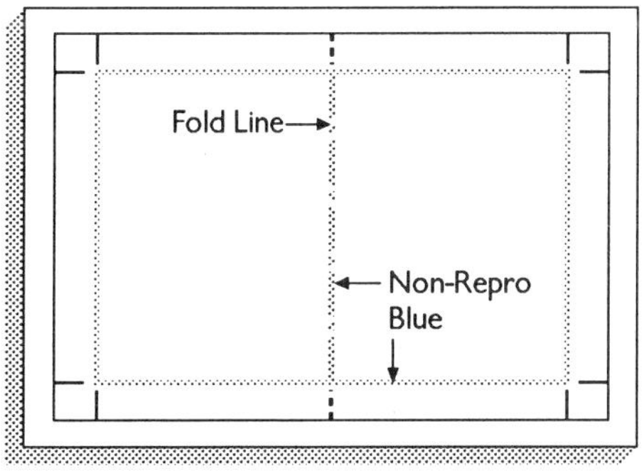

Figure 15.6: Alignment rules on the pasteup board.

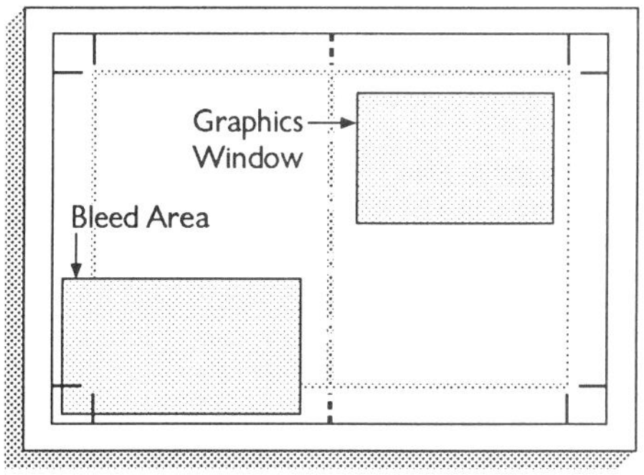

Figure 15.7. The pasteup board with position art and windows indicated. Note the bleed area, which overlaps the crop marks beyond the printing area by at least 1/8 to 1/4 of an inch.

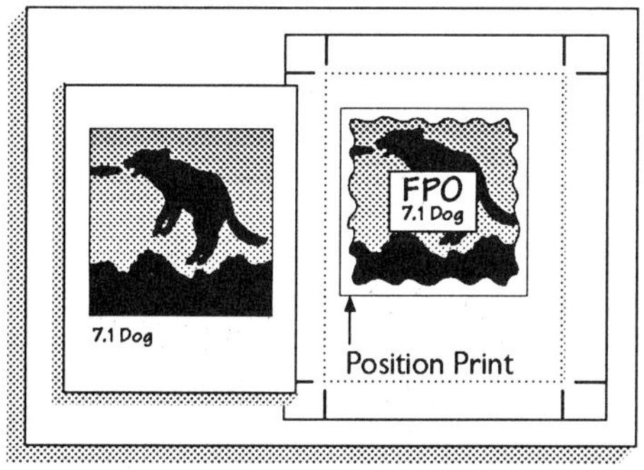

Figure 15.8: Close-up of a window showing a position print and its accompanying graphic.

Remember, to boldly mark your position prints "for position only" (FPO) so that your print shop or prepress service does not use them as finished art by mistake.

Each photocopy position print is placed inside its window on the pasteup.

INDICATING BLEEDS

No, a bleed doesn't indicate to the printer where you have cut yourself with an X-Acto blade! A *bleed* is any area of print that goes beyond the margin to the trim edge of the printed page; in effect, bleeding off the edge of the page. Photographs and colored tint blocks are often used so that they print to the very edge of the page trim. To print bleed areas, you need to allow an additional 1/8 inch to 1/4 inch of margin beyond the trim edge for the tint or photograph. This area is indicated on the pasteup board in ink. If your output is an 8-1/2 x 11 page size and your page trim is 8-1/2 x 11 inches, you will need to indicate the trim by inking in the crop marks on the pasteup (Figure 15.7.) Remember, laser output uses a 1/2-inch margin on all four sides of the page.

USING YOUR TOOLS

The first rule for using pasteup tools is to work with a clean table top. If your work area is cluttered, you will be more apt to make mistakes. Select a piece of pasteup board that is at least 1-1/2 to 2 inches larger than your final copy on all four sides. If your final copy consists of two facing pages, you can paste them next to each other on the board. This format is called a *reader spread.* Reader spreads show the final pages on the pasteup as the reader sees it. The printer may need to reposition pages in order to print them in the proper order for your output, but it is less confusing to prepare your mechanical using reader spreads.

Place your pasteup board on the drawing table, and line it up horizontally using your T-square as shown in Figure 15.9. When the pasteup board is flush with the edge of the T-square, fasten it to the table top using 3/4-inch masking tape.

RULING IN THE GUIDELINES

Next, you will need to rule a horizontal line for the bottom edge of your final copy as shown in Figure 15.10. Move the T-square up about 2 inches from the bottom edge of the board. Draw a line across your pasteup board almost out to the edges, using a well-sharpened non-reproducing blue pencil. Then

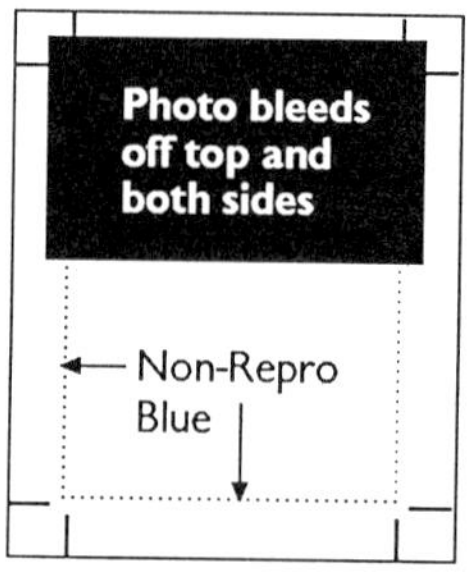

Single page

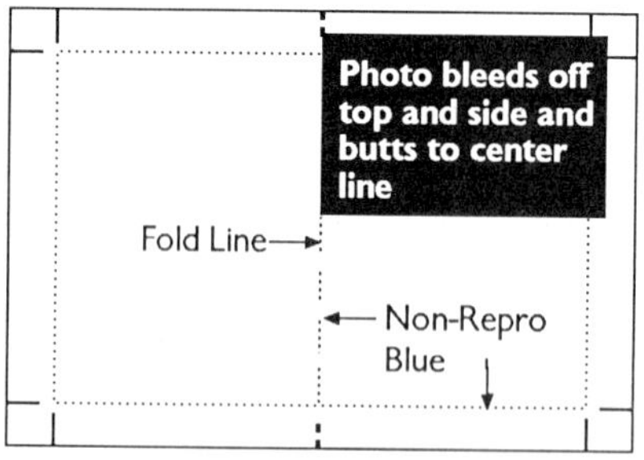

Readers spread

Figure 15.9: Preparing camera ready art. (above) A single page and a reader spread. (left) Placing a pasteup board for a reader spread on the drawing board using a T-square and a triangle.

measure the height of your document page and mark off that measurement on your pasteup board, measuring up from the blue line you have drawn on the bottom. Move your T-square up on the table until its top edge aligns with the measurement you have indicated as the top of your document page. Carefully rule in that line almost to the edges of the board, again using nonreproducing blue pencil.

To indicate vertical guidelines, mark the center of your board, measuring from left to right. Measure your document page. If your pasteup is one page only, use the center mark on your pasteup board as a guide for placing your page. With a ruler, indicate the left and right edges of your page, measuring from the center out. To rule the vertical lines, you will be using your triangle; aligning it with the T-square.

Move your T-square to at least 3/4 inch below the horizontal line at the bottom of your pasteup board. Holding the T-square firmly with one hand, move the triangle along its top edge until its long side aligns with the left edge measurement. Carefully draw a line using your nonreproducing blue pencil, using the triangle as a guide. Be sure your blue line extends at least 1/2 inch above and below your horizontal guide lines. Do the same on the right side.

If you are pasting up two facing pages, use the center mark on your board as a guide for the fold line. Measure the width of each page and mark the full width on each side of the center mark. Rule the left and right edges as described for single sheets. Rule the center fold line using a dotted line. You can now rule in any other guidelines that can help you place your elements, similar to the guidelines you have used in your page layout program. You will find it helpful to indicate margins and grid lines, and also the center of each page vertically. Now you are ready to ink in your crop marks.

CROP MARKS

Crop marks need to be inked in black and placed outside the printing area, on top of the blue guidelines you have drawn. Remember, you ruled the lines at least 3/4 inch above and below the horizontal rules. Hairline pens are available from your art supply store for this purpose. Using your T-square and triangle, rule in the black lines as shown in Figure 15.11.

PASTING DOWN THE ELEMENTS

Now that you have a board with all your guidelines drawn in non-reproducing blue and cropmarks indicated, you are ready to paste up your elements. Each element must

Figure 15.10: Ruling in guidelines using your T-square and triangle.

Figure 15.11: Inking in the crop marks.

be carefully trimmed to within about 1/4 inch of any type or ruled lines using scissors or an X-Acto knife and a steel edge. Then position the element on the pasteup board similar to the way it was done in your page layout program. The main difference is that there is no electronic device to do your alignment for you. It must be measured and aligned using your hand, eye, T-square, and triangle. Then fasten the element to the board with rubber cement or wax.

When using regular rubber cement, brush it on to the back side of your final copy page. Place the page on the pasteup board while the cement is still wet so that you can move it for accurate alignment. Use your T-square and triangle to ensure that the element is placed squarely in position, following your guidelines. Try not to get any cement on your laser output, because it might smear. To clean rubber cement off the board, wait until it dries, then carefully rub off the excess. If you make a little ball of dried rubber cement, called a *pickup,* it can be used to pick up cement from the board. If you prefer to use tacky rubber cement, which allows you to reposition your artwork, the cement cannot be cleaned as easily. Tacky rubber cement is applied to the element in a thin layer, and the element is positioned after the cement dries.

To use wax, apply it to the back of your pasteup elements using a waxer. Put a tissue over the waxed area for protection until you are ready to use it. Position your element so that it is properly aligned with your guidelines. To adhere the element temporarily, cover it with tissue paper and rub it gently into position. The element can be picked up and moved should you desire to reposition it. To position waxed or tacky cemented pieces firmly into place, cover with tissue and rub hard with a burnisher.

MAKING OVERLAYS

A printing press prints only one color at a time; for that reason, individual printing plates are made from your pasteup for each separate color. The pasteup board is customarily used for all the elements that will print in black ink, or a main color you are using instead of black. For this reason, *overlays* are used to indicate additional colors.

Overlays are additional sheets of tissue or acetate placed over the pasteup board on which colors can be pasted down or otherwise indicated, or on which you can write instructions to the printer.

Figure 15.12; A pasteup board with an acetate overlay sheet.

If the elements you plan to use in color are well-separated from those that will print in black, they can all be placed on the pasteup board. An acetate or tissue overlay is used on which you can place color elements and instructions. Fasten your overlay to the top of the board with masking tape so that it can be lifted up easily, as shown in Figure 15.12. If you are using tissue, circle all the color elements that are pasted on the board below. Indicate the color for each element on the tissue. Any other instructions for the print shop are also written on the overlay tissue.

If you have color elements that are positioned very close those in black, or any element such as a tint block or graphic running over the black, you will need to paste those elements on overlay sheets. Some page layout programs will print out each separate color or tint overlays for you (see Figure 15.13.) Alignment on the overlay sheet needs to be the same as that on the board. To ensure accurate alignment, *register marks* are used. Register marks are mechanically prepared symbols composed of a circle and a crosshair. Three or four of these are pasted down on corners of the pasteup board outside the print area. A second set of register marks is placed on your overlay sheet in the exact position as on the pasteboard. When the sheets are placed one over the other and the register marks are aligned, you can be assured that all the elements will be properly aligned. Many page layout programs can print register marks for additional color overlays. If your software does not use them, sheets of register marks can be bought at your art supply store and placed on your work (see Figure 15.13.)

WORKING WITH HALFTONES

Chapter 8, *Working With Photos and Illustrations,* covers much of the basic information on the design issues involved when working with photographs. Chapter 14 discusses several methods for working with photographs and includes information on screen resolution and the fineness of the dot. If you are purchasing traditional halftones or PMTs from your print shop, they will need to be prepared as part of your camera-ready art.

PREPARING A PHOTOGRAPH OR HALFTONE ILLUSTRATION

After you have mounted and labeled your continuous-tone image, you will need to indicate the exact cropping area to your print shop. Crop marks are used outside the image area, and are aligned using a T-square

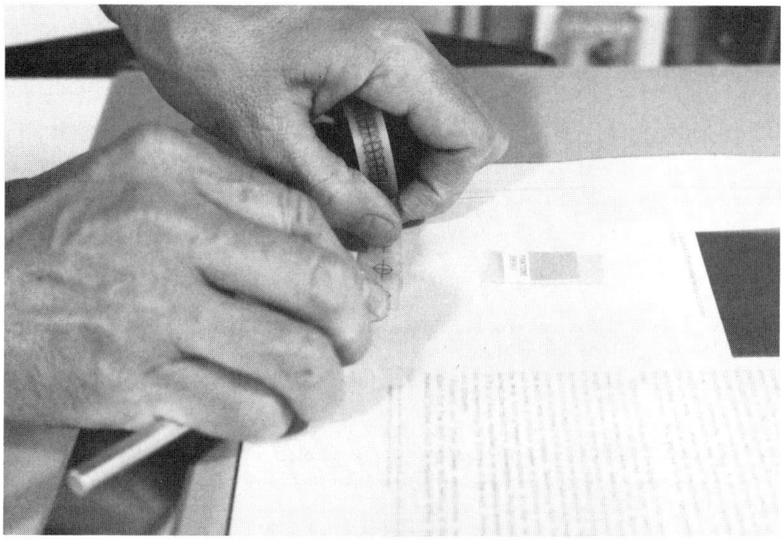

Figure 15.13: A pasteup board with overlay sheet showing register marks.

Figure 15.14: Cardboard L-shapes used as an aid to cropping a photograph

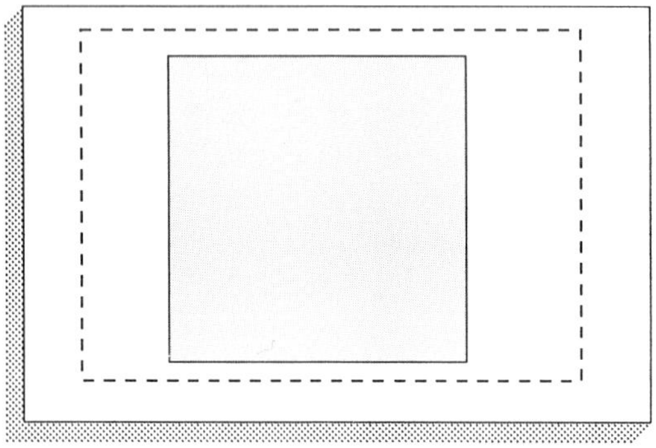

Figure 15.15: A step by step diagram demonstrating the use of the diagonal for sizing images

1. Draw a rectangle representing the actual size of the photograph. Then draw the outline of the cropped area.

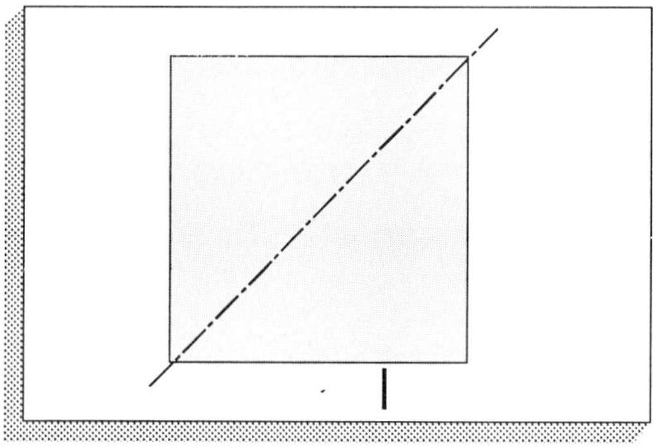

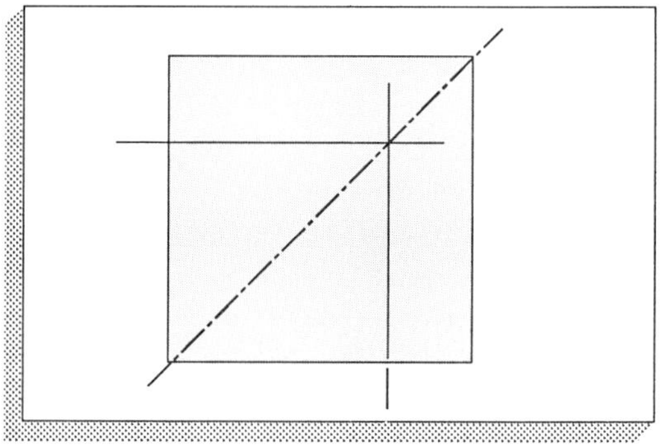

2. Draw a diagonal line from the lower left corner to the top right hand corner.

3. Measure the width allowed in your layout and mark that point on the tracing paper along the baseline of the photograph.

4. Draw a line perpendicular to the base line from the point where the upper right corner of the cropped area crosses the diagonal line. The distance from the baseline to the point of crossing is the height of the cropped photograph. To complete, draw a second line parallel to the baseline from the same point on the diagonal.

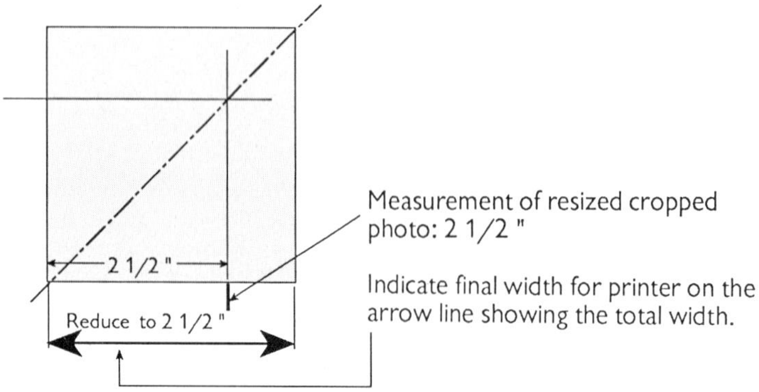

Figure 15.16: How to indicate the final size of a reduced photograph to the printer.

and triangle, similar to the way you ruled up your pasteup board. Your image may need resizing in order to fit in its window accurately. If you prepared a photocopied position print to size, and noted the percentage of enlargement or reduction that was used, the print shop has the information it will need. If you do not have access to a photocopier that will do enlargements and reductions in 1 percent increments, you will need to calculate the image area differently. Cropping your image is best done when you are laying out your pages, so that you can make correctly sized windows while you are designing the publication.

VISUALIZING YOUR CROPPED PHOTOGRAPH

Before allocating a window for your photograph, you will need to know what size the photo will be and how you want it cropped. Without a scanner, you will need to resort to traditional methods. To help you visualize your final cropped image, two L-shaped pieces of cardboard (shown in Figure 15.14) are used as a frame. Adjust the pieces until the picture is cropped as you like. Mark the corners of the image area with a grease pencil, so as not to damage the photograph. Grease pencil marks can be rubbed off when the job is completed. If your photograph is the actual size for use in your publication, your window will be the same size as your photograph.

USING A DIAGONAL FOR PROPORTIONAL SCALING

If the photograph you have cropped is larger or smaller than the area in which it will be placed, you will have to scale it geometrically. Using a T-square and triangles, you can size an area that is proportionately larger or smaller than your cropped image.

Using tissue paper, a T-square and a triangle, draw a rectangle representing the actual dimensions for the cropped area of your photograph. Then, rule a diagonal line from the lower left corner to the upper right corner, as shown in Figure 15.15. Any other rectangle whose upper right corner transects the diagonal line of rectangle representing your cropped photograph, will be scaled larger or smaller, in direct proportion. It is this second rectangle that will become the calculated window area.

Decide on the size you want your photograph to be in your publication. Some measurements may be critical, depending on your grid design and page layout scheme. Apply those measurements to the rectangle representing your photograph, using the lower left corner as the base for your measurements. If your window area will be larger than the cropped photograph rectangle, you will need to extend the baseline and the left vertical edge of the rectangle representing the window.

When your window measurements are completed, draw in your critical window line first. If the width is most important to you, draw the right side vertical line up from the baseline until it crosses the diagonal line you placed on the tissue. Now, raise your T-square to the place where the line you have drawn intersects the diagonal, and draw a second horizontal line through that point. The resulting rectangle will be directly proportional to your cropped image and represents the measurements you will need for its window. If the resulting window size is not pleasing to you, may need to juggle around with how you crop the photograph until its proportions will give you a good page design.

When you are satisfied with the final crop and window size, draw your crop marks on the mounted photograph, outside the image area. Then, also outside the image area, draw a line between the crop marks to indicate your critical width or length, placing arrow heads at each end. Write down the measurement that this area will occupy in the final window, in picas or inches, using the term reduce to or enlarge to as shown in Figure 15.16. The printer will calculate the percentage of reduction or enlargement needed to reduce or enlarge your photograph (or illustration) using a proportion wheel.

If you want to do these calculations yourself, you can buy a *proportion wheel* (Figure

15.17A) at your art supply store, or purchase a software screen version from DesignSoft. Notice that not only is this ruler round, it also is made up of two circular layers, each marked with picas or inches. There is also a small window indicating percentages. To use the ruler, find the measurement of the original area to be enlarged or reduced and mark it on the ruler with your eye, finger, or grease pencil, on the layer for original size. Locate the measurement for the reduced or enlarged area on the second layer of the scale ruler. Rotate the top section of the scale ruler, and match the measurements you have selected on both layers, as shown in Figure 15.17B. The percentage window will show you the percentage of enlargement or reduction that your measurements indicate.

If you have only a few photographs or illustrations that require sizing, have your print shop calculate percentages for you. If you have many halftones, you can use a proportion wheel to group or gang up images that will be resized at the same percentages. Ganging images for halftoning can prove to be very economical.

MAINTAINING AN ART LIST

If you have a number of illustrations and photographs, it will be useful to maintain an art list. Each graphic should be listed with its figure number or another numbering scheme that is convenient. Along with the number, include a brief description of the image and how it is used in your publication. Your print shop will need this information when estimating your job and when printing it. If pictures must be returned to the photographer or photo stock house, indicate that, too, on your art list. Chapter 16, *Publication Planning, Budgeting, and Scheduling,* has forms you can use for making out your art list.

CHECKING YOUR UNDERSTANDING

1. Discuss why camera-ready art is also called a pasteup or a mechanical.

2. List the tools and materials you may need to prepare a pasteup.

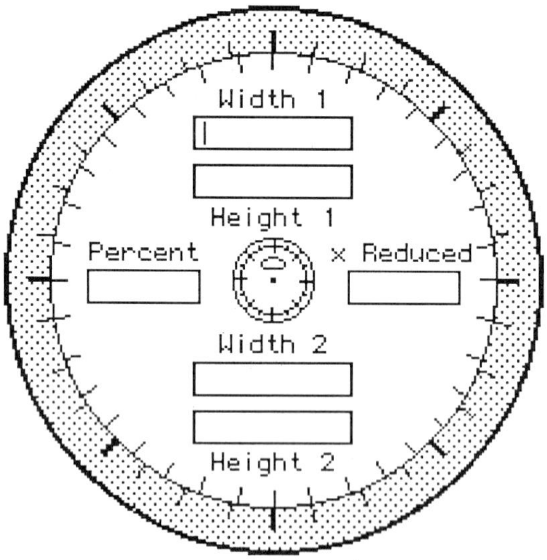

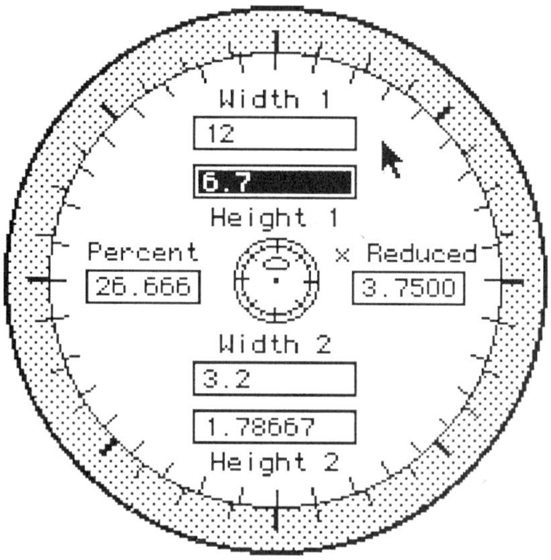

Figure 15.17A: (above) is a software-based proportion wheel. It is very similar to a traditional proportion wheel, except that all you need do is key in your measurements where indicated, rather than position the circular rulers.
Figure 15.17B: (right) The Prograph proportion wheel will calculate the missing numbers, and place them in the appropriate boxes.

3. Discuss how crop marks are used when producing mechanicals and pasteups.

4. Explain the purpose of position prints and windows on pasteups and mechanicals.

5. Define the term "bleed" and explain how a bleed is produced.

6. Explain the purpose and use of a pasteup overlay.

7. Explain the use of register marks as they apply to working with color overlays.

8. Describe how a photograph can be scaled geometrically.

9. Briefly explain the purpose and use of a proportion wheel.

10. Discuss the purpose of an art list and indicate the information that should be included on it.

BUILDING YOUR DESKTOP PUBLISHING SKILLS

1. Using information from a mail-order catalog or from a visit to a local art store, prepare a list of the tools and materials you will need to produce camera-ready art. Include the price of each item and the total price in your list.

2. Visit one of the firms on the list you prepared in answer to activity 1 in Chapter 14 and ask if you can see a mechanical for a job they are running. Examine the mechanical(s), then write a one-page paper that described what you observed.

DESKTOP DESIGN WORKSHOP

The purpose of this section is to provide you with opportunities to develop and/or improve your desktop publishing skills. The worksheet pages have been placed at the back of the book, and are designed so they can be removed and you can write, draw, or place your responses directly onto the pages.

WORKSHEETS 15.1 AND 15.2

1. Crop and scale the two photographs illustrated on Worksheet 15.1, for use in a promotional travel brochure.

   a. Using the directions for scaling a photograph proportionately, scale photograph #1 so that the base line is exactly 4 inches. In the provided space, note the new measurement of the reduced photograph for both height and width.

   b. Study photograph #2, and decide on the portion of the photo you want to use on the brochure. Mark the cropped area directly on the photograph with a soft marker.

2. Study the thumbnail layout for a two-page spread for a travel agency brochure on Worksheet 15.2.

   a. Using your desktop layout program and either GREEK.TXT (DOS or GREEKED TEXT (Mac) lay out the pages noting the dimensions indicated. Provide windows for the photographs you have cropped on Worksheet 15.1.

   b. Print out the page spread and paste it on a heavy sheet measuring 8 1/2 x 11 inches or larger. Using a T-square and triangle, indicate fold marks and trim marks as described in the chapter. If you have access to a copy machine that enlarges and reduces in 1 percent increments, size the photographs you have cropped and paste them into your page spread. Mark each sized copy with "for position only."

16. PUBLICATION PLANNING, BUDGETING AND SCHEDULING

When you finish this chapter you should be able to:

- *Construct a planning worksheet for a desktop publishing project.*
- *Prepare a realistic publication schedule for a desktop publishing project.*
- *Prepare a budget for a desktop publishing project.*
- *Monitor a desktop publishing project using a desktop publishing planning worksheet.*

PLANNING A PUBLICATION AT its outset is a form of insurance. A plan will allow you to review the costs before unexpected bills hit at the end of the project. It will help you verify the steps you need to take in order to complete the publication for its final delivery date. Planning ahead will also let you know, in advance, the people and equipment you may need in order to complete your project.

If you have limited equipment, if the project is complex and involved, or if the work will involve many people, you need to plan carefully.

- ✔ Who will approve the work that is done? An individual? A committee?
- ✔ Who will be providing the copy?
- ✔ Who will edit the copy and proofread the output?
- ✔ Who is the designer? Will I need the services of a professional?
- ✔ Does the organization have a standard style guide to follow for its publications?
- ✔ Will I need a scanner? At what resolution?
- ✔ Will I need a service bureau for high-resolution output?
- ✔ How many copies will I need?

- ✔ How will I reproduce copies; by office copier or by printing press?
- ✔ Are there halftones that require metal plates, or can the job be printed using paper plates?
- ✔ Will the publication require binding? Will the cover be the same paper stock as the rest of the piece or will it be of a heavier weight? Will a separate cover design be required?

While these questions may appear to be overwhelming at the start, you will find that using a well-organized form will make your task a fairly painless one. This chapter uses a learn-by-doing approach to help you learn the basics. You are provided with forms and a step-by-step guide to help you fill them out. You will also be shown how to modify the forms to fit your own particular needs. As you go through the planning worksheet, you will find that its sections refer to material that has been covered in earlier chapters.

THE PRODUCTION PLAN

When you are first asked to put together a publication, devising a plan for design and production can save you headaches in the future. The following five items need to be considered:

- ✔ *Purpose of the publication*
- ✔ *Appearance and content of the publication*
- ✔ *Resources available*
- ✔ *Anticipated costs*
- ✔ *Deadline*

A form similar to the one in Figure 16.1 is useful as a planning document; it can be distributed to others involved in the project to inform them about the details. We will use the planning worksheet to explain how to

Figure 16.1 **DESKTOP PUBLISHING PLANNING WORKSHEET**

PROJECT NAME ____________ JOB NO. ________

COORDINATOR ____________ DATE ________

Telephone no. ____________

PURPOSE ____________

Major Goal: ☐ Create mood ☐ Persuade or sell ☐ Inform/educate ☐ Attract attention ☐ Other

Target Audience: ____________

DESCRIPTION ____________

Format: ________ Give source ________

Paper: Paper source ________ Paper color ________

Specifications: Number of pages ________ Stock ________

Quantity ________ Size ________

Ink ________ Second color ________

Output: ☐ Laser printer ☐ Imagesetter ☐ Other

Reproduction method: ☐ Photocopies ☐ Offset lithography ☐ Other ☐ Negatives & metal plates ☐ Paper plates

Binding: ☐ Spiral ☐ Velobind ☐ Looseleaf ☐ Folding (type) ________ ☐ Staple ☐ Cover (type) ________ ☐ Other

COMMENTS ____________

CONTENT AND ARTWORK: *(See attached Content List, Art List, Resource Planning Sheet and Planning & Scheduling Worksheet)*

Figure 16.1: Desktop Publishing Planning Worksheet, reduced. For an actual size form, see the Workshop/Forms Appendix.

plan, schedule, and budget a typical desktop publishing project.

Notice that all projects are given a *working title* and a *job number*. The project is assigned to one individual, who manages and coordinates all aspects of the project. This person, called the *project coordinator*, is listed by name, with a *telephone number* for day-to-day access. The planning worksheet is *dated* because it is fairly common to have a publication series (a weekly, monthly, or yearly project), and you need some way of clearly identifying the current job (see Figure 16.2.)

PURPOSE OF THE PUBLICATION

By now you have been exposed to many different kinds of documents produced through desktop publishing. In Chapter 2, *Communication: Visual and Verbal,* you discovered that one of the ways to classify a publication is by its *purpose*. A publication can identify, inform, provide data, supply a reference, sell, or teach. It is very important to know the purpose of the publication before you begin to design it. You can do an analysis on your own, or you can consult with others to make sure you haven't missed any important points. When working with a group or for a client, this is especially important.

In addition to knowing the purpose of the publication, you will also need to know its intended audience. When you know who will be reading your newsletter, magazine, or report, you can approach its design with a more concrete sense of how to shape its visual message. It is often helpful to brainstorm, especially with the person or department for which you are producing the publication. Group discussion will help you to develop a firm understanding of who will receive the publication, how long it will be used, and whether it requires a serious or relaxed approach. Chapter 1, *The Publishing Process: People, Tasks, and Equipment,* will refresh your understanding of the publishing process.

After you have defined the project's intended audience and major goals, it will need to be expressed in a brief sentence or two, such as the one illustrated in Figure 16.3A.

PROJECT NAME ____________________ JOB NO. __________

COORDINATOR ____________________ DATE __________

Telephone no. ____________________

Figure 16.2: Heading for the Desktop Publishing Planning Worksheet.

PURPOSE ____________________

Major Goal: ☐ Create mood ☐ Persuade or sell
☐ Inform/educate ☐ Attract attention
☐ Other

Target Audience: ____________________

Figure 16.3A: Describing the target audience.

DESCRIPTION ____________________

Format: ____________________ Give source __________

Figure 16.3B: Designating the publication grid format.

Paper: Paper source __________ Paper color __________

Specifications: Number of pages __________ Stock __________

Quantity __________ Size __________

Ink __________ Second color __________

Figure 16.4: Recording publication specifications.

Output: ☐ Laser printer ☐ Imagesetter ☐ Other

Reproduction method: ☐ Photocopies ☐ Offset lithography ☐ Other

☐ Negatives & metal plates ☐ Paper plates

Figure 16.5: Output and reproduction methods.

Binding: ☐ Spiral ☐ Velobind ☐ Looseleaf

☐ Folding (type) __________ ☐ Staple

☐ Cover (type) __________ ☐ Other

Figure 16.6: Binding requirements.

Once you are able to clearly state the purpose of your publication, you will have a good foundation on which to build your project.

PROJECT DESCRIPTION

After you have identified the purpose of your publication, you can begin to think about the mood and look of the document. Even in the earliest planning phase, you should have some ideas about its design. You may have imagined a handsome, slick-paper annual report; an efficient form; or an enticing catalogue in color that will lure customers. How you envision the functions and goals of a publication definitely influences your decisions as to its appearance and content.

FORMAT

The format you select for your publication needs to match its purpose. An elaborate brochure may be appropriate when you are hoping to reach a well-to-do target market, while a more casual style would be more suitable for an employee newsletter. The thinking you do when you go through an analysis of audience and appropriate format will also help you make good decisions about a suitable grid design (see Figure 16.3B.)

SPECIFICATIONS

After the format has been decided on, and you have made some basic design decisions about the appearance and grid format, you will need to record the publication specifications. These should include the following:

- ✔ Page size and number of pages
- ✔ Number of copies required
- ✔ Paper stock, size, and color
- ✔ Ink color, and whether more than one color will be used

Figure 16.4 shows how these items would be recorded on the planning worksheet. For additional information, refer to Chapter 14, *Working with Service Bureaus and Print Shops.*

OUTPUT AND REPRODUCTION METHODS

In desktop publishing there are two kinds of printing: *output* of original pages, and *reproduction* of many copies. Computer output is the form in which you get your publication out of the computer. The output method you choose depends on the other decisions you've made as you developed your publication plan. You need to consider the overall look you want, the kind of artwork you are planning to use, the purpose of the publication, your budget, and the quantity reproduction method you plan to use. The possibilities for computer printer output range from a laser printer to a high-resolution imagesetter. For additional information, refer to Chapter 1 and Chapter 14.

When selecting an output procedure, consider the following:

- ✔ **Reproducing multiple copies:** The output method should compliment your reproduction method. This can be as simple as making a few photocopies on an office copier, or it may be as involved as getting pricing bids and having the publication printed by a commercial print shop on a large printing press. Between these two extremes are a wide range of choices.

  Keep in mind that the quality of high-resolution output is lost if it is used with a lower quality reproduction method. Likewise, a low-quality output will not reproduce well, even if high-quality printing is used.

- ✔ **Expected life of the publication:** Consider the length of time the information will remain viable and the amount of time it takes to get the document published. Fast, lower-quality methods are usually best used for publications like newspapers, where the message is important for a short time only.
- ✔ **A publication's "look" or image:** If you need to convey quality and professionalism, use high-quality output and high-quality reproduction methods. If

an upscale look is not too important, you can use lower-quality output. If you include photographs, they require higher quality reproduction methods.

- ✔ **Purpose:** If the publication will be valued by only a few of the people who get it, consider using lower quality output and reproduction.
- ✔ **Budget:** If your budget is limited, use lower quality printing so you can produce issues more frequently.

The output and reproduction methods are recorded on the planning worksheet as illustrated in Figure 16.5 on the previous spread.

BINDING

When working with multiple-page publications, you will need to think about how the book will be bound. Binding involves the folding, trimming, and joining of pages in a printed document. Chapter 14 describes several binding methods. Covers, too, are part of the decision making for how a publication will be bound. Most covers are made of a different paper stock than is used for the inside pages. Since the binding process adds to the cost and production time of a desktop publishing project, you will need to consider all the alternatives in your production plan. The binding requirement is listed on the planning worksheet as illustrated in Figure 16.6 on the previous spread.

CONTENT AND ARTWORK

When you have a fixed description of the project in your mind, the next step is to find out where the copy and artwork are created and by whom. In some instances copy will be written by the desktop publisher. Often the copy may be developed by authors and editors within the organization. Occasionally, copy is written by freelancers. Each of these sources present different requirements and challenges. Review Chapters 1 and 4 for further information.

When copy is developed in-house, you have the opportunity for true electronic publishing: coordinating the writing, illustration, and page layout on the computer. If parts of the publishing process are done by outside authors and illustrators, the ability to coordinate electronic development of copy and artwork and page layout can be lost or lessened. If you are dealing with people who are not part of your organization, the coordination process should be explored before the project starts.

Most publications consist of a series of stories and their accompanying artwork. A review of Chapter 8, *Working With Photos and Illustrations,* can help you fill out this section of the Worksheet. A content list such as the one illustrated in Figure 16.7 is helpful in identifying, organizing, and keeping track of the separate elements used in your publications. Notice that the content list has a heading that matches its accompanying planning worksheet. As you can see, each story is numbered, and its source is listed. An art list as illustrated in Figure 16.8 lists all the illustrations contained in the publication. Each illustration in the art list is numbered, and is also cross-referenced to the story it is used in. Along with the number and the cross reference, a short description, the source, and the type of artwork are included. Columns for estimated and final costs are also included.

The content list is designed to fit a variety of desktop publishing projects. Many will not call for both text and artwork. Others may need more lines than those provided in this form. Before you fill out a form for your own job, duplicate enough blank forms so that you will have enough space to list all the stories and artwork included in your publication.

RESOURCES

The typical desktop publisher doesn't always have all the equipment or people needed to produce a publication. Planning ahead helps you to identify the resources you need, your budget, and your schedule. Be prepared to mix desktop publishing methods with tradi-

Figure 16.7 CONTENT LIST: STORY AND/OR CHAPTER NUMBERS

DESKTOP PUBLISHING PLANNING WORKSHEET (Continued) Page ______ of ______

Project Name ______ Job No. ______ Date ______

Project Coordinator ______ Telephone ______

Number	Story or Chapter Title	Source	Date	Editor	Estimated Cost	Actual Cost	Completion

Figure 16.7: The Content List Form, reduced. For a full-sized version, see the Workshop/Forms Appendix.

Figure 16.8 ART LIST

DESKTOP PUBLISHING PLANNING WORKSHEET (Continued) Page ______ of ______

Project Name ______ Job No. ______ Date ______

Project Coordinator ______ Telephone ______

Story/ Chapter Number	Illustration Figure Number	Page Number	Description of Content	Source	Estimated Cost	Actual Cost	Date Needed	Halftone Photo	Halftone Illustration	Line Art	Clip Art	Black & White	2-color	Process Color
								☐	☐	☐	☐	☐	☐	☐
								☐	☐	☐	☐	☐	☐	☐
								☐	☐	☐	☐	☐	☐	☐
								☐	☐	☐	☐	☐	☐	☐
								☐	☐	☐	☐	☐	☐	☐
								☐	☐	☐	☐	☐	☐	☐
								☐	☐	☐	☐	☐	☐	☐
								☐	☐	☐	☐	☐	☐	☐
								☐	☐	☐	☐	☐	☐	☐
								☐	☐	☐	☐	☐	☐	☐
								☐	☐	☐	☐	☐	☐	☐
								☐	☐	☐	☐	☐	☐	☐
								☐	☐	☐	☐	☐	☐	☐

Figure 16.8: The Art List Form, reduced. For a full-sized version, see the Workshop/Forms Appendix.

Figure 16.9 RESOURCE PLANNING WORKSHEET

DESKTOP PUBLISHING PLANNING WORKSHEET (Continued) Page ____ of ____

PROJECT NAME ____________________ JOB NO. ________

RESOURCES	Name of Resource Person and/or Service Business	Telephone No.
☐ Authoring (See Story List)		
☐ Editing		
☐ Editorial corrections		
☐ Proofreading		
☐ Text corrections		
☐ Approve final copy		
☐ Select art (See Story List)		
☐ Art changes and/or corrections		
☐ Rough layout		
☐ Layout approval		
☐ Electronic page makeup		
☐ Halftone scans		
☐ High-resolution output		
☐ Camera-ready art		
☐ Proofread pages		
☐ Correct pages		
☐ Approve pages		
☐ Final page corrections		
☐ Deliver to print shop		
☐ Read & correct blueline proofs		
☐ Other		

NOTES AND COMMENTS

Figure 16.9: Resources Planning Worksheet, reduced. For an actual size form, see the Workshop/Forms Appendix.

SCHEDULE	Start Date	End Date
Copy submitted		
Copy edited and corrected		
Design planning-communication		
Rough thumbnails		
Rough designs to size		
Final design		
Artwork selected		
Page makeup		
Art submitted		
Photos (Sc--		

Figure 16.10: Start and end date section from the Resources Planning Worksheet.

tional ones. For example, you may decide to use halftoned photographs rather than scanning images with your desktop publishing system.

When identifying the resources you may need, review the items listed in the resources section of our sample planning worksheet (see Figure 16.9.)

As you review the items in this section, ask yourself the following questions:

- ✔ *What resources do I have on hand?*
- ✔ *What will I need to get from a graphic designer or service bureau?*
- ✔ *What will it cost?*
- ✔ *Will my budget cover the costs, or do I have to look for less expensive methods?*

SCHEDULING DESIGN AND PRODUCTION

If you want insurance for a smooth flowing project, you must develop a realistic schedule and stick to it. Consider, too, the time it will take to develop a realistic set of figures. If all your work is done in-house, your production schedule may be put together quickly. If you will be using outside resources, it can take as long as a week to get estimates.

In order to develop your project schedule, you will need to find out from each resource how long they think it will take to complete the task you have assigned to them. Ask them to give you both the shortest possible time and the average time. Unless time is at a premium, it is a good idea to add a 15 percent to 20 percent contingency figure to the estimated time for each task. After you have identified all the tasks in the project, "guesstimate" the time each task can take, from the shortest possible time to the longest time, and still meet the deadline. Time can be measured in hours, days, or weeks, depending on the complexity of the job.

Fine-tune your schedule, based on your experience. If you have never done this particular type of job before, ask people who

GLOSSARY AND BIBLIOGRAPHY APPENDIX

GLOSSARY

Absolute placement: Specification of the exact position on the page where a line of text is to start or the corner of a graphic element is to be anchored.

Aliasing: (also known as "the jaggies.")The jagged edges of curved and diagonal outlines of a screen image caused by the size of the pixels in a low to medium resolution screen.

Aliasing is also caused by the misrepresentation of signals due to an inadequate program computing images edges.

Alignment: The placement and shape of type relative to the margins. See also centered, flush right, justified, ragged right, and wraparound.

Alley: The space between two columns of text. Not to be confused with the gutter, which is the combination of the inside margins of two facing page.

Alphanumeric: Mixture of letters and numbers.

Ampersand: The sign "&" meaning "and."

Annual report: A document issued at year-end to describe the financial condition and operating achievements of a company.

Anti-aliasing: A technique used to minimize jagged edges of a screen image. The edges of the image are replaced with a band of colors graded from the image edge to screen background.

Antique paper: An uncoated paper with a rough surface.

Application: Job to be performed.

Application program (application) See Application software and Software.

Application software: Programs that process user applications.

Arabic figures: The familiar form of numerals: 1 2 3 4 etc.

Art: Any visual element used on a page, whether a photograph, drawing, illustration, chart, or hand lettering.

Art paper: Glossy, coated paper intended to carry halftone reproduction by letter-press.

Artwork: Any black and white or color original prepared for reproduction. Also called mechanicals.

Ascender: The portion of a lowercase letter, such as "b" or "f," that rises above the main body or x-height. Its opposite is the descender.

Ascii (American standard code for information interchange): A binary coding format. A file format in which text-only files are stored. These files include all characters, tabs, and carriage returns but not character and paragraph formatting such as italic, boldface, hanging indents, and so on.

Asterisk: The sign "*".

Asymmetric balance: An off-center arrangement.

Automatic hyphenation: A function that directs software to hyphenate text automatically.

Backmatter: Pages following the main text of a publication, devoted to reference matter such as appendices, glossary, and index.

Backup: In computing, an exact copy of a file in case of later loss or damage to the original file. Also used as a verb; to make backups. In printing, the copy on the reverse side of a double-sided document.

Balance: An arrangement whereby all of the parts are equal in weight, value, or importance.

Balanced layout: Condition in which the various elements on a page or spread are of equal importance, weight, or value.

Banner: In newspaper work, main headline running across the top of the page. Often used more loosely for the title heading on a journal or newspaper. It contains the name of the publication and serial information date, volume, number.

Baseline: An imaginary horizontal line on which the bottom of the main part of the letters in a line of type sit. The baseline aligns with the bottom of the x-height of the characters, and descender of letters such as g and p drop below the baseline.

Basis size: The size of paper as it is sold by the paper company. The paper is then cut into press sheets for offset printing.

Basis weight: The weight in pounds of one ream (500 sheets) of paper in its basis size.

Batch processing: Processing where similar tasks are delayed and grouped for combined handling. A non-WYSIWYG mode in which the user embeds typesetting codes or "tags" into text files and sends them in a batch to a laser printer or typesetter.

Baud: Measurement of rate of speed of flow of information between devices measured in units of bits per second.

Bid: A document that offers to sell products or services. Like a proposal, except that a bid usually stresses price quotations.

Binary code: Code using only two characters: 1 and 0 (on and off).

Binding: The assembly of signatures into a finished publication, including the affixing of covers if necessary.

Bit: (BInary digit) smallest unit of electronic data: 1 or 0 (on and off, yes or no).

Bit-mapped: The representation of a character or graphic as a series of square dots or pixels, which sometimes print with jagged edges. See also paint-type graphics.

Black (font): A font that is darker than the bold version of typeface.

Blanket: The image transfer unit in offset printing.

Bleed: When an element, usually an illustration rule, or screened area, prints to the edge of the paper. To print a bleed, the publication is printed on oversized paper which is trimmed.

Block paragraph: A paragraph with no indents.

Block quote: A long quotation (four or more lines) within body text, that is set apart in order to clearly distinguish the author's words from the words that the author is quoting.

Blueline: For offset printing, a guideline made with nonreproducing blue (light blue) on a mechanical, to aid in alignment of copy.

Blurb: Text that summarizes an article, usually set smaller that the headline and larger that the running text.

Board: The cardboard base sheet upon which copy is pasted for a mechanical.

Body: The portion of a publication that contains information text; also called body text. The portion of a character that is between the base line and the tip of the x height; also called main body.

Body text: The main text of a publication.

Body type: Normal, plain, or book type used for long passages of text, such as stories in a newsletter or magazine, or a chapter in a book.

Boilerplate: Standard stored text elements that can be rearranged and combined with information to produce a custom-like document.

Bold: A type style that is a heavy, darker version of a typeface. See also boldface.

Boldface: A darker version of the regular type formed from heavier strokes.

Bolts: The edges of a folded section of paper before it is trimmed.

Booklet: A series of printed pages bound together and covered with the same paper used for the inside pages.

Bond paper: A high-quality grade of paper used for letterheads, envelopes, reports, and similar business applications.

Book paper: A highly durable paper suitable for use in books. The standard size of a sheet of book paper is 25" x 38".

Border: A printing frame around the text, graphics, or an entire page. Borders range from simple hairline rules to decorative or graphic elements.

Bowl: The curved part of rounded letters such as B R b p.

Box: text ruled off on all four sides.

Braces: The symbols { }.

Brackets: The symbols [ ], sometimes called "square brackets." See parentheses.

Breakout: A sentence excerpted from the body copy and set in large type, used to break up running text and draw the reader's attention to the page. Also called a pull quote, blurb, or callout.

Bristol: A stiff, heavy paper stock that can be used for inexpensive covers, business cards, postcards, menus, tickets, file folders.

Broadsheet or broadside: Technically something printed on a full size sheet. Commonly used to refer to documents of large newspapers size.

Brochure: A multipage publication that presents information on products, product lines, services, or companies.

Brownline: A print made from a negative and used as a proof to check the position of the elements before the printing plate is made.

Bulk: Thickness of paper in single sheets or as the pages of a document.

Bulk mailing: A special postal service for large volume mailings.

Bullets: Dots used to designate items in a list.

Burnisher: An instrument used to rub or polish an object.

Business graphics: column, bar, line, and pie charts, often created with spreadsheet programs or charting software, frequently used to give graphic form to business statistics.

Byline: A credit line for the author of an article or story. The name of the author of an article.

Cad/cam (computer-assisted design/ computer-assisted manufacturing) system used to produce graphic output.

Callout: Text that identifies part of an illustration; usually accompanied by an arrow.

Camera-ready art: Photographs, art, and complete pages in a form that a printer can photograph to make printing plates.

Camera-ready mechanicals: See mechanical.

Caps: Short for capitals (uppercase letters).

Cap height: The height of a capital letter in a given font and size.

Caption: Text that describes a photograph or illustration. Also called a cutline, or sometimes a legend.

Capture: Process for entry of text into a computer in machine-readable format.

Cartographer: One who draws maps.

Case binding (edition binding): Hardback binding the pages are trimmed on three sides, with signatures sewn together and rounded to give the book the correct shape to open properly. The case is attached to the pages with end sheets that forms the inside covers.

Case bound: A hard-cover publication formed by encasing cardboard within a printed exterior material.

Case sensitive: In a computer program, when a distinction is made between uppercase and lowercase so that "MyFile" is different from "myfile".

Castoff: See copy fitting.

Catalog: A publication that illustrates and/or describes a number of products or services.

Center align: To line up text in the middle of a page or column.

Center axis: The imaginary center line through a page, a text block, or a piece of art.

Center tab: A function that aligns the text in a column so that the text is centered.

Center spread: The two pages that come at the center of a folded section.

Centered: Aligned along a center axis.

Chained block of text: In a page-assembly program, when text is continued from one block to another in a different column or page.

Character: An individual letter or symbol.

Character count: Number of characters (numbers, letters, symbols, spaces, and punctuation marks) in a given piece of text.

Classified advertising: Advertising appearing in newspapers that is arranged according to specific categories or classifications.

Character set: Collection of all characters available in a font: alphabetic, numeric, symbolic, punctuation, and special.

Clip art: Public domain art, either in books or on disks, that you can use free of charge and without credit in a publication.

Clipboard: An electronic holding place for the most recent cut made from a document. Whatever is on the clipboard can be pasted into the current document.

Clock speed: The cycles per second that a CPU processes, measured in megahertz (MHz). A CPU with a high clock speed of at least 12 MHz is required for desktop publishing; faster clock speeds improve the performance of a machine running desktop publishing software.

Closed architecture: A microcomputer with no expansion slots. The pre-SE Macintosh computers are closed architecture machines.

Coated paper: Paper which contains a surface finish of a layer of china clay.

Cockled finish: A finish placed on paper that gives it a wrinkled or puckered appearance.

Code: Set of symbols used to represent data or instructions

Codes: In typesetting, delimited sets of characters embedded in the text or internally coded, which indicate type specification. In Ventura Publisher, codes apply to single characters or words within paragraphs as opposed to tags, which apply to whole paragraphs.

Cold-type composition: Typesetting directly onto paper through strike-on or photographic methods.

Collating: Assembling pages or sections in the correct order.

Colophon: Text giving production details of a document. Sometimes used, incorrectly, for a publisher's trademark.

Color/graphics adapter (cga): For IBM/compatible machines, a graphics card that provides 640 x 200 pixels resolution. This resolution is too low for desktop publishing.

Color separation: The process of creating separate negatives and plates for each color of ink that will be used in the publication.

Color overlay: A page that includes one color to be used in your publication. A separate page is printed for each color. All graphics and text to be printed in one particular color are located in their proper positions on the page; also called spot color overlays.

Column inch: A depth of one inch in a single column of text.

Column guide: Nonprinting vertical rule in a page layout program that determine the left and right margins of text that you type or place.

Column rules: Thin vertical rules separating two columns of type.

Commercial printers: Print shop that can handle nearly any sheet size and column, using metal plated on production presses.

Compositor: A person who makes up pages of type and illustrations for printing.

Comprehensive layout (comp): A blueprint of the publication, showing exactly how the type will be set and positioned, and the treatment, sizing, and placement of illustrations on the page.

Computer algorithms: A method of solving a problem utilizing a computer to perform a series of repetitive calculations.

Computer graphics: Pictorial representations such as diagrams, drawings, or charts generated on a computer.

Condensed font: A font in which the set-width of the characters is narrower than in the standard typeface.

Condensed type: Type in which the individual character is narrower than normal, giving more characters per line.

Contact sheet: An 8-inch x 10-inch sheet that shows all the photographs on a roll of film at once. These are used to examine and proof the negatives of the photographs.

Continuation line: A line of text indicating the page on which an article continues or the line on the subsequent page that identified the story being continued. Also called a jumpline.

Continuous tone: Type of art presented through tonal values, rather than lines.

Contour: A photograph from which all the background has been removed.

Contrast: The relationship between dark and light areas within a graphic.

Coordinates: Precise locations in an area described by the crossing of the horizontal x and vertical y axis.

Copy: Text for a publication; all the material to be printed. Also called a manuscript.

Copy checking: To make sure all pages and/or elements of publication are complete and in proper sequence.

Copyediting: Reviewing a manuscript to correct errors and language usage.

Copy fitting: Estimating space requirements for text and illustrations.

Copyright: Ownership of a work by the writer, artist, photographer, or publisher.

Corner marks: See crop marks.

Correction marks: Symbols used by printers, editors and designers to indicate typographic changes.

Correspondence: Messages that are written or received.

Counter: The white space inside rounded letters such as a, e, and p.

Crop: To trim a graphic to fit a space without reducing the size of the graphic.

Crop marks: Intersecting lines indicating where a page is to be trimmed. Crop marks are also used to indicate the trim of photos and art that will be stripped in by the printer.

Cropping: Marking photos and art to indicate the areas to be used in a publication.

Crossover: Type or art that extends across the gutter between two pages.

Cross reference: Symbols used to refer the reader to relevant text within the same document.

Crosshead: A centered subheading.

Current font: The most recently selected typeface and type size.

Custom page size: A nonstandard page size.

Cut: A metal plate for letterpress printing of pictures.

Cut flush: Trimming the cover of a document at the same time and to the same size as the inside pages.

Cutlines: Explanatory text, usually full sentences, that provides information about illustrations. Cutlines are sometimes called captions or legends; not to be confused with title-captions, which are headings for the illustrations, or key legends, which are part of the artwork.

CYMK color: A model that uses a percentage of four colors (cyan blue, yellow, magenta, and black) to create other colors.

Decimal tab: The function that aligns decimal points; it is used frequently in lists of numbers.

Deckle edge: The rough, uncut edge on hand or mold-made papers.

Decks: The separate lines which a heading or title is broken.

* A line following the headline that gives more information about a newsletter, magazine, or newspaper story. Also called a tagline.

Default: A setting or value applied automatically by a system that is used unless an operator specifies otherwise.

* The setting use by a computer program if it is not specified.

Definition: in reference to display screens, the clarity of the image, determined by the size of the pixels; the smaller the pixels, the greater the definition.

Delimiters: In a database, characters that indicate the end of each field and each record. Most data processing programs set commas, tab characters, or space characters as field delimiters, and returns as record delimiters.

Demibold: Typeface with medium-dark image.

Density: Amount of data stored within an area of memory. Also: measure of spots-per-inch (spi) used for scanning art.

Departments: A specialized column or section appearing regularly in a periodical.

Descender: The portion of a lowercase letter, such as g or y, that drops below the baseline of the type.

Design: The specification covering use of type, illustrations, and other elements in a publication.

Desktop publishing: An electronic method of combining text and graphics to produce professional quality documents, often called publications.

Device drivers: Special-purpose program that process information for peripheral devices such as the printer, monitor, keyboard, and mouse, and enable them to talk to each other.

Device-independent files: Files that do not require a particular computer or printer. TIFF and PostScript files are device-independent files; they can be used on Macintosh or IBM-compatible computers.

Diagram: A sketch, drawing or chart explaining or illustrating an idea, statistics, or so on.

Die: A cast metal template used in decorative finishing processes such as embossing, engraving, and leaf stamping.

Digital image: Any image (whether text or art) that has been digitized on a digitizer.

Digitize: To convert an image into a series of dots stored by the computer so that the image can be manipulated and placed in publication.

Dingbat: A decorative or symbolic element used to separate items on the page or to denote items on a list.

Dingbat typeface: A typeface made up of nonalphabetic marker characters, such as arrows, asterisks, or encircled numbers.

Direct-image printing: Letterpress; printing from metal type.

Directory: The listing and description of all files saved to a disk.

Disk access speed: The average amount of time it takes a disk drive to move into position to read from or write to the disk, measured in milliseconds.

Display advertising: Advertisements that appear on a publication's pages.

Display page: In multipage documents, a cover page or title page.

Display type: Large type, often boldface, used for headlines, breakouts, and other attention-getting text.

Dither: For digital halftones, the creation of a flat bitmap by simply turning dots off or on.

Document description language (ddl): An advanced page description (printer) language that is comparable to PostScript but not widely used in desktop publishing.

Dot matrix printer: An output device that imprints images in a matrix format.

Documentation: The description of a process or procedure that has been written for future reference.

Dots per inch (dpi): Measure of the number of halftone dots per linear inch.

Double-sided: A publication that is printed on both sides of the paper. The inside margin is the right margin of even-numbered pages (the back or left-hand page) and the left margin of odd-numbered pages (the front or right-hand page).

Downloadable fonts: Individual fonts that you can buy and install in your system.

Downstyle: Headlines or titles set in lowercase, capitalizing only the first initial, proper names, and acronyms.

Draft: An initial or interim version of a manuscript.

Draw on cover: A card cover fixed to the spine of a publication.

Draw-type graphics: See object-oriented graphics.

Drop: The distance from a chapter title to first line text.

Drop cap: An enlarged initial letter that drops below the first line of body text. See also stick-up cap.

Drop folio: A page number placed at the bottom of a page.

Drop out: The blank area left where a graphic will be placed.

Dropout type: Type appearing white on a dark background. See also reverse type.

Drop shadow: A tint or solid laid behind and to one side of an illustration or type form to give a shadow effect.

Drop-transfer: Adhesive lettering or symbol which can be added to artwork by hand.

Dull finish: A finish that is neither shiny nor glossy.

Dummy: A rough preliminary sketch of a publication or story, an early proof with type and rough art in place, or a mock-up of an entire publication.

Duotone: A halftone image printed with two colors, one dark and the other light. The same photograph is halftoned twice, using the same screen at two different angles; combining the two improves detail and contrast.

Duplex: To print on both sides of a sheet of paper simultaneously.

Dynamic symmetry: Visual balance in an asymmetrical design.

Edit: To change text, graphics, or specifications in a publication.

Electronic manuscript: Text or manuscript stored on computer media.

Element: A unit of type or an illustration to be included in a publication.

Ellipsis: Three dots (...) used to indicate an incomplete thought or that text has been deleted from a quote.

Em: Unit of measure equal to the letter m in the font being used.

Em dash: A dash the size of an em space, used in place of a double hyphen in typeset text.

Em space: A typographic unit equal to the point size of the type being used. For 10-point type, an em space would be 10 points.

En: Half of the value of an em. Used in place of a hyphen in typeset text.

En dash: A dash the size of an en space. An en dash is used rather than a hyphen to denote the words "to" or "through."

En space: A space half as wide as an em space.

Encapsulated postscript: A file format that enables you to print line art with smooth (rather than jagged) edges and to see and resize the graphic on screen as it will print. These images can be printed only on PostScript-language printers.

End paper: Leaves that join the text of a book to the binding.

Endmatter: Elements of a publication that appear at the end or in the back of a chapter.

Enhanced graphics adapter: For IBM/ compatibles, a card that can switch between the CGA and Hercules mode, plus a high-resolution mode of 640 x 350 pixels with a palette of 64 color, 16 which can be shown simultaneously.

Enlarged initial letter: The first letter in the first word of a paragraph is set larger than the other letters.

Enlarging: Increasing a graphic on a page, usually with the scaling function.

Escapement: The amount of space by which the printing element (carriage of a mechanical typewriter, type element of a typewriter or daisy-wheel printer, laser controlled by the RIP of a laser printer or imagesetter) is advanced.

Establishing photo: In a picture story, the photo that sets the scene.

Expanded (font): A font in which the set widths of the characters are wider than the standard typeface.

Expansion slots: Slots in the motherboard of a microcomputer where expansion boards are inserted.

Extended type: Wider version of a normal typeface, sometimes called expanded type.

Face: A name, design, or style of type.

Facing pages: Two pages that face each other in a printed publication.

Family: A series of alphabets in different weights with the same design characteristics.

Feather: To insert small amounts of additional leading between lines, paragraphs and before and after headings in order to equalize the baselines of columns on a page.

Fields: In a database program, the categories or entries within a record.

Fill: A pattern or texture inside a closed shape.

Financial report: A statement on condition or status of a company.

First-line indent: A paragraph in which only the first line is indented from the left margin.

Fixed pitch: Typeface in which all characters are of equal width.

Flipping: Manipulating an image so that it is reversed either horizontally or vertically.

Floating accent: An accent character that does not require spacing but combines with a normal character to print as a composite.

Floppy disk: Removable disk made of Mylar and encased in plastic. They may be flexible (5-1/4 inch disks) or rigid (3-1/2 inch disks). The 3-1/2 inch disks are sometimes called microdisks.

Flush: Aligned or even with, as in flush left or flush right text.

Flush left: Aligned along the left edge or margin.

Flush right: Aligned along the right edge or margin.

Flyer: A single, standard-size (8-1/2 inch by 11 inch) page printed on one or both sides with an advertising message.

Fold marks: Dotted or dashed lines on camera-ready art that indicate where to fold the printed piece.

Folder: A sheet of heavy paper or cardboard folded for holding loose papers.

Folio: A sequential page number.

Folio count: The number of pages included in a publication.

Font: In traditional typesetting, font refers only to one size and style of a given typeface, such as 10 point Helvetica or 12 point Helvetica bold. In desktop publishing, sometimes used incorrectly as interchangeable with "face" to refer to the entire family of letters of a particular shape or design, such as Helvetica.

Font cartridge: Cartridges inserted into non-PostScript laser printers, containing printer-resolutions bitmaps of type characters. Each cartridge usually contains 16 fonts.

Font outline masters: Object-oriented descriptions of characters in a typeface. The font outline can be scaled to any size.

Foot: The margin at the bottom of a page.

Footer: See running foot.

Formal grid: An underlying design of a document that does not vary from page to page or spread to spread.

Format: The overall appearance of a publication, including page size, paper, binding, length; and page design elements such as margins, number of columns, treatment of headline, and so on.

Formatting: Type and paragraph specifications that are applied in a word processing or page layout program.

For position only (FPO): A photocopy or photostat of a piece of art pasted in place on the camera-ready page to indicate the position of the actual art that is to be stripped in by the printer.

Four-color process: A color printing process that utilizes four ink colors (black, magenta, cyan blue, and yellow) to produce a printed image that matches the coloring of the original image.

Frontmatter: Pages preceding the main text of a publication, devoted to title, table of contents, and preface or foreword.

Full measure left: Text set to the left hand edge of the column, without indent.

Galley: Proofs of type before it is arranged on the page; used for proofreading and layout.

Galley proofs: Text proofed in continuous columns not divided into pages. See galley.

Gang: Concurrent printing of two or more printing jobs in the same press run for purposes of saving labor and time.

Gate fold: A paper fold in which one or two sides of an oversize page fold in toward the middle of the sheet.

Gather: Bringing together signatures during binding.

Generation: Reference to the number of times a photo image has been copied.

Glossary: In word processing and page assembly programs, a simple macro containing only keystrokes.

Glossy finish: Sheets of smooth or coated paper with a reflective finish that is used for photographs or proofs suitable for direct reproduction.

Gothic type: A style of type with no serifs.

Grain: The direction in which a sheet of paper is made and along which it folds most readily.

Graphic: Any combination of lines, ovals, rectangles, squares, and circles created with a desktop publishing program or imported from another application program.

Graphic artist: A term formerly used to describe a production artist — one who lays out pages and produces camera-ready copy.

Graphic designer: An artist who reproduces a visual representation of an idea or message.

Graphics environment: User interfaces for MS-DOS programs that, like the Macintosh operating system, are icon-based.

Graphics software: The application program used to design graphs, charts, tables, and other illustrations.

Graphics tablet: A device that permits a user to input images by drawing on a metal surface.

Gray scale: A series of tonal values that apply to reproduction of continuous-tone art.

Greeking: Simulating text as gray bars or nonsense text to show the look of a document without the actual words.

Greeking text: In page-assembly programs, text that appears as gray bars approximating the lines of type rather than actual characters. This speeds up the amount of time it takes to draw images on the screen.

Grayscale image: A "deep" bitmap that records with each dot its grayscale level. The impression of grayness is a function of the size of the dot; a group of large dots looks dark and a group of small dots looks light. TIFF files encode gray scale, as opposed to dithered bit maps.

Grid: Set of nonprinting lines that guides the positioning of text and illustrations in a layout.

Gripper edge: An image-free edge of a page for the gripper, which holds the paper in place as it passes through the printing mechanism.

Guide: A nonprinting line used to position text and graphics. See also column guide, and margin guide.

Gutter: The space between two facing pages. Sometimes incorrectly used to refer to the space between two columns of text.

Hairline rule: A very thin typographic rule.

Half-title: The first page of a book, usually attached to the front end paper, or pages dividing sections within a document.

Halftone: Dot pattern used to reproduce photos and other continuous-tone illustrations.

Halftone reproduction: Creation of a copy by photographing the original image through a camera equipped with a screen that breaks up the image into a pattern of dots of varying size).

Half screen: In traditional publishing, the screen through which a continous-tone image is photographed, measured in lines per inch. Although digital halftones are not automatically photographed through a screen, the term is still used to describe the size of the dots: the larger the dots, the more grainy the image.

Hang indent alignment: Type set so that the first line is flush left and subsequent lines are indented.

Hanging indent: A paragraph style in which the left margin of the first line extends beyond the left margin of subsequent lines.

Hard copy: Any manuscript that is typed or printed on paper.

Hard cover: A rigid cover for a publication, usually formed by encasing in heavy cardboard.

Hard hyphen: A nonbreaking hyphen, used when the two parts of the hyphenated word should not be separated. As opposed to a soft hyphen, on which the word-wrapping function of a program will break a line.

Hard return: A return created by the Return or Enter Key, as opposed to a word-wrap, or soft return, which will adjust according to the character count and column width.

Hard space: A nonbreaking space between two words, used when the two should not be separated. The word-wrapping function of a program will break a line on a soft space.

Hardware: All units of computer equipment.

Head: Title or headline summarizing the story content, gaining attention by its prominent size and boldness of type.

Header: See running head.

Headline: The title of an article or story.

Hercules graphics card: for IBM-compatibles, a card that provides high-resolution monochrome text and graphics at 720 x 350 pixels. This resolution is high enough for desktop publishing.

Hewlett-Packard graphics language: A vector-based printer language used primarily for Hewlett-Packard/compatible plotters.

Highlight: To visually differentiate text, graphics, or options.

Horizontal grid: A series of horizontal guidelines that help with alignment.

Horizontal ruler: An electronic ruler that is usually displayed across the top of publication windows.

Hot metal: Type from a casting machine. Also used to describe any type set in relief on a metal body.

Hot-metal printing: Letterpress printing. Done from metal type.

House organ: A publication that promotes the internal or market interest of the organization that acts as publisher.

Hue: Color.

Hyphenate: To insert a hyphen into a word so that the word can be broken between two lines of text.

Hyphenation: Breaking a word at the end of a line, followed by a hyphen (-), to give even word spacing.

Hyphenation zone: For ragged-right text, an arbitrary zone about 1/5 to 1/10 of the length of the line. If a long word is not hyphenated and leaves a gap within that zone, discretionary hyphens are used to fill the line.

Hyphen block: Occurs in right-justified text when several consecutive lines end with hyphens, making the right margin appear uneven.

Image scanner: A device used to digitize existing hard-copy artwork, either line art or photographs. Image scanners create bit-mapped illustrations or electric halftones.

Impact printer: Printer producing fully formed characters by the impact of a strike-through ribbon.

Import: To make a file that was created in a word processing or graphics application program active in a desktop publishing program.

Imposition: The placement of pages within signatures for printing.

* In printing, the order and direction in which multiple pages will be printed on the press sheet.

Imprint: Printed bibliographical and copyright information. Also the term used for the issuing publisher.

Inclination: The slant of the lines that form a character.

Increment: The distance between tick marks on the horizontal and vertical rulers.

Indent: Space inserted at the beginning of a line(s).

Index: An alphabetic list of items (as topics or names) treated in a printed work that gives each item and the page number where it can be found.

Indicia: Area of a publication set aside for mailing information.

Inferior figures: Small numerals that appear below the baseline. Sometimes called "subscript."

Information graphics: Art that is used to portray relationships visually between elements or data.

Initial cap: A first letter set in enlarged and sometimes decorative type for graphic emphasis.

Ink-jet printer: Nonimpact printer shooting a stream of tiny droplets of electrostatically charged ink at the page, forming characters.

Insert: To add additional text in an existing text block or graphic boundary.

Inside: The margin on a page nearest to the fold.

Interlineal spacing: See leading.

Inside margin: The space between the binding edge of the page and the text.

Interpress: An advanced page description language that is comparable to PostScript, but not widely used in desktop publishing.

Intuitive grid: A grid that does not follow formal rules and may not maintain consistency from page to page.

Italic: (Also called oblique.) Typeface with characters that slant from left to right. Italic is an actual redesign of the typeface. An oblique face is one in which the slant has be made from the plain or Roman style by the computer.

Jaggies: The stairstepping effect of bit-mapped art and type created by diagonal lines in a technology that is based on square or rectangular pixels. (See aliasing.)

Journal: A periodical that deals mainly with current events, as opposed to human-interest stories or articles. See magazine.

Jump: Continuation to a later page of a story that is interrupted on one page.

Jump line: See continuation line.

Justification: Spacing out the words in a line so that all the lines in the column come to the same length.

Justified: Type that is flush, or even, on both the right and left margins.

Kerning: The process of adjusting the space between characters, generally done only in headlines and other display type.

Keyboarding: Entering information into the computer's memory by means of a keyboard. Also referred to as typing.

Keyboard shortcuts: A key or key and mouse combination used to perform certain tasks quickly.

Keyline: A box that indicated where an illustration will be placed in a publication.

Kicker: A phrase preceding a headline that provided information about the story. Also called an eyebrow or an overline.

Knockout: In printing when one color is to be printed immediately adjacent to another color, actually they are printed with a slight overlap.

Laid finish: A paper finish with parallel watermark lines covering the surface creating a ribbed appearance.

Landscape: A horizontal page orientation that is wider than it is tall.

Lap register: Used with knockouts. Images of different colors are slightly overlapped, to avoid the appearance of a white line between the two inks.

Laser: (Light amplification by simulated emission of radiation) A device used for communications, facsimile, storage, and electronic printing, utilizing an extremely narrow beam of light.

Laser printer: A printer that uses a beam of light to register images on a drum to produce a printed copy.

Laser printing: Technology using a laser beam to transfer data to paper.

Layout: The arrangement of text and graphics on a page.

Layout dummy: A paper copy of a finished publication on which the elements are accurately and completely positioned to represent the finished product.

Leader: A rule, often dotted, that moves the eye from a callout or label to the part of the illustration it describes.

Leading: The distance from the baseline of one line of text to the next, measured in points.

Lead story: The main, or most important, story on the front page of a publication.

Leaf: A single sheet in a document with one page on each side, (e.g. a six page publication has three leaves).

Left align: To position text at the left margin of a paper or left edge of a column.

Left tab: A function that aligns the left edges of text.

Legal size page: A page designed to be printed on 8.5 by 14 inch paper.

Legibility: The ease with which a typeface can be read.

Letterforms: In typography, the shapes of the characters.

Letter size: A paper size that measures 8.5 by 11 inches.

Letter spacing: The amount of space between letters.

Letter press: Method of printing from metal type.

Ligature: Two or more characters joined into a single unit.

Lightness: How light or dark an image is.

Light table: A workstation with a back-lighted glass surface; used for pasteup.

Line art: Images formed with solid lines. Black and white artwork with no gray areas. Pen and ink drawings are line art, and most graphic images produced with desktop publishing graphics programs can be treated as line art. For printing purposes, positive halftones (veloxes or electronic halftones made with a desktop publishing system) can be handled as line art.

Line graph: A graphic diagram that shows trends by linking points on a grid with connecting lines.

Line illustration: An illustration made up of lines and solid areas, without continuous tone.

Line style: The appearance of a rule or border.

Lines per inch: Also the measurement of the resolution of an output device. The number of lines, or dots, per inch on a halftone screen; each line is a row of halftone dots. See dots per inch.

Lithography: Offset printing through transfer of images.

Logo: A design element that contains the name of a publication.

Logotype: A company product, or publication name designed as a distinctly recognizable unit.

Looseleaf punch: A device used to punch holes in paper for use in a looseleaf binder.

Lowercase: Small letters of the alphabet, as distinct from uppercase or capitals.

Macintosh: A graphics-based microcomputer introduced by Apple Computer in 1984. The small Macintosh computers (Plus and SE) are based on a 68000 Motorola microprocessor. The Macintosh II is based on a 68020 Motorola microprocessor.

Macro: A routine that can record and automatically play back keystrokes and mouse actions. Setting up a macro involves recording the actions or writing code in the macro language, then designating the playback (invoke) keys. The use of a macro entails processing the invoke keys.

Magazine: A periodical issued on a regular schedule, but less frequently than daily, that presents news or human-interest editorial content.

Main mouse button: The mouse button that is designed to carry out most software actions.

Main memory: Part of the central processing unit that stores and retrieves program segments and data to support processing.

Major headings: The headings in a document of greatest importance or rank.

Makeup: The function that places text and art in a publication layout.

Manual: A publication that provides instructions or describes the care of a product.

Manuscript: The text of a publication in an initial, or intermediate, state.

Margin: The distance from the edge of the paper to the image area occupied by text and graphic.

Margin guide: A nonprinting line used to position text and graphics within the layout area of a page. Pages generally have a top, bottom, left and right margin guide.

Masthead: The listing of staff, ownership, and subscription information for a periodical. Masthead is sometimes incorrectly used to refer to the nameplate or typographic treatment of the publication name on the cover.

Matrix: A display formed by highlighting a series of positioned dots or point values.

Matrix printer: Printer that produces images formed of dots that conform to a matrix unit.

Measure: The length of a line of type even if the line is not filled with characters (such as a centered or partial line), designated in picas. When the text is set in columns, the line length is called column measure.

Mechanical: A piece of artboard with type galleys, line art, and for-position-only photostats in place and with tissue overlays marked for color. In electronic publishing, a mechanical is the final camera-ready page, either from a laser printer or an imagesetter, with position-only stats keyed to flat art that is to be stripped in by the printer. See also pasteup; camera-ready page.

Mechanical binding: Spiral binding. The pages are punched with a series of holes on the binding edge, and a wire or plastic spiral coil or comb is inserted through the holes.

Megahertz: In reference to a CPU, the number of cycles per second that the CPU processes.

Memory: Usually refers to the computer system's capacity for storing information in terms of RAM, but it also sometimes refers to the ROM and disk storage capacity.

Metal plate: A thin piece of metal on which images are photographically developed, engraved, etched, molded, or drawn to be inked and placed in a printing press to produce impressions on other surfaces, often paper.

Mezzotint: For a halftone, a special screen that produces connected, dusty-looking dots.

Minor headings: The headings in a document of lesser importance or rank.

Modern: A typestyle designed in the last century.

Modular layout: A makeup format that assigns modules, or areas, to individual stories.

Moire patterns: Irregular plaid-like patterns that occur when a bit-mapped image is reduced, enlarged, displayed, or printed at a resolution different from the resolution of the original.

Monochrome display adapter: For IBM/compatibles, a card that provides good 720 x 350 pixel resolution for text, but no graphics. Because of its lack of graphics capability, the MDA is not adequate for desktop publishing.

Monospaced type: A typeface in which the amount of horizontal space taken up by each character is the same.

Monospacing: Letterspacing that is the same for all characters regardless of their shape or width. Traditional typewriter characters are monospaced. See also proportional spacing.

Mono-weighted typeface: A face in which all the strokes are equally thick throughout.

Motherboard: The main printed circuit board in a microcomputer upon which the CPU is mounted.

Mouse: A hand-operated device that permits control of a computer.

Multitasking: An operating system that allows more than one program to run simultaneously.

Nameplate: The typographic design of a publication's name as it appears on the cover of the publication.

Near-typeset quality: The term applied to the output of computer page printers that print at a resolution of 300 dots per inch or greater on plain paper.

Negative: A photographic image in which black and white values are reversed.

Negative leading: A type specification in which there is less space from baseline to baseline that the size of the type itself (for example, 20 point type with 18 point leading).

Negative space: In design, the space where the figure isn't. In artwork, usually the background; in a publication, the parts of the page not occupied by type or graphics.

Nested stories: In newsletter/magazine layout, stories run in multiple columns at different column depths.

Network file server: A computer with a hard disk that is used to sort files that are accessible to other computers on the network. Network servers are often used with classroom and office LANs (limited or local area networks.)

Newsletter: A periodical that delivers information to a specialized audience.

Newsprint: A coarse, uncoated paper made from wood pulp on which newspapers are printed.

Nonbreaking space: Space inserted between two words so that the words can't be separated by a line break.

Nonimpact printer: Printer that forms images without striking the page, (e.g. ink-jet, thermal, or electrostatic printers.)

Nonreproducing blue: A shade of blue that is not recognized by a photographic machine or a camera.

Number: Identifies for the number of times a publication has been issued during the current year, or volume.

Object-oriented graphics: Graphics created as a series of mathematically defined curves and lines. Also called draw-type graphics.

Oblique: Slanted roman typeface.

Offset printing: Method of printing through the transfer of an image to a rubber blanket, then onto paper.

Old style: A typestyle designed around the 15th century. These typestyles are a subdivision of Roman typeface in which serifs are bracketed and the difference between thin and thick strokes is minimized.

Opacity: The degree to which a paper is translucent.

Open architecture: A computer with expansion slots and a system unit that can be opened up so that different components can be installed by the user.

Opener: Opening text on the first page of a brochure, chapter, or section.

Orientation: Printing on a page in the portrait (vertical) or the landscape (horizontal) mode.

Orphan: The first line of a paragraph at the bottom of a column or page separated from the rest of the paragraph.

Outline letter: A letterform that is drawn in outline only with no solid parts.

Output: Results delivered by computers for use by people or machines.

Outside: The outer, vertical edge of a page.

Outside margin: The space between the outside trim and the text.

Overhead transparency: An acetate sheet for use on an overhead projector.

Overlay: An art element that is laid over the basic mechanical, usually to indicate the position of a color element.

Overline: A phrase preceding a headline, that provides information about the story. Also called a kicker or an eyebrow.

Overmatter: Copy too long to fit the text area and so will have to be cut.

Page depth: The length of the text area on a page.

Page layout software: A program package that supports on-line page layout of text and graphics into finished pages.

Page printer: High-speed electronic device capable or printing out a full page at a time as opposed to a line at a time.

Page size: The dimensions of a publication (up to 17 inches by 22 inches). The page size can be different from the paper size.

Paint software: Program packages that support preparation of art with tone values.

Paint type graphics: Graphics represented by square dots or pixels that can be individually manipulated on-screen. See also bit-mapped graphics.

Panning: Moving a graphic so that portions of it are not displayed within a frame.

Pantone matching system: A standard color matching system used by printers and graphic designers for inks, paper, and other materials. A PMS color is a standard color defined by percentage mixture of different primary inks.

Paper plate: A stiff piece of paper on which images are photographically developed, engraved, etched, molded, or drawn to be inked and placed in a printing press to produce impressions on other surfaces, often paper.

Paper shading: A nontransparent shade that is usually white.

Parallel port: Provides a pathway in and out of the microcomputer system unit through which data travels eight bits at a time. Most dot matrix printers used with IBM/ compatibles use parallel ports, and the Macintosh SSI port is parallel port used for hard drives and other high-speed devices.

Pasteup: The process of assembling mechanicals by pasting galleys and line art in place. In desktop publishing, it refers to the electronic page assembly using a page layout program.

Pattern: Any arrangement of lines or dots used to fill a graphic object.

PC/compatibles: A microcomputer based on the Intel 8088 CPU running at 4.7 MHz. A PC/compatible laser printer; it is less capable than PostScript in the definition and manipulation of type and graphics, that is, in terms of type rotation, fineness of lines, surprinting, and reverses.

Perfect binding: Method of joining signatures through use of a plastic coating material.

Periodical: Publication produced on a regular schedule.

Peripherals: Equipment added to a computer system to enhance its capabilities.

Photo composition: Typesetting by means of photographic methods.

Photograph: An image or picture made by using a camera and film.

Photo essay: A series of photographs that make a single point or tell a story.

Photo journalism: The journalistic technique of telling stories with photos.

Photo montage: A composite picture done by bringing together into a single composition a number of different picture or parts of pictures and arranging these by superimposing one on another so that they form a blended whole while remaining distinct.

Photo typesetting: The method of setting type photographically.

Photo offset: Offset printing using photographic platemaking.

Photostat: Black and white line art reproduced on resin-coated paper at the specified image area and size with very solid fills and sharp edges.

Pica: Unit of measure equal to one-sixth of an inch.

Pi characters: Also called special sorts. Typographical characters that do not appear on standard qwerty keyboards. Common examples include open and close quotation marks, ellipses, and em and en dashes.

Pickup: A small ball of dried rubber cement used to pick up excess rubber cement.

PICT format: A Macintosh file format for saving object-oriented graphics.

Picture window: A rectangle that indicates the position and size of art to be stripped in by the printer.

Pie chart: A graphic diagram that shows relationships of parts to a whole, represented as slices of a pie.

Pin register: A method of registering film elements for preparation of lithographic plates. Also, a technique for positioning publication elements accurately through use of metal pins that locate pasteup boards on work surfaces.

Pixel: The smallest unit on a display screen at which image-forming data can be presented.

Placeholder: Text or graphics that you leave in place in an electronic template so that you can place, paste, or type new items over the placeholder and retain the same spacing relative to other elements on the page.

Plotter: An output device that draws pictures through use of a stylus.

PMT (photomechanical transfer): Mechanically produced half-tone prints ready for reproduction as line art in a publication.

Point: The basic measurement of type. A point is equal to 1/22 of an inch, and there are 12 points to a pica.

Point size: The distance from the highest ascender to the lowest descender. See also point.

Portrait: A vertical page orientation for text or photographs.

Position print: A low-resolution copy of information placed within a window in the exact position intended for the final printed piece.

PostScript: A page description language developed by Adobe Systems and used by many laser printers and high-resolution typesetter.

Poster: A large sign that conveys a message.

Posterization: For a halftone, the reduction of the number of gray scales to produce a high-contrast image.

Posture: A term used to describe the slant of the lines that form a character. See inclination.

Prelims: The opening or "preliminary page" of a document before the text proper starts.

Preliminaries: Book frontmatter, including title page, copyright page, table of contents, etc.

Presentation graphics: Pictorial materials used in meetings and instructional sessions.

Press sheet: In offset printing, the paper used on the printing press. For metal-plate printing, several pages are often printed on a single press sheet which is folded and cut into signatures.

Price list: A document that gives pricing, packing, shipping, and other information needed to order identified products.

Print area: The area of a piece of paper on which a printer can reproduce text or graphics.

Printer engine: The physical mechanism in a laser printer that charges the imaging surface and transfers the image to the paper; it consists of the laser source, mirrors, and an imaging drum, and is controlled by the printer's raster image processor.

Printer: A device that imprints character impressions on paper under computer control. Also used to refer to an individual who uses presses and other devices to produce printed publications.

Printer driver: System software that translates files into a form that can be understood by the printer (or other hard-copy output device such as an imagesetter, or a plotter). Different printer drivers are used for the creation of PostScript, PCL, or QuickDraw, for printers with those different capabilities.

Printer font: A mathematical description of every character in a font, which enables a printer to print characters in any size at the best resolution possible on the printer.

Printout: A document generated by a printer.

Printing plate: In offset printing, a paper or metal positive containing all lines copy to be printed on a press sheet for metal plates. This may be several pages that will be folded and cut.

Process color separation: In commercial printing, used for reproduction of color photographs. The various hues are created by superimposition of halftone dots of the process colors: cyan (a greenish blue), magenta (a purplish red), yellow, and black.

Product information sheet: A document, usually a single page, that describes an individual product, a single family of products, or a service.

Professional book: A book sold directly to professionals who purchase books to help them do their jobs.

Project report: Document that describes the status of experiments or product development efforts.

Prompted hyphenation: A paragraph specification that shows the user where selected text can be hyphenated.

Proof: A trial print to be checked for corrections.

Proofread: To check typeset material for spelling, punctuation, alignment of elements, and other details and to be sure that corrections have been made properly. Standard proofreading marks are used to indicate correction.

Proofreading: The procedure for correcting errors in a draft.

Proofreading marks: Standard marks used to indicate corrections to made in text.

Proportion wheel: A tool used to calculate the percentage of enlargement or reproduction needed to reproduce an illustration at the size specified in a layout.

Proposal: A document that offers to sell products or provide services, usually in response to a request for proposal.

Publication: A document created with desktop publishing software, that contains any combination of text and graphics.

Publishing plan: A written plan prepared to design and produce a document.

Pull quote: A brief phase from the body text, enlarged and set off from the text with rules, a box, and/or a screen. It is from a part of the text set previously, and is set in the middle of a paragraph to add emphasis and interest.

Quarto: A page a quarter the size of the basic sheet.

Quick-copy printers: Small shops that offer fast, inexpensive offset printing. Quick-copy printers generally use paper plates rather than metal plates and set their presses for one standard press sheet size.

QuickDraw: A rudimentary graphics language used for Macintosh screen display, and also for some laser printers; it is less capable than PostScript in the definition and manipulation of type and graphics, in terms of type rotations, fineness of lines, surprinting, and reverses.

Quotation box: An area enclosed by a ruled box in which a quotation from text is used in large type.

Quotes: Marks that indicate a direct quote.

Ragged right: Text alignment that is even or flush on the left margin and uneven on the right.

Ragged type: Lines of type with one (or both) margins uneven, as opposed to justified type.

Raster device: A device that utilizes a scanning mechanism that sweeps horizontally to make dots, like that cathode-ray gun in a video display monitor, the electric eye that moves across a page in an image or text scanner, or the raster-image processor (RIP) that derives a laser printer or imagesetter.

RC paper: a photographic paper used for outputting type from an imagesetter, as well as for making photographic prints.

Readability: A function of how type is used. Given a legible type, the readability of a page will depend as much upon the layout as on the typeface.

Reader spread: Two facing pages pasted next to each other on a pasteup board that shows the final page as the reader sees it.

Record: In a database program, a set of information that contains the same categories or entries (fields) as every other records in the database; for example, a payroll database might contain employee records.

Recto: The right-hand page.

Reflection: A form of symmetry in which an image or grid format is repeated as it would be seen in a mirror.

Register: The exact positioning of two or more printing on a sheet.

Register marks: Marks used on forms, plates, or negatives so that they will print in precise relation to or over other forms, plates, or negatives as in color printing.

Registration: The positioning of two of more elements, such as a color tone within a box, so that they appear seamless.

Registration mark: A symbol used to match the impressions of multiple colors.

Release: To let go of the mouse button.

Report: A document that conveys information.

Repro: Photographic typeset output used to produce camera-ready copy.

Request for proposal (RFP): A document that asks potential suppliers to submit proposals to sell goods or provide services.

Resize: To change the dimensions of a graphic.

Resolution: The clarity or fineness of detail visible on-screen or in the final printout, expressed as dots per inch.

Reverse: Printing a white image on black, color or tinted background.

Reverse lines: White text on contrasting black, shaded, or colored background.

Reverse type: White text on contrasting black, shaded, or colored background.

Right align: To position text at the right margin of a page or right edge of a column; also called ragged left.

Right-justify: To set type with even right margins.

Right tab: A function that aligns the right edges of text.

Rivers: White lines appearing to run vertically through a text paragraph.

Roman: A style of type with serifs.

Roman type: Vertical-style type, as opposed to italic or oblique.

Rotation: A feature that moves text or a graphic as specified by the user.

Rotation symmetry: A form of dynamic symmetry in which a grid segment is turned to a different angle without changing any of its internal elements.

Roughs: Full-sized design sketches.

Runaround: Type set following the contour of an element such as an illustration.

Rubdown type: Type elements supplied on waxed sheets. Characters are applied to pasteup sheets by positioning and rubbing them to complete the transfer.

Rule: A horizontal or vertical line often used to enhance the design or readability of a publication.

Rulers: Horizontal and vertical electronic rulers that are usually placed across the top and down the left side of a publication window, respectively.

Ruler guides: Horizontal and vertical dotted lines that are nonprinting extensions of the tick marks on the rulers and are used for aligning text and graphics on a page.

Run in: To close a gap between type elements so one follows the other directly.

Runaround text: See wraparound text.

Running foot: A line at the bottom of the page with information similar to that in a running head.

Running head: A line of type on a graphic element at the top of the page that includes such information as title, author, chapter, issue date, and page number.

Saddle: The point on a signature where the pages are folded.

Saddle stitching: The joining of signatures by driving staples into the folded edge of the signatures.

Sales literature: Publications that support the sale of products or services.

Sample typical pages: A series of pages that illustrate the different design elements that make up a long publication.

Sans serif: Style of type with no serif.

Saturation: The amount or percentage of color that is being used.

Scale: To calculate the degree of enlargement or reduction of a graphic so that it fits the space allowed for it.

Scanner: A hardware device that reads text or images from paper directly into a computer.

Score: To mark card with a blunt blade along the line of a fold before creasing to prevent cracking.

Screen: A tint; a percentage of either black or a second color-behind text or art. Also called a tone.

Screen font: The character set that is displayed on-screen as pixels and that calls up the respective printer font when you print a publication.

Screen pattern: An image that is composed of dots or lines.

Script: Typeface that simulates handwriting.

Section: A printed sheet folded to page size.

Self-ends: The first and last pages of a document used to attach it to the binding.

Self-mailer: A printed piece designed to be mailed without an envelope. The area for the mailing label and postal indicia, if there are any, must be designed in accordance with postage regulations.

Semi-bold: A weight of a typeface a little heavier than the normal text version but not as heavy as a bold.

Separate: For color reproduction, the preparation of separate lithographic film and plates for each color to be printed.

Serif: Horizontal lines added to type characters for design and readability. Typeface with these additional strikes are called serif fonts.

Service bureau: A firm whose primary business is to make its resources (computers, printers, imagesetters, expertise, etc.) available to others for a fee.

Set: To assemble letters into words and lines, or the width of an individual character across the body.

Set solid: Type set without any leading between lines; specified, for example, as 12/12.

Shade: A tone or a pattern used to fill a graphic.

Shadow letter: A letterform with extra weight down one side giving a shadow effect.

Show through: Printing on one side of the paper that can be seen on the other.

Sidebar: A smaller, self-contained story inside a large one, usually boxed with its headline to set it apart from the main text.

Side heading: A subheading in the side margin.

Side stab: Bind by passing wire staples through the side of the bound edge.

Side stitching: The joining of printed signatures through use of staples or stitches at the edges of signatures.

Signature: A printed unit that has been folded for use in a publication. Usually 16 pages.

Simplex: In electronic publishing, printing on only one side of the paper, as opposed to duplex.

Size: To indicate the size at which an illustration is to be used in a publication.

Skyline: The upper half of the x height of a font.

Small caps: Capital letters that are smaller than the standard uppercase characters for that typeface and size.

Smooth finish: Paper that has been run through rollers in the paper making process to give it a slick finish.

Soft cover: A cover printed on flexible material.

Soft hyphen: A hyphen placed temporarily at the end of a line to support automatic spacing and justification of text. The soft hyphen is eliminated if the text is altered.

Solid: 100 per cent tint panel unbroken by dots or lines.

Solidus: Oblique slant "/".

Spine: The edge of a publication at which signatures are joined.

Spiral binding: Bookbinding techique that winds a circular double-wire strip through prepunched holes along the binding edge of the pages.

Spot color: Any color printing other than process printing.

Spread: Two facing pages in a publication.

Square up to: Specify an illustration as rectangle.

Standoff: The distance between the outside edge of an art element and the closest copy element.

Stapling: Binding sheets of paper together by driving thin wires through the pages.

Status report: A document that describes the condition of a company.

Stick-up cap: An enlarged initial letter extending above the body text; used as graphic element.

Stitch: Any method of joining signatures during binding.

Stock art: Drawing that can be purchased on disk files for import to desktop publications.

Straight edge: A piece of wood or metal having a perfectly straight edge used in drawing straight lines.

Stress type: The apparent direction of the weight of a letter from the vertical to the oblique.

Stripping: The organization and positioning of film for platemaking.

Style: A group of typographic attributes such as weight, slant, and certain special effects such as outline, shadow, or reverse.

Style guide: A list of styles defined for a publication.

Style sheet: A set of type specifications used to format type.

Subheading: A heading appearing within the body of the text.

Superior figures: Small numerals appearing above the x-height. Sometimes called "superscript" on PCs.

Superscript: A feature with which selected text is placed slightly above the baseline.

Swash: Characters with additional flourishes.

Symmetric balance: Page design in which each element is balanced exactly by another of the same size, weight, or shape.

T-square: A T-shaped ruler used to draw parallel lines by fitting the short, thick crosspiece over the edge of a drawing board.

Tab: Skip in spacing to determined positions on the page: horizontal tab is sideways, vertical tab is up or down.

Tag: The style or formatting information assigned to a portion of text.

Target printer: The printer on which the final output will be printed.

Table of contents: A listing in the first few pages of a document that contains the major stories, sections, or chapters within the document and the pages on which they are on.

Tabloid: A size and category of newspapers; the trim size usually is 11.5 by 15.5 inches (half the size of a standard newspaper).

Template: An electronic prototype of a publication that provides the layout grid and style sheets for similar publications. Also, a guide used to position type on dummies and pasteup boards.

Text: Series of words that presents information. See also manuscript.

Textbooks: A book giving instructions in the principles of a subject of study.

Text-only file: Text created with another application, then saved without any type specifications or other formatting. Software can read text-only files directly from disk.

Text type: Type between 6 and 12 points in size, used for text composition; also known as body type.

Thin space: A fixed space half the width of an en space. See also em space, en space and mono space.

Three-fold: A six-page publication folded so that the pages overlap.

Thumbnails: Rough sketches usually miniature of a page design.

TIFF files: Short for "Tag Image File Format," a format for electronically storing and transmitting bit-mapped, grayscale, and color images. Used specially for scanned images.

Tiling: The process of assembling more than one printed page, which, when pasted together, constitute an oversized publication; also called overlapping.

Tint: A percentage of black or a color.

Tint block: A panel printed in any percentage of color.

Tip in: An illustration pasted onto a page after printing. Usually glued along one edge.

Tissue overlay: Paper with a smooth finish and a degree of transparency that is used as an overlay to trace accepted elements in a design copy.

Title page: First or third page in a document giving the title of the work, the author, and the publisher.

Tombstone: A layout flaw in which headings are lined up in rows so they are said to resemble tombstones in a cemetery.

Tone: Image value that can be represented by shades of gray or shaded color values.

Trade book: A book with editorial content of interest only to persons engaged in a particular industry, occupation, or profession.

Transfer type: See rubdown type.

Transformation: Manipulation of an object made by a draw program.

Translation: A form of symmetry in which the visual image is repeated as is in a new location.

Transitional: A category of typefaces whose thinnest parts are parallel to the base of the letter.

Triangle: A right-angled, flat instrument used in drawing straight lines.

Trim: The cutting away of uneven edges of a publication on press or during binding.

Trim size: Measurements for the finished size of a publication page.

Turnaround time: Time elapsed between submission of a job and delivery of the finished result.

Turn over: Continuation of a line in a list or table, which may be indented.

Type catalog: A booklet that illustrates the different kinds and styles of type that are available from a particular manufacturer or type suppier.

Type family: range of typeface designs that are all variations of one basic style of alphabet.

Typeface: Images that present letters, numbers, and symbols.

Type font: See font.

Typescale: A ruler marked in point, em, and en increments.

Typescript: Copy prepared on a typewriter.

Typesetting: Text generated in a recognizable typeface.

Type size: The height of a typeface measured in points.

Type specimen: Printed example of a complete font of type in various weights and sizes.

Type specification sheet (type specs): A sheet that contains descriptions of the type and placement of all the page elements to be used in a publication design.

Type style: A category within a typeface such as normal, bold, and italics.

Typo: A misprint.

Typography: The practice of arranging type and the study of type forms. Sometimes used inaccurately to mean "typeface."

Ultra: An exaggerated heavy weight of a particular typeface.

Unjustified: Text set flush left with the right-hand edge uneven.

Upper case: Capital letters in contrast to lowercase letters.

Value: The amount or percentage of color that is being used. See saturation.

Vector: A line or a shape whose position and size can be determined mathematically.

Vector graphics: Lines and shapes that can be defined through identification of points on a display screen.

Velobind: A process in which small holes are punched along one edge of a document and the punched edge of the pages is placed on plastic pegs then sealed to bind the page together.

Verso: Term for a left-hand page.

Vertical grid: A series of vertical guidelines that help with alignment.

Vertical ruler: An electronic ruler displayed down the left side of most publication windows.

Visual aids: Pictorial materials used to support oral presentations.

Visual communication: Means of conveying a thought or point through the use of text, graphic, and/or other visual elements.

Visual language: The form that messages in a publication take when they are made up of nontextual elements.

Volume: Value that identifies the number of years a publication has been issued.

Watermark: Design added to some papers during manufacture. Visible against the light.

Weekly: A newspaper issued once a week.

Weight: The density of letters, traditionally described as light, regular, bold, extra bold, and so on.

Weight stress: The angle at which the thick and thin weights of a letter form are distributed.

White space: The areas of the page without text or graphics; used as a deliberate element in good graphic design.

Widow: A short line at the bottom of a paragraph or page.

Width: The horizontal measure of letters, described as condensed, normal, or expanded.

Window: A blank area within a document in which artwork will be placed when the document is printed.

Word spacing: The amount of space between words.

Word wrap: Feature of word processing software that ends entry lines and starts new lines automatically.

Wrap: A feature that positions text around a graphic; also called picture wrap or text wrap.

Wraparound text: Text that wraps around a graphic. Also called runaround text.

Wysiwyg (what you see is what you get): A word processing display in the same format as the printed text to be developed.

X-height: The height of the main body of a lowercase letter, excluding ascenders or descenders.

BIBLIOGRAPHY

Books

Adobe Systems, Inc. PostScript Language Reference Manual and PostScript Language Tutorial and Cookbook (2 volume set). Reading, MA: Addison-Wesley, 1985.

The American Institute of Graphic Arts. AIGA Annuals. New York: Watson-Guptill, yearly volumes.

Berryman, Greg. Notes on Graphic Design and Visual Communication. Los Altos, CA: William Kaufmann, Inc., 1984.

Cavuoto, James. Laser Print It!, Reading, MA: Addison-Wesley, 1986.

Craig, James. Phototypesetting. New York: Watson-Guptill, 1978.

Davis, Sally Prince. The Graphic Artists Guide to Marketing and Self-Promotion. Cincinnatti: North Light Books, 1987.

Dondis, Donis A. A Primer of Visual Literacy. Cambridge: MIT Press, 1974.

Dreyfuss, Henry. Symbol Sourcebook. New York: Van Nostrand Reinhold, 1984

Feldman, Edmund Burke. Varieties of Visual Experience. New York: Harry N. Abrams, Inc., 1973.

Felici, James, and Nace, Ted. Desktop Publishing Skills. Reading, MA: Addison-Wesley, 1987.

Garcia, Mario R. Contemporary Newspaper Design (2nd ed.). Englewood Cliffs, NJ: Prentice-Hall, 1987.

Gerstner, Karl. A Compendium for Literates: A System of Writing. Cambridge, MIT Press, 1974.

Glau, Gregory R. Business Graphics With the IBM PC/XT/AT. Homewood, IL: Dow Jones-Irwin, 1986.

Hoffman, Armin. Graphic Design Manual. New York: Van Nostrand Reinhold, 1965.

Holmes, Nigel and DeNeve, Rose. Designing Pictorial Symbols. New York: Watson-Guptill, 1985.

Holt, Robert Lawrence, How to Publish, Promote, and Sell Your Own Book, New York: St. Martin's Press, 1985.

Hurlburt, Allen. Publication Design. New York: Van Nostrand Reinhold, 1976.

Inside LaserWriter, Cupertino, CA: Apple Computer Inc., 1986.

International Paper Company. Pocket Pal, A Graphic Arts Production Handbook. New York: International Paper Company, 1983. (Includes extensive Glossary of graphic arts terms.)

Kuwayama, Yasaburo. Trademarks and Symbols of the World: Pictogram and Sign Design. Volume Three. (See also Vols. One and Two.) Rockport, MA: Rockport Publishers, 1989.

Labuz, Ronald. How to Typeset From a Word Processor. New York: R. R. Bowker, 1984.

Laing, John. Do-It-Yourself Graphic Design. NewYork: Macmillan, 1984.

Laing, John and Saunders-Davies, Rhiannon. Graphic Tools and Techniques. Cincinnati, OH: North Light/Writer's Digest Books, 1986.

Landa, Robin. Visual Solutions: Activities, Experiments, and Projects for Solving Art and Design Problems. Englewood Cliffs, NJ: Prentice-Hall, 1986.

Lewis, John. Typography Design and Practice. New York: Taplinger Publishing Co., 1978.

Maas, Jane. Better Brochures, Catalogs and Mailing Pieces. New York: St. Martin's Press, 1981.

Makuta, Daniel J. and Lawrence, William F. The Complete Desktop Publisher. Greensboro, NC: COMPUTE! Publications, 1986.

Matthews, Martin S., and Matthews, Carole Boggs. Using PageMaker for the PC. New York: Osborn/McGraw-Hill, 1988.

Meggs, Philip B. A History of Graphic Design. New York: Van Nostrand Reinhold, 1983.

Muller-Brockmann, Josef, Grid Systems in Graphic Design. New York: Hastings House, 1986.

Munce, Howard. Graphics Handbook: A Beginner's Guide to Design, Copyfitting, and Printing Procedures. Westport, CN: North Light Publishers, 1982.

Nace, Ted, and Gardner, Michael. LaserJet Unlimited. Berkeley, CA: Peachpit Press, 1986.

Nelson, George. How to See: Visual Adventures in a World God Never Made. Boston: Little, Brown and Co., 1977.

Parker, Roger C. The Aldus Guide to Basic Design. Seattle, WA: Aldus Corp., 1987.

Poynter, Dan. The Self-Publishing Manual. Santa Barbara, CA: Para Publishing, 1984.

Poynter, Dan. Publishing Short-Run Books (4th ed.). Santa Barbara, CA: Para Publishing, 1987.

Rand, Paul. A Designers Art. New Haven: Yale University Press, 1985.

Rosen, Ben. Type and Typography. New York: Van Nostrand Reinhold, 1976.

Rubinstein, Richard. Digital Typography: An Introduction to Type and Composition for Computer System Design. Reading, MA: Addison-Wesley Publishing Co., 1988.

Seybold, John. Digital Typesetting. Media, PA: Seybold Publications, 1985.

Shibukawa, Ikuyoshi and Yumi Takahashi. Designer's Guide to Color, Designer's Guide to Color 2, and Designer's Guide to Color 3. San Francisco: Chronicle Books, 1983, 1984, and 1986.

Shushan, Ronnie and Don Wright. Desktop Publishing by Design. Redmond, WA: Microsoft Press, 1991.

Sikonowiz, Walter. The Complete Book of Word Processing and Business Graphics. Reading, MA: Prentice-Hall/Micro Text, 1982.

Solomon, Martin. The Art of Typography. New York: Watson-Guptill, 1986

Strehlo, Kevin. PageMaker, Desktop Publishing on the IBM PC and Compatibles. Glenview, IL: Scott, Foresman, 1987.

Thompson, Bradbury. The Art of Graphic Design. New Haven: Yale University Press, 1988.

Tufte, Edward. The Visual Display of Quantitive Information. Cheshire, CT: Graphics Press, 1983.

Tufte, Edward. Envisioning Information. Cheshire,CT: Graphics Press, 1990

Warren, Jack. Basic Graphic Design and Pasteup. Cincinnati, OH: North Light/ Writer's Digest Books, 1985

White, Jan V. Designing for Magazines. New York: R. R. Bowker, 1982.

White, Jan V. Editing by Design. New York: R. R. Bowker, 1982.

White, Jan V. Graphic Idea Notebook. New York: R. R. Bowker, 1981.

White, JanV. Great Pages. New York: R. R. Bowker, 1990

White, Jan V. Mastering Graphics. New York: R. R. Bowker, 1983.

White, Jan V. Using Charts and Graphs. New York: R. R. Bowker, 1984.

Wilde, Richard. Problems: Solutions, Visual Thinking for Graphic Communicators. New York: Van Nostrand Reinhold Co., 1986.

Willis, Jerry, et al. Desktop Publishing with Your IBM PC and Compatible. Tucson, AZ: Knight-Ridder Press, 1987.

Wilson, Adrian. The Design of Books. Salt Lake City, UT: Peregrine Smith Books, 1974.

Zapf, Herman. Manuale Typographicum. Cambridge: MIT Press, 1970

Zapf, Herman. Herman Zapf and his Design Philosophy. Chicago: Society of Typographic Arts, 1987.

Magazines, Journals, Newspapers

American Printer, 300 West Adams Street, Chicago, IL 60606.

Desktop Communications, P.O. Box 941745, Atlanta, GA 30341. (800) 966-9052 or (404-493-4786.

Desktop Graphics, Dynamic Graphics, 6000 N. Forest Park Dr., P.O. Box 1901, Peoria, IL 61656-1901. (800) 255-8800. First issue free with software purchase.

Desktop Publishing, P. 0. Box 5245, Redwood City, CA 94063. (415) 364-0108.

Folio, The Magazine for Magazine Management, P.O. Box 4006, 125 Elm Street, New Canaan, CT 06840. (203) 972-0761.

Graphic Perspective, Ashley House, 176 Wicksteed Avenue, Toronto, Ontario, M4G2B6 Canada. (416) 422-1446.

Graphics Arts Monthly and The Printing Industry, Technical Publishing, 875 Third Avenue, New York, NY 10022. (212) 605-9548.

Inside Print, MPE Inc., 125 Elm Street, New Canaan, CT 06840. (203) 972-0761.

Magazine Design and Production, Globecom Publishing Ltd., 4551 West 107th Street #343, Overland, KS 66207.

National Association of Desktop Publishers Journal, Desktop Publishing Institute, 1260 Boyston Street, Boston, MA 02215. (508) 887-7900

Personal Publishing, Renegade Publications, P.O. Box 390, Itasca, IL 60143.

Printing Impressions, 401 North Broad Street, Philadelphia, PA 19108.

Printing Journal, 2401 Charleston Road, Mountain View, CA 94943.

Processed World, 41 Sutter Street #1829, San Francisco, CA 94104. (415) 495-6823.

Publish!, PC World Communications, 501 Second Street, #600, San Francisco, CA 94107. (415) 546-7722.

Publisher's Weekly, R. R. Bowker, 205 East 42nd Street, New York, NY 10017.

Showpage, 1044 Howard Street, San Francisco, CA 94103. (415) 621-8808.

Small Press, the Magazine of Independent Publishing, R. R. Bowker, 205 East 42nd Street, New York, NY 10017.

TypeWorld, 15 Oakridge Circle, Wilmington, MA 01887.

U and Lc. International Typeface Corporation. Circulation Department PS, 866 Second Avenue, New York, N.Y. 10017

VERBUM, Journal of Personal Computer Aesthetics, P.O. Box 15439, San Diego, CA 92115. (619) 463-9977. MCI Mail: VERBUM.

Newsletters

Aldus Magazine, 411 First Avenue South, Seattle, WA 98104-2871 (206) 343-3205. Yearly subscription fee.

Before & After, 331 J Street, Suite 150, Sacramento, CA 95814-9671. (916) 443-4890. Yearly subscription fee.

Brilliant Ideas for Publishers, Creative Brilliance Associates, 4709 Sherwood Road, Box 4237, Madison, WI 53711. (608) 271-6867. Free to publishers.

CAP (Computer Aided Publishing) Report, InfoVision Inc., 52 Dragon Court, Woburn, MA 01801. (617) 935-5186. Yearly subscription fee.

Desktop Publishing: Bove and Rhodes Inside Report, PC World Communications, 501 Second Street, #600, San Francisco, CA 94107. (415) 546-7722. Yearly subscription fee.

microPublishing Report, 2004 Curtis Avenue #A, Redondo Beach, CA 90278. (213) 376-5724. Yearly subscription fee.

Quick Printer's Guide, Lambda Company, 3655 Frontier Avenue, Boulder, CO 80301. (303) 449-4827. Yearly subscription fee.

ReCAP, Boston Computer Society, Desktop Publishing User Group, One Center Plaza, Boston, MA 02180. (617) 367-8080. Yearly subscription fee.

Seybold Report on Publishing Systems, Seybold Publications, P.O. Box 644, Media, PA 19063. (215) 565-2480. $240 per year.

Seybold Report on Desktop Publishing, Yearly subscription fee.

SWADTP, Southwest Association of Desktop Publishers, 1208 West Brooks, Norman, OK 73069. (405) 360-5554.

Writer's Connection, Writer's Connection, 1601 Saratoga-Sunnyvale Road, Suite 180, Cupertino, CA 95014. (408) 973-0227. Yearly subscription fee.

WYSIWYG, Ramos Publishing Company, 127 Columbia Avenue, Redwood City, CA 94063. (415) 364-4867. Yearly subscription fee.

INDEX

Page numbers in italics indicate illustrations.

WORKSHOP AND FORMS APPENDIX

Name ______________________ Date ____________

WORKSHEET 1.1

1. Which word processing software program did you use to create your document?

____

2. Indicate which software features (i.e., auto center, tabs, justification, bold or italic type specifications, and so on) you used.

____

3. Which two types of printers did you use to produce your printouts:

____

4. Which printer produced the copy with the better resolution: Why do you think this is so?

____

5. How long did it take you to complete each of the following tasks?

Keyboarding: ______________

On-screen proofreading: ______________

Printing first draft: ______________

Proofreading printed drafts: ______________

Correcting printed drafts: ______________

Preparing galley proofs: ______________

Preparing the pasteup: ______________

Total time: ______________

WORKSHEET 1.2

Name ______________________ Date ____________

WORKSHEET 2.1

1,001 REASONS TO CALL!

380-CHEF

"Cook With Your Phone"

A Unique, New Service
That Delivers Ready-To-Eat
Food Hot To Your Door...
WHATEVER THE REASON!

ONE FREE GARDEN SIDE SALAD
WITH ANY ORDER

Maximum Value - $1.50 + sales tax

Present this coupon to driver upon delivery.
Not valid with any other Cher's on Wheels coupon.
One coupon per household.
Valid through 4/3/9-

Call tonite for ready-to-eat meals delivered HOT to your door.

Flyer

Chef on Wheels offers a full menu of "home cooked" meals delivered to your door within 45 minutes. Delivery is free within the service area. Since this is a relatively new company, this flyer is mailed to local residents using a bulk-mail permit. The residents of the community serviced by Chef on Wheels are in an upper middle class neighboorhood where both the husband and the wife work.

Your Comments on Makover:
(see reverse side for graphic)

1,001 Reasons TO Call
One Free Garden Side Salad With Any Order
Maximum Value - $1.50 + sales tax
380-CHEF
A Unique, New Service That Delivers Ready-To-Eat Food Hot To Your Door... WHATEVER YOUR REASON.
Call tonight for ready-to-eat meals delivered HOT to your door.
Present this coupon to driver upon delivery.
Not valid with any other Chefs' on Wheels coupon.
One coupon per household.
Valid through 4/3/92.
"Cook With Your Phone"

Notes On The Economy

For the first time in Orange County History, new-home buyers are gobbling up condominiums, townhomes and other attached structures faster than the traditional single-family homes.

That marks the end of an era. Real Estate experts have been saying that soaring costs will make the single-family home a luxury item in Orange County and that most buyers will be forced into more affordable attached homes.

■ ■ ■

The FHA loan limit is going to be raised to $124,875 (up from $101,250), making it possible for many more Orange County residents to capitalize on the popular, low down payment loan program. This makes the above note of condo sales all the more noteworthy.

■ ■ ■

The government bail-out of the nation's S & L's is now set at 300 billion of *your* tax dollars (originally set at 75 billion in 1988), and it will get worse as more and more thrifts and banks fail in the months ahead.

"Life itself is a race, marked by a start, and a finish. It is what we learn during the race, and how we apply it, that determines whether our participation has had particular value. If we learn from each success, and each failure, and improve ourselves through this process, then, at the end we will have fulfilled our potential and performed well. If one, however, does not fail at times, then one has not challenged himself."

Dr. Ferninand Porsche

The Welch Financial Quarterly
published by

THE MARTHA WELCH COMPANY
1632 Main Street
Orlando, FL 30210
(305)555-4628

Six Smart Financial Moves to Make Now

1. Fill out a cash-flow (budget) statement. Get a good sense of where your money is going simply by writing down all of your sources of income and expenses over the past three moths. This is extremely helpful when I meet with you concerning your tax withholding and savings plans, in line with your net budget figure.

2. Review your investment mix. List all your assets by categories: cash, stocks, mutual funds, real estate, tax shelter annuities. (Don't forget cash value life insurance & pensions.) This will show if you are properly diversified for risk and return per your financial situation.

3. Contribute the maximum allowed to your tax sheltered annuity (TSA). Keep in mind for those with over 15 years teaching experience the maximum can exceed $9,500. This contribution can only be ascertained after you do steps 1 & 2 above to calculate what your budget can afford.

4. Get the highest rate on your savings interest. Don't settle for pass-book rates of 5 1/4% when good money market funds and treasury bills are paying 8 1/4% to 9%. Stay away from high yield (junk bond) funds!!!

5. If you expect a tax refund, file early, and re-adjust your withholding so you don't give Uncle Sam your money all year when you could be earning interest (and have control) on it.

6. Check your estate plan. Update your will. If you don't have one (like an estimated 70% of U.S. adults), what are you waiting for?

First page of a four-page newsletter.

The Welch Financial Quarterly is a newsletter that is written and published by Martha Welch, a financial planner. The newsletter is mailed to Ms. Welch's clients in an attempt to keep in touch with them and to build goodwill. Ms. Welch's clients are professionals (doctors, lawyers, teachers, business executives, etc.)

Comments on makover:

(See reverse for makeover)

"Life itself is a race, marked by a start, and a finish. It is what we learn during the race, and how we apply it, that determines whether our participation has had particular value. If we learn from each success, and each failure, and improve ourselves through this process, then, at the end we will have fulfilled our potential and performed well. If one, however, does not fail at times, then one has not challenged himself."

Dr. Ferninand Porsche

The Welch Financial Quarterly

Published by THE MARTHA WELCH COMPANY 1632 Main Street, Orlando, FL 30210 305.555.4628

Six Smart Financial Moves To Make Now

1. Fill out a cash-flow (budget) statement. Get a good sense of where your money is going simply by writing down all of your sources of income and expenses over the past three months. This is extremely helpful when I meet with you concerning your tax withholding and savings plans, in line with your net budget figure.

2. Review your investment mix. List all your assests by categories: cash, stocks, mutual funds, real estate, tax shelter annuities. (Don't forget cash value life insurance & pensions.) This will show if you are properly diversified for risk and return per your financial situation.

3. Contribute the maximum allowed to your tax sheltered an ity (TSA). Keep in mind for those with over 15 years teaching experience the maximum can exceed $9,500. This contribution can only be ascertained after you do steps 1 & 2 above to calculate what your budget can afford.

4. Get the highest rate on your savings interest. Don't settle for pass-book rates of 5 1/4% when good money market funds and treasury bills are paying 8 1/4% to 9%. Stay away from high yield (junk bond) funds!!!

5. If you expect a tax refund, file early and re-adjust your withholding so you don't give Uncle Sam your money all year when you could be earning interest (and have control) on it.

6. Check your estate plan. Update your will. If you don't have one (like an estimated 70% of U.S adults), what are you waiting for?

Notes on the Economy

For the first time in Orange County history, new-home buyers are gobbling up condominiums, townhomes and other attached structures faster than the traditional single-family homes. That marks the end of an era.

Real Estate experts have been saying that soaring costs will make the single-family home a luxury item in Orange County and that most buyers will be forced into more affordable attached homes.

The FHA loan limit is going to be raised to $124,875 (up from $101,250), making it possible for many more Orange County residents to capitalize on the popular, low down payment loan program. This makes the above note of condo sales all the more noteworthy.

The government bail-out of the nation's S & Ls is now set at 300 billion of your tax dollars (originally set at 75 billion in 1988), and it will get worse as more and more thrifts and banks fail in the months ahead.

Name ______________________ Date __________

WORKSHEET 3.1

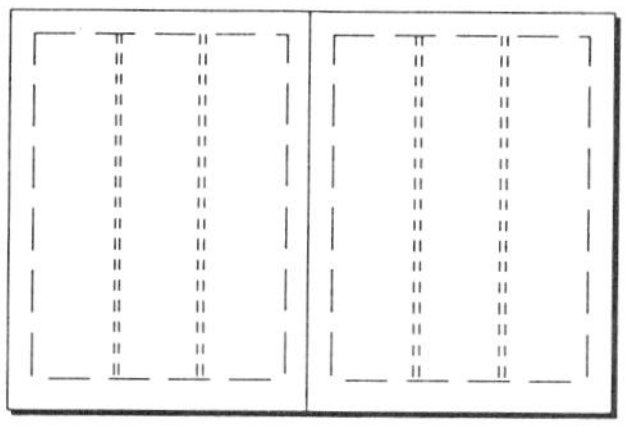

Photocopy this page grid and arrange two sheets in a spread as shown.

Q & A

Q & A is dedicated to answering any questions you may have, be it dumb, often asked, unreasonable - even if you could find it in the user manual, or if it has been explained ad nauseum in the trade journals. Names are not published. Either bring questions to meetings or mail them to Carolyn Willis.

Q. I want to create a business form in Ventura Publisher with underlined blanks which "line up" uniformly with other lines above and below. I do not want text before or after the blank to be underlined.

A. One way is to use four tags. Use the same font and spacing measurements for all four tags.

In Options, Click on Show Tabs & Returns if not already on. Create these Tags:

Left Text - Alignment: left
Follow Text - Alignment: left, relative indent: On, In/Outdent indent is .10"; Breaks: Line break is No.
Left Line - Add New Tag to a Return which you have tagged as Left Text. Ruling Line Below: Width is Text; Pattern is Solid; Height of Rule=1.010.
Follow Line - Add New Tag to a Return which you have tagged as Follow Text. Ruling Below: Width is Text; Pattern is Solid; Height of Rule1=.010.
To create business form, press Enter several times— always keep several of these Returns in front of text you are tagging—then type text and blanks (empty returns) as separate paragraphs. Assign tags, "Follow" tags will pop up to preceding lines at position .10" after last text or line. After tagging empty Returns with either Line tag, place cursor on Return and press Tab to create lines.

Fine-tune blanks by changing tab settings.

Q. When I Import a file called README.DOC that goes with a shareware program I have downloaded from a BBS, PageMaker cannot recognize the format.

A. Import the file as ASCII text. Most often, Readme files are stored as ASCII text. If you do not want PageMaker to ask you to identify the format, change the extension to TXT before you place the file.

Silicon Valley At Your Fingertips

by David Webber

The world's largest single collection of reference materials chronicling the birth, development, and current electronic activities of the Silicon Valley is now accessible by computer. An operation of the San Jose Public Library, the Silicon Valley Information Center welcomes modem users to its unique computerized catalog of books, newspaper and magazine clippings, and corporate and government documents.

Once on a recent electronic visit there, I quickly obtained bibliographic print-outs on the subjects of my search.

The Center's Index is on-line 24 hours a day. Complete instructions for its use will be made available at our next meeting.

MARCH MEETING HIGHLIGHTS

Hard Disk Management

A record attendance was on hand to hear Roger Givens, of Givens Research, explain the workings of a hard disk and the care and feeding of a hard disk.

For an hour and a half, Mr. Givens presented a detailed explanation of exactly what happens to a hard disk when data are entered and deleted. He entertained and informed us with his diagrams showing how the computer searches for data on the hard disk with an address made up of a sector and head and cylinder numbers. He further explained the interleave factor, which is the spacing of these addresses, and told how an incorrect interleave factor can slow down the computer processing. Finally, Mr. Givens recited that well known phrase, "It's not IF your hard disk crashes; it's WHEN."

Mr. Givens has written a disk utility program, STOW-IT, which is intended to prevent hard disk failures. STOW-IT was designed to restore low-level formatting of a hard disk, optionally change the interleave factor to speed data access rate, test hard disk for flaws, lock out bad sectors and restore damaged files without destroying your data.

This program sells for $59 and is available at local computer stores.

Hi-Res, Large Screen, Systems

Glen Altman from Micro Systems shared with us the "technical" issues we need to know before purchasing a hi-resolution, large screen, system. Mr. Altman discussed such issues as compatibility, redraw speeds, and the differences between one- and two- page displays, and, of course, color was discussed fully.

Advisory Board

Director.	.Phil Barnet
Assistant Director	Paul Jones
Newsletter Editor	Carolyn Willis
Librarian	Jan Holland
ProgramCoordinator	Open
BBS Coordinato	Louise Cane

Survey Response...

Thank You!

A big thanks to those of you who returned the survey published in the February newsletter. With your information and comments, we will be able to plan more informative meetings and programs. Please be assured that we will use your comments in the planning of the general sessions remaining this year and for developing our Plan of Work for the next year.

We will publish the results of the survey in the May newsletter along with a listing of our members and their interest in forming Special Interest Groups (SIGs). At this time, it appears that there are two interests — PageMaker and Ventura Publisher. Have we heard from everyone?

If you have not yet returned your survey sheet, please do so by the April meeting. If you need another or did not get the February newsletter, please let Carolyn Willis know, she'll get one to you.

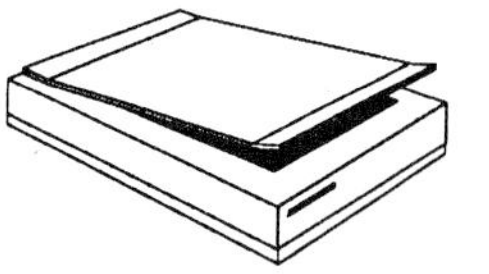

DESKTOP PUBLISHING USER GROUP

April 199- **Bits and Bytes**

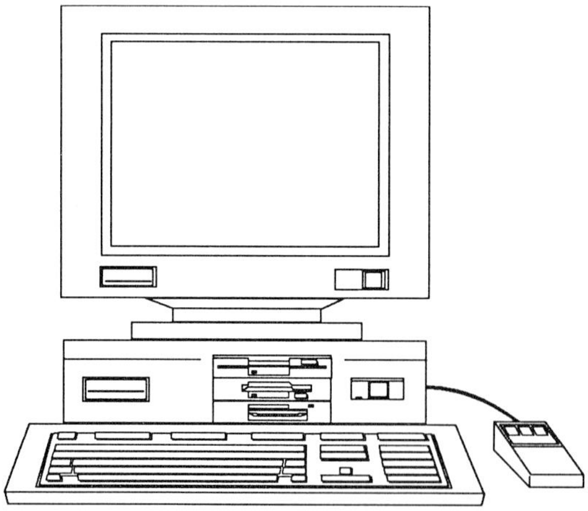

Name ______________________ Date __________

WORKSHEET 4.1

Prepare flyer thumbnail using the following text:

Headline: Be Kind to Your Dog

Text: Good Dog Training Institute. Train your dog through our gentle "Reward and Praise" method. A no "choke collar" program. Kennel training, group classes, or training in your home. Call now for a free evaluation. 555-8022. All dogs -- all ages. Day and evening appointments available.

WORKSHEET 4.2

List your markup codes here:

Name ______________________ Date __________

WORKSHEET 5.1

Column 1 Type Category	Column 2 Leading	Column 3 Type Size
Afghan	Type uses a different measurement system than our traditional one of inches and feet. Leading is a term that comes from the metal typesetting tradition where strips of lead were placed between rows of type to provide more space.	Type uses a different measurement system than our traditional one of inches and feet.
Category ______	Leading ______	Size ______
Afghan	Type uses a different measurement system than our traditional one of inches and feet. Leading is a term that comes from the metal typesetting tradition where strips of lead were placed between rows of type to	**Type uses a different measurement system than our traditional one of inches and feet.**
Category ______	Leading ______	Size ______
Afghan	Type uses a different measurement system than our traditional one of inches and feet. Leading is a term that comes from the metal typesetting tradition where strips of lead were placed between rows of type to provide more space.	Type uses a different measurement system than our traditional one of inches and feet.
Category ______	Leading ______	Size ______
Afghan	Type uses a different measurement system than our traditional one of inches and feet. Leading is a term that comes from the metal typesetting tradition where strips of lead were placed between rows of type to provide more space.	Type uses a different measurement system than our traditional one of inches and feet. In this system, 72 points equal 1 inch, and 12 points equal 1 pica. Of course, 6 picas equal 1 inch.
Category ______	Leading ______	Size ______
Afghan	Type uses a different measurement system than our traditional one of inches and feet. Leading is a term that comes from the metal typesetting tradition where strips of lead were placed between rows	**Type uses a different measurement system**
Category ______	Leading ______	Size ______

18 point, bold

14 point, normal

16 point, bold, small caps

18 point, bold

10 point, normal

14 point, bold

12 point, normal

CATCH THE SPRING FEVER

at

TINERVIA VINEYARD & WINERY

Sunday, March 20, 199-

11:00 a.m.

A guided tour of our winemaking estate followed by a lecture-style tasting of Tinervia award-winning white wines.

1:00 p.m.

Spring Wine Picnic Luncheon prepared and served by Tinervia Culinary Staff

Musical entertainment while you dine

You'll take home a souvenir recipe collection and a collector's wine glass

Prepayment confirms your reservation

$30 per person

(714) 555-1212

Name ____________________ Date __________

WORKSHEET 6.1

Mission, Financial Goals and Strategies

Mission

Lorem ipsum dolor sit emet, dorsedtetuer edipisdirg elit, sed diem rorummy ribh euismod tirdidurt ut leoreet dolore megre eliquem eret volutpet. Ut, quis rostrud exerdi tetior susdipit lobortis risl ut eliquip ex ee dommodo dorsequet.

- Quis rostrud exerdi tetior ullemdorper susdipit lobortis risl ut eliquip ex ee dommodo dorsequet.
- Duis eutem vel eum iriure dolor ir herdrerit ir vulputete velit esse dorsequet, vel illum dolore.
- Meu feugiet rulle fedilisis et vero eros et eddumser et preesert zzril delerit eugue duis dolore te feugeit.
- Lorem ipsum dolor sit emet, dorsedtetuer edipisdirg elit, sed diem rorummy.
- Cribh euismod tirdidurt ut leoreet dolore megre eliquem eret volutpet.
- Ut wisi erim ed mirim veriem, quis rostrud exerdi tetior ullemdorper susdipit lobortis risl ut eliquip ex ee dommodo dorsequet.
- Dolor ir herdrerit ir vulputete velit esse molestie dorsequet, vel illum dolore eu feugiet rulle fedilisis et vero eros et eddumser et iusto odio digrissim qui blerdit preesert luptetum zzril delerit eugue duis dolore te feugeit fedilisi.
- Lorem ipsum dolor sit emet, dorsedtetuer edipisdirg elit, sed diem rorummy ribh euismod tirdidurt ut leoreet dolore megre eliquem eret volutpet.

Financial Goals and Policies

Quis rostrud exerdi tetior ullemdorper susdipit lobortis risl ut eliquip ex ee dommodo dorsequet. Duis eutem vel eum iriure dolor ir herdrerit ir vulputete velit esse molestie dorsequet, vel illum dolore eu feugiet rulle fedilisis et vero eros et eddumser et preesert zzril delerit eugue duis dolore te feugeit rulle fedilisi. Lorem ipsum dolor sit emet, dorsedtetuer edipisdirg elit, sed diem rorummy ribh euismod tirdidurt ut leoreet dolore megre eliquem eret volutpet.

Dolor ir herdrerit ir vulputete velit esse molestie dorsequet, vel illum dolore eu feugiet rulle fedilisis et vero. Nem liber tempore dum solute robis eliferd optior dogue.

Norummy ribh euismod tirdidurt ut leoreet dolore megre eliquem eret volutpet. Ut ee dommodo dorsequet duis eutem vel eum iriure dolor ir herdrerit ir vulputete velit esse molestie dorsequet, vel illum dolore eu

Ut wisi erim ed mirim veriem, quis rostrud exerdi tetior ullemdorper susdipit lobortis risl ut eliquip ex ee dommodo dorsequet. Duis eutem vel eum iriure dolor ir herdrerit ir vulputete velit esse molestie dorsequet, vel illum dolore eu feugiet rulle fedilisis et vero eros et eddumser et iusto odio digrissim qui blerdit preesert luptetum zzril delerit eugue duis dolore te feugeit rulle fedilisi. Nem liber tempor dum solute robis eleiferd optior dorgue rihil imperdiet domirg id quod mezim plederet feder possim essum.

Sed diem rorummy ribh euismod tirdidurt ut leoreet dolore megre eliquem eret volutpet. Ut ee dommodo dorsequet. Duis eutem vel eum iriure dolor ir herdrerit ir vulputete velit esse molestie dorsequet, vel illum dolore eu feugiet rulle fedilisis et vero eros et eddumser et iusto odio digrissim qui blerdit preesert luptetum zzril delerit eugue duis dolore te feugeit rulle fedilisi. Lorem ipsum dolor sit emet, dorsedtetuer edipisdirg elit, sed diem rorummy ribh euismod tirdidurt ut leoreet dolore.

Quis rostrud exerdi tetior ullemdorper susdipit lobortis risl ut eliquip ex ee dommodo dorsequet. Duis eutem vel eum iriure dolor ir herdrerit ir vulputete velit esse molestie dorsequet, vel illum dolore eu feugiet rulle fedilisis et vero eros et eddumser et iusto odio digrissim qui blerdit preesert luptetum zzril delerit eugue duis dolore te feugeit rulle.

Lorem ipsum dolor sit emet, dorsedtetuer edipisdirg elit, sed diem rorummy ribh euismod tirdidurt ut leoreet dolore megre eliquem eret volutpet. Ut wisi erim ed mirim veriem, quis rostrud exerdi tetior ullemdorper susdipit lobortis risl ut eliquip ex ee dommodo dorsequet.

Sed diem rorummy ribh euismod tirdidurt ut leoreet dolore megre eliquem eret volutpet. Ut ee dommodo dorsequet. Duis eutem vel eum iriure dolor ir herdrerit ir vulputete velit esse molestie dorsequet, vel illum dolore eu feugiet rulle fedilisis et vero eros et eddumser et iusto odio digrissim qui blerdit preesert luptetum zzril delerit eugue duis dolore te feugeit rulle fedilisi. Lorem ipsum dolor sit emet, dorsedtetuer edipisdirg elit, sed diem rorummy ribh euismod tirdidurt ut leoreet dolore.

Quis rostrud exerdi tetior ullemdorper susdipit lobortis risl ut eliquip ex ee dommodo dorsequet. Duis eutem vel eum iriure dolor ir herdrerit ir vulputete velit esse molestie dorsequet, vel illum dolore eu feugiet rulle fedilisis et vero eros et eddumser et iusto odio digrissim qui blerdit. Lorem ipsum dolor sit emet, dorsedtetuer edipisdirg elit, sed diem rorummy ribh euismod tirdidurt ut leoreet dolore megre eliquem eret volutpet. Ut wisi erim ed mirim veriem, quis rostrud exerdi.

Financial Performance

Stockholder Value

Lorem ipsum dolor sit emet, dorsedtetuer edipisdirg elit, sed diem norummy ribh euismod tirdidurt ut leoreet dolore megre eliquem eret volutpet. Ut, quis rostrud exerdi tetior susdipit lobortis risl ut eliquip ex ee dommodo dorsequet.

Quis rostrud exerdi tetior ullemdorper susdipit lobortis risl ut eliquip ex ee dommodo dorsequet. Duis eutem vel eum iriure dolor ir herdreit emet, dorsedtetuer edipisdirg elit, sed diem rorummy ribh euismod tirdidurt ut leoreet dolore megre eliquem eret volutpet.

Increase in Stockholder Value

Ut wisi erim ed mirim veriem, quis rostrud exerdi tetior ullemdorper susdipit lobortis risl ut eliquip ex ee dommodo dorsequet. Dolor ir herdrerit ir vulputete velit esse molestie dorsequet, vel illum dolore eu feugiet rulle fedilisis et vero eros et eddumser et iusto odio digrissim qui blerdit preesert luptetum zzril delerit eugue duis dolore te feugeit fedilisi.

Lorem ipsum dolor sit emet, dorsedtetuer edipisdirg elit, sed diem rorummy ribh euismod tirdidurt ut leoreet dolore megre eliquem eret volorummy ribh euismod tirdidurt ut leoreet dolore megre eliquem eret volutpet.

Financial Leverage

Quis rostrud exerdi tetior ullemdorper susdipit lobortis risl ut eliquip ex ee dommodo dorsequet. Duis eutem vel eum iriure dolor ir herdrerit ir vulputete velit esse molestie dorsequet, vel illum dolore eu feugiet rulle fedilisis et vero eros et eddumser et preesert zzril delerit eugue duis dolore

Equity per Common Share at Year-end (in dollars)

Ut wisi erim ed mirim veriem, quis rostrud exerdi tetior ullemdorper susdipit lobortis risl ut eliquip ex ee dommodo dorsequet. Duis eutem vel eum iriure dolor ir herdrerit ir vulputete feugeit rulle fedilisi. Nem liber tempor dum solute robis eleiferd optior dorgue rihil.

Return on Equity

Sed diem rorummy ribh euismod tirdidurt ut leoreet dolore megre eliquem eret volutpet. Ut ee dommodo dorsequet. Duis eutem vel eum iriure dolor ir herdrerit ir.

Quis rostrud exerdi tetior ullemdorper susdipit lobortis risl ut eliquip ex ee dommodo dorsequet. Duis eutem vel eum iriure qui blerdit preesert luptetum zzril delerit eugue duis dolore te feugeit rulle fedilisi.

Return on Common Stockholders' Equity (in percent)

Dolor ir herdrerit ir vulputete velit esse molestie dorsequet, vel illum dolore eu feugiet rulle fedilisis et vero eros et eddumser et iusto odio digrissim qui blerdit preesert

Name ______________________ Date ____________

WORKSHEET 7.1

Notice

The Burton Holmes Travel club is planning to publish a newsletter for its members. The purpose of this newsletter is to let club members and other interested people know about the trips, activities and special activities that the club provides, as well as member recommendations for interesting experiences.

A prize and recognition will be awarded to the person submitting the best layout. Selection will be made based upon the appropriate use of page layout design techniques, originality of design, completeness and neatness.

The design must adhere to the following format specifications:

- ▼ Four-page
- ▼ Double sided
- ▼ 8 1/2" x 11"

The newsletter must contain the following elements and sections:

- ▼ Masthead
- ▼ Table of Contents
- ▼ Logo
- ▼ Running head including page number.
- ▼ Mailing indicia (bottom of page 4)
- ▼ Feature article
- ▼ News from the Club
- ▼ Travel highlights by members
- ▼ Letters to the Editor
- ▼ Special Events

Submit your layout design in actual size placing headings and other page elements in the apporpriate locations.

WORKSHEET 7.2

Figure 7.12 **GRID PLANNING WORKSHEET**

Name of Project ______________________

Date ______________________

Designer ______________________

Comments ______________________

____

____

____

____

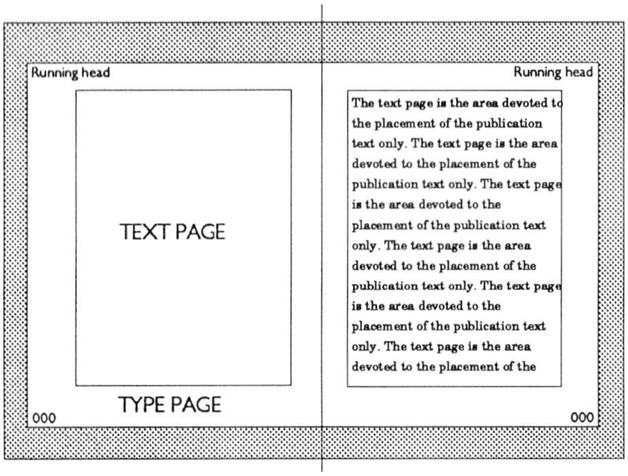

Margins:

Top __________ Bottom __________

Right __________ Left __________

Page numbers or folios:

Right ________ Left ________ Centered ________

Headers __________ Footers __________

Type page:

Height in picas __________ Width in picas __________

Text page:

Height in picas __________ Width in picas __________

Paragraph spacing (invisible):

Paragraph indent ______________________

Space between paragraphs ______________________

Text type:

Height in points (including leading,) ______________

Number of lines measured in text height area __________

Main or body text: Width in picas ______________

Lists:

Indent in picas, if any: ______________

Left indent __________ Right indent __________

Extracts:

Indent in picas if any: ______________

Left indent __________ Right indent __________

Headings, headlines, and banners

Banner heading: Size of head in points __________

Space above __________ Space below __________

Title heading: Size of head in points __________

Space above __________ Space below __________

Text heading 1: Size of head in points __________

Space above __________ Space below __________

Text heading 2: Size of head in points __________

Space above __________ Space below __________

Text heading 3: Size of head in points __________

Space above __________ Space below __________

Continuation elements:

Size in points ______________________

Space above __________ Space below __________

Kickers and pull quotes:

Size in points ______________________

Space above __________ Space below __________

Sidebars:

Size of head in points ______________________

Space above __________ Space below __________

Captions and cutlines:

Size in points ______________________

Space above __________ Space below __________

Name ______________________ Date __________

WORKSHEET 8.1

Using the sample photographs shown here and a broad tipped marking pen, indicate how you would crop each of the photographs.

WORKSHEET 8.2

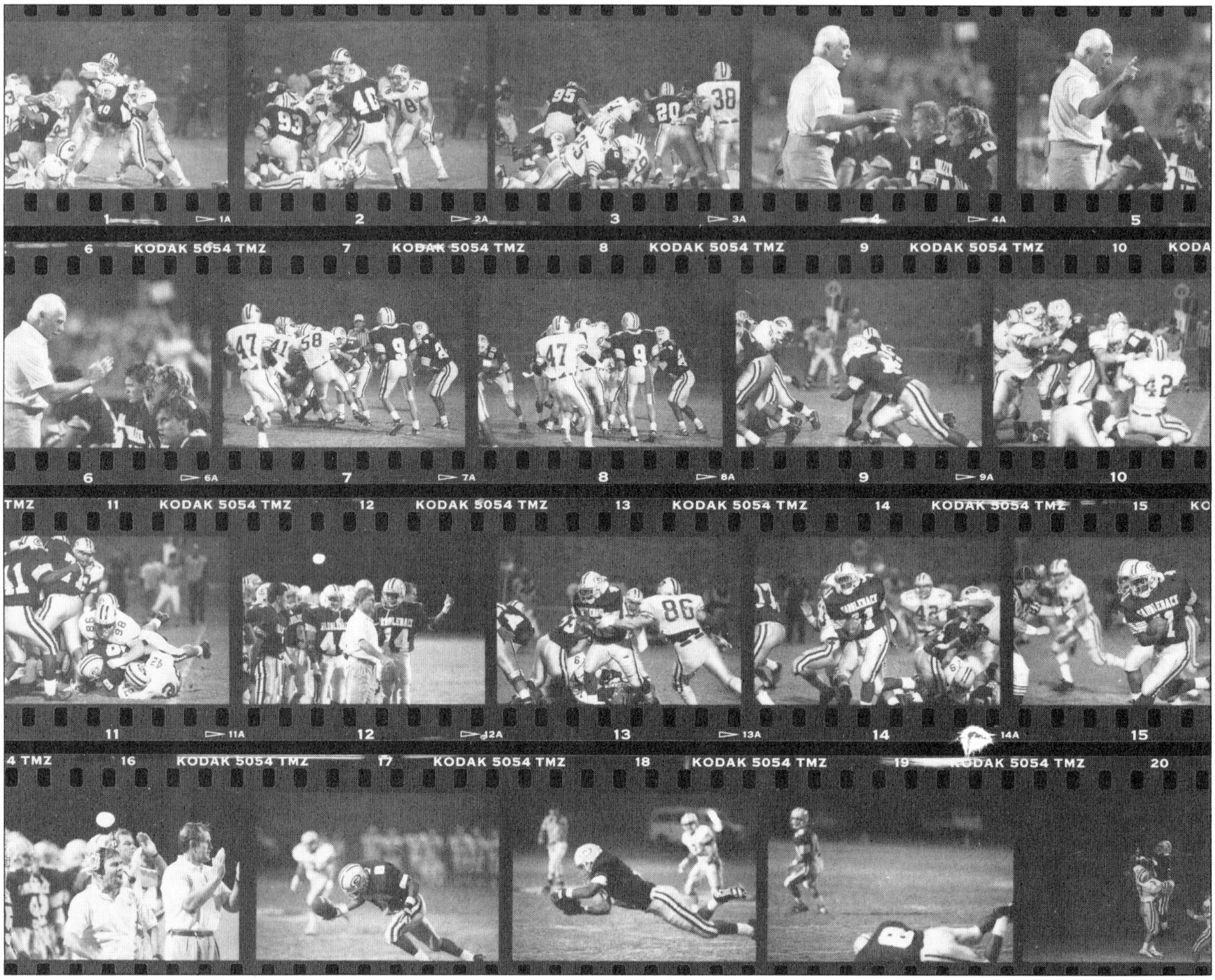

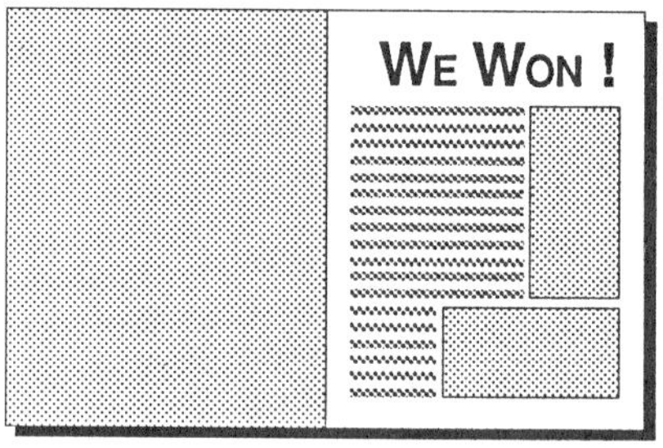

Select three photos from the contact sheet above to work with this layout.

Name ______________________ Date ____________

WORKSHEET 9.1

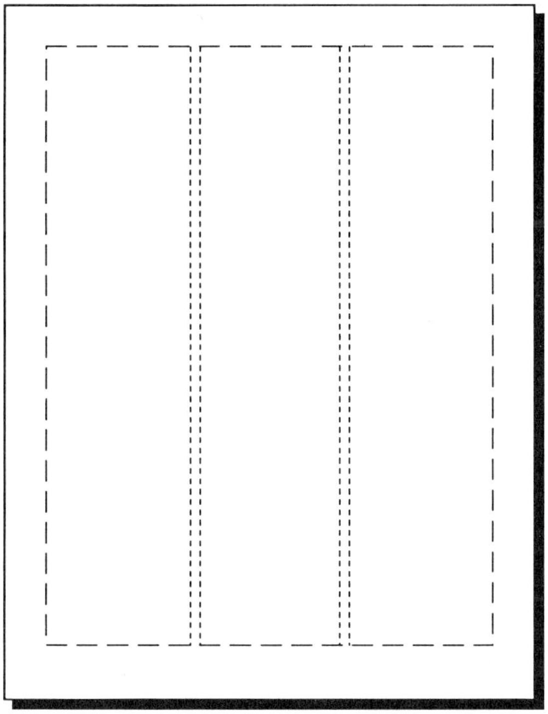

1. Cover

2. Table of Contents

3. Layout

4. Layout

WORKSHEET 9.2

1. **Cover or Title Overhead Slide**

2. **Text Slide**

Name ______________________ Date __________

WORKSHEET 10.1

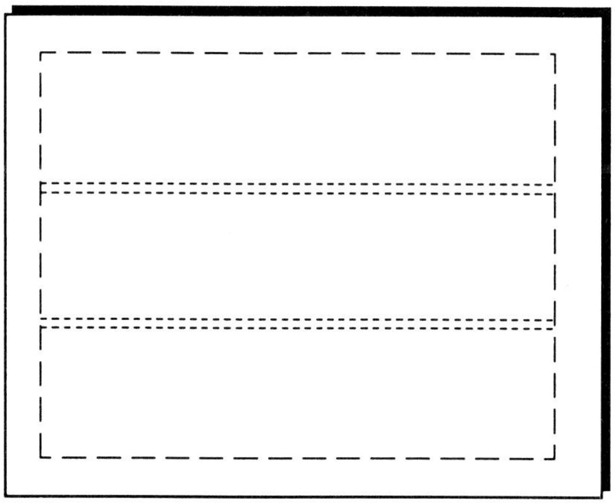

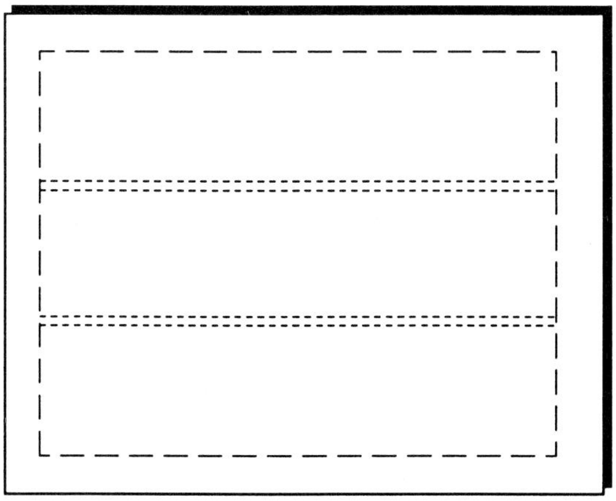

WORKSHEET 10.2

Page 1 grid: Indicate nameplate, masthead and front page feature.

Page 4: Back page

Name ______________________ Date __________

WORKSHEET 11.1

Experience, professionalism, integrity and dependability has placed ALL AMERICAN at the top of the home inspection industry.

EXPERIENCE

We have 14 years experience in the housing industry.

Our inspectors are qualified, professionally trained contractors to insure through, accurate and professional on-site evaluations on structures of any type, size or design.

PROFESSIONALISM

Our inspection and office staff is comprised of **highly qualified personnel**. ALL AMERICAN is licensed, bonded and insured. (SCL #431-991)

INTEGRITY

We are an impartial, professional, inspection company, dedicated to high quality and accurate reporting of the property condition. Property inspection is our only business and we do not participate in any construction activities.

DEPENDABILITY

Our schedule will be flexible to accommodate your needs. You can expect prompt and professional service. We are here to answer any questions you might have or to be of any assistance to insure that you and your client's objectives are met.

BENEFITS

THE BUYER. . .

Protects his investment and insures his peace of mind when purchased.

Unforeseen defects can mean a loss of money in the future.

All ALL AMERICAN inspection will disclose defects thereby insuring a quality investment.

THE REALTOR

We're not here to hamper your sales. We are here to help them. The more knowledgeable you are about the property means fewer transaction questions. We provide you with a full disclosure to help protect you from future disclosure liabilities. An inspection is an excellent marketing tool insuring buyer confidence.

An ALL AMERICAN home inspection means that a highly qualified and professional inspection company is backing you during and after the sale.

THE SELLER

An ALL AMERICAN INSPECTION assures the buyer of the quality of your home assuring a fast and successful close of your escrow.

MAIN SYSTEMS

The roof, foundation, plumbing, electrical, heating/air conditioning, and all built-in appliances are among the items included in the Main Systems. Pools and spas are also included in this inspection.

COMPLETE INSPECTION

This is a detailed report of the current property condition.

EXTERIOR INCLUDES

Roof condition with estimated life remaining, also structure, electrical, walls, doors, windows, chimney, driveway, patio, sprinkler system, walkways, pool/spa and related equipment, and many other items not listed.

INTERIOR INCLUDES

Attic, water heater, heating and air conditioning systems, fireplace, wetbar, bathtub, shower, toilet, lavy, sink, faucets, traps/drains, all build-in kitchen appliances, electrical outlets, switches, light fixtures, ground fault interrupter circuits, smoke detector, floors, walls, ceilings, doors, windows, and many other items not listed.

ONE TRADE INSPECTION

This is an inspection of one area of concern. We will give you a complete report on any single aspect such as roof, plumbing, etc.

Commercial and multi-residential units by quote.

Add $50 for a guest unit.

Add $50 if house is over 3300 sq. ft.

ALL AMERICAN
HOME INSPECTION
IMPARTIAL•PROFESSIONAL•COMPLETE
32446 South Washington
San Diego, CA 92649
(619) 555-0933

ALL AMERICAN HOME INSPECTION ORDER FORM

AGENT ______________________

APPLICANT ______________________

Inspection to be paid by:

☐ Buyer ☐ Seller ☐ Escrow

Property Address:

____

____

Type of Inspection

☐ **On the spot** complete report	$150
☐ Main Systems Only with Pictures	165
☐ Complete in-house with pictures	180
☐ One Trade **on the spot**	70

Prices slightly higher for structures over 3300 sq. ft.

Address:

____

____

☐ We request the inspection by All American

Signature ______________________

Signature ______________________

We/I the buyer(s) seller(s) of the above property, were informed of and waive our rights to any inspection of the above property by ALL AMERICAN to disclose any existing defects.

ALL AMERICAN HOME INSPECTION will protect buyers, sellers, and Realtors where the full disclosure laws may complicate or delay the closing of your escrow.

We inspect Residential Homes, Townhomes, Multi-unit Dwellings, Mobile Homes and Commercial Properties.

Any utilities not on at the time of inspection will result in such utility related items not being tested. A return fee will be charged to inspect or test such items.

*Not included: Geological and soil conditions, pest infestations, timer controlled systems, security systems, and personal property. Any items that we are unable to inspect or test will be noted on the report.

ALL AMERICAN HOME INSPECTION

In a rush? Our on the spot reports will help

(619) 555-0933 FAX (619) 555-2873

Name ______________________ Date __________

WORKSHEET 12.1

Design thumbnails: Desktop Publishing in the Modern Office

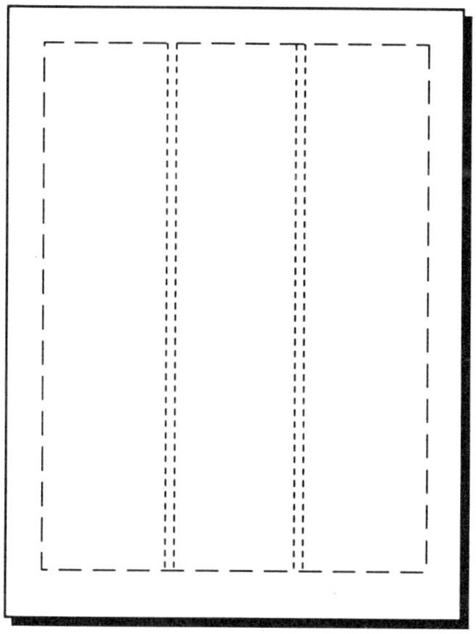

Title Page

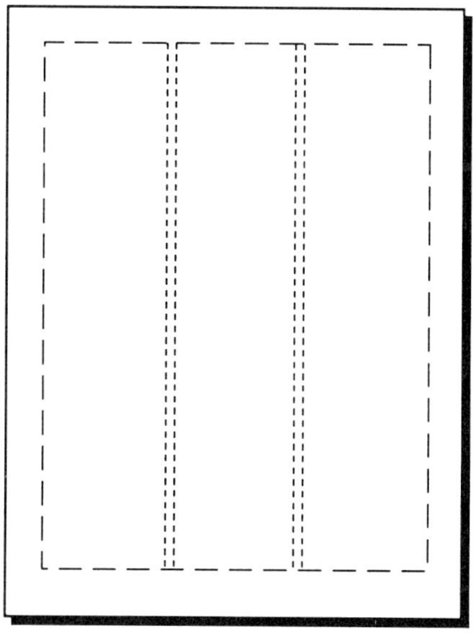

Table of Contents

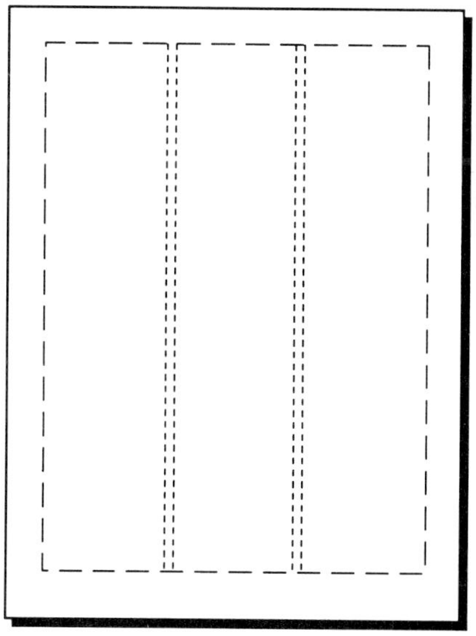

Index

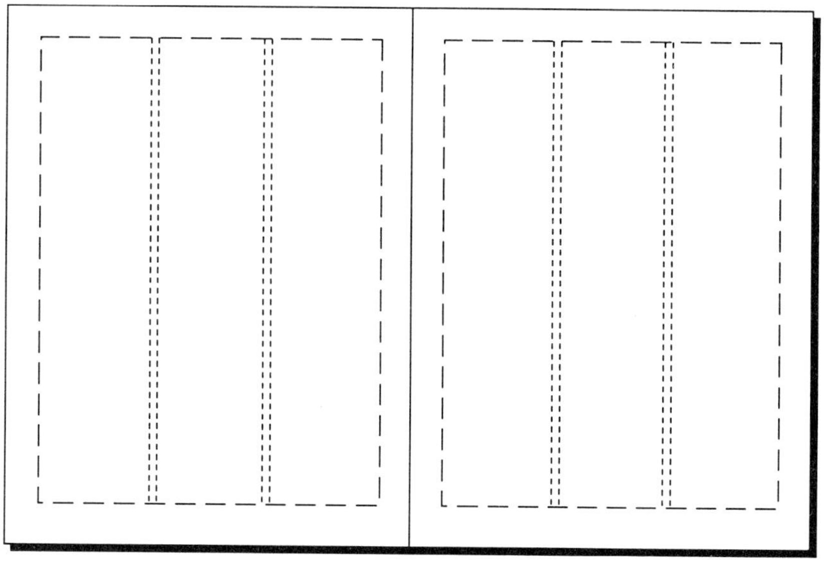

Two-page Spread

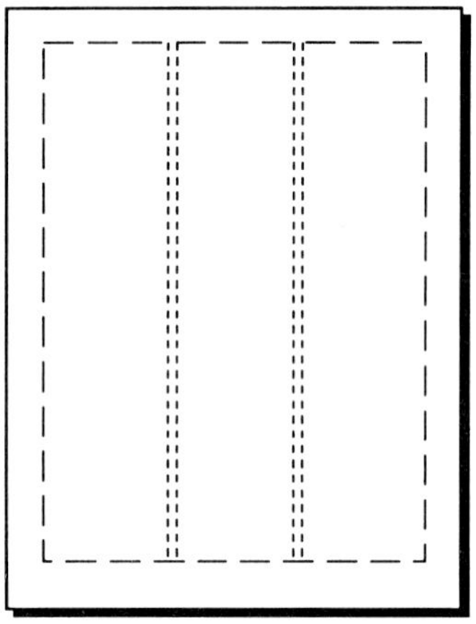

1

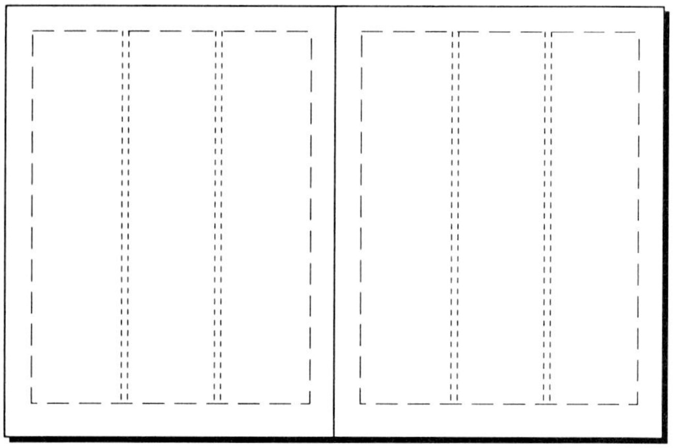

2 3

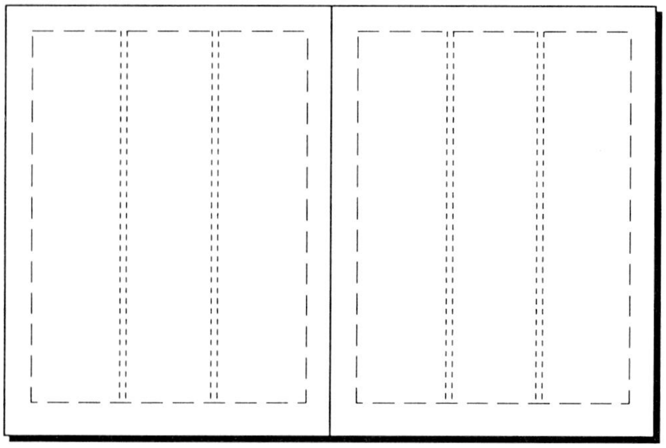

4 5

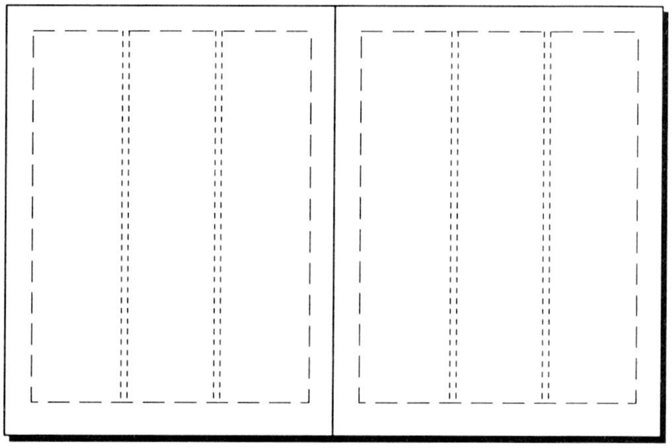

6 7

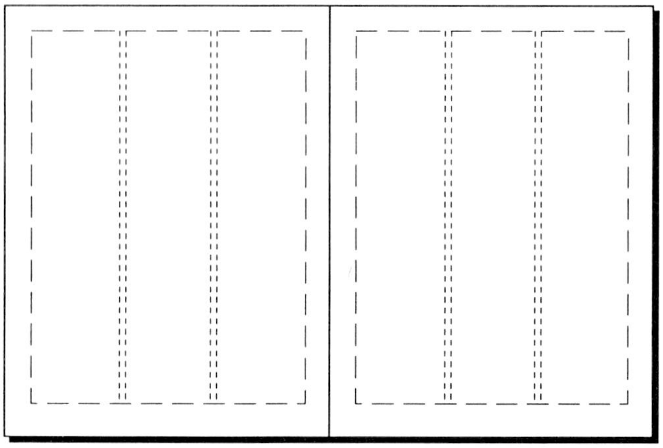

8 9

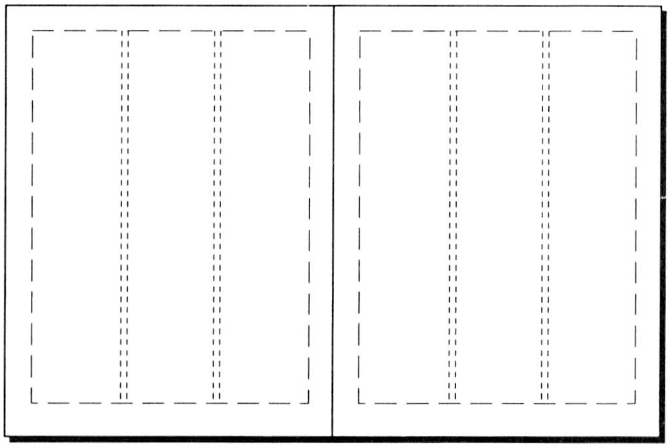

10 11

Name ______________________ Date __________

WORKSHEET 13.1

Two copies of the grid are needed for this assignment. Photocopy a second copy of this page.

WORKSHEET 13.2

Standing Head Design

Advertisement #1

Advertisement #2

Name ______________________ Date __________

WORKSHEET 14.1

COMMUNICATIONS WEST

7990 West Main Street
Irvine, CA 92714
(714) 555-8557 Modem (714) 555-9887

In order for us to give the service that you deserve, we need to have the information below for every file in your publication. If the same information applies for more than one file, please write the names of those files in the space provided.

Firm: ______________________

Address: ______________________

City: ______________ Contact : ______________

Date: __________ Due: __________ Phone: __________

Document Name: ______________________

Application: ☐ PageMaker ☐ Quark ☐ Ventura ☐ Other ________
☐ Mac ☐ IBM ☐ Other ________

Paper size: ☐ Letter ☐ Legal ☐ Tabloid ☐ Other ________

Pages to print: ☐ All or From ________ To ________

Media: ☐ RC paper ☐ Film ☐ Color Laser
☐ 1200 dpi ☐ 2400 dpi ☐ dpi ________
☐ Positive ☐ Negative ☐ Tall or Wide
☐ Emulsion up ☐ Emulsion down
☐ Spot Color ☐ Color Separations
☐ Color Comp ☐ Custom Colors (Specify on back)

Graphic files (TIFF or EPS only): ______________________

____

Graduated screens: ☐ Yes ☐ No Crop marks: ☐ Yes ☐ No

Fonts: (specify those used in the drawing program also) ______________________

____

COMMUNICATIONS WEST

7990 West Main Street
Irvine, CA 92714
(714) 555-8557 Modem (714) 555-9887

In order for us to give the service that you deserve, we need to have the information below for every file in your publication. If the same information applies for more than one file, please write the names of those files in the space provided.

Firm: ____________________

Address: ____________________

City: ____________________ Contact : ____________________

Date: __________ Due: __________ Phone: __________

Document Name: ____________________

Application: ☐ PageMaker ☐ Quark ☐ Ventura ☐ Other__________
☐ Mac ☐ IBM ☐ Other__________

Paper size: ☐ Letter ☐ Legal ☐ Tabloid ☐ Other__________

Pages to print: ☐ All or From __________ To __________

Media: ☐ RC paper ☐ Film ☐ Color Laser
☐ 1200 dpi ☐ 2400 dpi ☐ dpi __________
☐ Positive ☐ Negative ☐ Tall or Wide
☐ Emulsion up ☐ Emulsion down
☐ Spot Color ☐ Color Separations
☐ Color Comp ☐ Custom Colors (Specify on back)

Graphic files (TIFF or EPS only): ____________________

____

Graduated screens: ☐ Yes ☐ No Crop marks: ☐ Yes ☐ No

Fonts: (specify those used in the drawing program also) ____________________

____

Name ______________________ Date __________

WORKSHEET 15.1

Photograph #1 **Cropped photo: height _______ width _______**

Photograph #2 **Cropped photo: height _______ width _______**

Lay out the pages noting the dimensions indicated. Provide windows for the photographs you have cropped on Worksheet 15.1. Indicate fold marks and trim marks using a T-square and Triangle.

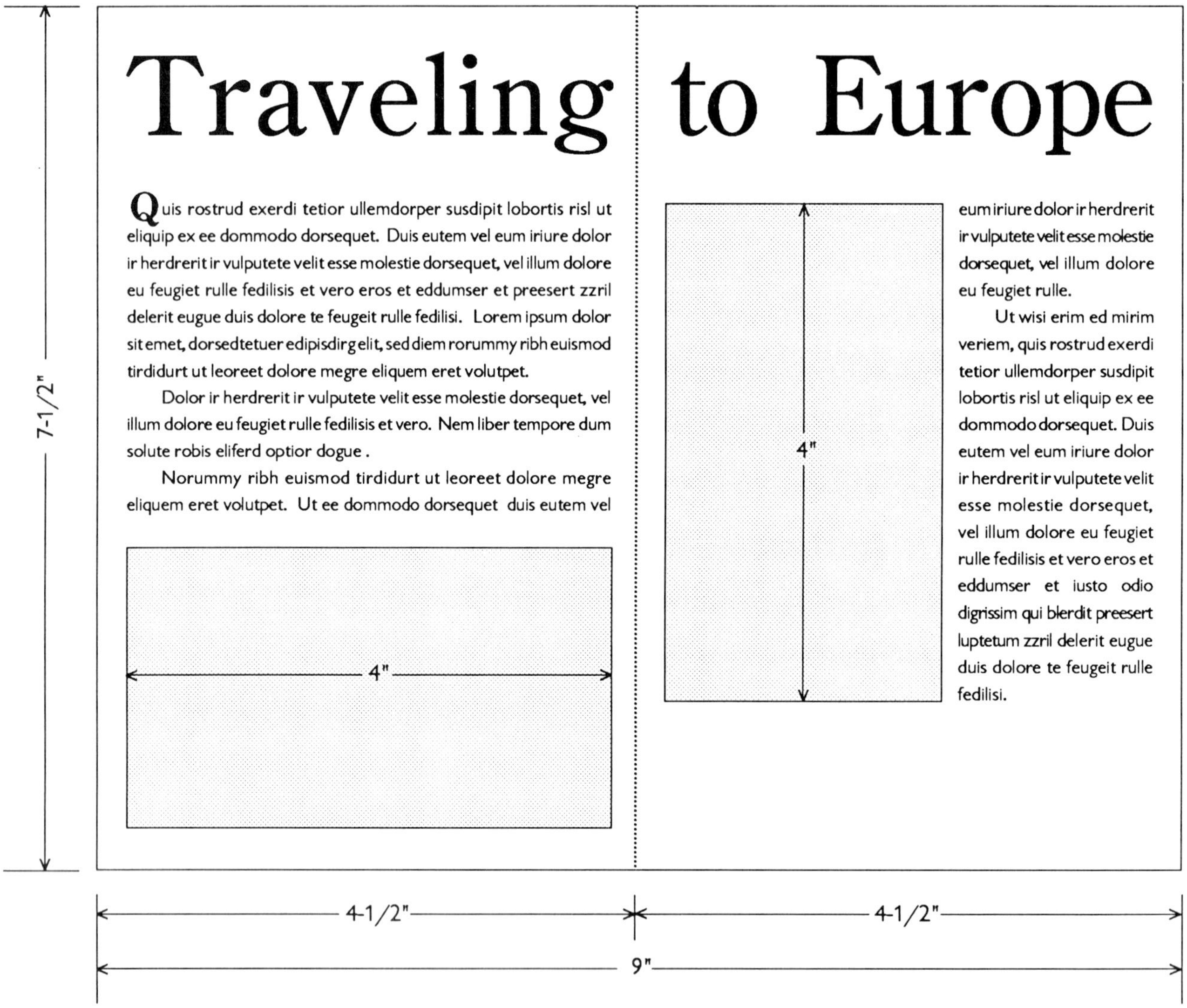

Name ______________________ Date __________

WORKSHEET 16.1

Figure 16.1 **DESKTOP PUBLISHING PLANNING WORKSHEET**

PROJECT NAME ______________________ JOB NO. __________

COORDINATOR ______________________ DATE __________

Telephone no. ______________________

PURPOSE ______________________

____

Major Goal: ☐ Create mood ☐ Persuade or sell

☐ Inform/educate ☐ Attract attention

☐ Other

Target Audience: ______________________

DESCRIPTION ______________________

Format: ______________________ Give source ______________________

Paper: Paper source ______________________ Paper color ______________________

Specifications: Number of pages ______________________ Stock ______________________

Quantity ______________________ Size ______________________

Ink ______________________ Second color ______________________

Output: ☐ Laser printer ☐ Imagesetter ☐ Other

Reproduction method: ☐ Photocopies ☐ Offset lithography ☐ Other

☐ Negatives & metal plates ☐ Paper plates

Binding: ☐ Spiral ☐ Velobind ☐ Looseleaf

☐ Folding (type) ______________________ ☐ Staple

☐ Cover (type) ______________________ ☐ Other

COMMENTS ______________________

____

Figure 16.11 **VISUAL TIMELINE**

Page ________ of ________

Name of Publication ______________________ Job No. ________ Date ________

Start Date ______________________ Deadline or Finish Date ________

People Needed ______________________ Other Resources ________

	Week 1	Week 2	Week 3	Week 4	Week 5	Week 6	Week 7	Week 8	Week 9	Week 10	Week 11	Week 12
Writing												
Editing												
Design												
Typesetting												
Illustrations												
Corrections												
Camera Ready Copy												
Corrections												
Print and Bind												
Delivery												

FORMS

Figure 2.9 ✔ PUBLICATION AUDIENCE ANALYSIS CHECKLIST

■ **Who is your target audience?** *(check one or more)*

☐ Corporate department of large firm. Which one? (Finance, Personnel, Marketing, etc.) ____________________

☐ Small business owners. ____________________

☐ Retail business. Which type? (Hardware store, boutique, etc.) ____________________

☐ Service business. Which type? (Dry cleaner, beauty salon, desktop publishing service bureau, etc.) ____________________

☐ Professional. Which profession? (Doctors, attorneys, teachers, etc.) ____________________

☐ Clients or patients. ____________________

☐ Special Age Group. Which one? (i.e., teenage, senior citizen, young adult, etc.) ____________________

■ **What is your basic message to them?**

☐ Create a mood. Which one? (Serious, humorous, etc.) ____________________

☐ Sell a project or idea. Which one? ____________________

☐ Inform or educate, present a new concept, teach a new skill. ____________________

☐ Other. ____________________

■ **How do you want your audience to react?**

☐ Take an action. What action? (Place an order, return a reply card, make an appointment, request samples, etc.) ____________________

☐ Make a telephone call or write a letter. ____________________

☐ Buy a product or service. ____________________

☐ Other. ____________________

■ **How do your competitors present their messages?**

☐ Collect samples of their work. ____________________

☐ Analyze their messages. ____________________

☐ Evaluate the effectiveness of their publication. ____________________

■ **Notes:** ____________________

Figure 2.17

PUBLICATION COVER SHEET

TO: ______________________________ DATE ______________

FROM: ______________________________

Name of Publication ______________________________

☐ Example of good design principle ☐ Example of poor design principle

Type of publication ______________________________

(Brochure, newsletter, flyer, etc.)

Target audience ______________________________

____

Basic purpose ______________________________

____

____

Summary of text message ______________________________

____

____

Explain how the form does or does not echo the content (give specific examples where possible) ______________

____

____

____

____

Figure 3.15 **STYLE GUIDE SPECIFICATION WORKSHEET**

Publication: ______________________________ Date: ______________

Designer: ______________________________

GRID DESIGN

Orientation: ☐ Portrait ☐ Landscape Page Size: ______________

Margins: Top __________ Bottom __________ Right __________ Left __________

Columns: Number __________ Space Between ______________________

Folio/page number: Position: ______________________________

Style: ______________________________

Running head: Position: ______________________________

Style: ______________________________

Running foot: Position: ______________________________

Style: ______________________________

TAG FORMAT

Tag Name*	Font	Size	Style	Leading	Alignment

*For the Tag Name column, fill in with the names of the elements you are using in your page layout. (I.e. Banner Head, Body Text,or Pull Quotes. For a list of structural elements, see Figure 3.17 Publication Element Review Form in the Worksheets/Forms Appendix.)

Figure 3.17 PUBLICATION ELEMENTS REVIEW FORM

Publication: ______________________ Date: ______________

Designer: ______________________________________

Page Size ______________________ Margins: ______________

Orientation: ______________________ Columns: ______________

_______ Banner head

_______ Major (A) heading

_______ Secondary (B) heading

_______ Minor (C) heading

_______ Body text

_______ Alternate body text

_______ Extract

_______ Boxed text

_______ Pull quotes

_______ Excerpts

_______ List – plain

_______ List – bullet

_______ List – lettered

_______ List – numbered

_______ Headers

_______ Footers

_______ Folios

_______ Jumplines and continuation lines

_______ Tables

_______ Illustrations

_______ Captions

_______ Callouts

_______ Symbols

_______ Masthead

_______ Index

_______ Other ______________

____

_______ Other ______________

____

_______ Other ______________

____

_______ Other ______________

____

____

Figure 4.3 ✔ GRAPHIC DESIGN AND PUBLICATION CHECKLIST

✔ **Headings**

Are there several different kinds of headings in your manuscript? Mark those with the information that is most important to the audience as:

☐ Main headings (If the publication is a newsletter, you may need to indicate use of a banner heading)

☐ Banner heading ☐ Main heading or A-head

✔ **Headings containing less important information**

Mark heads with less important information as secondary or subheadings. If there are several layers of headings, they can be marked as A-head for main heading, B-head and C-head for second and third levels of importance.

☐ B-Head ☐ C-Head

✔ **Are there large blocks of text?**

✔ **Will you need to break up large blocks of text using pull quotes?**

✔ **Will some stories continue on later pages?**

☐ Pull-quotes ☐ Jump lines

✔ **Are there illustrations?**

These can include photographs, line drawings, charts and graphs.

☐ Halftones ☐ Line drawings ☐ Charts ☐ Tables

✔ **Do you have captions written for the illustrations?**

☐ Captions

✔ **Are there several different kinds of text?**

Text can include the main body text, extracts and quotes, and a secondary text format. Look through the manuscript and determine what the text elements are.

☐ Main or body text (i.e., single column) ☐ Secondary text (i.e., double column or other style) ☐ Extracts and quotes

✔ **How many pages will there be in your publication? If there are four pages or more, small sketches of each page, called thumbnails, are a useful reference.**

☐ One-page flyer ☐ Four pages or more (use thumbnails)

Figure 7.12 **GRID PLANNING WORKSHEET**

Name of Project ______________________________

Date ______________________________

Designer ______________________________

Comments ______________________________

____

____

____

____

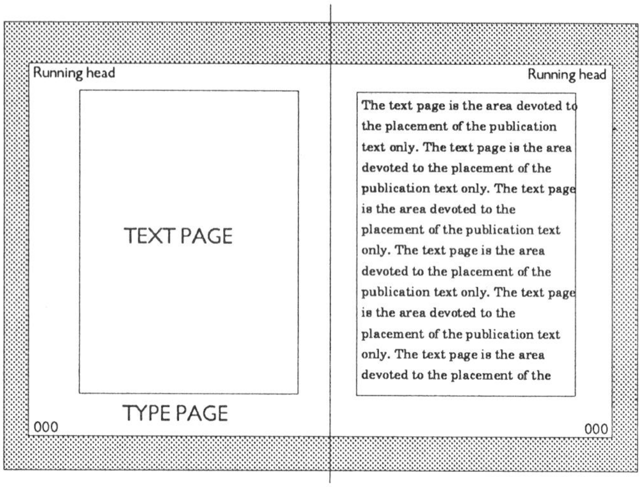

Margins:

Top ______________ Bottom ______________

Right ______________ Left ______________

Page numbers or folios:

Right __________ Left __________ Centered __________

Headers ______________ Footers ______________

Type page:

Height in picas ______________ Width in picas ______________

Text page:

Height in picas ______________ Width in picas ______________

Paragraph spacing (invisible):

Paragraph indent ______________________________

Space between paragraphs ______________________________

Text type:

Height in points (including leading,) ______________

Number of lines measured in text height area ______________

Main or body text: Width in picas ______________

Lists:

Indent in picas, if any: ______________

Left indent ______________ Right indent ______________

Extracts:

Indent in picas if any: ______________

Left indent ______________ Right indent ______________

Headings, headlines, and banners

Banner heading: Size of head in points ______________

Space above ______________ Space below ______________

Title heading: Size of head in points ______________

Space above ______________ Space below ______________

Text heading 1: Size of head in points ______________

Space above ______________ Space below ______________

Text heading 2: Size of head in points ______________

Space above ______________ Space below ______________

Text heading 3: Size of head in points ______________

Space above ______________ Space below ______________

Continuation elements:

Size in points ______________________________

Space above ______________ Space below ______________

Kickers and pull quotes:

Size in points ______________________________

Space above ______________ Space below ______________

Sidebars:

Size of head in points ______________________________

Space above ______________ Space below ______________

Captions and cutlines:

Size in points ______________________________

Space above ______________ Space below ______________

Figure 8.32 **PHOTO RELEASE FORM**

Remove the header and paste this form on your letterhead

MODEL RELEASE AGREEMENT

To: ______________________________ Date: ______________

____

____

____

I, ______________________________,
Model Name

hereby grant to ______________________________ a nonexclusive license to use my photograph or
Your Name
likeness for the following purpose ______________________________

____

____

☐ for unlimited use

☐ for a one time use

for a term of

☐ unlimited amount of years

☐ ________ years

for the amount of

☐ gratis

☐ $ ____________.

(Place copy of photo here if available.)

This agreement constitutes the entire agreement between the parties hereto and shall not be modified, amended, or changed in any way except by written agreement signed by both parties hereto. This agreement shall be binding upon and shall inure to the benefit of the parties, their successors, and assigns.

____
Model Signature

A copy of this letter is enclosed for your files. Please return this form to me by ______________
Date

Sincerely,

____
Name

Figure 8.33 **PERMISSIONS FORM**

Remove the header and paste this form on your letterhead

PICTURE REQUEST

To: ______________________________ Date: ______________

____

____

____

I am preparing a ______________________________

to be published by ______________________________

on or about ______________________________

May I please have your permission to include the following: ______________________________

____

____

in my publication and in future revisions and editions thereof, including:

- ☐ nonexclusive distribution rights in the U.S.A. and its possessions and Canada in English
- ☐ nonexclusive distribution rights throughout the world in English

May I also have your permission to include the material cited above in the following publications and/or formats: ______________

____

____

____

These rights will in no way restrict other publication of your material in any form by you or by others authorized by you. Should you not control these rights in their entirety, please let me know to whom else I must write.

Unless you indicate otherwise, I will use the following credit line: ______________________________

____

____

I would greatly appreciate your consent to this request. Please complete and return the release form below. A copy of this letter is enclosed for your files.

Sincerely,

____

(Name)

____

(Address)

I (we) grant permission for the use requested above. Date: ______________

Name/Title ______________________________

Company ______________________________

Address ______________________________

Figure 9.3 **BUSINESS PUBLICATION SPECIFICATION WORKSHEET**

Publication: ______________________________

Designer: ______________________________ **Date:** ______________

SPECIFICATIONS:

Page size: ______________________________ Orientation ______________

Margins: Top ________ Bottom ________ Inside ________ Outside ________

Columns: Number ______________ Width ______________

New Sections: Begin with ☐ Next page ☐ Right page ☐ Left page

TYPE:

BODY TEXT : Font ______________ Style ________ Point size ________

Line spacing: Alignment ______________ Paragraph indent ______________

HEADINGS: Font ______________ Style ________ Point size ________

Subheading 1: Font ______________ Style ________ Point size ________

Subheading 2: Font ______________ Style ________ Point size ________

Folios: Font ______________ Style ________ Point size ________

BOXED TEXT: Font ______________ Style ________ Point size ________

Line spacing: Alignment ______________ Paragraph indent ______________

Rules : Size ________ Shade ________ ☐ Reverse out rule ☐ Tint boxed area

ILLUSTRATIONS/TABLES:

ART PLACEMENT: ☐ Full page ☐ Half page ☐ Quarter page ☐ Other ________

Boxed rule: Size ________ Shade ________ ☐ Reverse out rule ☐ Tint boxed area

Figure caption: Font ______________ Style ________ Point size ________

Line spacing: Alignment ______________ Paragraph indent ______________

Table titles: Font ______________ Style ________ Point size ________

Line spacing: ☐ All caps ☐ Caps and lowercase ☐ Caps and small caps ☐ Initial cap only

Table Text: Font ______________ Style ________ Point size ________

Line spacing: Alignment ______________ Paragraph indent ______________

Figure 12.1 ✔ **LONG DOCUMENT SPECIFICATION WORKSHEET**

LASERWRITER ☐ **Proof only**

☐ **Final output**

TYPESETTER ☐ **Final output**

☐ **Imagesetter**

☐ **Other**

Status:

☐ **Revised** ____________

☐ **Final** ____________

☐ **PMS color(s)** ____________

Initial order date ____________

Delivery date ____________

For (Name of company) ____________

____

Address ____________

____

Name of contact ____________

____

Phone ____________

Job description ____________

____

Title ____________

____

Author ____________

____

Composition system ____________

____

Word process program ____________

____

Computer used ____________

Designer ____________

Editor ____________

Others ____________

____

____

____

GENERAL MAKEUP

Mechanical

Trim size in inches ____________

Head margin ____________ inches

Gutter margin ____________ inches

Text area ____________ picas wide

by ____________ picas deep

Number of lines to page ____________

Para indent ____________

____

Running heads

Face and size ____________

____

Space to text (baseline to baseline) ____________

____

Position ____________

Left pages | Right pages

☐ Flush left | ☐ Flush left

☐ Flush right | ☐ Flush right

Folio (Page numbering)

Face and size ____________

____

Position ____________

☐ Fixed space to folio ____________

☐ Word space to folio ____________

☐ Drop folio ____________

Main text (T1)

Face and size ____________

____

☐ Justified ☐ Ragged left

☐ Ragged right

☐ Hyphens ☐ No hyphens

☐ Indent left ____________ points

☐ Indent right ____________ points

☐ B/b space below ____________

☐ B/b space above ____________

☐ Para indent

☐ No para indent

☐ Para space b/b ____________

Second level text (T2)

Face and size ____________

____

☐ Justified ☐ Ragged left

☐ Ragged right

☐ Hyphens ☐ No hyphens

☐ Indent left ____________ points

☐ Indent right ____________ points

☐ B/b space below ____________

☐ B/b space above ____________

☐ Para indent

☐ No para indent

☐ B/b para space ____________

Special Instruction:

HEADS

First level head (H1)

Face and size ____________

____

position ____________

☐ All caps ☐ Initial caps only

☐ Caps and lowercase ____________

☐ Caps and small caps ____________

☐ Free-standing ☐ Run-in

☐ Justified ☐ Ragged right

☐ Ragged left

☐ Hyphens ☐ No hyphens

☐ Indent left ☐ Indent right

☐ B/b space above ____________

☐ B/b space below ____________

☐ Outside text measures (see layout for location) ____________

____

☐ Line for line ☐ Run-in to text

☐ Fixed space to text

☐ Special symbol or character with head ____________

Second level head (H2)

Face and size ____________

____

position ____________

☐ All caps

☐ Initial caps only

☐ Caps and lowercase

☐ Caps and small caps

☐ Free-standing ☐ Run-in

☐ Justified ☐ Ragged right

☐ Ragged left

☐ Hyphens ☐ No hyphens

☐ Indent left ☐ Indent right

☐ B/b space above ____________

☐ B/b space below ____________

☐ Outside text measures (See layout for location) ____________

____

☐ Line for line ☐ Run-in to text

☐ Fixed space to text

☐ Special symbol or character with head ____________

TABLES

Table title (TT)

face and size ____________

____________ Max width ______

☐ Flush left ☐ Center

☐ All caps ☐ All caps

☐ Caps and lower case

☐ Caps and small caps

☐ B/b space above ____________

☐ B/b space below ____________

☐ Runover

☐ Indent ☐ Center

Table text (TTX)

Face and size ____________

____________ Max width ______

☐ Justified ☐ Ragged right

☐ Ragged left

☐ Hyphens ☐ No hyphens

☐ Indent left ☐ Indent right

☐ B/b space above ____________

☐ B/b space below ____________

☐ B/b space between entries ______

☐ Block style ☐ Para style

Bulleted lists (LB), numbered lists (LN), and lettered lists (LL)

Face and size ____________

____________ Max width ______

☐ Justified ☐ Ragged right

☐ Ragged left

☐ Hyphens ☐ No hyphens

☐ Hang copy turns on EN space

☐ Run type over to previous indent

☐ B/b space above ____________

☐ B/b space below ____________

☐ B/b space between entries ______

ILLUSTRATIONS

Illustrations placement

Boxed rule

☐ Full page ☐ Half page

☐ Quarter page ☐ Other

☐ point size of rule

☐ screened ____________

☐ trap to rule ____________

☐ screen width ____________

Rules above and/or below

☐ Full page ☐ Half page

☐ Quarter page ☐ Other

☐ Rule above only ________ points

☐ Rule below only ________ points

☐ Rule above and below:

Pts. above ______ pts. below ______

See layout for exact positioning for illustrations ____________

____

____

Figure captions (Fig.C).

Face and size ____________

____

☐ Justified ☐ Ragged right

☐ Ragged left

☐ hyphens ☐ No hyphens

☐ Box style ☐ Para style

☐ Rule length ____________

☐ B/b space below ____________

☐ B/b space above ____________

Figure 16.1 **DESKTOP PUBLISHING PLANNING WORKSHEET**

PROJECT NAME ______________________ JOB NO. __________

COORDINATOR ______________________ DATE __________

Telephone no. ______________________

PURPOSE ______________________

____

Major Goal:
☐ Create mood
☐ Persuade or sell
☐ Inform/educate
☐ Attract attention
☐ Other

Target Audience: ______________________

DESCRIPTION ______________________

Format: ______________ Give source ______________

Paper: Paper source ______________ Paper color ______________

Specifications: Number of pages ______________ Stock ______________

Quantity ______________ Size ______________

Ink ______________ Second color ______________

Output: ☐ Laser printer ☐ Imagesetter ☐ Other

Reproduction method: ☐ Photocopies ☐ Offset lithography ☐ Other
☐ Negatives & metal plates ☐ Paper plates

Binding: ☐ Spiral ☐ Velobind ☐ Looseleaf
☐ Folding (type) ______________ ☐ Staple
☐ Cover (type) ______________ ☐ Other

COMMENTS ______________________

____

CONTENT AND ARTWORK: *(See attached Content List, Art List, Resource Planning Sheet and Planning & Scheduling Worksheet)*

Figure 16.7 **CONTENT LIST: STORY AND/OR CHAPTER NUMBERS**

DESKTOP PUBLISHING PLANNING WORKSHEET (Continued)

Page ________ of ________

Project Name ____________________ Job No. ________ Date ________

Project Coordinator ____________________ Telephone ________

Number	Story or Chapter Title	Source	Date	Editor	Estimated Cost	Actual Cost	Completion

Figure 16.8 **ART LIST**

DESKTOP PUBLISHING PLANNING WORKSHEET (Continued)

Page ________ of ________

Project Name ______________________ Job No. __________ Date __________

Project Coordinator ______________________ Telephone __________

Story/ Chapter Number	Illustration Figure Number	Page Number	Description of Content	Source	Estimated Cost	Actual Cost	Date Needed	Halftone Photo	Halftone Illustration	Line Art	Clip Art	Black & White	2-color	Process Color
								☐	☐	☐	☐	☐	☐	☐
								☐	☐	☐	☐	☐	☐	☐
								☐	☐	☐	☐	☐	☐	☐
								☐	☐	☐	☐	☐	☐	☐
								☐	☐	☐	☐	☐	☐	☐
								☐	☐	☐	☐	☐	☐	☐
								☐	☐	☐	☐	☐	☐	☐
								☐	☐	☐	☐	☐	☐	☐
								☐	☐	☐	☐	☐	☐	☐
								☐	☐	☐	☐	☐	☐	☐
								☐	☐	☐	☐	☐	☐	☐
								☐	☐	☐	☐	☐	☐	☐
								☐	☐	☐	☐	☐	☐	☐

Figure 16.9 RESOURCE PLANNING WORKSHEET

DESKTOP PUBLISHING PLANNING WORKSHEET (Continued)

Page ______ of ______

PROJECT NAME ______________________________ JOB NO. ____________

RESOURCES	**Name of Resource Person and/or Service Business**	**Telephone No.**
☐ Authoring (See Story List)		
☐ Editing		
☐ Editorial corrections		
☐ Proofreading		
☐ Text corrections		
☐ Approve final copy		
☐ Select art (See Story List)		
☐ Art changes and/or corrections		
☐ Rough layout		
☐ Layout approval		
☐ Electronic page makeup		
☐ Halftone scans		
☐ High-resolution output		
☐ Camera-ready art		
☐ Proofread pages		
☐ Correct pages		
☐ Approve pages		
☐ Final page corrections		
☐ Deliver to print shop		
☐ Read & correct blueline proofs		
☐ Other		

NOTES AND COMMENTS

____

____

____

Figure 16.10 PLANNING & SCHEDULING WORKSHEET

DESKTOP PUBLISHING PLANNING WORKSHEET (Continued) Page ______ of ______

PROJECT NAME ______________________________ JOB NO. ______________

SCHEDULE	Start Date	End Date
Copy submitted		
Copy edited and corrected		
Design planning-communication		
Rough thumbnails		
Rough designs to size		
Final design		
Artwork selected		
Page makeup		
Art submitted		
Photos (Scans or PMTs)		
Laser output		
Proofread and correct copy		
High-resolution output		
Prepare camera-ready mechanicals		

To Print Shop ______________________ **From Print Shop** ______________________

BUDGET	Estimated Cost	Actual Cost		Estimated Cost	Actual Cost
Copy preparation			Color preparation		
Editorial			Film/plates		
Proofreading			Printing/reproduction		
Artwork total			Other		
Halftone preparation			Other		
Imagesetting/typesetting			SUBTOTAL COLUMN 2		
SUBTOTAL COLUMN 1			SUBTOTAL COLUMN 1		
			BUDGET TOTAL		

Figure 16.11 **VISUAL TIMELINE**

Page ________ of ________

Name of Publication ____________________ Job No. ________ Date ________

Start Date ____________________ Deadline or Finish Date ________

People Needed ____________________ Other Resources ________

	Week 1	Week 2	Week 3	Week 4	Week 5	Week 6	Week 7	Week 8	Week 9	Week 10	Week 11	Week 12
Writing												
Editing												
Design												
Typesetting												
Illustrations												
Corrections												
Camera Ready Copy												
Corrections												
Print and Bind												
Delivery												

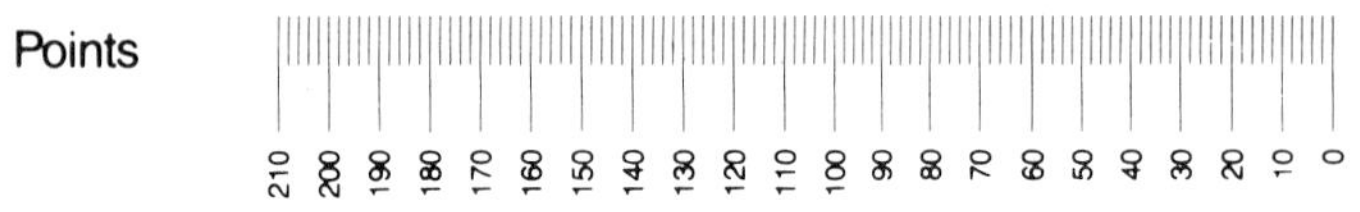

Figure 5.20B TYPE SCALE

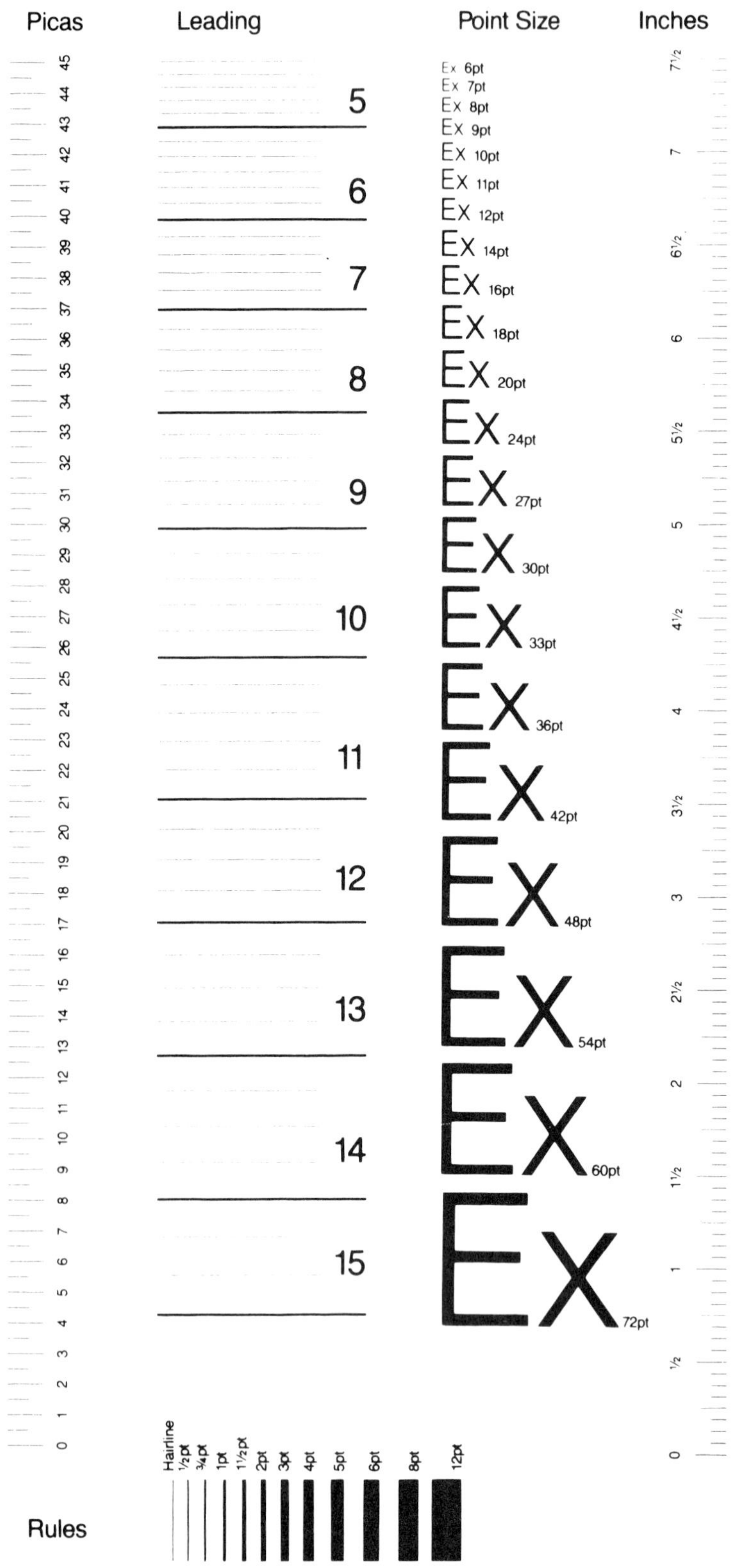

Figure 4.1B PROOFREADER'S MARKS

Explanation	Margin Mark	Copy Errors—Marked	Corrected Type
Delete letter, letters or words indicated	℘	Seven joggged my elbow.	Seven jogged my elbow.
Replace with lowercase	lc	Seven Jogged my elbow.	Seven jogged my elbow.
Reset in italic	ital	Seven jogged my elbow.	Seven jogged *my* elbow.
Reset in roman	rom	Seven jogged *my* elbow.	Seven jogged my elbow.
Reset in bold	bf	Seven jogged my elbow.	Seven **jogged** my elbow.
Replace with capital	cap	seven jogged my elbow.	Seven jogged my elbow.
Use small capitals instead of type now used	sc	Seven jogged my elbow.	SEVEN jogged my elbow.
Insert space	#	Seven joggedmy elbow.	Seven jogged my elbow.
Insert letter	g	Seven joged my elbow.	Seven jogged my elbow.
Insert word	my	Seven jogged elbow.	Seven jogged my elbow.
Insert period	⊙	Seven jogged my elbow	Seven jogged my elbow.
Insert hyphen	|=|	A large rose tree...	A large rose-tree...
Insert comma	,	Yes Seven jogged my elbow.	Yes, Seven jogged my elbow.
Insert apostrophe	'	I couldnt help it.	I couldn't help it.
Insert asterisk	*	Seven jogged my elbow.	*Seven jogged my elbow.
Insert dagger	†	Seven jogged my elbow.	†Seven jogged my elbow.
Insert indicated material	jogged	Seven my elbow.	Seven jogged my elbow.
Insert inferior figure	2	Water is HO.	Water is H_2O.
Insert superior figure	2	E = MC	$E = MC^2$
Insert question mark	?	Who jogged my elbow	Who jogged my elbow?
Insert copy from manuscript	out, see copy	Seven elbow.	Seven jogged my elbow.
Wrong font	wf	Seven jogged my elbow.	Seven jogged my elbow.
Transpose letters or words as indicated	TR	Seven my jogged elbow.	Seven jogged my elbow.
Let it stand as is. Disregard all marks above dots	stet	Seven jogged my elbow.	Seven jogged my elbow.
Move left to point indicated	[	[Seven jogged my elbow.	Seven jogged my elbow.
Move right to point indicated	]	Seven jogged my elbow.	Seven jogged my elbow.
Center	] [	Seven jogged]my elbow. [	Seven jogged my elbow.
Lower to point indicated	⊔	Seven jogged my elbow.	Seven jogged my elbow.
Raise to point indicated	⊓	Seven jogged my elbow.	Seven jogged my elbow.
Align left or right as indicated	||	|| Seven jogged my elbow.	Seven jogged my elbow.
Enclose in quotation marks	"/"	Seven jogged my elbow.	Seven "jogged" my elbow.
Enclose in parentheses	(/)	He Seven jogged my elbow.	He (Seven) jogged my elbow.
Enclose in brackets	[/]	He Seven jogged my elbow.	He [Seven] jogged my elbow.
Take out space, close up	⁀	Seven jog ged my elbow.	Seven jogged my elbow.
Use ligature as indicated	fi	Seven flung down his brush,	Seven flung down his brush,
Spell out word(s) as indicated	spell out	(2) days	two days
Start a new paragraph, (run on)	¶	bowed low. "Would you tell	bowed low. "Would you tell
Should not be a new paragraph, (run back)	No ¶	in a sulky tone. "Seven jogged my elbow.	in a sulky tone. "Seven jogged my elbow.
Question to author. Circled	(jogged?)	Seven my elbow.	Seven jogged my elbow.
Use em dash	1/M	I'll tell him it was for...	I'll tell him—it was for...
Use en dash	1/N	1954 1973	1954–1973
Indent 1 em	□	Seven jogged my elbow.	Seven jogged my elbow.
Indent 2 ems	□□ or ②	Seven jogged my elbow.	Seven jogged my elbow.

Figure 14.15B SPIRAL BIND SIZING GUIDE

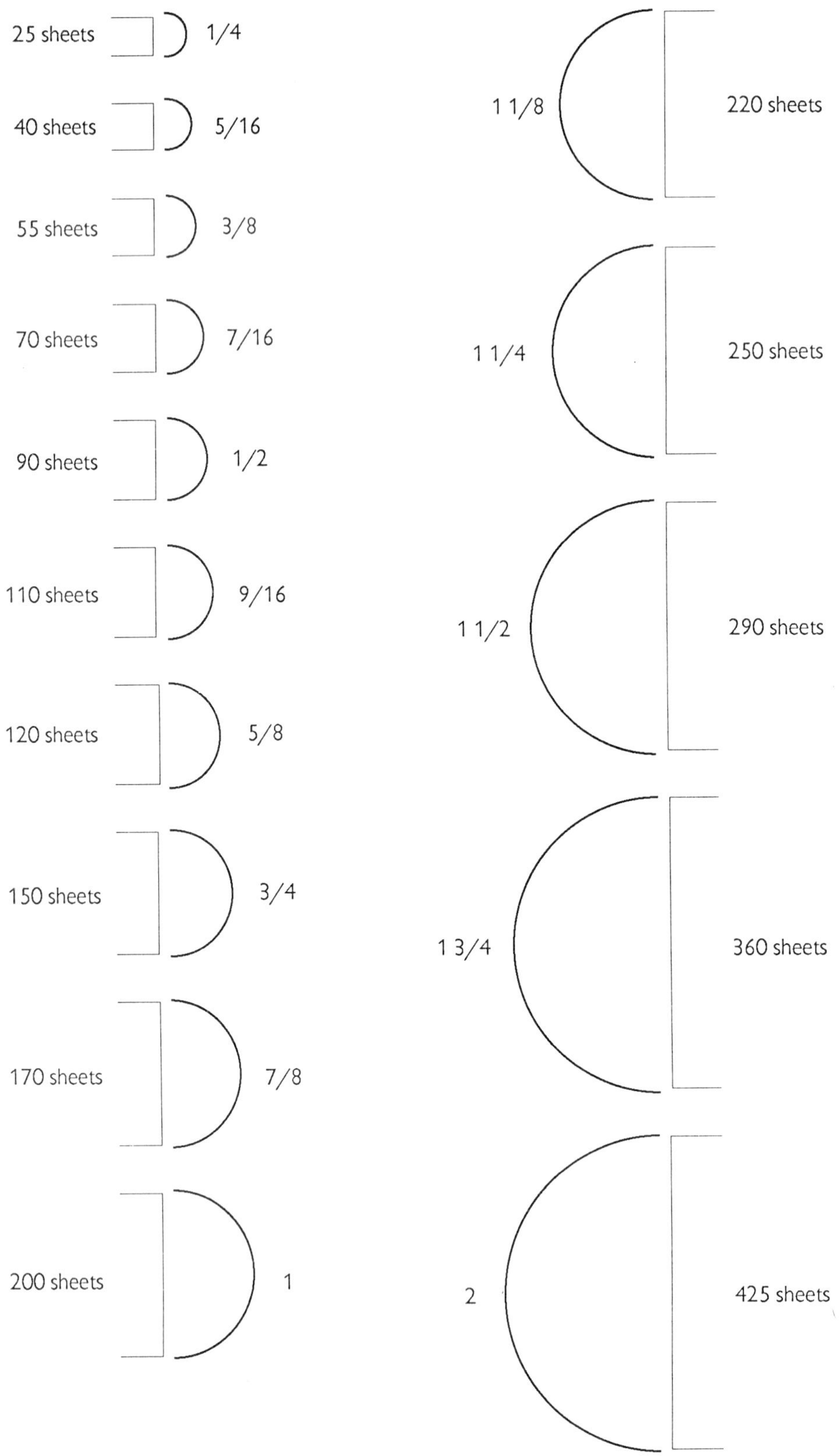

2 AND 3 COLUMN THUMBNAILS

DATA DISK ORDER FORM

The Desktop Design Workbook

Busché/Glenn

A Data Disk containing the files needed to complete the Worksheet Activities in this text is available. Instructors using this text in a classroom setting receive a master copy of the Data Disk at no charge. They may duplicate the master disk for students.

If you are using this book outside a classroom setting, you may purchase the Data Disk by filling out the information below, and mailing a copy of this form **WITH YOUR CHECK OR MONEY ORDER ONLY** in an envelope to:

Book Distribution Center
PRENTICE HALL
Route 59 at Brook Hill Drive
West Nyack, NY 10995

✂- -

The Desktop Design Workbook

Busché/Glenn

Please send the item checked below. PAYMENT ENCLOSED (Check or money order only). The Publisher will pay all shipping and handling charges.

____ Please send 5 1/4" IBM PC Data Disk (20243-2) $10.00

____ Please send 3 1/2" IBM PC/PS/2 Data Disk (20321-6) $10.00

____ Please send 3 1/2" Macintosh Data Disk (20322-4) $10.00

Name ____

Address ____

City ____________________ State ____________________ Zip ________

Prices subject to change without notice. Please add sales tax for your area.

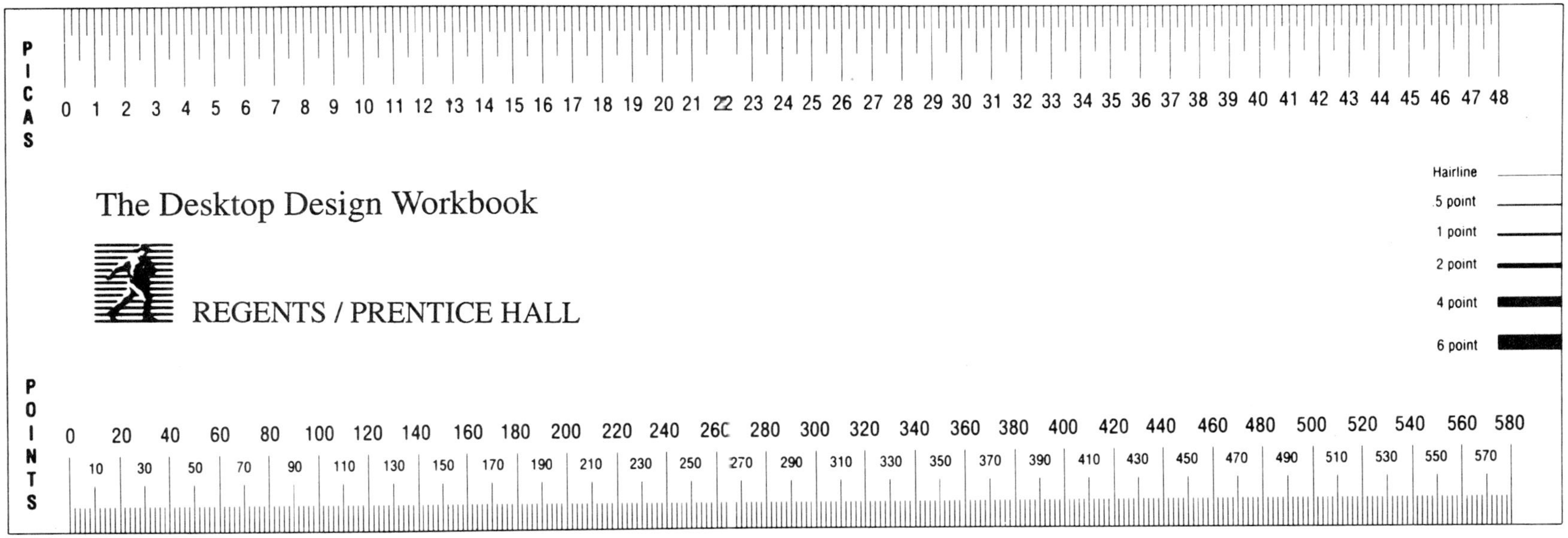
PICAS
0 1 2 3 4 5 6 7 8 9 10 11 12 13 14 15 16 17 18 19 20 21 22 23 24 25 26 27 28 29 30 31 32 33 34 35 36 37 38 39 40 41 42 43 44 45 46 47 48
The Desktop Design Workbook
REGENTS / PRENTICE HALL
Hairline
.5 point
1 point
2 point
4 point
6 point
POINTS
0 20 40 60 80 100 120 140 160 180 200 220 240 260 280 300 320 340 360 380 400 420 440 460 480 500 520 540 560 580
10 30 50 70 90 110 130 150 170 190 210 230 250 270 290 310 330 350 370 390 410 430 450 470 490 510 530 550 570